13.95

M000306685

After Pluralism

RELIGION, CULTURE, AND PUBLIC LIFE

Religion, Culture, and Public Life

Series Editors: Alfred Stepan and Mark C. Taylor

The resurgence of religion calls for careful analysis and constructive criticism of new forms of intolerance, as well as new approaches to tolerance, respect, mutual understanding, and accommodation. In order to promote serious scholarship and informed debate, the Institute for Religion, Culture, and Public Life and Columbia University Press are sponsoring a book series devoted to the investigation of the role of religion in society and culture today. This series includes works by scholars in religious studies, political science, history, cultural anthropology, economics, social psychology, and other allied fields whose work sustains multidisciplinary and comparative, as well as transnational analyses of historical and contemporary issues. The series focuses on issues related to questions of difference, identity, and practice within local, national, and international contexts. Special attention is paid to the ways in which religious traditions encourage conflict, violence, and intolerance, as well as support human rights, ecumenical values, and mutual understanding. By mediating alternative methodologies and different religious, social, and cultural traditions, books published in this series will open channels of communication that facilitate critical analysis.

After Pluralism: Reimagining Religious Engagement

Edited by Courtney Bender and Pamela E. Klassen

COLUMBIA UNIVERSITY PRESS
NEW YORK

Columbia University Press
Publishers Since 1893
New York Chichester, West Sussex
Copyright © 2010 Columbia University Press
All rights reserved

Library of Congress Cataloging-in-Publication Data
After pluralism : reimagining religious engagement / edited by Courtney Bender and Pamela E. Klassen.
p. cm. — (Religion, culture, and public life)
Includes bibliographical references (p.) and index.
ISBN 978-0-231-15232-7 (cloth : alk. paper) ISBN 978-0-231-15233-4 (pbk. : alk. paper)
ISBN 978-0-231-52726-2 (e-book)
1. Religious pluralism. 2. Pluralism. 3. Religions. I. Bender, Courtney. II. Klassen, Pamela E. (Pamela Edith), 1967– III. Title. IV. Series.

BL85.A45 2010
201'.5—dc22 2010018854

Columbia University Press books are printed on permanent and durable acid-free paper.
This book is printed on paper with recycled content.
Printed in the United States of America
c 10 9 8 7 6 5 4 3 2 1
p 10 9 8 7 6 5 4 3 2 1

References to Internet Web sites (URLs) were accurate at the time of writing. Neither the editors nor Columbia University Press is responsible for URLs that may have expired or changed since the manuscript was prepared.ISBN

"God Bless America" by Irving Berlin. © Copyright 1938, 1939 by Irving Berlin. © Copyright Renewed 1965, 1966 by Irving Berlin. © Copyright Assigned the Trustees of the God Bless America Fund. International Copyright Secured. All Rights Reserved. Reprinted by Permission.

"I Whistle a Happy Tune" by Richard Rodgers and Oscar Hammerstein II. Copyright © 1951 by Richard Rodgers and Oscar Hammerstein II. Copyright Renewed. WILLIAMSON MUSIC owner of publication and allied rights throughout the World. International Copyright Secured. All Rights Reserved. Used by Permission.

"Life Upon the Wicked Stage," from SHOW BOAT. Lyrics by Oscar Hammerstein II. Music by Jerome Kern. Copyright © 1927, 1928 UNIVERSAL-POLYGRAM INTERNATIONAL PUBLISHING, INC. Copyright renewed. All Rights Reserved. Used by permission. *Reprinted by permission of Hal Leonard Corporation.*

"Make Believe," from SHOW BOAT. Lyrics by Oscar Hammerstein II. Music by Jerome Kern. Copyright © 1927 UNIVERSAL-POLYGRAM INTERNATIONAL PUBLISHING, INC. Copyright renewed. All Rights Reserved. Used by permission. *Reprinted by permission of Hal Leonard Corporation.*

"My House Is the Red Earth" by Joy Harjo. Reprinted by permission of the poet.

"That's the Place Indians Talk About" by Simon Ortiz. Reprinted by permission of the poet.

"There's No Business Like Show Business" by Irving Berlin. © Copyright 1946 by Irving Berlin. © Copyright Renewed. International Copyright Secured. All Rights Reserved. Reprinted by Permission.

CONTENTS

Acknowledgments vii

Introduction: Habits of Pluralism 1
PAMELA E. KLASSEN AND COURTNEY BENDER

Part I. Law, Normativity, and the Constitution of Religion

1. Ethics After Pluralism 31
JANET R. JAKOBSEN

2. Pluralizing Religion: Islamic Law and the Anxiety of Reasoned Deliberation 59
ANVER M. EMON

3. Religion Naturalized: The New Establishment 82
WINNIFRED FALLERS SULLIVAN

4. The Cultural Limits of Legal Tolerance 98
BENJAMIN L. BERGER

Part II. Performing Religion After Pluralism

5. The Birth of Theatrical Liberalism 127
ANDREA MOST

6. The Perils of Pluralism: Colonization and Decolonization in American Indian Religious History 156
TRACY LEAVELLE

7. A Matter of Interpretation: Dreams, Islam, and Psychology in Egypt 178
AMIRA MITTERMAIER

8. The Temple of Religion and the Politics of Religious Pluralism: Judeo-Christian America at the 1939–1940 New York World's Fair 201
J. TERRY TODD

Part III. The Ghosts of Pluralism: Unintended Consequences of Institutional and Legal Constructions

9. Native American Religious Freedom Beyond the First Amendment 225
MICHAEL D. MCNALLY

10. Saving Darfur: Enacting Pluralism in Terms of Gender, Genocide, and Militarized Human Rights 252
ROSEMARY R. HICKS

11. What Is Religious Pluralism in a "Monocultural" Society? Considerations from Postcommunist Poland 277
GENEVIÈVE ZUBRZYCKI

12. The Curious Attraction of Religion in East German Prisons 296
IRENE BECCI

Selected Bibliography 317

Contributors 325

Index 331

ACKNOWLEDGMENTS

First hatched in a Cambridge, Massachusetts, coffee shop, *After Pluralism* is the result of four years of collaboration, supported by many individuals, institutions, and foundations. As the editors, we would like first to thank the contributors to the volume, who entered into this multiyear project with great collegiality and commitment and whose writing and conversation have taught us both a great deal. We also thank the keynote lecturers and participants from the two After Pluralism workshops whose work does not appear here (although their influence certainly does): Tomoko Masuzawa, Kenneth Mills, Natalie Zemon Davis, James Tully, Kent Greenawalt, Janice Boddy, Charles Stewart, Ananda Abeysekara, Shari Golberg, Derek Williams, and Peggy Levitt.

This project depended on the support of several funding agencies and institutes in Canada and the United States, which we gratefully acknowledge. For awarding us competitive grants, we thank the Social Sciences and Humanities Research Council of Canada Workshop Fund and the Connaught Fund of the University of Toronto. At the University of Toronto, we also benefited from the support of the Department and Centre for the Study of Religion, the Centre for the Study of the United States, the Bissell-Heyd Chair, the Centre for Diaspora and Transnational Studies, the Munk Centre for International Studies, the Jewish Studies Program, and Ethnic and Pluralism Studies. At Columbia University, the Department of Religion; the Center for Democracy, Toleration, and

Religion; and the Institute for Religion, Culture, and Public Life supported this project in numerous ways.

The work of convening three international workshops was made remarkably smooth by the expert assistance of several graduate students: Rebekka King and Frances Anne Cation at the University of Toronto and Erika Dyson, Daniel Vaca, and Joseph Blankholm at Columbia University. We would like to thank several colleagues and administrative staff in our respective institutions, including James Dicenso and John Kloppenborg, successive chairs of the Department for the Study of Religion, and Irene Kao, the department's business officer at Toronto. Pamela Klassen would especially like to thank Ruth Marshall, her colleague at the University of Toronto, for her careful reading and criticism of the first chapter. At Columbia, Mark C. Taylor, Al Stepan, Robert Thurman, and Philip Hamburger provided valuable support at important junctures; Emily Brennan at the Institute for Religion, Culture, and Public Life assisted with administrative issues with precision and aplomb. We also thank Travis McCauley for designing and administering our Web site.

Turning *After Pluralism* into a book extended its collaborative web further. Ada Jeffrey, a graduate student in the Centre for the Study of Religion at the University of Toronto, worked tirelessly on formatting and proofreading multiple versions of the manuscript, and Rajiv Sicora at Columbia University assisted heroically with a number of last-minute details. We are deeply grateful for the support and enthusiasm of Wendy Lochner, religion editor at Columbia University Press.

Finally, we would like to thank our families. Pamela Klassen, as always, thanks John Marshall for his perfect blend of collegiality, critique, and comfort, and her children, Magdalene, Isabel, and Georgia, for their encouragement and for being such great hosts whenever academics fill up the house. Courtney Bender thanks Jonathan Dworkin for his careful editorial eye and ear, and for his unending support of this book project and everything else. She also thanks her children, Solomon and Hope, for not complaining too much when she travels to Toronto without them (we will all go together soon, I promise) and for their perceptive observations about the social and religious worlds around them.

After Pluralism

INTRODUCTION

Habits of Pluralism

PAMELA E. KLASSEN AND COURTNEY BENDER

Throughout the world, "Parliaments of Religion" are no longer experiments held at a World's Fair but instead are everyday assemblies occurring in schools, hospitals, and city streets throughout North America, Asia, and Europe. At the same time, combatants in new "wars of religion" base their legitimacy on claims to defend religious traditions or worldviews, in such diverse places as Pakistan, Nigeria, and (in a less overtly militarized zone) Washington, D.C. Religion is proliferating; academics, journalists, and policymakers increasingly take religion as a subject of inquiry, and laypeople of all sorts consider it a rubric by which to understand shifting social forces in local neighborhoods and around the globe. Part of this proliferation has come in the guise of religious pluralism, in which a multiplicity of individuals and communities recognize each other as parallel forms of the phenomenon called religion. Whether considering the ways religion secures the diversity of identities in liberal democracies or the ways religion fosters antagonisms in war zones, thinking about how people construct and live with religious difference has clearly become a necessary task for states, scholars, and neighbors.

Pluralism, variously specified as cultural, political, legal, or religious, has come to represent a powerful ideal meant to resolve the question of how to get along in a conflict-ridden world. The authors in *After Pluralism* consider various definitions and discourses of pluralism, but put most simply, in this book we focus on pluralism defined as a commitment to recognize and understand others across perceived or claimed lines of religious difference.[1] For example, civic and academic organizations have lately adopted pluralism as an ideal model or doctrine for bringing about tangible social engagement across religious differences. From Harvard University's "Pluralism Project," through the proposed cooperation between the Aga Khan Foundation and the Canadian government in the Global Centre for Pluralism, to the European Union's quest for "A Soul for Europe," politicians, religious leaders, and academics in North American and Europe have converged on pluralism as the best path for proceeding into an admittedly uncertain future.[2]

We start with the understanding that modern practices of religion take place in the wake of this doctrine of pluralism, that is, after pluralism has become a widely recognized social ideal embedded in a range of political, civic, and cultural institutions. Our goal is to examine the grounds on which religious difference is itself constructed as a problem that has pluralism as its solution. Working comparatively across both national and disciplinary borders, the essays in this volume invite readers into a conversation about the conditions that have made pluralism a dominant frame in which diversity and heterogeneity can be recognized and engaged.

As our title suggests, *After Pluralism* takes this convergence on the doctrine of pluralism as its beginning but not its end. We thus consider what comes *after* pluralism in both temporal and theoretical terms. The episodic and genealogical analyses in *After Pluralism* explore the ways pluralism works as a "term of art," in Anver Emon's words, casting prescriptive norms of identity and engagement, creating new possibilities and curtailing others. We inquire into what comes after the recognition that current forms of religious pluralism are not naturally occurring ones and what comes after we begin taking account of the historical emergence and institutional production of certain practices and peoples as plural forms of religion. By querying the genealogy and effects of the concept of pluralism within a range of national and transnational contexts, this book generates new sets of questions for engaging and imagining the collective worlds and multiple registers in which religion matters.

EXPLAINING *AFTER PLURALISM*

Several scholars of religion have shown how contemporary articulations of religious pluralism have reproduced older distinctions among "world religions" that in their very origins exercised or abetted various forms of colonial and imperial control over foreign ideological, cultural, and legal systems (Asad 2003; Dirks 2001; Masuzawa 2005; Mitchell 2000; Said 1978). They rightly caution that the revivification of religious difference within frames of pluralism carries with it the violence of these earlier encounters. Political theorists have similarly questioned the ways in which the concept of political pluralism has been used to celebrate American exceptionalism and, more recently, have asked about the unexamined ontological grounding of the concept as it has served dual purposes as both a political ideal and an analytical tool (Campbell and Schoolman 2008).

Our own interests in this multidisciplinary volume are not to reproduce arguments that have taken shape within political theory or to rehash the well-documented story of the construction of pluralism. Rather, the authors in this volume take these positions as the obvious ground on which to pose our questions about what happens after pluralism. With an awareness of the construction of the category of religion at the fore, we ask the following: What does pluralism look like in practice, as a set of tools, projects, and political claims? We consider how the frame of pluralism recognizes some kinds of religious interactions and encounters and some kinds of religions (but not others) as normal and natural. We thus proceed by asking how pluralism is at work in the world, considering how pluralist aspirations and pluralist logics shape modes of public engagement and the various religious and nonreligious subjects that can take part within them. The specific sites in which our collective inquiry proceeds are themselves heterogeneous and include legal systems, theaters, prisons, interfaith coalitions, dream interpretation, and public memorials. Considering these realms as sites of the performance and policing of religious difference, we have compared conclusions about projects of pluralism in Canada, the United States, Egypt, Poland, and Germany.

Our focus on comparative cases and on specific examples allows close scrutiny of social processes that often appear to be more theoretical than concrete and more global than local. Many of the most contentious sites of debates about religious pluralism are simultaneously home to processes of transnationalism, globalization, and postwar (or intrawar) state formation. None of these are new phenomena, but they have taken new forms within current networks of global capitalism (Sassen 2006). Recent debates over immigration legislation in Europe and North America, conflicts over the legitimacy of religious legal systems within secular or multireligious states, and a variety of other flashpoints (including controversies over comic strips and religiously marked attire) all point to the ways in which the movement of peoples and ideas reveals the power relations within polities and communities. These revelations are not the simple consequence of certain religious actors and organizations showing up in new places, necessitating the response of host societies. Multinational religious corporations and networks are actively involved in both developing and critiquing religious pluralism at every level. While citizenship in a nation-state remains an unavoidable necessity for survival and stability, religious leaders make transnational claims to authority over increasingly dispersed universal communities, and the production and circulation of religious objects and media pay little heed to national borders (Jain 2007; Levitt 2007; Meyer and Moors 2006).

Shaped by this flurry of mediated images of religion and by the claims to authority made in the name of particular texts, histories, or lineages, public discussions of religion and religious pluralism within nation-states that consider themselves modern often carry with them a welter of tacit concerns about changing norms of political and moral authority. In many discussions of religious pluralism, what is "religious" itself appears as newly unsettled and out of place. The rules of what counts as recognized and recognizable religious difference (and shared notions about the privatization or laicization of religion within secular cultures) are ever more diversely challenged, whether from neo-pagan Wiccans or practitioners of Cuban Santeria. For some commentators, religious pluralism requires either new rules for public engagement or better enforcement of the old rules.[3]

The urgency surrounding the current manifestations of religious pluralism can therefore be partly explained by the ways they challenge, or even produce, what it means to be a multicultural, modern citizen (Modood and Levey 2008). "New" religious diversity becomes a condition through which commentators, politicians, and scholars can focus their various concerns about how personal liberties and minority self-determination will shape the futures of modern democratic engagement.[4] These are not just matters for pundits and politicians: Many prominent scholars are reopening debates about what constitutes the ideal relationship between religious claims and state power in liberal democracies (Chambers 2007; Habermas 2006; Taylor 2007). One of the most prominent of these scholars, Charles Taylor, has offered his perspective in the form of a lengthy scholarly book and a government-sponsored report. Taylor's *A Secular Age*, in which he argues that a secular "modern social imaginary" robustly undergirds and shapes the conditions through which people can be religious in both intimate and public arenas, has inspired academic blogs and much scholarly rethinking of the structures of religious identity in secular societies. With historian and sociologist Gérard Bouchard, Taylor has also coauthored a report commissioned by the government of Québec, dealing with the question of the state's accommodation of "cultural differences," which in the report largely took the form of religious differences. Based on four months of public consultations that the authors held across Québec, the report makes a case for "open secularism" as the best means for protecting freedom of conscience and religion along with a flexible practice of state neutrality (Bouchard and Taylor 2008). Histories of Christian establishment and political power in Europe and North America cast a long shadow over Taylor's academic and policy interventions. At the same time, the future of states in which many religious imaginaries are newly in cohabitation animates his work.

The debates about how far any particular liberal democratic state should go in accommodating religious difference are not merely about theological or ritual divergences. They are also about the distribution of resources. In this frame, religion acts as a "mediating symbol," to use Courtney Jung's term. According to Jung (2001:226), ethnicity, race, language, and religion should be understood as waxing and waning with respect to political identity, which remains the principal site of "organized struggle for the control over the allocation of resources and power residing in the state." This resource- and power-based approach explains a great deal about what is at stake in recent discussions of possibilities and perils of religious pluralism, but by articulating religion as one more exploitable set of positions, Jung's analysis does not go far enough in questioning how religiousness itself becomes a recognizable ground for a new type of negotiation of state power and civic actors.

What interests us in this volume is where and whether the rubric of pluralism helps to create religion as an affiliation that is about more than organizing to achieve a class of economic and political interests. Emerging in new public settings and in disconcertingly plural ways, religion presents a threat to the stories nations, communities, and families tell about themselves, whether tales of laicité, mosaics, spiritual kinship, or gender equality (Fessenden 2007; Most, chap. 5, this volume). At the same time, the frame of religious plurality is undergirded by the unifying notion of religion as something shared between diverse groups, whether as articulated in the language of harmonious interfaith coalitions or in the terminology of secular detractors who decry both evangelical Christians and Muslim terrorists as equally religious zealots (Todd, chap. 8, and Hicks, chap. 10, this volume; Hitchens 2007). The mutually constitutive relations between plurality and unity—between celebrating the plurality of religious diversity and organizing under the unity of the category of religion—produce complicated political effects in a range of arenas. These include legal contexts in which Native Americans struggle for sovereignty partly through the guise of religion, and spaces of incarceration in which Muslim prisoners are pastored by Protestant chaplains in German jails (Leavelle, chap. 6, McNally, chap. 9, and Becci, chap. 12, this volume). Ironically, in most of the nation-states represented in this book's cases, the growing presence of a wider range of religious actors is often pointed to both as the triumph of tolerant and liberal democratic projects and as evidence of threats to the secular spaces that undergird those projects.

As the essays in this volume demonstrate, the sites and spaces in which avowedly secular and religious groups encounter and shape pluralism are historically emergent. We pay particular attention to the considerable and often vexed diversity within particular overarching religious identities in particular national settings, whether one considers Christianity, Islam, Judaism, or religious and spiritual traditions among Native American communities. Pluralisms have taken shape in different national, transnational, legal, and cultural contexts, where different constellations of institutions and actors shape the conditions of interaction and the terms of religiousness or secularity recognized within them (Baumann and Behloul 2005; Berger et al. 2008; Eisenberg 2005; Mortensen 2003).

Thinking comparatively about pluralisms in a range of national contexts seems especially necessary when many recent discussions of pluralism vaunt the vitality of U.S. religious pluralism as "the greatest contribution made by the United States to global religious life" (Lippy 2000:162).[5] David Hollinger (2001:243) goes even further in his recommendation of the "demographically unruly case" of the United States as particularly "worthy of the world's scrutiny" when debating pluralism. Critiquing the work of Canadian philosopher Will Kymlicka, Hollinger (2001:243) explicitly argues against taking "Quebec-preoccupied Canada as a basis for a liberal theory of group rights applicable to the world," suggesting that where the Canadian example is too particular, the U.S. case is more revealing of the contemporary "species experience" of migration and mixing.[6] Although scholars rarely endorse the United States as a model for global emulation, they often come close to privileging it as a starting point for cross-national comparison. Our comparative work strives to remain self-reflexive about what we can (and cannot) learn from particular examples. After reading about how effectively the concept of pluralism can be applied to Canada, Poland, East Germany, or Egypt, one might conclude that there is something particularly American about the concept of religious pluralism after all. This particularity would suggest that it functions less as a model for export than as a doctrinal ideal embodied in particular historical, political, and theological conditions of possibility.

PLURALISM: A BRIEF GENEALOGY

In our reading, pluralism is a fully modern concept arising in concert with the equally modern ideas of secularity and religion. Genealogies of pluralism grant the word a range of progenitors, from eighteenth-century German philosopher Immanuel Kant, in *Anthropology from a Pragmatic Point of View*, to twentieth-century U.S. philosopher Horace Kallen, who coined the phrase "cultural pluralism" (Hutchison 2003; Kühle 2003). In its English usage, *pluralism* was first coined to address an issue of church–state relations, although it held less salutary associations than it currently enjoys. Initially, *ecclesiastical pluralism* named the situation in which a cleric in the state-supported Church of England held two or more offices simultaneously, often neglecting one for the other, while being paid for ministering to all the parishes in question. In 1772, W. Pennington decried the "turpitude of Pluralism" for causing parishes to lack resident clergy and for fostering greedy priests. For Pennington (1772:54, 69), the "summit of corruption" lay in pluralism's Roman Catholic past, when parishes, or benefices, could be bought and sold to the highest bidder.

In his 1818 work *Church-of-Englandism and Its Catechism Examined*, Jeremy Bentham, better known for his theories of economics and the Panopticon, also commented on how the practice of ecclesiastical pluralism was a "relick" left over from the "yoke of Popery." Bentham (1818:249) argued that pluralism was an irrefutable example of the vicious "mendacity and insincerity" of the established Church of England and was proof that state-established religion was untenable for both moral and practical reasons. That a cleric could claim payment for leading his flock while being entirely absent from it was akin to shoplifting and swindling for Bentham, with the same viscerally harmful effects. Pluralism was "a sin the guilt of which is as real, as that of *Simony* is imaginary" (Bentham 1818:337). Considering this work with his earlier appeal to France to *Emancipate Your Colonies!*, we can see that Bentham's strategies of argumentation against pluralism were similar to his critique of (at least) French colonialism. In this 1793 address, Bentham called on France to live up to its own declaration of rights by renouncing its claim to its colonies. Bentham (1830) argued that contrary to its claims, colonial governance was characterized not by "solicitude" but by tyrannical absence: "What picture can you so much as form to yourselves of the [colonized] country? What conception can you frame to yourselves of manners and modes of life so different from your own? When will you ever see them? When will they ever see you? If they suffer, will their cries ever wound your ears?" Just as colonial governments extracted resources by "leading" people they neither knew nor cared for, so did the pluralist priest.

Ecclesiastical pluralism soon came to hold another connotation, that of Christian churches that attempted to live with some degree of mutual compatibility in the wake of the Reformation. Tracing what he called "official pluralism" in early modern Europe, historian Benjamin Kaplan (2007) has recently demonstrated the multitude of ways in which Christians of divergent theologies and loyalties found ways to share space across Europe while alternately "emancipating," segregating, or expelling Jews and Muslims from these spaces of toleration. Economist Murat Iyigun (2006) further highlights the processes that shaped eighteenth-century European ecclesiastical pluralism as an intra-Christian unity in diversity, prompted in response to the threat of Ottoman—and Muslim—military conquest (see also Baer 2008).

Unburdening pluralism of its etymological roots in eighteenth-century Church of England debates, nineteenth-century philosophers adroitly commandeered it for their own purposes. Counterposed with monism and dualism, pluralism eventually became identified with William James's articulation of philosophical pluralism, in which he argued against philosophical monism, where everything could (if only ultimately, or ideally) be contained within a single system. James (1909:321–322) writes in *A Pluralistic Universe*, "The pluralistic world is thus more like a federal republic than like an empire or a kingdom. However much may be collected, however much may report itself as present at any effective centre of consciousness or action, something else is self-governed and absent and unreduced to unity." Read against Bentham's wrath for the church- and state-funded absent pluralists, James's political metaphor of the republican freedom of irreducibly pluralist absence shows just how profoundly the meanings of the word had changed.

In the twentieth century, pluralism truly found its crossover appeal. Political theorists debating questions of state sovereignty applied *pluralism* as a term to describe multiparty political systems, and anthropologists also used it to describe societies in which more than one group sought cultural recognition. Despite his argument for the irreducibility of philosophical plurality, William James's work on religion and mysticism ended up lending itself to project of unification, as mid-twentieth-century Protestant theologians discussed religious pluralism as a kind of "global theology" (Kühle 2003:427), in which many paths to led to the same divine truth (Schmidt 2003).

With such a plethora of meanings and ends, it is not surprising that pluralism has retained both descriptive and prescriptive burdens and that it is not always easy to tell them apart. Those who use the term *pluralism* have not always acknowledged the limits necessary for its operation. It should therefore not come as any surprise that the current use of *pluralism* also has its own limits and that those who use it are only intermittently aware of these limits. Because the current frame of pluralism is often expansive in its aspirations and (as examples noted earlier indicate) often used within systems of state power, it is all the more necessary to continue to consider its work in the world. Suffice it to say that pluralism, like the related concepts of secularism and religion, emerged in response to particular challenges in the development of Western liberal democracies. In turn, pluralism has gone global, creating the paradox that with its expanding reach, invocations to celebrate difference may themselves breed a hegemonic unity.

LOCATIONS OF PLURALISM

Empirical studies of religious pluralism in the United States have worked with dual purposes: first, to identify the shifts in the types of religious actors active in

America, thereby mapping a newly diverse religious terrain, and second, to use such knowledge to promulgate practices of tolerance and respect. The project of mapping the "new" religious pluralism has been most visibly and actively developed by Harvard University's Pluralism Project, a multiyear program to map the religious landscape of the United States and its diversity. Other projects have similarly followed this path, working to identify the location of U.S. religious diversity by focusing on congregations and religious communities in American cities, a project that in itself articulates religious pluralism as organized via existing and clearly demarcated voluntary societies and associations.[7] Similarly, projects such as the one summarized in Robert Wuthnow's *America and the Challenges of Religious Diversity* (2005) investigate how American Christians understand religious diversity and what they think it means for them and for their nation.

Although these projects have described some elements of the changing religious landscape, they often embed prescriptive models of interaction and normative understandings of religious communities. Indeed, Martin Marty suggests that the language of religious pluralism always embeds a normative goal: It is not merely descriptive of varieties but indicative of the proper relations that should take place between them. Marty (2007:16) observes that "careful listening to scholars and public figures who devote themselves to the subject would reveal that 'pluralism' implies and involves a polity, a civic context which provides some 'rules of the game,' refers to an ethos, and evokes response" (see also Porterfield 2008). Thus Diana Eck defines pluralism as an "energetic engagement with diversity" that is "achieved" only through a "dialogue" rooted in "the encounter of commitments." Pluralism is "the active seeking of understanding across lines of difference" (Eck 2007). Similarly, Robert Wuthnow (2005) calls religious leaders to more active engagement with their religious neighbors and suggests that teaching their faithful about the theologies and the beliefs of neighbors will ultimately help to cultivate better interactions between religious individuals and groups. And political scientist Thomas Banchoff (2007:5) most recently writes that although "religious pluralism describes a social and political phenomenon," it nonetheless remains a central understanding that "religious pluralism should be peaceful" and that, furthermore, "a preference for nonviolence . . . is shared in principle across religious faiths and institutionalized in democratic orders."

The discourse on religious pluralism does not encompass the whole of contemporary discourse on pluralism, which often refers to other kinds of difference and other kinds of prescriptive interactions. Political theorist William Connolly's (2005:66) book *Pluralism* draws on a similar kind of understanding of interaction as that of Eck, where "deep pluralism" is about "layered practices of connection across multiple differences," differences that could be based in religion, philosophy, or politics. Connolly, long both a critic and a poet of pluralism in its liberal democratic political forms, has more recently articulated his critique and construction of the normative bases of pluralism through a nontheistic yet theological language. Arguing that deep pluralism requires both "a politics of *agonistic respect*" and an "ethos of *critical responsiveness*," Connolly simultaneously recognizes that the very concepts scholars choose for debating pluralism are themselves "laced with onto-theological differences that might not be fully susceptible to definitive resolution." Operating from his own explicitly nontheistic ontology that the world is constituted by a "fundamental diversity of being," Connolly understands his capacious notion of pluralism to be rooted in a diversity of diversities, held to by their adherents with deep "affective intensity." To refuse to take the step from academic description to normative engagement is ethically intolerable, concludes Connolly (2008:307, 309); "to bypass the pursuit of deep diversity is to fail an elemental test of fidelity to the world."

In Canada, *pluralism* is a less common—and less passionately argued—term, replaced with the notion of diversity. Projects that deal with questions of diversity have often been less explicitly concerned with religious difference, instead focusing on issues of multiculturalism or cultural recognition. This is partly because the defining contexts in which pluralism has been adjudicated in Canada have involved First Nations and Québec, both of which consider themselves nations that existed in some form long before the Canadian nation (1867) and certainly long before the patriation from Great Britain of the Canadian Constitution in 1982. Although the United States shares similar "multinational" contexts, whether in the case of Native American groups or territories such as Puerto Rico, these nations within a nation have not been a predominant feature of the discourse of pluralism in the United States. Instead, U.S. discourse has focused largely on how individual rights and cultural recognition intertwine, with the "freedom of religion" as one of the gold standards of individual rights (Kymlicka 2001:271). When religion has been a focus of discussion of pluralism or multiculturalism in Canada, it has often been discussed as a facet of ethnicity or as one particularly tricky case study for the dilemmas of living in a multicultural society. Nevertheless, even in Canada an American-style prescriptive message has grown prominent of late, as scholars increasingly position their work as a contribution to the fostering of harmonious relations between religions (e.g., Seljak and Bramadat 2005).[8]

The European contexts of pluralism are found both in particular nation-states and in the wider polity of the European Union. With very different histories of how the state conceived of and supported religious groups—from the established churches of Germany and England to the avowed secularism and anticlericalism at France—no single answer has emerged for the question of how to bring together democratic politics and religious commitments. However, the demographics of immigration in European countries have provoked some similarities in discussions of religious diversity. German "guest workers" who were once known as "Turks" and immigrants from France's former colonies who were once known as Algerians or North Africans are now both largely subsumed under the religious marker *Muslim*. In many European countries, Judaism remains a historically remembered though largely physically absent marker of religious difference (Zubrzycki, chap. 11, this volume). Increasingly, however, demographics dictate that religious difference is imagined through Islam, embodied in such forms as separate education systems, a growing presence in urban architecture and soundscapes, attire recognized as religious and not "fashionable," and discussions of legal pluralism in family law (Baumann 2005). This religious difference is marked against twin "inheritances" of Christianity and secularism, which various actors in the political field of the European Union claim—with much debate—as particularly European heritages.

The question of how the European Union will acknowledge the significance of religion, both in terms of its "Christian heritage" and in terms of the current presence of Islam and other more marginalized religions, is being actively debated. Some groups claim precedence for Catholic or Protestant influences, and others define their interventions as a defense of the legacy of European traditions of secular toleration and pluralism. José Manuel Barroso, then president of the European Commission, took the latter course in a speech to the 2006 conference of the European Commission–supported initiative, "A Soul for Europe":

> Europe, which "invented" tolerance for individuals, for their opinions, for their beliefs and for their differences, must make its own special voice heard. Let us not hesitate and then one day regret that we did not say "no" in time and out loud. So it is important to defend respect for diversity. But at the same time we must not lose sight of the fact that this respect is based on a deeper respect for certain principles which cannot be negotiated. Freedom of expression, freedom of religion, or the right not to be religious, and freedom of creation are simply not negotiable.

Understanding the principle of respecting diversity as respecting the right to be or not to be religious puts a particularly European cast on the matter that is less often found in U.S.-based discussions of pluralism.

Pluralism, then, must be understood as emerging in specific contexts and places, as a discourse of the future that cannot escape the past. Our inclusion of Amira Mittermaier's analysis of dream interpretation in Egypt reveals the limits of what contexts and places can fruitfully be understood by the concept of pluralism, a term less naturalized in Egyptian political or religious discourse. The North American and European focus of the other chapters allows the authors to engage with doctrines of pluralism as more or less indigenous discourses, operating in particular ways in cultures with an embedded Christian past (or present). Muslim dream interpretation in Egypt, though shaped by interactions with Freudian psychoanalytic theory and to a lesser extent Coptic Christian visionary traditions, is concerned largely with negotiating a plurality of Muslim approaches to the significance and consequence of dream visions. Mittermaier's appraisal of the utility and effects of the concept of pluralism in thinking about Muslim dreaming demonstrates another model for imagining what it is to cross over realms of difference.

The goal of deep engagement across difference, as articulated by Connolly and Eck, is an attractive and even laudable goal in many ways. However, the doctrines and programs of pluralism that dominate contemporary academic and public conversations do not constitute a theory of understanding religious interactions as they take place in the world. Nor do these starting points adequately acknowledge the great diversity (and sometimes conflict) within particular religious traditions or the ways in which the political projects of pluralism (whether religious or otherwise) hinge on exclusions and occlusions of various religious and political actors. This volume's goal is to set the normative, prescriptive foundations of projects of pluralism in comparative perspective, by presenting multiple empirical studies, historical reflections, and theoretical reassessments.

With all this in mind, this volume is guided by several underlying questions. First, given that pluralism functions as a prescriptive discourse, what assumptions and power relations condition its rhetorical authority? Second, to what degree have the prescriptive and normative understandings embedded in these pluralistic frameworks reified the very differences that pluralism hopes to engage, for example by defining "religions" more coherently than historical or ethnographic accounts might warrant? Finally, as we investigate transnational and historical contexts, what contrasting patterns of power and difference might we identify in the practices of religious encounter, exchange, and conflict?

The Toronto and Columbia conferences where these papers were first presented began by questioning the types of religiousness imagined within the frameworks of pluralism. When prescriptive pluralisms imagine religions as discrete and recognizable traditions with explicit and observable boundaries across which interchange or conflict occurs, they often leave the messy and unpredictable character of religious practice unrecognized. Messiness and unpredictability, whether in conflicts within a particular religious community over questions of gender and sexuality or in the development of unexpected alliances, borrowings, or transformations effected among "religious traditions" when defined as such by the state or the law, are as constitutive of living religious groups in the modern period as are their claims to purity and distinctiveness. The goals articulated within contemporary commitments to religious (or deep) pluralism enjoin rigorous debate. Our proceedings did not start out on the path of that debate, although we necessarily stepped onto it at times. Instead, we began with a shared view that the time has come to investigate the effects of current descriptive and prescriptive assessments of pluralism through sustained comparative inquiry.[9]

CONCEPTUAL PARTNERS, ALTERNATIVE CONCEPTS

As we embarked on this inquiry, we considered several sets of conceptual apparatuses for engaging religion that we believed would set our inquiry into religious interactions and engagements on different trajectories than those suggested by pluralism. Although none of these approaches remove us from the worlds shaped by pluralist discourses, and none are any less ideologically embedded or pure than pluralism, they nonetheless present alternative coordinates for assessing ongoing social processes and imagining religious engagement. Mapping out these partners and alternatives at the beginning crystallizes a range of ways to develop arguments that move beyond the well-rehearsed genealogical critiques to contribute a better platform on which to ground future research and debate.

HYBRIDITY

A large part of the impetus for the conferences on which this volume is based was the degree to which the editors' research into American and Canadian religious mixtures failed to fit with conventional stories of religious interaction. While we encountered religious diversity and intersections, we found few examples of neat borders and boundaries between religious groups, nor did we find that exchange necessarily took place through dialogue or even recognition of the other. Klassen researched twentieth-century liberal Protestants, who she found had a robust supernaturalism unlike the bureaucratic rationality ascribed to them in many scholarly accounts. For example, a twentieth-century Anglican missionary confidently wrote of himself as a psychologist engaged in the science and spirituality of a kind of telepathic healing that bore many unstated resemblances to the spiritual practices of his First Nations neighbors and sometime converts. Bender similarly encountered early-twenty-first-century metaphysical and mystical seekers whose varied practices, including Reiki, yoga, spiritual belly dancing, and shamanic "soul singing," resonated deeply with earlier

American and European religious crossings, borrowings, and transformations. The knotty genealogies of these activities continued to raise to the fore the realities of shifting temporal politics of religious borrowing, thus making clear the limits of simple designations or claims about any practice's authenticity or origins. In each of these cases, religious people trafficked in claims of authenticity shaped by an openness and acceptance of others' religious views, drawing on rhetoric that was indistinguishable from liberal political discourse about cultural and religious tolerance (Bender 2007, 2010; Klassen 2007, 2011).

We realized that understanding the mixtures that characterized our research subjects would require clear and rigorous theoretical approaches that allowed us to consider innovative and often controversial religious borrowing, appropriation, and combination in historical and cultural contexts. We not only began to draw on the burgeoning literature on the constitutively hybrid nature of religious traditions but likewise asked how and through which social and political processes the facts of these hybrid forms are obscured (or at best ridiculed) in public discourse and effaced from the public (symbolic, ritual, and political) construction of religious authority. The "facts" of our hybrid subjects pressed us to consider what social processes shaped them as such: What kinds of social distinction, political arguments, and religious imaginations articulated the boundaries that designated (if not created) some practices and traditions as hybrid and, for that matter, designated others as nonhybrid? What events, practices, and discourses shaped these entities? To paraphrase sociologist Andrew Abbott (1995), what kinds of social boundaries make what kinds of religious things?

In a variant of this approach, political theorist James Tully (an "After Pluralism" participant) has argued that modern constitutionalism—with its primary focus on equality between self-governing nations and equality between individual citizens in a nation—has been unable to adequately grapple with the politics of cultural recognition driven by groups within a nation, such as aboriginal peoples, new immigrants, and feminist organizations. Tully contended that modern constitutionalism remains profoundly shaped by a desire for cultural uniformity and by a "billiard ball" model of cultural diversity, in which national identity is held as the preeminent form of belonging and cultures are imagined as coherent groups. Instead, Tully (1995:11) suggests, we live in times of "strange multiplicity" in which "cultures are continuously contested, imagined, and reimagined, transformed and negotiated, both by their members and through their interaction with others. The identity, and so the meaning, of any culture is thus aspectival rather than essential. . . . Cultural diversity is a tangled labyrinth of intertwining cultural differences and similarities, not a panopticon of fixed, independent and incommensurable worldviews in which we are either prisoners or cosmopolitan spectators in the central tower." Modern constitutionalism has applied this Benthamite billiard ball model to its dominant conceptions of religion as well, using the law to reify or acknowledge only certain practices or communities as "religious," as several of our contributors note. The assumptions about religion and culture within models of constitutionalism (and the varying "sacredness" or unchangeable nature ascribed to the constitutions of particular nations) are thus extremely important to any negotiations or reimagining of religious difference and interaction, whether among scholars or citizens.

Studies of hybridity and multiplicity continue to compel us to investigate the ways in which actors and institutions fashion themselves as religious through the interplay and friction between overlapping identities and communities. Similarly, hybridity calls attention to the ways in which such identities are shaped in various interactions with apparently nonreligious institutions, including law, medicine, and popular entertainment. These studies and approaches compel persistent reflexivity about the fluidity or fixity of the categories by which we label people, practices, and texts as "Christian," "Muslim," "Jewish," "Buddhist," or "secular." Likewise, they compel our ongoing attention to the various historical trajectories of religious mixtures, taking place under the name of syncretism, hybridity, creolization, or other charged rubrics (Bhabha 2004; Stewart 1999; Stewart and Shaw 1994). These perspectives remind us that our labors take shape in the wake of an ideology of pluralism that articulates and naturalizes the very boundaries of difference that it seeks to diminish, overcome, or mediate.

ENCOUNTER

Another conceptual partner to pluralism is the metaphor of encounter as a meeting place of religious difference (McCarthy 2007). A powerful image applied readily to the political and intimate spaces of many present-day liberal democracies, whether kitchen tables, classrooms, or streets, the metaphor of encounter conveys the sense of making space for new actors and communities (Kurien 2007). A metaphor that lends itself to a vision of a collision of purities, whether billiard balls or individuals, encounter also risks imagining a level playing field in which all religious actors and groups are similarly oriented in relation to secular forms. In the frame of political theory, the level playing field model echoes a Rawlsian veil of ignorance, or what Courtney Jung (2001:223) has called the "liberalism of neutrality." Instead of endorsing neutrality that excludes from public debate such kinds of difference as religion, ethnicity, and language, however, the metaphor of encounter encourages an understanding of meeting across lines of difference that grants neutrality to difference itself. Histories of colonialism, differential social and economic capital, and gendered divisions of labor and political power are just some of the factors that mitigate against any lines of difference, religious or otherwise, being equally arrayed, encountered, porous, or bounded for all. In European and North American liberal democracies, the playing field, as shaped by secular civic institutions, has undoubtedly, even if ambivalently, favored some forms of religion over others.

Beginning with tales of the pilgrims and Pocahontas, the metaphor of encounter has been particularly applied to the context of the United States. Imagined and proclaimed as a place where the vitality of pluralism has naturally and uniquely flourished, the United States has been repeatedly held up as a model for other nations seeking to deal with diversity (Hollinger 2001; Lippy 2000). Although some admirers of the U.S. model prefer the metaphor of the marketplace to that of the encounter, both metaphors have become revitalized in the wake of European confrontations with Islam and other religious groups (free church Pentecostals, for example) (Graf 2003). However, *encounter* is a metaphor that cannot fully address the history of America as a settler colony in which many of those with political power—but not all—worked hard to displace the native inhabitants.[10]

Martin Marty (2007:22–23) again provides a useful historical corrective: "That pluralism found encouragement in the new United States occurred not because everyone strove to realize it, believed firmly in its base, or nicely stepped out of the path of each other. Much of the move toward embracing it was prudential and practical." Here, we add that such "practical" pluralism was guided by historically realized secular and religious impulses, including those of a Protestant elite, and became naturalized in the courts, public schools, and a variety of other civic and political institutions. These historical conditions contributed to the framework wherein our understanding of pluralism (and various related ideas of multiculturalism, interfaith, and ecumenism) begins with visions of socially contained and organized encounters. A fuller historical understanding of religious pluralism would necessarily include not just these developing articulations of pluralism in various institutions but also the bitter contests, conflicts, and violence that have informed the ideals and the collective memories and imaginations of both liberal democracies and ecumenical organizations, as well as the ability of states to contain religious actors and mediate their divergent claims.

With this in mind, studies of religious diversity must attend to the historically variable practices and techniques that constitute and objectify collective visions of appropriate religious interaction. Among other things, this will entail holding together stories of harmonious religious cooperation with tales of religious conflict, the repression of religious minorities, and other nonpeaceful events in order to consider how they conjointly shape imaginings of the religious and the possibilities of dialogue. A focus on encounter likewise demands broadening our conceptual and empirical investigations into sites of encounter, to include the numerous encounters that religious individuals and groups have with legal structures and other secular institutions and organizations that powerfully articulate the very terms on which religious actors, interests, and understandings are recognized as such. How and when interests and ways of life are recognized as religious or cultural, as belief or attribute, as group or individual matter for the fashioning or contention of religious identities in political, economic, and cultural contexts. Expanding our vision of what counts as encounter means attending to the range of daily interactions and practices of translation, interpretation, and mutual indifference that shape the lived experience of religious diversity as a shared project in pluralistic, and often postcolonial, societies.

SECULARISM

Secularism is more than a conceptual partner of normative models of pluralism; it is one of its conceptual grounds. Several scholars have squarely positioned "secular formations" as profoundly shaping and articulating the boundaries that are encountered or hybridized in religious encounters. This view, evident in many of the chapters in this volume, raises in a new way a question about the relationships in our contemporary world between formations of the secular and formations of plural religions and religious plurality (Most, chap. 5, this volume; see also Asad 2003; Jakobsen and Pellegrini 2008).

The relations between the secular and the plural are not clear, however: We might find in some cases that the "problem" of the religious other is developed by political and social actors as a political problem that justifies the development of a secular state. Such has often been suggested to be the case in Europe, where the Peace of Westphalia (1648) is often referred to as a singular moment in shaping both the emergence of secular states, the privatization of religion, and nascent forms of tolerance of religious pluralism. That tolerance and its abode of citizenship were not extended to all is well recognized (Hurd 2007; Philpott 2002). Yet the fact that these early moments, which linked the development of European secularity to religious privatization and tolerance, simultaneously organized, distinguished, and excluded religious groups along new vectors of public and private would have deep consequences for distinguishing various groups' capacities to become modern, private, secular citizens. These arguments continue to rage in Europe and the United States, where (as Mahmood Mamdani and many others have argued) the conditions of secularism have actively created sets of (Islamic and other religious) people whose religious natures render them incapable of participating in secular politics (Mahmood

2006; Mamdani 2004; Scott 2007). To put it another way, when William Connolly's deep pluralism defines the pursuit of deep diversity as an act of fidelity to the world, any individual or group that does not take agonistic respect as its starting point can only be considered infidel on a global scale.

The details of European and North American cases reveal greater complexity and complication, if not contradictions, in the formations of pluralism. In the United States, for example, a secular state that is presumed to neither encourage nor discourage religious identity unites some variants of religious plurality as admissible under law while excluding other religious groups as insufficiently tolerant. At the same time, the idioms of tolerance, multicultural or religious celebrations, simultaneously depoliticize and depublicize particular religious interests. In the face of these normative paths to "religious" recognition, scholars must acknowledge and inquire further into the processes by which gaining religious recognition in the United States requires that groups take a seat at a multireligious table. The stories told in this volume call attention to a growing recognition that the varying cultures of religious pluralism in which we live are always directed toward and galvanized by multiple fields of knowledge and power.

This volume depended on our willingness to engage with localized discussions of mixture and encounter while also stepping back from them to think comparatively and with the benefit of several theoretical lenses. With the perspectives of both the global and the local at hand, we came to new awareness of the structures that have made pluralisms possible, moving us beyond a focus on discussions of religion and the political to also include the legal and constitutional, the literary and performative (see also Bramen 2001; Fessenden 2007; Pecora 2006; Viswanathan 2008). Where does the production of religious distinction take place: at what social and cultural points, at what practical, discursive, institutional, or structural levels? What makes certain religious groups and their actions observable and others not? Focusing on these questions has taken us closer to reassessing and even observing the varied, fine-grained modes of engagement through which we act and imagine our worlds and those of others.

THE SCOPE OF THE VOLUME

The contributors to this volume share a commitment to empirical research in specific communities, institutions, and movements. Their shared attention to the messy business of religious action, interaction, and engagement allows a vantage point on the varieties of ways in which groups, individual actors, and institutions shape and draw on logics of pluralism. Together, these chapters provide ample evidence that the human interaction expressed in the language of religion rarely follows a straight path. In some of the essays we find groups, actors, or states playing on or with the motifs of religious pluralisms. In others, explicitly religious and secular groups are caught up short by those logics and find themselves limited and contained in problematic ways, whereas others carry on with indifference to them. Spanning a range of locations and disciplines, this volume presents multiple sites for the critique of existing discourses while generating numerous questions and possibilities for engagement with the quandaries and challenges that confront us after pluralism.

As we begin to look at the ways in which our understandings of religious pluralism emerge historically in various contexts, we also begin to question the strategies and politics that accompany contemporary views of religious pluralism. We take it as given that although religious differences and the boundaries between religious groups are not natural, they are no less powerful or important because of it. An important focus of many essays in this volume is to trace how and when religious groups and communities are able to make claims, pursue their aims, build coalitions, or mark boundaries within the structures and limits of these "pluralistic" worlds and what they might gain or sacrifice in the process of constructing themselves as singular religions in a such a pluralistic world. The chapters on Native American religions and U.S. law demonstrate this most clearly. At the same time, the papers also attend to other varied and unexpected sites for the negotiation of religious identities and difference, such as theater, prisons, debates about dream interpretation, and largely "uniform" religious societies such as Poland.

The book is divided into three related sections that we arrived at collectively during three meetings in 2007 and 2008. In these meetings, authors, editors, and keynote speakers presented, discussed, and revised the chapters and contributed toward our developing collective argument. *After Pluralism* is thus the fruit of two years of collaborative conversation that included all the contributors and several workshop participants who were unable to contribute chapters to the volume. We have learned from each other in many ways over this time, and we hope that the intensity and exchange of our conversations are evident in the writing that has found its way to these pages.

The first section, "Law, Normativity, and the Constitution of Religion," brings together four chapters that focus on the power of legal discourses and rulings, as well as broader forms of normativity, to shape what and who counts in the construction of human activity as "religious." In "Ethics After Pluralism," ethicist, queer theorist, and scholar of religion Janet Jakobsen questions how norms and practices of sexuality trouble the presumption of a level field on which religious difference can be negotiated within a society. Arguing that secularism, with its Protestant groundings, cannot adequately function as such a level field, Jakobsen addresses the specific quandary of how sexuality acts as a crucible for conflicts about what constitutes "ethics" in the religiously diverse United States. In a very different context, legal historian Anver Emon's chapter, "Pluralizing Religion: Islamic Law and the Anxiety of Reasoned Deliberation," considers the circumstances of colonialism and encounters with Western legal systems that have led to the codification of Islamic legal traditions. Arguing that "legal pluralism" characterized premodern Islamic legal traditions, Emon traces the varying interests and communities that work against such plurality today in both Islamic and Western states. In " Religion Naturalized: The New Establishment," another scholar of law and religion, Winnifred Fallers Sullivan, turns back to the U.S. context, demonstrating how inadequate current disestablishment laws are for regulating the new scope of religious activities in the United States, including the case she presents of challenges to the constitutionality of government-sponsored and funded "spiritual assessments" integrated into Veterans Administration hospitals. Sullivan suggests that a legal system wary of "naturalizing" Christianity in a world of pluralism has now come to naturalize a more diffuse yet still particular notion of spirituality. Finally, legal scholar Benjamin Berger argues that the meeting of law and religion in U.S. and Canadian contexts is best understood as a cross-cultural encounter in itself. "The Cultural Limits of Legal Tolerance" traces the way in which current legal formations of rights and religion often contribute to rather than solve problems that inhere in multicultural societies and offers suggestions for how legal scholars might rethink this dilemma.

The second section, "Performing Religion After Pluralism," groups four chapters that consider public sites in which the performance of rituals, identities, or doctrines has provoked open debate or implicit discomfort about the effects and place of religion in public. Drawing on recent genealogical critiques of secularism, including that of Janet Jakobsen, scholar of American literature Andrea Most investigates what she calls Jewish "theatrical liberalism." Most demonstrates how twentieth-century musical theater was a primary site for liberal Jews to enact their encounter with dominant liberal Protestant ideals of the relationship between individual and community. Her chapter, "The Birth of Theatrical Liberalism," takes the notion of "performing religion" seriously, as she argues that the theater was a key site for Jews to establish and often implicitly argue for a public sphere in which religious diversity was accepted and normalized. In another context, historian Tracy Leavelle traces the legacies of Christian predominance, in coordination with state power, as he analyzes several attempts by Native American groups to reclaim lands on the bases of religious practice and ritual that required them to perform religion in ways recognizable to the eyes of U.S. law. In "The Perils of Pluralism: Colonization and Decolonization in American Indian Religious History," Leavelle pays particular attention to the ways in which Native activists have used the category of religion to claim authenticity and legal standing in the context of a supposedly secular framework.

Moving to twenty-first-century Egypt, a site rarely considered under the rubric of pluralism, anthropologist and religion scholar Amira Mittermaier considers how divergent perspectives on dream interpretation—that of Western-trained psychologists and that of Sufi masters working from Islamic traditions—contend with each other for popular and official recognition. Her chapter, "A Matter of Interpretation: Dreams, Islam, and Psychology in Egypt," concludes that these "different epistemes" for understanding dreams end up in an interplay of interpretation rather than a clash of modern and religious views of the self. Mittermaier's research, rooted in ethnographic research that considers personal narratives and mediated encounters among proponents of both psychological and Islamic approaches, allows her to make a strong case for the processual nature of "ontotheological" engagement, in which commitments to "deep pluralism" are not equally shared. Finally, religious studies scholar Terry Todd's chapter, "The Temple of Religion and the Politics of Religious Pluralism: Judeo-Christian America at the 1939–1940 New York World's Fair," takes us to the civic and business organizations that shaped an interfaith chapel at the 1939–1940 New York World's Fair, tracing the emergence of a new symbolic display—and the very construction—of "Judeo-Christian" religious cooperation that sought to mitigate and overcome chronic Catholic–Protestant conflicts, but at the expense of other religious coalitions. All four of these chapters demonstrate the necessity—and rewards—of looking for religious contest and formation in supposedly secular places, such as the commercial theater, psychoanalytic practice, U.S. law, and temples to capitalism.

Our final section, "The Ghosts of Pluralism: Unintended Consequences of Institutional and Legal Constructions," includes chapters that focus on the often unacknowledged specters that haunt the celebratory air of projects of pluralism: legacies of Christian domination, the continual presence of gender as a threat to pluralist engagement across religious difference, and the legacies of explicitly antireligious ideologies in newly pluralist postcommunist countries. Religious studies and legal scholar Michael McNally argues in "Native American Religious Freedom Beyond the First Amendment" that in the case of Native Americans working within the constraints of the First Amendment of the U.S. Constitution, legal arguments based on religious identity have not been as efficacious as those based on "cultural property." McNally shows how diverse, not easily classifiable Native American traditions pose one of the greatest challenges to the concept of religion itself, not only as it is used by scholars but also as it is implemented in the legal and political rubrics of pluralism.

Similarly, in "Saving Darfur: Enacting Pluralism in Terms of Gender, Genocide, and Militarized Human Rights," scholar of religion Rosemary Hicks asks how norms of gender worked within the development of the Save Darfur Coalition, an interreligious coalition of Christians, Muslims, and Jews who focus specifically on exposing sexualized violence to develop support for their cause. Interrogating both the possibilities and the implicit assumptions of such coalition building, Hicks situates this construction of pluralism in transnational contexts in which humanitarianism carries its own religious ghosts. In a very different context characterized by religious homogeneity, sociologist Geneviève Zubrzycki's chapter, "What Is Religious Pluralism in a 'Monocultural' Society? Considerations from Postcommunist Poland," discusses the uses of discourses of pluralism in overwhelmingly Catholic Poland. Centering her argument on her ethnographic study of the controversy over installing crosses next to the grounds of Auschwitz, Zubrzycki demonstrates how the ghosts of religious difference—the massacred Jews of Auschwitz—and religious suppression under communism have led to ideologically charged uses of pluralism in a largely monocultural country.

The final chapter, sociologist Irene Becci's "The Curious Attraction of Religion in East German Prisons," considers the ways in which religious practice has, or has not, been accommodated in postcommunist prisons in eastern Germany. Based on ethnographic research, Becci has found that as these prisons try to redress policies of official atheism in their recent past by introducing the possibility of varieties of religious practice, prisons have become the first point of entry into religious identity for many prisoners. Her analysis of the construction of religion in spaces of incarceration reveals much about how norms of pluralism rooted in Christian modes of religious practice are the grounds for religious recognition in secular, state contexts.

ABSENCE AND PRESENCE

We began our project with the goal of reimagining models of religious engagement. But as Benjamin Berger reflected at one moment in our October 2008 discussions, the models of religious pluralism that circulate in public ceremonies, public discourse, and legal and constitutional spaces have imaginative failure built into them. Modern secular fields encourage frequent appeals to the epistemological autonomy of religion and locate that autonomy in particular, recognized historically constituted traditions. As a result, the norms and practices of pluralism are as much about reifying difference and autonomy as about confusing or challenging such claims. Recognizing this imaginative failure, we suggest that thinking after pluralism requires careful attention to the ways in which yearning for transparent and authentic communication across lines of religious difference has long been a goal of Western theories and practices (Peters 1999). We present these multiple and intersecting projects of analysis as a way to see anew and, we admit, recalibrate the fields of theory and practice through which we locate and engage the religious, the secular, and the multiple.

We would be foolhardy to claim that the projects of pluralism or deep diversity have not also formed our questions and our desires. All the contributors to *After Pluralism* work and live within cultures of pragmatic pluralism, characterized by a commitment "to talk things through with citizens unlike [our] selves . . . prior to all theorizing, in the habits of the people" (Stout 2004:297). It is precisely for this reason that we consider our work to require fidelity to methods of inquiry that demand us to question how being after pluralism has cultivated particular habits of talking and acting things through, and with what consequence. Perhaps the affinities between Jeremy Bentham's critique of pluralism and his condemnation of colonialism have their echoes in our own collective goals. Instead of decrying the tyranny of ecclesiastical or colonial absence, however, we trouble the forced unity of presence, in which showing up at the table requires wearing religion as a marker of difference that obscures all others as the truly universal embodiment of human sociability.

NOTES

1. Perhaps tellingly, the categories of gender, sexuality, class, and race are less prominent lines of difference in discussions of pluralism. For example, we may speak of sexual diversity but rarely, if ever, of sexual pluralism.

2. For the Pluralism Project, see http://pluralism.org; for the Global Centre for Pluralism see http://www.pluralism.ca; for "A Soul for Europe" see http://www.berlinerkonferenz.eu. See also the references to pluralism in the European Union president's opening speech at the 2004 Soul for Europe conference, http://europa.eu/rapid/pressReleasesAction.do?reference=SPEECH/07/77&format=HTML&aged=0&language=EN&guiLanguage=en (all accessed May 11, 2009).

3. New polities are also forced to confront religion in new ways, as in the case of Afghanistan and the European Union (Rivers 2004).

4. Examples of this increasing interest in grappling with relations between religion and secular polities as a problem include "The Immanent Frame," the Social Sciences Research Council's blog, launched in 2007 (see http://www.ssrc.org/blogs/immanent_frame/, accessed June 2, 2009), and a recent poll ordered by the Canadian news magazine *Maclean's* (Geddes 2009).

5. We note that both of these examples of what might be called American exceptionalism were written before the attacks on the World Trade Center towers and the U.S.-led war against Iraq that followed. The optimistic climate of discussion about

religious diversity—with specific focus on Islam and the conception of the United States as a Christian nation—changed markedly in the wake of these two events.

6. The Canadian government and the Aga Khan seemingly disagreed with Hollinger's argument, because in 2006 both committed $30 million to found the new Global Centre for Pluralism, declaring Canada to be an ideal site for such a center, "a country that epitomizes what can be achieved through a commitment to pluralism," http://www.pluralism.ca/backgrounder.shtml (accessed May 7, 2009).

7. For example, the Pew Charitable Trusts Gateways initiative funded multiple geographically centered studies on religious diversity (and the religions of new immigrants) in the 1990s. A good number of these projects focus primarily on religious congregations and community centers, thus placing strong emphasis on the voluntary and organizationally defined worlds of religious interaction (Ebaugh and Chafetz 2000; Kniss and Numrich 2007). Wendy Cadge and Elaine Ecklund's (2007) review article surveys the larger literature and likewise notes the limitations of congregationally based studies for understanding religious diversity.

8. That said, Paul Bramadat's introduction is an excellent starting point for thinking about issues of religious difference in Canada.

9. Wendy Brown's recent critical assessment of "tolerance" and her call for continuing "shrewdness" in tracing the power of this discourse resonate strongly for us as well. This means "becoming shrewd about the ways that tolerance operates as a coin of liberal imperialism, intersects with racialized tropes of barbarism or of the decline of the West, and at times abets in legitimizing the very violence it claims to abhor or deter. It means apprehending how tolerance discourse articulates normal and deviant subjects, cultures, religions, and regimes, and hence how it produces and regulates identity" (Brown 2006:204).

10. In an example that considers contemporary American religious interaction as a pluralist model, sociologist Nancy Ammerman (2005:256) suggests, "Some non-Protestant traditions have complained that they have been 'Protestantized' as they have accommodated to American culture. Whatever else that has meant, they are right that they have been pushed to adopt a basic commitment to live peacefully alongside religious others. The idea that a religious group could both celebrate its unique identity and recognize the limits of its power is a continuing legacy of the Protestants who dominated the early European settlements in North America." For a discussion of multiple approaches to American encounters with native peoples, see James Tully's discussion of the forced removal of the Cherokees in *Strange Multiplicity* (1995). See also Fessenden (2007).

WORKS CITED

Abbott, Andrew. 1995. Things of Boundaries. *Social Research* 62:857–882.

Ammerman, Nancy. 2005. *Pillars of Faith: American Congregations and Their Partners*. Berkeley: University of California Press.

Asad, Talal. 2003. What Might an Anthropology of Secularism Look Like? In *Formations of the Secular: Christianity, Islam, Modernity*, 21–66. Stanford, Calif.: Stanford University Press.

Baer, Marc David. 2008. *Honored by the Glory of Islam: Conversion and Conquest in Ottoman Europe*. New York: Oxford University Press.

Banchoff, Thomas. 2007. Introduction. In *Democracy and the New Religious Pluralism*, ed. Thomas Banchoff, 3–15. New York: Oxford University Press.

Barroso, José Manuel. 2006. Introductory address at "A Soul for Europe," Berlin conference. http://europa.eu/rapid/pressReleasesAction.do?reference=SPEECH/06/706&format=HTML&aged=0&language=EN&guiLanguage=en (accessed May 12, 2009).

Baumann, Martin. 2005. Religionspluralität in Deutschland: Religiöse Differenz und kulturelle "Kompatibilität" asiatischer Zuwanderer. In *Religiöser Pluralismus: Empirische Studien und analytische Perspektiven*, ed. Martin Baumann and Samuel M. Behloul, 123–144. Bielefeld: Transcript.

Baumann, Martin, and Samuel M. Behloul, eds. 2005. *Religiöser Pluralismus: Empirische Studien und analytische Perspektiven*. Bielefeld: Transcript.

Bender, Courtney. 2007. American Reincarnations: What the Many Lives of Past Lives Tell Us About Contemporary Spirituality. *Journal of the American Academy of Religion* 75:589–614.

Bender, Courtney. 2010. *The New Metaphysicals: Spirituality and the American Religious Imagination*. Chicago: University of Chicago Press.

Bentham, Jeremy. 1818. *Church-of-Englandism and Its Catechism Examined*. London: E. Wilson.

Bentham, Jeremy. 1830. *Emancipate Your Colonies! Addressed to the National Convention of France, Anno 1793*. London: R. Heward.

Berger, Peter, Grace Davie, and Effie Fokas. 2008. *Religious America, Secular Europe? A Theme and Variations*. Aldershot: Ashgate.

Bhabha, Homi. 2004. *The Location of Culture*. Routledge Classics edition. London: Routledge.

Bouchard, Gerard, and Charles Taylor. 2008. *Building the Future: A Time for Reconciliation*. Abridged report, Commission de Consultation sur les Pratiques d'Accommodement Reliées aux Differences Culturelles. Montréal: Gouvernement du Québec.

Bramen, Carrie. 2001. *The Uses of Variety: Modern Americanism and the Quest for National Distinctiveness*. Cambridge, Mass.: Harvard University Press.

Brown, Wendy. 2006. *Regulating Aversion: Tolerance in the Age of Identity and Empire*. Princeton, N.J.: Princeton University Press.

Cadge, Wendy, and Elaine Howard Ecklund. 2007. Immigration and Religion. *Annual Review of Sociology* 33:359–379.

Campbell, David, and Morton Schoolman, eds. 2008. *The New Pluralism: William Connolly and the Contemporary Global Condition*. Durham, N.C.: Duke University Press.

Chambers, Simone. 2007. How Religion Speaks to the Agnostic: Habermas on the Persistent Value of Religion. *Constellations* 14:210–223.

Connolly, William. 2005. *Pluralism*. Durham, N.C.: Duke University Press.

Connolly, William. 2008. An Interview with William Connolly. In *The New Pluralism: William Connolly and the Contemporary Global Condition*, ed. David Campbell and Morton Schoolman, 305–336. Durham, N.C.: Duke University Press,

Dirks, Nicholas. 2001. *Castes of Mind: Colonialism and the Making of Modern India*. Princeton, N.J.: Princeton University Press.

Ebaugh, Helen Rose, and Janet Saltzman Chafetz. 2000. *Religion and the New Immigrants: Continuities and Adaptations in Immigrant Congregations*. Walnut Creek, Calif.: Alta Mira.

Eck, Diana. 2007. *What Is Pluralism?* The Pluralism Project. http://www.pluralism.org/pluralism/what_is_pluralism.php (accessed March 21, 2007).

Eisenberg, Avigail. 2005. Identity and Liberal Politics: The Problem of Minorities Within Minorities. In *Minorities Within Minorities: Equality, Rights, and Diversity*, ed. Avigail I. Eisenberg and Jeff Spinner-Halev, 249–270. Cambridge: Cambridge University Press.

Fessenden, Tracy. 2007. *Culture and Redemption: Religion, the Secular and American Literature*. Princeton, N.J.: Princeton University Press.

Geddes, John. 2009. What Canadians Think of Sikhs, Jews, Christians, Muslims. *Maclean's* 122, no. 16:20–23.

Graf, Friedrich Wilhelm. 2003. Cultivating Corporate Identity: Transformation Processes in Postmodern Religious Markets. In *Theology and the Religions: A Dialogue*, ed. Viggo Mortensen, 14–25. Grand Rapids, Mich.: Eerdmans.

Habermas, Jürgen. 2006. Religion in the Public Sphere. *European Journal of Philosophy* 14:1–25.

Hitchens, Christopher. 2007. *God Is Not Great: How Religion Poisons Everything*. New York: Twelve Books.

Hollinger, David. 2001. Not Universalists, Not Pluralists: The New Cosmopolitans Find Their Own Way. *Constellations* 8:237–248.

Hurd, Elizabeth Shakman. 2007. *The Politics of Secularism in International Relations*. Princeton, N.J.: Princeton University Press.

Hutchison, William. 2003. *Religious Pluralism in America: The Contentious History of a Founding Ideal*. New Haven, Conn.: Yale University Press.

Iyigun, Murat. 2006. *Ottoman Conquests and European Ecclesiastical Pluralism*. Discussion Paper no. 1973. Bonn: Forschungsinstitut zur Zukunft der Arbeit/Institute for the Study of Labor.

Jain, Kajri. 2007. *Gods in the Bazaar: The Economies of Indian Calendar Art*. Durham, N.C.: Duke University Press.

Jakobsen, Janet R., and Ann Pellegrini. 2008. *Secularisms*. Durham, N.C.: Duke University Press.

James, William. 1909. *A Pluralistic Universe*. London: Longmans, Green.

Jung, Courtney. 2001. The Burden of Culture and the Limits of Liberal Responsibility. *Constellations* 8:219–235.

Kaplan, Benjamin. 2007. *Divided by Faith: Religious Conflict and the Practice of Toleration in Early Modern Europe*. Cambridge, Mass.: Harvard University Press.

Klassen, Pamela E. 2007. Radio Mind: Christian Experimentalists on the Frontiers of Healing. *Journal of the American Academy of Religion* 75:651–683.

Klassen, Pamela E. 2011. *Pathologies of Modernity: Medicine, Healing, and the Spirits of Protestantism*. Berkeley: University of California Press.

Kniss, Fred, and Paul Numrich. 2007. *Sacred Assemblies and Civic Engagement: How Religion Matters for America's Newest Immigrants*. New Brunswick, N.J.: Rutgers University Press.

Kühle, Lena. 2003. Religious Pluralism in Multireligiosity. In *Theology and the Religions: A Dialogue*, ed. Viggo Mortensen, 419–429. Grand Rapids, Mich.: Eerdmans.

Kurien, Prema. 2007. *A Place at the Multicultural Table: The Development of an American Hinduism*. New Brunswick, N.J.: Rutgers University Press.

Kymlicka, Will. 2001. *Politics in the Vernacular: Nationalism, Multiculturalism, and Citizenship*. Oxford: Oxford University Press.

Levitt, Peggy. 2007. *God Needs No Passport*. New York: New Press.

Lippy, Charles. 2000. *Pluralism Comes of Age*. Armonk, N.Y.: Sharpe.

Mahmood, Saba. 2006. Secularism, Hermeneutics, and Empire. *Public Culture* 18, no.2:323–347.

Mamdani, Mahmood. 2004. *Good Muslim, Bad Muslim: America, the Cold War, and the Roots of Terror*. New York: Pantheon.

Marty, Martin. 2007. Pluralisms. *Annals of the American Academy of Political and Social Science* 612:13–25.

Masuzawa, Tomoko. 2005. *The Invention of World Religions: Or, How European Universalism Was Preserved in the Language of Pluralism*. Chicago: University of Chicago Press.

McCarthy, Kate. 2007. *Interfaith Encounters in America*. New Brunswick, N.J.: Rutgers University Press.

Meyer, Birgit, and Annelies Moors, eds. 2006. *Religion, Media and the Public Sphere*. Bloomington: Indiana University Press.

Mitchell, Timothy, ed. 2000. *Questions of Modernity*. Minneapolis: University of Minnesota Press.

Modood, Tariq, and Geoffrey Levey, eds. 2008. *Secularism, Religion, and Multicultural Citizenship*. Cambridge: Cambridge University Press.

Mortensen, Viggo, ed. 2003. *Theology and the Religions: A Dialogue*. Grand Rapids, Mich.: Eerdmans.

Pecora, Vincent. 2006. *Secularization and Cultural Criticism: Religion, Nation and Modernity*. Chicago: University of Chicago Press.

Pennington, W. 1772. A *Free Inquiry into the Origin, Progress, and Present State of Pluralities. By W. Pennington*. London, 1772. Based on information from *English Short Title Catalogue. Eighteenth Century Collections Online*. Gale Group. http://galenet.galegroup.com/servlet/ECCO (accessed May 11, 2009).

Peters, John Durham. 1999. *Speaking into the Air: A History of the Idea of Communication*. Chicago: University of Chicago Press.

Philpott, Daniel. 2002. The Challenge of September 11 to Secularism in International Relations. *World Politics* 55:66–95.

Porterfield, Amanda. 2008. Religious Pluralism, the Study of Religion, and "Postsecular" Culture. In *The American University in a Postsecular Age*, ed. Douglas Jacobsen and Rhonda Jacobsen, 187–202. New York: Oxford University Press.

Rivers, Julian. 2004. In Pursuit of Pluralism: The Ecclesiastical Policy of the European Union. *Ecclesiastical Law Journal* 7:267–291.

Said, Edward. 1978. *Orientalism*. New York: Vintage.

Sassen, Saskia. 2006. *Cities in a World Economy*. Thousand Oaks, Calif.: Pine Forge Press.

Schmidt, Leigh Eric. 2003. The Making of Modern Mysticism. *Journal of the American Academy of Religion* 71:273–302.

Scott, Joan Wallach. 2007. *The Politics of the Veil*. Princeton, N.J.: Princeton University Press.

Seljak, David, and Paul Bramadat. 2005. *Religion and Ethnicity in Canada*. Toronto: Pearson Longman.

Stewart, Charles. 1999. Syncretism and Its Synonyms: Reflections on Cultural Mixture. *Diacritics* 29, no. 3:40–62.

Stewart, Charles, and Rosalind Shaw, eds. 1994. *Syncretism/Antisyncretism: The Politics of Religious Synthesis*. New York: Routledge.

Stout, Jeffrey. 2004. *Democracy and Tradition*. Princeton, N.J.: Princeton University Press.

Taylor, Charles. 2007. *A Secular Age*. Cambridge, Mass.: Harvard University Press.

Tully, James. 1995. *Strange Multiplicity: Constitutionalism in an Age of Diversity*. Cambridge: Cambridge University Press.

Viswanathan, Gauri. 2008. Secularism in the Framework of Heterodoxy. *PMLA* 123, no. 2:466–476.

Wuthnow, Robert. 2005. *America and the Challenges of Religious Diversity*. Princeton, N.J.: Princeton University Press.

PART I

Law, Normativity, and the Constitution of Religion

1. ETHICS AFTER PLURALISM

JANET R. JAKOBSEN

It seems there could not be a better time to consider the status of pluralism, particularly of religious pluralism, in the United States. The election of President Barack Obama in 2008 has been taken by some commentators to mean that the United States is "post-racial" and perhaps we could say "post-pluralism," given Obama's multiracial parentage and extended family as formed by his siblings. However, other commentators, such as former CNN host Lou Dobbs, continue to complain about the supposedly lenient policies of the U.S. government toward immigration, and immigration reform is not a policy on which the Obama administration is moving quickly. Rather, immigration reform seems to be one of the policies that, though no longer a hot issue, is still considered politically volatile and hence to be approached with caution by the highly pragmatic Obama administration. In the academic world, we see a similar divide between commentators who take the increasing demographic diversity of the American populace as evidence enough that pluralism has (or will) triumph, and those such as the late Harvard professor Samuel Huntington (2004), who argued that the United States should act to protect the singularity of its cultural heritage by openly recognizing and supporting a dominant—Protestant—identity and culture, particularly against the threat posed by Latino immigration.[1] In some ways it seems that we in the United States are not "after pluralism"; rather, we have yet to reach any agreement that pluralism is possible or, for some like Dobbs, Huntington, and their followers, desirable.

If this is the current state of things, in the United States at least, what does it mean to be "after pluralism"? As Pamela Klassen and Courtney Bender note in the introduction to this volume, the "after" indicates a number of different aspects of the times in which we find ourselves. We are "after" the moment in which the discourse of pluralism has become part of mainstream political discourse, as have its ethical imperatives, which involve a commitment to democratic engagement across differences. And yet we have also reached a point where it may be necessary to recognize that the spread of the discourse of pluralism has not produced the realization of its ethical promises. To be "after pluralism" is to recognize the value of social difference to democratic ethics but also to recognize that neither the demographic fact of pluralism nor its meaningful invocation by advocates of pluralist ethics has produced the United States as a society in which differences are recognized with equality rather then taken as markers of inequality, in which segregation in housing, schooling, and labor markets does not continue to be the order of the day, and in which the mainstream has moved much beyond token recognition of difference, particularly of religious difference.[2] The question that Klassen and Bender put to us is not whether public recognition of religious difference is desirable or even whether it is a central part of democracy but whether the model of pluralism is the best route for the realization of that much-desired recognition.

THE PROBLEM OF PLURALISM

One of the fundamental problems for the realization of these democratic goals is that the model of pluralism often presumes clearly delineated "units" of religious difference, most often located in well-recognized institutions of religious tradition with identifiable authorities who speak for the members of said tradition. Thus the model of pluralism can fail to recognize both diversity within religious traditions and forms of religious difference that do not fit this model of organization, for example, those that are not organized around authorities who can act as spokespersons, that are not institutionalized in recognizable (and hierarchical) structures, and that are delineated by practice or land rather than by beliefs about which one might speak. Moreover, as Andrea Most (chap. 5, this volume) shows, the boundaries between different traditions are often quite permeable and are perhaps more accurately described as mutually constitutive than as pluralistic.

I am wholly in sympathy with this critique, having argued in my first book on feminist alliance politics (Jakobsen 1998) that it is precisely the assumption of separable "units" of difference, whether delineated along lines of race, class, or religion, that undercuts the possibilities for connection and understanding across difference so often sought by advocates of alliances (and of pluralism). The analytic problem is clear enough: Pluralism does not adequately describe the complexity of religious differences. Because it obscures both internal diversity and external connections, pluralism cannot provide an adequate model for those hoping to improve interactions.

The ethical problem, which has long been my concern, follows from this analytic problem. The promise of democracy is that people in their differences can come together and through nonviolent interaction move forward on public issues. Yet if religious differences block public participation—if the representation of a plurality of religious participants in the public sphere is not possible, for example—then the promise of democracy remains unfulfilled.

Yet when we imagine the public sphere as divided into "units" of difference, we tend to undercut the possibilities for interaction that might actually facilitate democratic processes. We are trapped between a politics of representation in which we try (and repeatedly fail) to find the perfect formula for providing representation to any and all groups (or groups within groups) and a politics of blindness to differences—in other words, between the difficulties of identity politics and the historic failures of acting as though social differences do not exist or do not matter. So with religious pluralism, for example, how do we fully represent religious differences in the public sphere? Who are the appropriate representatives of religious communities? The institutional leaders of those communities? Charismatic leaders? Someone else? And if those leaders also happen to be all men or all of one race, who represents the racial minorities or women of this group? The traditional leaders? Those who are not directly represented but who agree with the leaders? Those who disagree?[3] In other words, crosscutting differences make it difficult if not impossible to use a unit of identity (whatever that unit might be) to find a means of representing everyone.

Does this failure mean that we should (and could) all just represent ourselves as individuals?[4] Among other problems, this approach would tend to erase the serious and continuing exclusions that group identities, including religious differences, have created in U.S. public life. For example, although Barack Obama's election to the presidency represents a truly significant change in the racial politics of American democracy, his Christian identity was crucial to the possibility of his election. Unfounded rumors circulated throughout the campaign that he was secretly a Muslim, and although his supporters repeatedly denied these rumors, neither the campaign nor these supporters raised the question of why it might be such a problem that a Muslim would be running for president of the United States of America.

In the post–September 11 atmosphere, where many Americans continue to identify Islam as a legitimating force in the attacks, perhaps it's obvious why a Muslim cannot now be elected president of the United States, but that "obviousness" points to an even deeper problem facing the ethical vision of pluralism.[5] For some, including analysts such as Huntington, the events of the past decade have raised or renewed the question of whether adherents to multiple religious perspectives can even live together in peace. This focus on violence was set off not just by the attacks of September 11, 2001, and the resultant proclamation of a "clash of civilizations" but also by the bombings of July 7, 2005, in London, in which the bombers had grown up in and were fully a part of a supposedly pluralistic Britain.

Enter secularism. Secularism was invented—or so the story goes—to solve the problem of violence emanating from pluralistic religious viewpoints. As one prominent version of the secularization thesis goes, it was the European "wars of religion" produced by the Protestant Reformation that eventually made clear the need for a social space not determined by any particular religion, within which different religious traditions could coexist peaceably.[6] The secular framework that was created by what is called the separation of church and state allows for religious pluralism by providing a framework within which different voices can interact. Because secularism is not expressive of any particular religious voice, it can provide the framework for general interaction, interaction that in moral terms is undertaken through the protocols of universal reason. Public deliberation and debate, then, can take place under terms that can be universally shared regardless of the particular religious commitments of the participants. And interaction can take place peacefully. Decisions can be made not by the force of violence but by the "force of the better argument" (Habermas 1984:87) in situations of open communication and free expression.

This is a very powerful story, one that has had powerful effects in our world, leading to repeated telling of the story.[7] And this story is deeply entwined with the problem of pluralism. If there is no general secular discourse within which pluralistic religious voices can interact, then how can the moral promises of pluralism, including peaceful coexistence, be realized? And yet, as a spate of recent scholarship has shown, there are serious reasons to doubt that secularism can provide the type of framework for interaction on which pluralism depends.[8]

In *Secularisms* (Jakobsen and Pellegrini 2008), an anthology produced from a project that brought together scholars working on secularism in various parts of the world, my co-editor, Ann Pellegrini, and I have asked whether secularism is general after all or whether there are particular secularisms. For example, Ann and I are Americanists, and can one really say that public secularism in the

United States, especially the secularism of the state that is supposed to be so separate from the church, is general? Or is it a particular form of secularism, one that both expresses and enacts in law the values of Protestantism that have so long been dominant in U.S. history?[9] In our study of sexual regulation in the United States (Jakobsen and Pellegrini 2003), which we pursued parallel to the secularisms project, we found that, at least when it comes to sexual regulation, the basis of U.S. law is almost always and everywhere, whether in the executive, legislative, or judicial branches of government, based on Christian values.[10] And the political affiliation or philosophy of the lawmaker doesn't much matter in terms of this outcome. Whether it is George W. Bush speaking of his Christian views in a Rose Garden press conference to explain his support of an anti–gay marriage amendment to the Constitution before the 2004 election or the Democratic presidential candidates in that same year and in 2008 trying to explain their stance on gay marriage through their own religiosity; whether it's Republican Senate majority leader Trent Lott proclaiming that as Americans we should "love the sinner and hate the sin" or Democratic Senator Robert Byrd reading from his family Bible on the floor of the Senate in the debate over the Defense of Marriage Act—when it comes to sex, a particular set of Christian assumptions informs the law of the land.

In the secularisms project, we found that this Christian secularism has ramifications that reach far beyond the regulation of sexuality in the United States. With the development of capitalist globalization, it has implications for the structure of life and work globally. With colleagues who work on areas of the world ranging from India to China to Iran to Turkey to Britain and the United States, we found that Christian secularism has global implications in relation to capitalist practice, which perhaps should not surprise us given that of all the calendars in the world, it is the Christian calendar that is the basis of operation for world financial markets.[11] But unlike others who understand Christian values to be constitutive of global secularism and who therefore see all secularism and all secularisms as somehow variants of Christianity, we did not find Christian secularism to be the only form of secularism active in the world today. For example, Geeta Patel (2008) offers a meditation on the workings of secularism in India during the government of the Bharatiya Janata Party (BJP), and she shows how, by suturing Hindu nationalism to Hindu secularism to the secularism of global capitalism, the BJP was able to accomplish the production of India as simultaneously the true site of Hindu identity and an ultramodern capitalist powerhouse. As Banu Subramaniam (2008) shows in her essay on battles over Hindu science and education, the reascension of the Congress Party into government has changed very few aspects of this formation or of the policies associated with it. Even with the ostensibly more secular Congress Party, the governing secularism in India remains a Hindu secularism.[12] Christian secularism may be the dominant secularism in the contemporary world, but it is not the only secularism with world historical consequences.

So if secularism is particular to the context in which it is formed and of a particular form in the global context, what of the story of universal secularism as a framework for religious pluralism? And perhaps even more urgently, what of the moral narrative in which universal reason provides a framework for the peaceful adjudication of moral claims from competing religious traditions? If there is no universal secularism, there is no foundation for universal moral reason, and then there is a moral, as well as a practical, problem. Thus, the problem of pluralism exists on two levels: We cannot assume autonomous units of religious tradition as a basis for pluralistic interaction, and we cannot assume a secular framework that provides general and reasonable rules, rules that because general can be accepted by all no matter their tradition (at least all who are reasonable) so as to maintain peaceful interactions.

GENDER, SEXUALITY, AND ETHICS AS A SITE FOR ALTERNATIVES

As a result, in this chapter I would like to explore possible alternatives to the moral order offered by the dominant narrative of religious pluralism and its secular framework. To do so, I turn to the realm of sexuality studies and in particular to the possibilities presented by queer ethics. Given that this is not the usual place to turn for an anthology made up of legal scholars and sociologists of religion, let me first explain this particular choice. One of the things that the editors of this book have encouraged us to do is to look to the sites where religious pluralism is actually negotiated in contemporary societies—the law, the media, and the street—and I am happy to take up this encouragement. In nearly all these places, one of the points at which negotiations of difference occur is around issues of gender and sexuality. If one looks at the primary examples of the negotiation of religious difference provided in the initial description of the "After Pluralism" conference, for example, one finds that two of the three cases focus on the institution most associated in our society with gender and sexuality: the family. The organizers rightly point out, "As demonstrated by debates about the uses of Shari'a within Canadian family law, global conflicts over democratic principles of free speech and blasphemy, and government funding of religious family planning groups in the United States, numerous religions share (often uncomfortably) similar economic, legal, and media positions, in both national and global arenas" (Bender and Klassen 2007). This choice of examples is neither unusual nor misplaced, because gender and sexuality are often at the center in debates over religious difference. In fact, religious difference is often reduced to difference over sexuality.

To illustrate this point, I would like to provide a brief description of an opinion piece from *USA Today* (a newspaper that, as its title suggests, is particularly useful at distilling U.S. public discourse). The essay in question, an op-ed by radio talk show host Michael Medved (2007), expresses outrage at the release of a film, *September Dawn*, that purports to be a historical account of the 1857 Mountain Meadows Massacre, in which a Mormon militia attacked a wagon train headed through the territory of what is now the state of Utah, killing much of the party. In its lurid depictions of nineteenth-century Mormonism, the film expresses a disregard for, indeed a prejudice toward, a religious community that has since that time been a model of American uprightness—in other words, a perfect player in the drama of American religious pluralism. And if Medved's description of the film is correct (I haven't seen it), then it is indeed an example of Hollywood's willingness to exploit and even inflame religious animus. However, the point of the article is not that one should not be prejudiced toward minority religious communities in the United States but rather that Hollywood, at least, has failed to be prejudiced toward the right religionists, who are of course Muslims.

According to Medved, even as Hollywood has supposedly given a pass to Muslim Americans, motion pictures have maintained a prejudice toward Mormons "that is not only unjust but downright Un-American—violating the cherished pluralistic traditions by which we judge religious communities." Americans know that Mormons are worthy of respect because Mormons do not currently respond to this injustice with violence, and they adhere to appropriate sexual practices. Having earlier dismissed the idea that Mormons are "sexually repressed," Medved brings home his point as follows: "Despite the turbulence of their founding generation, Mormons have been conspicuously peaceful, patriotic, hardworking and neighborly for at least the past 117 years (since the church repudiated and banned polygamy)." And so the complex history of the Mormon battle with the federal government over the independence of religious authority from the federal government and the status of the territory of Utah (the very battle of which the Mountain Meadow Massacre was a part) is reduced to a question of sexual practice.[13] And here, in the tie between sex and violence—Mormons' contemporary status as nonviolent minority is intimately tied to their having given up sexual deviance—we have an all-too-American idea of pluralism and its limits. The boundaries of sexual regulation also form the boundaries of religious pluralism.

Why should gender and sexuality be brought into play so frequently in negotiating religious difference and its appropriate boundaries? Many answers have been offered to this question from a variety of disciplines and perspectives. Several of the most helpful come from the sociology of religion. For example, one explanation argues that religion is associated with the private sphere as is sexuality, and so religion has particular purview when it comes to sexual questions (Ammerman 1987).[14] These sociological explanations are undoubtedly helpful, but the field of ethics also offers a potential answer to this question that focuses on why gender and sexuality are so often taken to stand in for morality as a whole.[15] Turning to the field of ethics can help to explain the persistence of both religion and sexuality as public (as well as private) issues, as sites of major cultural, legal, and political debates in the United States.

By looking at the place of sexuality in modern ethics, not only can we learn something about why sexuality is so important to American public and religious discourse, but we might also see our way to alternative solutions to the very modern problem of religious pluralism. Turning to this type of queer theoretical exploration for the resolution of problems in religious studies may be unusual, but given the recurrent (but often unremarked) dependence on cases having to do with gender and sexuality, it might be helpful if queer theory or at least gender and sexuality studies were taken up more frequently. Queer theory is certainly not the only or even the necessary site for the type of response I will suggest, but it is a site where the ethics of modernity has been pursued from a perspective that could be helpful beyond the field of sexuality per se.[16]

Queer theory has focused on the problem of sex as the problem of normativity. Drawing on a Foucaultian understanding, normativity is understood to be a means of organizing moral life in relation to social power. With regard to sexuality, for example, scholars have identified the ways in which heterosexuality is established as the normative sexuality through what Lauren Berlant and Michael Warner (1998) call heteronormativity. Berlant and Warner list the myriad ways in which heterosexuality is established and reinforced as a dominant sexuality—not just through direct moral exhortation and the proclamation that other forms of sexuality are wrong but through daily reinforcement in popular culture, on morning television programs, or through an obsessive focus on the sexuality, marriages, and childbearing of celebrities (including politicians), casual conversations about families and children at work, and entire industries producing self-help books or diet and exercise regimens all aimed at increasing one's attractiveness to the "opposite sex." Since the publication of Berlant and Warner's article, some of these normative operations have opened up to gay and lesbian people (in some places), at least to those who are willing and able to participate in normative practices—to form social units recognizable as families, to get married and have children, to participate in the self-help and wedding industries. This shift has prompted scholars such as Lisa Duggan (1994) and Jasbir Puar (2007) to speak of a move to "homonormativity," to signal the ways in which some gay and lesbian people can participate in normative society to the exclusion of queer people who do not fit the model of white, middle-class normality.

Importantly, then, normativity is not a problem that is specific to sexuality. Several scholars, including Roderick Ferguson (2004), Amy Villarejo (2005), and Puar (2007), have described how heteronormativity is itself a matrix that brings together norms of race, class, nation, and religion to produce the heteronormative individual. To belong to a nonnormative racial or religious group is also to be suspected of being sexually deviant and vice versa.[17] Given this mutually constitutive matrix of difference, the queer focus on normativity does not produce an analysis of what's distinctive about sexual identity and thus what queers can add—pluralistically—to other forms of moral critique. To take this approach would be to produce sexuality as yet another autonomous unit of difference, to be added to race and religion or gender and class in an attempt to produce a holistic picture of social life. Rather, the idea of a matrix of normativity provides a means of understanding the ways in which various means of social differentiation are not simply intertwined but are dependent on and produced through each other. Thus the social processes that produce differentiation cannot be separated into individual units and then somehow added back together to produce a coherent whole.

What the critique of normativity, as conceptualized by Foucault and taken up by queer theory, provides is an analysis of the tie between the articulation of norms and the operations of power, including the social forces that create these mutually reinforcing differences. In describing normativity specifically in relation to mental illness, Foucault says that it is "a normative system built on a whole technical, administrative, juridical and medical apparatus."[18] Foucault understands the moral problematic of modernity as the connection between this apparatus and a particular form of moral discourse, one in which the moral ideal and what we now call the statistical norm converge. When it comes to sex, for example, marriage was long the norm in terms that we would now define statistically, but it was not the ideal of sexual morality within Christian societies; the ideal was the celibacy of monastic life. It is only in modernity that marriage becomes both statistical norm and moral ideal. Foucault is interested in the modern convergence between norm and ideal because it sets up a particular type of moral problem. Normative discipline—rather than, for example, the cultivation of virtue—becomes the centerpiece, the dominant understanding, of moral life.

This new moral order is tied to new, specifically modern, forms of governance through what Foucault calls biopower. No longer is the Crown's capacity to threaten subjects with death the center of the state's power; rather, in the modern period it is control over life, over the ways and means by which life is produced, that maintains the state. Keeping watch over the population and managing its activities is what is required, and normative self-discipline prompted in part by the exhortations of watchful experts is the means of accomplishing this management. Because sex is the site of the literal production of bodies and also a potent site for figuring self-discipline and control of one's individual body, it facilitates both normative discipline and the mechanics of biopower.

In other words, sex is not just an accidental site of moral concern, a handy marker of moral standing (or religious pluralism) in modernity. Sex works in particular ways within the modern regime of power. It works to produce modern individuals, both literally and subjectively. As a result, sex is a site for determining what's normal in modernity.

For Foucault, the problematic of normativity means that the central question of sexual ethics is not the one that obsesses the American public—whether the ethic is liberatory or regulatory—but how the ethic is sutured to the operation of normative power. For Foucault, a focus on sexual liberation, in which sex is presumed to be the route to freedom, is as much an operation of modern power as is state regulation. A modern ethical life that is organized around normativity can discipline subjects either through state regulation or through market imperatives to freely choose one's sexual lifestyle. In both cases, sex is a central means by which an individual produces himself or herself as recognizable within society. This queer critique suggests that gender and sexuality are constitutive elements of the imagination of the moral self, and Foucault argues that in terms of modern norms to be such a self is to be one who is fundamentally self-willed, who is autonomous.

The connection between these norms and biopower means that sex works to produce not just the autonomous individual but also the autonomous nation. Why else would the moral health of an entire nation be seen as depending on whether a small minority of the population engaged in particular sex acts? And yet, to hear American politicians talk, this is precisely the case for the United States. In his biblically based speech on the Senate floor, Senator Robert Byrd used not just the Bible but also the King James phrasing in proclaiming "woe betide" the nation that turns from the path of monogamous marriage. It's important to note that in this speech he is depending on the text of what he calls the "Old Testament" while ignoring that the patriarchs of the Hebrew Bible did not define marriage as between one man and one woman but were actively polygamous. This is more than just a casual oversight or ironic hypocrisy. When politicians proclaim the status of monogamous marriage as supposedly unchanged for the last 5,000 years, they are projecting the modern discourse of sexuality back over a varied history of religious complexity, and in so doing they suture a sense of religiosity to a modern secular vision. Byrd's use of his family Bible in the halls of government articulates his modern Protestantism with secularism (in this case secular law) so as to make Protestant monogamy normal and other sexual ethics, religious or not, distinctly abnormal. The suturing of religious and secular concern makes modern sexual norms particularly powerful because they appear to be natural. They seem so natural, in fact, that they can lay claim to millennia of unchanging force and religious coherence (despite actual changes in sexual morality over time and differences between religious ethics).[19]

To develop an ethic that shifts away from modern normativity is not do away with norms—any activity has its norms of action—but to shift the relationship between norms and the operation of power and to challenge the way in which norms are embedded in the "whole technical, administrative, juridical and medical apparatus" of power (Foucault 1984:336). In the third volume of his *History of Sexuality* (1988), Foucault seeks such an alternative through the historical example of the practice of "care of the self" among some Greek citizens. Foucault is not suggesting that the example of the care of the self is one that should be taken up in the present day; rather, he is exploring the ways in which ethical systems and norms might be differently configured. Thus the question for contemporary queer theorists such as Michael Warner in *The Trouble with Normal* (1999) or feminist ethicists (since the critique of normativity is not just queer) such as Ewa Ziarek in *An Ethics of Dissensus* (2001) is what types of ethical approaches might disarticulate norms from biopower.

AUTONOMY: AT THE INTERSECTION OF PLURALISM AND SEXUALITY

What does the queer critique of normativity offer to thinking about ethics "after pluralism"? First, such an analysis asks us to consider the ways in which the production of autonomous "units" of difference, such as religious difference, are implicated in the type of power relations that make for modern normativity. In particular, the production of autonomy also invokes a series of hierarchies, both within and between autonomous "units" (whether they be selves, communities, religious traditions, or nations). The critique of normativity asks us to consider the way norms and power relations contribute to the construction and defense of these hierarchies, whether we are speaking of individual human beings or of the autonomous religious communities presumed to be the basis of religious pluralism. For example, how do the norms of gender and sexuality contribute to defining who is part of a religious community and who is not? How does the normative idealization of autonomy itself enlist moral force on behalf of such boundary-defining exercises (and their deployment of gendered or sexual norms)?

The issues raised by this problem are manifold, and I do not have the space in this brief essay to go into all of them, so I will focus on a longstanding feminist critique of the problem of autonomy, which is that the ideal of autonomy tends to elide the ways in which autonomous individuals (or social groups) do not actually exist autonomously.[20] Rather, those to whom autonomy is attributed and who tend to understand themselves as existing autonomously actually depend on the labor of others. In what is now called the "traditional" family, for example, they depend on the labor of wives and servants.

The problem here is one of imagination. Autonomy is imagined or presented as an ideal, even as it is achieved through the appropriation of labor from others. For example, the modern nation-state came into existence at a time of the consolidation of the labor of human beings toward producing the nation (rather than the feudal estate, for example) and as the nations that became the hallmark of modern nationalism were pursuing colonial projects around the world that supported their supposedly autonomous existence. With regard to the production of separable religious communities, nineteenth- and early-twentieth-century feminist Charlotte Perkins Gilman probably put it most succinctly in the title of her book *His Religion and Hers: A Study of the Faith of Our Fathers and the Work of Our Mothers* (1923). Gilman argued that the labor required in producing religious communities as particular and autonomous communities of faith, like the labor of producing the family, depended primarily on the appropriation of the labor of women within the faith, who put in the work but did not make the norms. Moreover, the assertion of autonomy will also invoke hierarchies, for example, between the self who is autonomous and those whose labor is appropriated. Or hierarchies will be produced within a community, between those who set the norms and those who bear the burden of maintaining them.

In terms of religious pluralism, norms become imbricated with the operation of power because of the need to create community self-discipline so as to produce publicly articulable and authentic versions of religious difference. Thus, even communities whose ethical commitments might be critical of autonomous individualism, when representing themselves in the modern public, may still produce themselves precisely as authentically autonomous communities.[21] For example, communitarian ethics might critique autonomous individualism, but they may also just raise the problem of modern normativity to a different scale. Instead of the individual, it is the community whose boundaries must be protected, and it is the community and its members that must be disciplined in producing that coherence. Not surprisingly, those who are different within the community (who are in some way queer) are also differentially affected by the demand for community coherence. And this problem of community normativity is as true of the frequently invoked "gay and lesbian community" as it is of religiously defined communities, as indicated by the persistent struggles over the respectability of those who publicly represent gays and lesbians.[22] Thus, although queer critique is indebted to (or, as David Halperin [1997] says, "haunted by") issues of sexuality, and of homosexuality in particular, queer critique parts company with the idea of identity and community politics, even those of a homosexual community.

The queer alternative to this ethical regime is to ask whether it is possible to imagine both moral action and moral subjectivity outside the bounds of normativity, and in particular of normative autonomy. Is it possible to recognize the penetrability of boundaries, the influences of others on the self, or, to go a step further, the ways in which the self is constituted relationally with others? And is it possible to do this in a way that does not replicate the power relations of normativity at another level? Is it possible to recognize mutual constitution at the level of public representation? With regard to sex specifically, can we imagine a society in which sexual practice is not tied to the demands of producing the modern ethical self, a society in which sex is not unimportant but is also not burdened with what Gayle Rubin (1993) calls the oversignification of sex in modernity? Can we imagine a public life in which sexual ethics has meaning for sexual practice but is not burdened by having to account for the health of the nation, the status of a civilization, or the state of the world?

My analysis suggests that to do this U.S. public discourse would also have to give up the imagination of communities, of religious traditions, of nations, or of civilizations as autonomous entities. Part of what the oversignification of sex makes possible is the imagination of autonomy not just for the individual but also for his or her community. For example, one reason that homosexuality is taken as a threat to the health of the nation is because nonnormative sexual practice within the United States is seen to undercut the unity of the nation and in so doing is also understood to undermine the ability of the nation to defend itself and its borders.[23] The alternative I have been sketching is to ask whether it is really the case that such aspirations to autonomy are necessary or even desirable for national or for individual well-being.

Similarly, the possibility of imagining the nonautonomous but nonetheless ethical agent could contribute to a world after pluralism, not just a world in which there is negotiation at the boundaries, whether in the streets or in the courtroom, but rather a world in which the relational and co-constitutive nature of different religious traditions and of religion and secular modernity could be acknowledged as a starting point. This type of relational reading suggests that unlike the model of pluralism and its close cousin, interreligious dialogue, which are often focused on building relationships where none are presumed to exist, we should not pass over the ways in which religious communities are already in relation, with each other and with secular states and global capitalism. These relations might not be the happy and peaceful relations desired by those of us who advocate equality and democracy; in fact, they may be openly conflictual relationships. But these conflicts have to be produced, and they are produced relationally. They also have to be maintained, and as anyone who has been embroiled in conflict knows, the more intense the conflict, the more intense the relation. The queer intervention I have sketched here suggests that rather than thinking that conflict can be resolved by looking at each party independently and then trying to bring them together, we should look at the relational production of the conflict itself. Specifically, queer theory is interested in the way in which such a perspective makes it more difficult to hide the relational production of the self, as if the self had no part in the production of the conflict but rather came to the conflict wholly self-contained, unaffected by the other and having had no effect on the other before the conflict began.

This shift in perspective is one that might maintain many of the values advocated by proponents of pluralism—equality, openness, democracy, freedom, justice—but that understands a different basis for these values and their realization. If pluralism hopes for peaceable relations between different communities, the approach I've been sketching here focuses not so much on interrelation as on mutual constitution—on the flow across boundaries that makes selves and relations possible. Although I have named this approach a queer one (and there are certainly other possible queer approaches),[24] it does not necessarily focus on sexuality per se and certainly is not based on something that is supposed to be inherent in sexuality. Rather, it is based on a critique of the effects of normativity, which include a heteronormative politics but go much beyond sexuality. Therefore, it shouldn't be a surprise that the focus on interdependence or even a similar type of critique is found elsewhere, nor will a focus on sexuality provide some knowledge that is not available elsewhere. Queer lives may produce alternative social forms, but so also may disabled lives or queer disabled lives, or the lives of those who are simply different. Spaces of queer cultural production are not the result of something inherent in sexuality but are a means of living in relation to normative social formations. Thus, to line up sexuality as yet another difference in the parade of pluralism may produce gay pride, but it won't allow us to alter the terms by which there must always be shame handed out to some so as to enable the pride of others. To change that particular dynamic, we would need to change the relation not just between heterosexuality and homosexuality but also between norms and power.

DIFFERENT POSSIBILITIES

Given this analysis, the response I would offer to antipluralists such as Dobbs and Huntington is that we consider the value of living "after pluralism." Rather than a simple defense of pluralism or an appeal to reality—to the fact that the United States is already (demographically at least) radically pluralistic—we might pursue a step beyond pluralism and its assumptions. For Huntington, for example, the problem with the scale of Latino immigration to the United States is that it will undercut the "Anglo-Protestant" core of American culture, a core that includes liberty, equality, and democracy, all of which he associates with the Protestant heritage of the United States. For Huntington, the "Latino-Catholic" culture that contemporary immigrants bring with them signals religious difference that could undermine the country and its core values. The model of modern pluralism would encourage Huntington to see immigration as an enactment of American values of freedom and democracy and to see religious difference as strengthening those values.

Benjamin Berger's analysis (chap. 4, this volume) of the limits of Canadian legal promises of tolerance also holds for U.S. public discourse, however. As Berger points out, the demand that you can participate as long as you match the specific values of U.S. democracy or of the Canadian legal system is itself a contradictory demand: Immigrants can be equal to "Americans" as long as they live according to values that are "American." But what happens when those values—of freedom, equality, and individual autonomy, for example—are not the values shared by immigrants? For example, what if immigrants do not value the equality or autonomy of women? In such cases the limits of tolerance are reached, and as Berger succinctly argues, "when toleration of a given religious commitment would require the law [or the purveyors of 'American' values] to actually cede normative or symbolic territory, law trumps it in the name of procedural fairness, choice, autonomy, or the integrity of the public sphere" (Berger, chap. 4, this volume). This is the trick of liberal values: The liberal values of freedom, equality, and justice are a specific set of values, held by some and not by others, *and* they are supposed to be the universal frame within which conflicts of values can be adjudicated. This trick means that some values (such as equality) are more equal than others, and thus the invocation of equality can actually create a hierarchy, such as the one between Americans and immigrants espoused by Huntington.[25] The basic paradox here is that the openness espoused by the discourse of pluralism can also be used, as Huntington uses it, to shut down openness to immigrants or to any form of religious difference.

Huntington sees the United States as a unique site of openness and worries that religious difference will undermine this openness in favor of a society that no longer primarily values dissent (in the Protestant form). And certainly as pluralists, we would not argue that he is entirely wrong. Immigration may very well change "American" values. It would be quite an illiberal moment indeed if the boundaries of social life were so impermeable as to admit of no effects across the boundaries of difference. In other words, Huntington's worries are not without grounding. However, they are based on the presumption that United States is a Protestant nation and that its values have one source, rather than being born of the very conflicts between different value systems that Huntington so greatly fears.

The norms of freedom, equality, and justice play out very differently if we presume a relational context from the start rather than assuming that values—whether those of liberal modernity, Canadian law, or U.S. culture—come from a single source that is only later brought into conflict by the encounter with "difference." Huntington is not just a mistaken purveyor of anxieties about those with whom he has yet to interact. He is actively writing out of the social relations, including the conflicts, that produced the values he sees as simply Anglo-Protestant and American. In the pluralist model, interaction and knowledge of the other, including the other's values, is required; the relational model requires recognition of an entire set of social relations that have gone into the production of those values. And as historians such as Eric Foner (1998) and Robin D. G. Kelley (2002) have shown, the histories that have produced American values are highly conflictual, both in terms of social relations and in terms of the ways in which these relations have violated the proclaimed values of America, from the founding national violence against Native Americans, to the history of slavery, to the restrictive and unjust treatment of immigrants, to the contemporary economic injustices that fuel immigration. The idea that values come from social conflict rather than from dialogue between separate and preexisting groups is a much more demanding idea of how we might come to live together in peace. Because this model is based on existing relations, it is also one that is much more likely to produce both peace and justice in the long run.

A queer critique also suggests that we look at such conflicts not just as they are relationally produced by the parties involved but also in the context of the prevailing normativity. This is not to say that communities in conflict do not have their own norms and values but that these norms and values are in relationship to normative systems of power. A clear example of the way in which the operations of power constitute certain norms as vitally important is the way in which gender and sexuality have become crucial to contemporary religious ethics. The fact that contemporary religious traditions so often distinguish themselves in terms of sexual ethics is not intrinsic to something called "religion," nor is it an accidental formation; it is, at least in part, an effect of power.

For example, consider how the treatment of gender is used as a chip in the game of geopolitics, as illustrated by the sudden concern of President Bush and First Lady Laura Bush for the women of Afghanistan just before the American invasion of that nation.[26] By using women's status in defining themselves as the home of freedom and equality, Western powers such as the United States connect liberal values with the exercise of power, including exercises in illiberality and inequality such as military invasion and occupation.

In other words, although modern secularism is often presented as the answer to the problem of gender and sexual regulation by religious forces—as the site where the liberalism of secular America is evident—the type of analysis I have been presenting, influenced as it is by queer theory, argues that secular modernity produces a normative discourse of sexuality that is the driving force behind making sexual politics so central. If liberal, secular norms of sexuality are deployed, particularly by the secular state, as legitimation of state actions on behalf of inequality (including invasion and occupation), then arguing for more progressive norms and values alone will not address any of the myriad conflicts that come up around these issues. Rather, the invocation of such norms will simply be seen as an imposition of secular (read: Western) norms that have no special claim to promoting equality or justice. In fact, such invocations may provide inducements to assert "traditional" gender and sexual norms as a means of asserting difference from such "Western" impositions.[27] Suddenly because of their implication in the operation of power, gender and sexuality are more rather than less important to conflicts between secular and religious advocates, and it becomes harder to resolve such conflicts.[28]

How might conflicts over gender and sexuality be resolved differently, in ways that are open to religious differences and yet after pluralism? A useful conceptual starting point for such a project is to place religious differences, including the difference from religion that is secularism, actually on the same plane rather than placing religious differences within the framework of modern secularism.[29] In other words, secularists, particularly those whose norms are articulated with the secular state, must give up the position of secularism as the framework for resolving conflicts and be willing to enter the conversation on terms of equality.

However, we cannot simply assume equality through either the good will of the participants or the supposed neutrality of the secular state. Instead, such equality must be produced. The critique I have outlined suggests that one necessary step toward equality is to remove the norms of freedom and equality from the modern normativity in which these norms are embedded. This shift does not mean that secular norms must be removed from discussion; they may still offer valuable contributions to relations across differences. However, their contribution will be different (and possibly more valuable in resolving conflicts) when these norms are one set of possible norms advocated by the participants to the conflict rather than the norms that claim to frame all possible discussions.

A potential step in disengaging secular norms from modern normativity would be for proponents of secularism to acknowledge the conflicts within their own invocation of values. In particular, we would have to acknowledge our own commitments to gender and sexual hierarchy. For example, why should the secular state expect religious communities to make shifts on their less progressive values regarding gender and sexuality when, as I argued earlier, the way in which the liberal state uses gender and sexuality to normatively construct the nation produces hierarchies organized around gender and sexuality? This question is only intensified by the recognition that the way in which the secular state deploys gender and sexuality induces responses that make conservative positions on gender and sexuality a likely site for the expression and maintenance of difference. In other words, if those of us whose values are identified with the secular, liberal state are to understand the illiberal position of others, we have to take into account the illiberality of our position and our contributions in relationally producing the forms of illiberality that we claim to oppose. In particular, we must recognize that the invocation of norms such as freedom and equality can be as much about the invocation of normative power as about the invocation of equality.

Such a recognition does not imply that freedom and equality cannot be useful norms in situations of conflict. Queer analysis implies that the effects of appealing to particular norms depend not just on the norms but on their relation to normative power. Just as we must see the ways in which secular norms actually contribute to conflicts, we can also look at the ways in which these same norms and values—and those of religious communities—might contribute to the resolution of conflict.

If we hope to shift the valence of interaction across difference from a secular position, then secular norms must be both less and more present to the conflict than they are understood to be in the model of pluralism. The norms of secular liberalism are less present because they are not presumed to frame the conflict but to be up for debate. They are more present because, like those of religious communities, they must be seen as a party to the conflict, and because they are articulated with the power of the secular state they have a particular responsibility in the formation of the conflict. Recognition of this presence can also open the door to the productive engagement of these norms precisely because once removed from the framework and brought into the conflict, the norms of secularism are no longer sutured into the prevailing normativity.

In such an interaction, liberal norms are not brought into play for the production of an autonomous secularism but, to put it in queer terms, for the fulfillment of desire, of desires that are not set in advance and that are themselves fluid and mobile without being shapeless (normless). Queer theory does not propose the suspension of one's norms but rather a suspension of their connection to particular operations of power. The queer combination of presence and fluidity allows for forms of solidarity with those within communities whose norms and values may overlap with or otherwise touch on secularist values.[30] These points of connection will not necessarily be with the official representatives of "the community." Yet as Bender and Klassen suggest, it may be precisely by looking to sites other than those of official representation that models for interacting across religious difference after pluralism are to be developed.

My queer theoretical intervention adds to this suggestion the idea that this appeal to nonofficial interaction will be successful in producing sustainably peaceable relationships across difference only if such interaction takes into account not just the norms and values of the participants but the prevailing normativity that frames their interaction. Queer theory also suggests that we cannot resolve contemporary problems of religious difference without addressing either the gender question or the sex question, not just within religious communities but also within the liberal state.

NOTES

1. For a clear response to Huntington's argument from the perspective of pluralism, see Eck (2007).

2. The most recent field in which the stark lack of diversity has become an issue is financial management, where women are just 10 percent of mutual fund managers and less than 3 percent of hedge fund managers (Basch 2009). Similar statistics show the United States behind much of the rest of the world in other indicators as well. In 2007, of the 535 current members of Congress, a mere 87 (or 16.3 percent) are women; 16 of these are in the Senate, and 71 are in the House of Representatives. The proportion of women in state legislatures is 23.5 percent ("Women in Elective Office 2007" http://www.cawp.rutgers.edu). In a 2007 World Economic Forum report on the global gender gap, the U.S. ranked twenty-seventh out of 130 countries (well behind countries such as Lesotho, no. 16; Mozambique, no. 18; and Moldova, no. 20), based on assessment of jobs, education, politics, and health as a measure of gender parity (Hausman et al. 2007).

3. These questions have produced an extensive literature. One round of such arguments is gathered in the anthology of responses to Susan Moller Okin's (1999) provocative essay, "Is Multiculturalism Bad for Women?"

4. Iris Marion Young (1990) in *Justice and the Politics of Difference* makes the point that such a position assumes a form of self-presence, of knowing oneself and one's interests, that is not necessarily possible. Similarly, Gayatri Spivak (1988) presents a blistering critique of the idea that one can simply know and represent one's interests

in "Can the Subaltern Speak?" As she says at the end of the article, "The problem of representation has not withered away."

5. On the "obviousness of the obvious," see Althusser (1971).

6. For the recent iterations of this narrative, see Mark Lilla's book *The Stillborn God: Religion, Politics and the Modern West* (2007), which generated a great deal of attention in the U.S. press (see *New York Times Magazine*, August 19, 2007, for example, and approbation by Stanley Fish [2007] in his column for the *New York Times*). The most influential book on secularism of late has been Charles Taylor's (2007).

7. Talal Asad (2003:13) makes the point that the retelling of the secularization narrative can actually be prompted by the failure of secularism to materialize as described in the dominant secularization narrative. Because the narrative is at once descriptive and prescriptive, the less secularism is realized descriptively, the more it is invoked prescriptively as a political goal that should be sought and enforced through various means, including the clash of civilizations.

8. Doubts about the validity of the secularization thesis have been raised in a wide range of fields and for some time. Some of the crucial volumes in addition to Asad (2003) in the scholarship that questions the assumptions of the secularism narrative include Bhargava (1998), Casanova (1994), Connolly (2000), Martin (1969), and Needham and Rajan (2007).

9. As Jakobsen and Bernstein (2009) argue, even when shorn of its explicitly religious aspects, secular American law continues to depend on a Christian, explicitly Protestant history and to ensure that Protestant presumptions undergird the political process (Campbell 2007; Green 2007; Layman 2001). For example, Philip Hamburger (2004) argues that even the idea of the separation of church and state, which is usually traced to eighteenth-century founders Thomas Jefferson and James Madison, developed as it is used in contemporary American political discourse mainly in the nineteenth century as part of Protestant efforts to ensure that state funds would not go to Catholic projects, organizations, and schools. Steven Newcomb (2008) argues that the very claim to dominion over the United States is based "on Old Testament narratives of the chosen people and the promised land, as exemplified in the 1823 Supreme Court ruling *Johnson v. McIntosh*, that the first 'Christian people' to 'discover' lands inhabited by 'natives, who were heathens,' have an ultimate title to and dominion over these lands and peoples." Tracy Fessenden (2007:33) has traced the development of this presumption in American culture from Puritan ideas of God-given dominion over the Native Americans as foundational to the United States to a larger project of "equating American Protestantism with American culture," such that "those religious sensibilities that do not shade invisibly into 'American sensibilities' fail to command our attention as foundational to our national culture, while those that *do* shade imperceptibly into American sensibilities fail to command our attention as religious."

10. In *Love the Sin* (2003), Jakobsen and Pellegrini make this argument through close readings of key Supreme Court decisions on sexuality and on religious freedom. We show how some of the rulings directly use Christian language and enact Protestant presumption, such that Christianity is interpreted in ways that often align with Protestantism and only sometimes with Catholicism: accepting contraception

and abortion but until the *Lawrence v. Texas* (2003) decision opposing sodomy. In a more recent project with Elizabeth Bernstein, I have also tracked the ways in which Protestant presumption works in congressional and Clinton administration appeals to sexual regulation as the legitimation for "welfare reform" (a policy that directly contradicted the lobbying efforts of the Catholic Bishops Conference and Catholic Organizations) and in Bush administration trafficking policy. Of course, there are various ways in which the Catholic Church has been influential in promoting sexual conservatism in the United States if not in shaping the form of legal regulation, and so Bernstein and I argue for an analytic frame of Protestant hegemony that sees Protestantism as overdeterminative, but not determinative, and thus takes into account the suturing of different, potentially contradictory strands, into a commonsense understanding of sexuality (Jakobsen and Bernstein 2009).

11. U.S. foreign policy also has had a crucial influence on how secularism has developed around the world, as Afsaneh Najmabadi (2008) relates in a heartbreaking history of the imposition of a ban on veiling in Iran and its implications for both religious and secular possibilities in Iran.

12. Rajeswari Sunder Rajan analyzes the particular dilemma this creates for feminists when the possibility of a Uniform Civil Code (UCC) is debated in India. On one hand, a UCC might address some of the gender inequities in India's personal laws; on the other hand, a UCC would also be likely to reinforce the dominance of the Hindu majority as the assumptions of Hinduism are codified into law in the name of "uniformity" and "secularity." For more on these questions, see Needham and Rajan's (2007) anthology on secularism in India.

13. And notably, Medved focuses on a question of sexual practice that can be linked to the understanding of Islam in the popular imagination. Not only are Muslims supposed to respond violently to insults, but also they have not renounced polygamy.

14. For an alternative explanation, see Martin Riesebrodt's (1993) study of fundamentalism in the United States and Iran. And for an alternative reading of the relationship between evangelicalism and the politics of gender and sexuality, see Watt (1991).

15. A good example of gender and sexuality as representing morality tout court was provided by the *New York Times* coverage of the role played by so-called values voters in the 2004 presidential election. The polls on which the claim that "values voters" swung the election were based did not ask for any specification of the meaning of *values*, and yet the *Times* went on to name a set of values defined by conservatism on two issues, both of which deal with gender and sexuality: opposition to abortion and to "recognition of gay and lesbian couples" (Zernike and Broder 2004).

16. This focus on normativity as the problem of and for sex reflects the ways in which sexuality studies in general and queer theory in particular have been deeply influenced by the work of Michel Foucault, most prominently *The History of Sexuality* but also the writings that have been collected in *Ethics: Subjectivity and Truth* (1998). It is significant that at the time this collection of the "essential" works began to be published, *Ethics* rather than, for example, *Power* was the first volume. Although Foucault pursued this moral problem not just through the study of the discourse of sexuality but also through studies of crime and punishment (1977) and the treatment of mental

illness (1994), he is best known in the United States for his *History of Sexuality* (1980), and it is the field of sexuality studies that has most actively responded to his readings of modern ethics.

17. Ferguson, a sociologist, focuses on the ways in which racial difference becomes marked as sexual deviance in many sociological studies, particularly those focused on impoverished communities; Villarejo takes up the question of how to represent sexual difference through the media as anything other than pathology; and Puar analyzes the ways in which the sexualization of religious difference in post–September 11 security discourses produces a particularly threatening picture of the religious "other."

18. See Foucault's preface to *The Use of Pleasure*, quoted in *The Foucault Reader* (1984:333).

19. The U.S. Supreme Court's opinion in *Bowers v. Hardwick* produced just such a continuous history of moral and religious proscription of homosexual sodomy from its "very ancient roots" through a "Judeo-Christian tradition" (based only on the mention of Christian sources) to the Georgia sodomy law, first passed in 1816 and upheld in 1986. The Court skips over not only religious variation but also differences in the meaning of *sodomy* between the 1816 version of the Georgia law and its revision in 1968 (the version that the Court actually upheld). *Bowers v. Hardwick* 478 U.S. 186 (1986), 196–197. For a more extensive reading of *Bowers*, see Jakobsen and Pellegrini (2003).

20. For example, see Pateman (1988), Armstrong (1990, 2005), and Chow (2002).

21. In other words, what's interesting about the problem of autonomy is not just that it's shared by societies and communities who maintain a normative vision of individualism but that communities that might otherwise critique individualism nonetheless are interpolated into the demand for autonomous self-representation at the level of a community, just as all nations, whatever their national culture, produce themselves as the modern unit of the nation-state (as they must to be recognized in the modern system). Similarly, religious traditions tend to be produced and to produce themselves as autonomous units whether or not they ascribe to an ethics of autonomy. Such self-production is the power of normativity. Laura Levitt's (2008) essay in *Secularisms*, for example, details the ways in which secular Judaism became difficult to sustain in the United States in part because of the presumption in public life that Jewish difference must represent an authentically religious difference, autonomous from the secular. And particularly interesting from a queer perspective is the way in which gender and sexuality are so often used to produce this unit, so that women and their sexuality bear the burden of community distinctiveness.

22. These fights often occur over how representative gay pride parades are and how they are represented. Because it is often the most flamboyant participants who are represented by the media, questions are raised nearly every year about whether the parades or these particular participants in the parades should be taken to represent the community. For a recent version of this argument, see Mutchnick (2009).

23. See Mary Pat Brady's (2008) analysis of the connections between the control of sexuality and the control of immigration.

24. For example, see Judith Butler's (2004) Levinasian approach in *Precarious Life*, particularly chapter 5.

25. For an extended argument about the ways in which this trick of liberal values was used to support colonialism, see Kazanjian (2003).

26. Laura Bush first expressed her support for women's well-being in Afghanistan in November 2001 by giving the weekly presidential radio address on this topic. For the full text of her address, see http://www.presidency.ucsb.edu/ws/index.php?pid=24992 (accessed December 13, 2009). In 2005, Mrs. Bush made her first visit to Afghanistan, where she spent six hours and extolled women's education (Gall 2005).

27. Geeta Patel's essay in the *Secularisms* project (Jakobsen and Pellegrini 2008) on the BJP shows how leaders of the Hindu nationalist party used gender and sexuality to establish their vision of India simultaneously as modern and progressive and as distinctly Hindu. In a close reading of a speech by one-time BJP leader Atal Behari Vajpayee, Patel shows how a progress narrative is created through the invocation of specifically gendered forms of subjectivity: the farmer who establishes a rural–urban progress narrative, the militarized youth as the embodiment of a future that is at once fragile and determined, and a domesticated woman who desires and represents both timeless tradition and modern commodities. Patel notes how the speech brings into play colonial and missionary (specifically Christian) images, modern secularist images of capitalist production, and Hindu nationalist claims to construct a Hinduism in India that is supposedly counter to Western secularism even as it embraces that secularism in the form of capitalism, as well as capitalism's Christian roots. In the reading offered by Patel (and by Banu Subramaniam) the appeals to gender and sexuality taken up by the BJP are not to separate Hindu nationalism from modernity but to give that modernity a particular form. In other words, the forms of patriarchy constructed by some contemporary religious movements are not symptomatic or strategic antitheses to modernity but ways of appropriating modernity and moving forward.

28. A profile of Asma Jahangir in the *New Yorker* (Dalrymple 2007:33) illustrated this point when Jahangir took up the discussion of so-called honor killing, the killing of women who are supposed to have strayed sexually in order to preserve the "honor" of murdered woman's family. Jahangir is quoted as saying, "Honor killings are not a specifically Islamic tradition. . . . They are just a bad tradition that must be stopped." And as reporter William Dalrymple notes, "Before Zia came to power, honor killings were restricted mainly to Pakistan's tribal regions and other remote areas. But the practice has since spread to the rest of the country, and is now widely seen as something linked with religion as well as with the old notions of tribal honor." The import of this shift in the social landscape is that the defense of sexual honor even to the point of murder is not a throwback to less modern times and traditions but has actually spread and intensified in the last several decades, and such actions can now be deployed as a chip in conflicts between religious and secular actors.

29. Akeel Bilgrami (1994) has made a similar suggestion. Bilgrami emphasizes that taking secularism to be the Archimedean point for cross-communal interaction is socially unsustainable because many parties to such interactions find the secularist framework to be imposed from without. Bilgrami's argument is particularly interesting because this critique does not lead him to give up on secularism but to argue for a secularism that might emerge from the bottom up out of negotiation between communities through a process of

what he calls internal reasoning. In a postscript to a longer version of this essay, published subsequently in *Secularism and Its Critics*, Bilgrami (1998) explains more fully what he means by "negotiation" and "internal reasoning," which is a method that would require secularists and, specifically for Bilgrami in this case, the "secular state" to give reasons for their claims that would be acceptable internally to different religious communities. This is an exciting suggestion because it opens the possibility of shifting the status of secularism and of *producing* a secularism that might be more sustainable: "If secularism transcends religious politics in the way that I am suggesting, it does so *from within*, not because it has a shimmering philosophical existence separate from religious political commitments." But despite the emphasis on the process of negotiation and internal reasoning, there is still a sense that the secularist or the secular state never has to fully own his commitments (he is always reasoning internally to others' discourse) or accept the possibility of internal reasons that might shift the meaning of secularism. As a result, it can seem as if the outcome is predetermined toward a reestablishment of the contemporary hierarchy that privileges secularism. For example, the passage quoted earlier concludes, "[If secularism] does [transcend religious politics] *after* climbing up the ladder of religious politics (via dialogue among acknowledged substantive religious communities in politics), this emergent secularism might be in a position to kick the ladder away." There are also practical problems, as Bilgrami points out: "What a secular state, trying to cope with communitarian political voices on specific issues of the kind mentioned above [including issues involving gender and sexuality], can do to give those voices the confidence to attend to the conflicts within their own thinking and values, and then internally reason them toward progressive and secular commitments is not an easy question" (Bilgrami 1998:223–224). This is, indeed, a difficult question, but the queer alternative to liberal autonomy suggests some possible answers. First, the secular state would have to give up the position that it was reasoning them toward it. Such a position on the part of the secular state once again establishes secularism in an unequal position in relation to other parties to conflict and would be bound to reinforce the claims of those who create their positions most strongly against the inequalities set up by a secular state that claims (progressively) to value equality.

30. William E. Connolly (2000) makes a similar suggestion based on Deleuze and Guattari's (1987) idea of "rhizomatic" connection. Connolly develops the idea of such connections between different participants in public debate when it is not presumed that the debate is framed by modern secularism. Aihwa Ong (2006) also considers the prospects for a connective social solidarity in the context of transnational feminism. For another approach through the idea of queer "touch" across difference, including across the differences of time, see Dinshaw (1999).

WORKS CITED

Althusser, Louis. 1971. Ideology and Ideological State Apparatuses. (Notes Towards an Investigation). In *Lenin and Philosophy*, trans. Ben Brewster, 127–186. New York: Monthly Review.

Ammerman, Nancy. 1987. *Bible Believers: Fundamentalists in the Modern World*. New Brunswick, N.J.: Rutgers University Press.

Armstrong, Nancy. 1990. *Desire and Domestic Fiction: A Political History of the Novel*. New York: Oxford University Press.

Armstrong, Nancy. 2005. *How Novels Think: The Limits of Individualism from 1719–1900*. New York: Columbia University Press.

Asad, Talal. 2003. *Formations of the Secular: Christianity, Islam, Modernity*. Stanford, Calif.: Stanford University Press.

Basch, Linda. 2009. More Women in Finance, a More Sustainable Economy. *Christian Science Monitor*, June 24. http://www.csmonitor.com/2009/0624/p09s02-coop.html (accessed December 10, 2009).

Bender, Courtney, and Pamela Klassen. 2007. After Pluralism workshop description. http://www.columbia.edu/cu/afterpluralism/about.html (accessed December 13, 2009).

Berlant, Lauren, and Michael Warner. 1998. Sex in Public. *Critical Inquiry* 24, no. 2:547–566.

Bhargava, Rajeev, ed. 1998. *Secularism and Its Critics*. Delhi: Oxford University Press.

Bilgrami, Akeel. 1994. Two Concepts of Secularism. *Yale Journal of Criticism* 7, no. 1:211–227.

Bilgrami, Akeel. 1998. Secularism, Nationalism and Modernity. In *Secularism and Its Critics*, ed. Rajeev Bhargava, 380–417. Delhi: Oxford University Press.

Brady, Mary Pat. 2008. The Homoerotics of Immigration Control. *Scholar and Feminist Online* 6.3 http://www.barnard.edu/sfonline/immigration/brady_01.htm.

Butler, Judith. 2004. *Precarious Life: The Powers of Mourning and Violence*. London: Verso.

Campbell, David E., ed. 2007. *A Matter of Faith: Religion in the 2004 Presidential Election*. Washington, D.C.: Brookings Institution Press.

Casanova, José. 1994. *Public Religions in the Modern World*. Chicago: University of Chicago Press.

Chow, Rey. 2002. *The Protestant Ethnic and the Spirit of Capitalism*. New York: Columbia University Press.

Connolly, William E. 2000. *Why I Am Not a Secularist*. Minneapolis: University of Minnesota Press.

Dalrymple, William. 2007. Days of Rage. *New Yorker*, July 23, pp. 26–34.

Deleuze, Gilles, and Félix Guattari. 1987. *A Thousand Plateaus: Capitalism and Schizophrenia*. Trans. Brian Massumi. Minneapolis: University of Minnesota Press.

Dinshaw, Carolyn. 1999. *Getting Medieval: Sexualities and Communities, Pre- and Postmodern*. Durham, N.C.: Duke University Press.

Duggan, Lisa. 1994. Queering the State. *Social Text* 39:1–14.

Eck, Diana. 2007. Prospects for Pluralism: Voice and Vision in the Study of Religion. *Journal of the American Academy of Religion* 75, no. 4:743–776.

Ferguson, Roderick. 2004. *Aberrations in Black: Toward a Queer of Color Critique*. Minneapolis: University of Minnesota Press.

Fessenden, Tracy. 2007. *Culture and Redemption: Religion, the Secular, and American Literature*. Princeton, N.J.: Princeton University Press.

Fish, Stanley. 2007. Liberalism and Secularism: One and the Same. *New York Times*, September 2. http://fish.blogs.nytimes.com/2007/09/02/liberalism-and-secularism-one-and-the-same (accessed December 10, 2009).

Foner, Eric. 1998. *The Story of American Freedom*. New York: Norton.

Foucault, Michel. 1977. *Discipline and Punish: The Birth of the Prison*. Trans. Alan Sheridan. New York: Vintage.

Foucault, Michel. 1980. *The History of Sexuality*. Vol. 1, *An Introduction*. Trans. Robert Hurley. New York: Vintage.

Foucault, Michel. 1984. *The Foucault Reader*. Ed. Paul Rabinow. New York: Pantheon.

Foucault, Michel. 1988. *The History of Sexuality*. Vol. 3, *The Care of the Self*. Trans. Robert Hurley. New York: Vintage.

Foucault, Michel. 1994. *Birth of the Clinic: An Archaeology of Medical Perception*. New York: Vintage.

Foucault, Michel. 1998. *Ethics: Subjectivity and Truth*. Ed. Paul Rabinow. Vol. 1 of *Essential Works of Foucault, 1954–1984*. New York: New Press.

Gall, Carlotta. 2005. Laura Bush Carries Pet Causes to Afghans. *New York Times*, March 31. http://query.nytimes.com/gst/fullpage.html?res=9404E3DB133FF932A05750C0A9639C8B63&cp=2&sq=carlotta%20gall%20%20+%202005%20+%20Laura%20Bush&st=cse (accessed December 10, 2009).

Gilman, Charlotte Perkins. 1923. *His Religion and Hers: A Study of the Faith of Our Fathers and the Work of Our Mothers*. New York: Century.

Green, John Clifford. 2007. *The Faith Factor: How Religion Influences American Elections*. Westport, Conn.: Praeger.

Habermas, Jürgen. 1984, 1987. *The Theory of Communicative Action*. Trans. Thomas McCarthy. 2 vols. Boston: Beacon.

Halperin, David. 1997. *Saint Foucault: Towards a Gay Hagiography*. New York: Oxford University Press.

Hamburger, Philip. 2004. *Separation of Church and State*. Cambridge, Mass.: Harvard University Press.

Hausman, Ricardo, Laura Tyson, and Saadia Zahidi. 2007. *The Global Gender Gap Report 2007*. Davos, Switzerland: World Economic Forum.

Huntington, Samuel. 2004. *Who Are We? The Challenges to American National Identity*. New York: Simon and Schuster.

Jakobsen, Janet R. 1998. *Working Alliances and the Politics of Difference: Diversity and Feminist Ethics*. Bloomington: Indiana University Press.

Jakobsen, Janet R., and Elizabeth Bernstein. 2009. *U.S. Country Report: Religion, Politics, and Gender Equality*. United Nations Research Institute for Social Development. http://www.unrisd.org/.

Jakobsen, Janet R., and Ann Pellegrini. 2003. *Love the Sin: Sexual Regulation and the Limits of Religious Tolerance*. New York: New York University Press.

Jakobsen, Janet R., and Ann Pellegrini, eds. 2008. *Secularisms*. Durham, N.C.: Duke University Press.

Kazanjian, David. 2003. *The Colonizing Trick: National Culture and Imperial Citizenship in Early America*. Minneapolis: University of Minnesota Press.

Kelley, Robin D. G. 2002. *Freedom Dreams: The Black Radical Imagination*. Boston: Beacon.

Layman, Geoffrey. 2001. *The Great Divide: Religious and Cultural Conflict in American Party Politics*. New York: Columbia University Press.

Levitt, Laura. 2008. Other Moderns, Other Jews: Revisiting Jewish Secularism in America. In *Secularisms*, ed. Janet R. Jakobsen and Ann Pellegrini, 107–138. Durham, N.C.: Duke University Press.

Lilla, Mark. 2007. *The Stillborn God: Religion, Politics and the Modern West*. New York: Knopf.

Martin, David. 1969. *The Religious and the Secular: Studies in Secularization*. New York: Schocken.

Medved, Michael. 2007. Hollywood's Terrorists: Mormon, Not Muslim. *USA Today*, August 13, p. 13A.

Mutchnick, Max. 2009. Where's My Martin Luther Queen? *Huffington Post*, June 18. http://www.huffingtonpost.com/max-mutchnick/where-is-my-martin-luther_b_217426.html (accessed December 10, 2009).

Najmabadi, Afsaneh. 2008. Feminism Unveiled. In *Secularisms*, ed. Janet R. Jakobsen and Ann Pellegrini, 39–57. Durham, N.C.: Duke University Press.

Needham, Anuradha Dingwaney, and Rajeswari Sunder Rajan, eds. 2007. *The Crisis of Secularism in India*. Durham, N.C.: Duke University Press.

Newcomb, Steven T. 2008. *Pagans in the Promised Land: Decoding the Doctrine of Christian Discovery*. Golden, Colo.: Fulcrum.

Okin, Susan Moller, ed. 1999. *Is Multiculturalism Bad for Women?* Princeton, N.J.: Princeton University Press.

Ong, Aihwa. 2006. *Neoliberalism as Exception: Mutations in Citizenship and Sovereignty*. Durham, N.C.: Duke University Press.

Patel, Geeta. 2008. Ghostly Appearances. In *Secularisms*, ed. Janet R. Jakobsen and Ann Pellegrini, 226–247. Durham, N.C.: Duke University Press.

Pateman, Carole. 1988. *The Sexual Contract*. Stanford, Calif.: Stanford University Press.

Puar, Jasbir. 2007. *Terrorist Assemblages: Homonationalism in Queer Times*. Durham, N.C.: Duke University Press.

Riesebrodt, Martin. 1993. *Pious Passion: The Emergence of Modern Fundamentalism in the United States and Iran*. Trans. Don Reneau. Berkeley: University of California Press.

Rubin, Gayle. 1993. Thinking Sex: Notes for a Radical Theory of the Politics of Sexuality. In *The Lesbian and Gay Studies Reader*, ed. Henry Abelove, Michèle Aina Barale, and David Halperin, 3–44. New York: Routledge.

Spivak, Gayatri Chakravorty. 1988. Can the Subaltern Speak? In *Marxism and the Interpretation of Culture*, ed. Lawrence Grossberg and Cary Nelson, 271–315. Urbana: University of Illinois Press.

Subramaniam, Banu. 2008. What Tangled Webs We Weave: Science, Secularism, and Religion in Contemporary India. In *Secularisms*, ed. Janet R. Jakobsen and Ann Pellegrini, 178–205. Durham, N.C.: Duke University Press.

Taylor, Charles. 2007. *A Secular Age*. Cambridge, Mass.: Harvard University Press.

Villarejo, Amy. 2005. Tarrying with the Normative: Queer Theory and Black History. *Social Text* 84–85:69–84.

Warner, Michael. 1999. *The Trouble with Normal: Sex, Politics and the Ethics of Queer Life*. Cambridge, Mass.: Harvard University Press.

Watt, David Harrington. 1991. A *Transforming Faith: Explorations of Twentieth-Century American Evangelicalism*. New Brunswick, N.J.: Rutgers University Press.

Young, Iris Marion. 1990. *Justice and the Politics of Difference*. Princeton, N.J.: Princeton University Press.

Zernike, Kate, and John M. Broder. 2004. War? Jobs? No, Character Counted Most to Voters. *New York Times*, November 4, p. P1.

Ziarek, Ewa. 2001. *An Ethics of Dissensus: Postmodernity, Feminism and the Politics of Radical Democracy*. Stanford, Calif.: Stanford University Press.

2. PLURALIZING RELIGION

Islamic Law and the Anxiety of Reasoned Deliberation

ANVER M. EMON

The authors in this volume remind us not only of the theme of this collection but also of a major challenge in our world today: Religious pluralism is here to stay. As a demographic fact, it is everywhere, as Winnifred Sullivan writes. But of interest in this volume is how *religious pluralism* is not merely a descriptive label. Rather, it is a term of art that is used to raise various questions about the potential for conflict and peace and about the best modes for good governance. In their introduction to this volume, Pamela Klassen and Courtney Bender remind us that the variety of themes that emanate from the phrase *religious pluralism* attest to the importance of exploring the impact of the facts of pluralism on our ability to contend with our rapidly globalizing world in which the increased movement of peoples has heightened the potential for religious conflict.

Benjamin Berger (2007, chap. 4, this volume) offers an important contribution to the study of religious pluralism when he uses the fact of pluralism as a flashpoint for critiquing the assumptions underlying liberal rule of law. He shows how juridical and academic approaches to the law fail to account for how the liberal rule of law is more than a dispassionate moderator in a pluralist setting but rather is a normatively thick instrument that creates and polices the boundaries of acceptable pluralist expression. He also argues that contemporary scholarship fails to account for how the liberal rule of law draws those boundaries based on certain predispositions of what religion is, can, and should be.

For the liberally minded, religion is something that inheres in people rather than an arena for reasoned deliberation. This essentialization arises in part from how an uncritical embrace of liberal tolerance as value neutral covers the way in which liberal governance essentializes religion and thereby marginalizes it from general debate. For Wendy Brown, who writes in a context of a liberal theory of governance, the conception of the religious in a discourse of tolerance is reductive and will often blind others from understanding how members of a faith community understand both their God and their world through a thick, rational vocabulary founded on religious traditions that either speak directly or are made to speak to issues affecting the public weal. It has contributed to a climate in which the religious is deemed to have little or no place in public debate and discourse, on either principled or pragmatic grounds (Brown 2006:4, 10, 24).

Those with a religious framework may not view their religious system as purely subjective, private, and individual. Rather, they may rely on it as a lens through which to view and understand their world. Therefore, to problematize liberal discourses of tolerance and religion will require us, in part, to understand how religious traditions such as Islamic law were not rarefied traditions but instead offered a framework for understanding, characterizing, and ultimately ordering the world.

But accepting Berger's and Brown's critiques can have anxiety-producing implications for the religiously minded who might not want to contend with the indeterminacy that comes with rendering religion a site of reasoned deliberation. Those with a religious framework may want their framework to be so determinate as to be outside the bounds of reasoned deliberation. Indeed, Roxanne Euben (1999) suggests that for Islamic fundamentalists, having a uniform set of guidelines aids in cementing an Islamic identity positioned against a hegemonic liberal West. Therefore, to undermine the rarefied image of a religious tradition such as Islamic law may pose a threat to both liberals and Islamists whose agendas of governance and community identity benefit from the rarefaction of a tradition such as Islamic law.

Nonetheless, the fact remains that Islamic legal history is replete with theoretical inquiries into the nature of knowledge, the scope of moral agency and legal interpretation, and the authority of law. These inquiries are perhaps a product of the anxiety that comes with recognizing a religious tradition as a site of reasoned deliberation. This chapter provides a brief account of how premodern Muslim jurists theorized about the inevitable interpretivism in the juridical enterprise. The way in which they gave license to jurists to reason to conclusions of law raised fundamental questions of theology, moral agency, and legal authority.

Their philosophical exposition on these issues assumed a metaphysics that rendered aspects of the observed world objective and thus distinct from the observing human eye. The world and the human experience of the world were two separate things for them, but they could be linked through a naturalist account of human interpretation. Akin to natural law theorists in the West, Muslim jurists fused fact and value in the created world, by which they could render reasoned deliberation as an authoritative source for normative ordering.[1] As we will see, their naturalist accounts invoked a theory of an objective and normatively thick nature that may have been so implicit in their worldview as to render it nearly veiled from critique. But a critique of objectivity, akin to that adopted by Berger regarding the liberal rule of law, will allow us to challenge premodern metaphysical assumptions and begin to reflect on the importance of ongoing, often anxiety-producing moral agency (and thereby reasoned deliberation) in the framework of Islamic legal analysis. This chapter will briefly review premodern Muslim arguments on natural law, question the underlying assumptions about objectivity and determinacy, and consider what such challenges might mean for a Shari'a-based theory of legal authority and moral agency.

TEXT, LAW, AND INTERPRETIVE AGENCY: THE TEXT AND BEYOND

For premodern Muslim jurists, the authority of a Shari'a rule, also known as *fiqh*, might be linked to a particular source text, such as the Qur'an or *Hadith* of the Prophet.[2] The rules of *fiqh* are so called because they represent the human attempt at understanding the divine law. Between the source texts and the *fiqh* rules lies the jurist as interpreter who derives from authoritative sources the rules of law that, when applied within a rule of law system, are intended to have coercive effects on those subjected to the law.

A significant debate in Islamic jurisprudence concerns situations in which there is no source text to aid a jurist's interpretive activity.[3] Although one refrain in Muslim apologetic literature is that there is no issue unaddressed by a source text in Islamic law, premodern Muslim jurists disagreed. In their works on legal philosophy (*usul al-fiqh*), jurists raised the philosophical question about the ontological authority of human reason in the law.

The debate is often phrased in terms of how one determines a governing rule where there is no revelatory source text (*min qabla wurud al-shar'*). Some have interpreted this phrase to refer to a counterfactual hypothetical state of humanity lacking revelation (Crone 2004:263–264). However, I suggest that the phrase raises the question of whether human moral inquiry into the good (*husn*) and the bad (*qubh*) can be an authoritative basis for asserting a rule of law consonant with the divine will. This is not to suggest that this debate ignores the existence of source texts. Rather, it arguably recognizes that source texts are finite. Therefore, jurists queried about the authority of human reason alone within the Shari'a framework.

Muslim jurists of competing theological persuasions equally adopted natural teleological philosophies to authorize and contain the scope of human reason as a source of law. Yet their jurisprudence could not ignore the differences in theology they each held. In particular, they were concerned with preserving the omnipotence of God's will amidst human reasoning to the law. We find two naturalist theories—hard and soft naturalism—that come to similar teleological conclusions but with important theological differences.[4]

THE THEOLOGY AND JURISPRUDENCE OF HARD NATURALISM

Hard naturalism is reflected here in the works of Basran Mu'tazilites and is built on theological first principles about God and the ontology of nature, as well as epistemic concerns with objectivity and determinacy in the law. Relying on a theology of divine justice in which God only does good and is incapable of evil, hard naturalists argued that God created the world for the purpose of benefiting humanity. God has no need for any benefits from creation; the theology of God's omnipotence precludes the possibility that God created the world for His own benefit. Nor would God create it to cause pain and suffering for others, because that would be unjust to those adversely affected. Because God is only just, creation must therefore pose a benefit. Hard naturalists fused the value arising from God's justice and will with the facts of a natural order to invest nature with both objectivity and normative value. Nature is objectively good for humanity, given the assumption of a just creator who does only good and needs nothing. Consequently, hard naturalists argued that one could rationally deduce the good from nature and transform that finding into a normative Shari'a value because the empirical goodness of nature embodies the willful intent of God. Hard naturalists such as Qadi 'Abd al-Jabbar (d. 415/1025) and Abu al-Husayn al-Basri (d. 436/1044) fused fact and value in nature and thereby embraced an ontology of law founded on source texts *and* the reasoned deliberation of human beings.

Hard naturalists generally framed their discussion using the specific terms *husn* (good) and *qubh* (bad). They asked whether human beings could reason their way from the good and the bad to obligations and prohibitions under the Shari'a. A significant theological implication of their inquiry was whether their rational analysis of the good and the bad obligated God to punish and reward.

But if God is omnipotent, how can he essentially be bound by human reasoning to reward or punish conduct that mere humans designate as obligatory and prohibited (i.e., *wajib* and *mahzur*)? To make their argument, hard naturalists needed a theology of God that linked his will to human reasoning. Nature became the means by which they made that link.

FUSING FACT AND VALUE: THE PRESUMPTION OF PERMISSIBILITY

Qadi ʿAbd al-Jabbar asserts as a first principle that God created the world as a bounty (*rizq*) for humanity. ʿAbd al-Jabbar (n.d.:*Taklif* 27) and premodern lexicographers defined *rizq* as something from which one benefits (see also al-Zabidi 1994:13:162). As a first-order principle, creation is a benefit to all of humanity. With the act of divine creation arises the assumption that God's creative endeavors do not benefit any one person in particular but rather are meant to benefit all of humanity together (*jumlat al-ʾibad*) (ʿAbd al-Jabbar n.d.:*Taklif* 27). No rule of law exists at this primordial moment to distribute rights and entitlements in an exclusive manner.

For ʿAbd al-Jabbar, at the primordial moment of creation, nature poses a benefit that all can enjoy. Whether we enjoy creation is not relevant for his argument (ʿAbd al-Jabbar n.d.:*Taklif* 27). The sheer possibility of using creation as we see fit is by itself a positive good (i.e., *hasan*) rather than value neutral. This first principle, the principle of permissibility, is the means by which ʿAbd al-Jabbar fuses both fact and value in nature.

Notably, al-Basri reaches the same position but situates it within a larger epistemic concern about legal deduction and analysis. According to him, we reason about the good and the bad by inquiring into nature. Nature presents both an empirical base for investigation and a normative foundation given God's creative goodness, both of which allow al-Basri to fuse fact and value to thereby uphold the authority of naturalistic reasoning, akin to ʿAbd al-Jabbar's argument. Nature becomes the medium by which rational observations about the good and the bad gain normative content. But for al-Basri, the naturalistic analysis is the first step of legal analysis. The second step concerns the scope and limits of naturalistic analysis. Any naturalistic legal conclusion will yield to countervailing evidence from source texts. Al-Basri's approach both liberates moral agency and provides a textually based framework to limit and direct the legal inquiry.

For al-Basri the existence and nature of a legal norm will depend on the type of sanction it conveys. Some acts that are prohibited may nevertheless invoke minor sanctions, whereas others pose harsher ones. Likewise, other acts that are obligatory may offer limited rewards or more significant rewards. Among the bad acts (*qabih*) are those that entail praise if omitted and blame if committed and others that involve praise if omitted but have no consequences if committed. Al-Basri (n.d.:1:335) calls these acts, respectively, *muharram* (prohibited) and *makruh* (reprehensible).[5] Among the good acts (*hasan*) are those that entail praise if they are committed and blame if they are not, whereas others involve only praise if committed but no consequence if omitted. Because of the varying normative consequences, these acts are respectively known as *wajib* and *nadb*, or obligatory and recommended (al-Basri n.d.:1:335). These categories of norms are important because they allow al-Basri to use inherited concepts of legal values (e.g., *al-ahkam al-khamsa*)[6] within the framework of a rationally based inquiry into the good and the bad and the consequences of obligation that arise therefrom.

The final normative category involves acts (including omissions) that entail neither praise nor blame. This act would seem normatively neutral. But for al-Basri this last category provides the naturalistic foundation for reasoning that allows him to move from rational observations of the good and the bad to normative assertions of obligation, prohibition, the recommended, and the reprehensible. He argues that what may seem like a value-neutral act on its face is actually an affirmative good (*hasan*). Therefore, he infuses it with positive normative value. By suggesting this type of act is affirmatively good, al-Basri follows the same reasoning of ʿAbd al-Jabbar, who also fused fact and value to fashion his principle of permissibility.

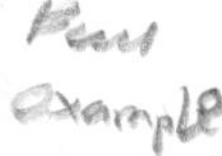

To illustrate his fusion, al-Basri referred to the example of eating food. He argued that one can reason that eating food is permissible because of the benefit that arises from eating. Furthermore, this type of benefit poses no presumptive evil (al-Basri n.d.:2:315). According to al-Basri (n.d.:2:315), eating is good because "the benefit (*manfa'a*) beckons [one to do] the act and permits it since [gaining benefit] is one of the purposes [of the act]." The term *manfa'a* and others like it embrace both the empirical determination of a benefit and the dispositional tendency to attain that benefit as a good: They fuse fact and value. In the absence of evidence to the contrary, any empirical benefit that invites one to do and achieve the good should be pursued as a good.

LIMITING THE PERMISSIBLE, REASONING TO LAW

Both ʿAbd al-Jabbar and al-Basri recognized that a mere principle of permissibility is insufficient for a naturalist jurisprudence. Both relied on the principle of permissibility to fuse fact and value and thereby to offer ontological authority to human reasoning in the law. But more was needed to move from the ontology of reason to an epistemology of law. The two jurists adopted different approaches, but they were attempting to reach similar results.

For ʻAbd al-Jabbar, although creation is a benefit for humanity, not all its uses are necessarily permissible. First, some uses of a *rizq* might cause harm to us or someone else. ʻAbd al-Jabbar argues that any use posing harm to someone can rebut the presumption of permissibility. He states, "We know through reason that we can utilize everything that benefits us, where there is neither temporal nor eternal harm imposed on us for doing so, nor on someone else" (ʻAbd al-Jabbar n.d.:*Taklif* 33). Second, ʻAbd al-Jabbar uses the concept of property to restrict who can and cannot make use of certain resources. If I make a specific claim on a particular resource, and my use poses no harm to anyone, I become the owner of that resource (*sara malikan lahu*) and can exclude others from making competing claims (ʻAbd al-Jabbar n.d.:*Taklif* 34).

One might ask why anyone might or even should make a claim on specific resources. According to ʻAbd al-Jabbar (n.d.:*Taklif* 44), to seek out benefits in ways that cause no harm is an independent good (*hasan*) to be pursued, even though doing so may involve some hardship (*al-amr al-shaqq*). Pursuing self-fulfillment involves both avoiding harm and pursuing benefits; but benefits are not pure or devoid of hardship.

According to ʻAbd al-Jabbar, to make a claim on *rizq* is to pursue the telos of self-fulfillment. For ʻAbd al-Jabbar (n.d.:*Lutf* 9), one's telos of fulfillment is captured by the term *lutf*, which is "what beckons [one] to an act of obedience under circumstances in which one chooses [to act] or where one will most likely do so. Under these two sets of circumstances, the active element is *lutf*. . . . It is what beckons [one] to an act." God places the *lutf* in us as a guide toward the good, which thereby renders any of our determinations of obligations to be products of teleological reasoning. According to ʻAbd al-Jabbar, the function of the *lutf* is akin to the function of the prophets. God provided humanity with prophets as divine guidance. The prophets issued laws to guide people to the good. Although the prophets' laws were embedded in their own experiences, the law itself was ultimately from God (ʻAbd al-Jabbar n.d.:*Lutf* 10). In this sense, says ʻAbd al-Jabbar, the prophets were a divine *lutf*. By implication, human dispositions are a form of divine guidance. Although they may reflect the contingency of the human condition, they nonetheless embody divine guidance. The significance of the *lutf* lies in the fact that because God created human dispositions, we can refer to them and thereby claim to know what pleases God (ʻAbd al-Jabbar n.d.:*Lutf* 10).

Our obligation to pursue the good is fundamentally tied to our own self-fulfillment. Anything else would lead to a utilitarian, consequentialist teleology that would undermine the meaningfulness that comes from individual moral agency. As 'Abd al-Jabbar (n.d.:*Lutf* 46) states, "It is not obligatory on Zayd to bring about benefits (*iltimas al-masalih*) for someone else or to avoid harms (*daf' madarr*) accruing to someone else." Rather, Zayd must embrace such goods and avoid such evils when they affect himself. To require otherwise would render Zayd an instrument for someone else's good and benefit.

However, this does not mean that we will always and necessarily follow our dispositional traits to do good and avoid evil ('Abd al-Jabbar n.d.:*Lutf* 15). We might do evil acts, avoid good acts, or even remain paralyzed in a state of indecision. 'Abd al-Jabbar admitted this discontinuity between one's *lutf* and one's actualized behavior. But he never intended to suggest that human beings always follow their dispositional traits. Rather, his point is more general and abstract (*'ala jihat al-tawassu'*), that one's disposition "contributes to [doing] the good, but does not suggest that the individual actually does the good because of it" ('Abd al-Jabbar n.d.:*Lutf* 20). The *lutf* directs one to the good because God's justice precludes Him from creating human dispositions that lead us to evil or harm ('Abd al-Jabbar n.d.:*Taklif* 64). Consequently, humans are endowed with dispositions to the good, thereby giving them the *potential* of inquiring into the divine will to find guidance, although they may not always succeed in doing so.

Our dispositions therefore are less products of our desire and choice than structures that lie within us. They speak to the human condition at a general level and are distinct from any personal desires or whims we have. For example, no criminal wants to be punished. It causes pain and harm that he will want to avoid. But individual desire does not negate the overall systemic good that arises from inflicting pain and suffering on the criminal. If someone is sentenced to suffer punishment (*'iqab*), his suffering is good in the sense that he deserves it (*li kawnihi mustahaqq*) ('Abd al-Jabbar n.d.:*Taklif* 85). This example illustrates that 'Abd al-Jabbar's emphasis on the desire principle is not intended to empower mere whimsy or idiosyncrasy. Rather, he assumes the *lutf* is a deep structure that can be harnessed for constructing and perfecting a *general* normative. Reason is used to understand that telos in light of the specific goods or bounties we can enjoy.

'Abd al-Jabbar's principles of inquiry, his emphasis on the philosophy of law (as opposed to the psychology of human whimsy), and his assumptions of human nature allow him to construct a framework of inquiry that relies on human reason. According to 'Abd al-Jabbar (n.d.:*Taklif* 384), "knowledge of justice is not possible without [reason] because when [one] does not know the difference between the good and the bad, he cannot dissociate the eternal divine from evil, or associate Him with the good. Much of the divine guidance and the social goods (*masalih*) cannot be realized without [reason]." Reason is the means by which one identifies the good and the bad, understands one's natural dispositions (*altaf*), and identifies the goods in the world that can justify obligations and prohibitions within a larger normative ordering.

Al-Basri limits the authority of reason by reference to countervailing evidence. We can use reason to make decisions about the good and the bad and thereby justify our actions in Shari'a value terms. But we can do so only to the extent that there is no countervailing evidence in source texts reflecting the divine will or prophetic example. As noted earlier, al-Basri presumed that nature is good. But this presumption stands only as long as it is not rebutted by countervailing, authoritative evidence. Therefore, al-Basri (n.d.:2:315) held that God provides the essential evidence required for us to determine whether the presumptive goodness of something is rebutted by evidence to the contrary (*lau kana fihi mafsada la dallana Allahu 'alayha*). To hold otherwise would undermine his presumption of the good in nature, not to mention impose on the individual an impossible standard of analysis. When no contrary evidence exists, we can pursue the good as we see fit.

To illustrate his schema of natural law reasoning, he used the example of breathing air (*al-tanaffus fi al-hawa'*). To determine the goodness of this act, the investigator "presumes that the goodness of this activity exists in the absence of evidence of the bad. He ascertains it involves no corruption (*mafsada*), [presuming that] if there were corruption, we would have knowledge of its corrupt nature. [This presumption] negates evil in [the act, but will] . . . change if evidence is offered" (al-Basri n.d.:2:316).

Investigating God's created natural order thereby involves certain basic presumptions. First, God does only the good (al-Basri n.d.:2:343). Second, human beings must be capable of knowing the difference between the good and the bad and of pursuing the good. Third, because of God's goodness, creation and nature are presumptively good unless evidence exists to the contrary. And fourth, if an act poses a harm, we can presume God would have provided evidence to illustrate that harm (al-Basri n.d.:2:343). To hold otherwise not only would challenge the presumption of the good but also would require the impossible from us. These presumptions involve a theology of God, a philosophy of humanity, and a theory of nature, all of which link the divine will to human rational agency.

Al-Basri by no means suggests that reason can be a source for all laws of God. One cannot rationally know that a Muslim must fast the first day of Ramadan but not the day before (al-Basri n.d.:2:323). Rather, reason is one of many sources for legal analysis. Reason, experience (*idrak*), accepted traditions (*khabar mutawatir*), and other evidence (*dalil*) are part of any method (*tariqa*) of legal deduction (al-Basri n.d.:2:323). We may first begin with a rational determination of the good as a starting point. Thereafter we inquire whether any source text might contradict our reasoned conclusion. "If one does not find [in source texts] anything that changes [the determination] from the rationally based rule, he decides in accordance with the [rational rule]" (al-Basri n.d.:2:343). But where source texts contradict our reasoned findings, the reasoned rule must change. "Reason attests to those rules on condition that a source-text does not alter [our decision]" (al-Basri n.d.:2:343).

For both 'Abd al-Jabbar and al-Basri, naturalistic reasoning relies on various presumptions about God, nature, and the human capacity to acquire knowledge and make judgments. Certainly from the preceding discussion, 'Abd al-Jabbar's approach has a highly philosophical flavor, whereas al-Basri's model is designed to explain the epistemic mode for deriving a rule of law. Nonetheless, both models rely on a conception of nature that is unchanging in its presumed goodness, assuming no evidence to the contrary. For both, the naturalist fusion of fact and value is a starting point that allows them to move from empirical findings to assertions of norms and law.

THE VOLUNTARIST CRITIQUE OF HARD NATURALISM

Those who opposed hard naturalism, most notably Ash'arite theologians, founded their position on two fundamental points. First, they argued that nature is not sufficiently determinative, objective, or foundational to ground a theory of moral reasoning that fuses fact with value. Second, although they agreed that human beings make rational moral judgments all the time, those determinations cannot assume the normative authority of a divine rule whereby God is bound by human reason to reward or punish.

Voluntarists opposed any fusion of fact and value by citing verses of the Qur'an, such as Q. 17:15, which states, "We do not punish until We send a messenger." This verse enshrines the idea that divine sanction requires an express statement of will, not a reasoned inquiry into the good and the bad. To reason from nature, they argued, assumes too much of both God and human understanding of the divine will. For instance, eleventh-century jurist Ibn Hazm (1984:1:54), never one to mince words, argued that the hard naturalists' fusion of fact and value in nature was "plain pomposity" (*makabirat al-iyan*). By their very nature, human beings are prone to sexual licentiousness, drunken debauchery, and lapses in religious observance. These are natural dispositions that God expressly prohibits. Consequently, one cannot argue from the facts of nature to moral norms and obligations with the imprint of the divine.

The voluntarist Ash'arites also attacked the hard naturalist theology of God's justice. For nature to be a bounty and source of goodness, one had to assume that God only does good with the purpose of benefiting humanity.[7] Voluntarist jurists retorted that this theology of God undermines God's omnipotence. If God can do only good for humanity's benefit, and human reason can determine what is good, then humans can require God to reward and punish certain behavior. This possibility undermines the idea that God is beyond any limits. Jurists such as Abu Ishaq al-Shirazi (d. 1083) argued vociferously that God was not limited in any way. Rather God does as He wishes and rules as He desires (*yaf'alu Allah ma yasha' wa yahkumu ma yuridu*) (al-Shirazi 1988:2:983–984).

For voluntarist jurists, where no source text addresses an issue, no one can assert a divine rule of law. Voluntarist jurists did not deny that a rule of God exists; they argued instead that humans are not in an epistemic position to determine what the law is.[8] Consequently in situations where there is no source text, voluntarists held that the divine law is in a state of suspension (*tawaqquf*), such that one cannot authoritatively assert a rule of obligation or prohibition (Ibn Hazm 1984:1:52; al-Khatib al-Baghdadi 1977:192–194; al-Sam'ani 1997:2:46–47, 52; al-Shirazi 1988:2:977).[9]

However, hard naturalists countered that the position of suspension is substantively no different from the hard naturalist presumption of permissibility. Both positions implied that one suffers no consequence for acting (al-Jassas 2000:2:103). But voluntarists countered that the hard naturalists' presumption of permissibility relies on an affirmative rational assumption of the fusion of fact and value in nature. The voluntarist position of suspension makes no such rationalist assumption. It only asserts the absence of an authoritative source text that could justify finding an obligation (al-Baji 1995:2:689; al-Ghazali n.d.:1:133; Ibn Hazm 1984:1:56; al-Sam'ani 1997:2:52; al-Shirazi 1988:2:979–980).

This is not to suggest that voluntarists denied that humans can and do make moral judgments about the good and the bad all the time. For instance, Shafi'ite-Ash'arite jurist al-Juwayni (d. 478/1085) recognized that people constantly make judgments about how best to avoid harm (*ijtinab al-mahalik*) and enjoy various benefits in nature (*ibtidar al-manafi'*). This tendency lies in the very nature of humanity (*haqq al-adamiyyin*); to deny it would be entirely unreasonable (*khuruj 'an al-ma'qul*) (al-Juwayni 1997:1:10). But making moral determinations of the good and the bad is entirely different from identifying a ruling of God (*hukm Allah*). Whether something is obligatory or prohibited depends on whether God has provided a sanction for violation of the given norm. Without a sanction, we cannot meaningfully speak of obligations and prohibitions. Surely we might reason to the good or the bad, but we cannot effectively impose on God the obligation to punish or reward someone for performing or omitting a particular act. As al-Juwayni (1997:1:10) said, "It is not prohibited [for people] to investigate these two characteristics [i.e., *husn* and *qubh*] where harm may arise or where benefit is possible, on condition that [their determination] not be attributed to God or obligate God to punish or reward."

THE VOLUNTARISTS' SOFT NATURALISM

Voluntarist jurists who rejected hard naturalism were not so jurisprudentially naive as to assume that sufficient source texts exist to address every potential legal issue. Certainly issues would arise for which no source text provides guidance. Their response to this situation required a balance between their theological commitment to God's omnipotence and the need to endow juristic reasoning with sufficient authority to justify the creative determination of law.

Their theory of legal authority relies on a conception of nature that is, just as for the hard naturalists, beneficial for human beings. But the benefit that nature provides is not a consequence of God's eternal goodness and His inability to do evil. Rather, nature's goodness is a product of God's grace (*tafaddul*). On one hand, God's grace renders nature a positive good that can be a foundation for naturalistic reasoning. On the other hand, God's grace is subject to change if God so desires. By relying on a theory of divine grace, voluntarists were able to preserve God's omnipotence while fusing fact and value in nature to provide an authoritative basis for reason as a source of law.

For instance, Abu Hamid al-Ghazali (d. 1111) intuitively held that God's goals in legislating the Shari'a are to uphold five basic interests: life, lineage, property, mind, and religion.[10] For al-Ghazali these five values can be found in any legal system. However, the way in which he justifies his position illustrates how his soft naturalism differs from the hard version noted earlier. Al-Ghazali (1971:162–163) states,

> Reason determines and decides upon [the five values], whether or not there are source-texts (*lau la wurud al-shara'i'*). [They are values] that no legal system can do without, according to those who speak of the good and the bad in rationalist terms.[11] We say: It is for God . . . to do as He wishes with His servants. It is not obligatory for Him to uphold the good. [But] we do not deny the power of reason to indicate the beneficial and the corrupt, to warn against harm, and desire bounties and fulfillment. Nor do we deny that the prophets . . . were sent for the benefit of humanity concerning worldly and otherworldly affairs, as a mercy and grace (*rahma, fadl*) from God for creation, but not because of an imposition or obligation on Him. . . . Indeed we

have explained [our position] to this degree in order to distinguish ourselves from the Mu'tazilite position (*i'tiqad al-i'tizal*).

Al-Ghazali accomplishes four main theoretical goals in this paragraph. First, he invokes the debate about the good and the bad, thus situating his theory in opposition to the hard naturalists. Second, he emphasizes the centrality of God's omnipotence in his theory. Third, he recognizes that human beings make reasoned determinations of the good and the bad all the time. And fourth, our ability to reason to the law is due to the mercy and grace of God. For voluntarist jurists such as al-Ghazali, God need not have provided such guidance, but because he did out of his grace, humans can rely on it. But they do so not because of some rationalist theological assumption about the limits of God's power. Instead, we can authoritatively reason about the law because of God's willful and gracious creation of our ability to discern such things from nature.[12]

This particular naturalist theory seems softer than the hard naturalism noted earlier because of how it undermines one's confidence in nature as an indubitable good. Certainly al-Ghazali considered nature to be a basis for moral inquiry and thus fuses fact and value in nature. But the theology of God's grace renders that nature contingent in a way that was not the case in the hard naturalist tradition. The theory of God's grace allows soft naturalists to reason about Shari'a where source texts are otherwise silent, without violating their fundamental commitment to God's omnipotence.

THE LIMITS OF NATURALISM IN KNOWING THE LAW

The preceding accounts of soft and hard naturalism in premodern Islamic jurisprudence were offered to make the following points:

- Islamic jurisprudence was a discipline of law that was tied to source texts, context, and theological presumptions of God and his relationship to humanity as a lawgiver.
- The history of Islamic jurisprudence illustrates diverse philosophies of knowledge and reasoning in law.
- Even though soft and hard naturalists disagreed theologically about the nature of God's justice, jurists from both camps recognized that the natural order of the world provides a factual and normative basis for reasoning about God's law.

Of crucial significance is the fact that both hard and soft naturalists resorted to nature as a source of evidence for the divine will, whether on pure rational grounds or textualist ones. In the end, both considered nature objective, normative, and, most importantly, distinct from the individual observing what it can and does "say."

However, the objective quality of nature in both hard and soft naturalism raises questions about their ongoing tenability. Suggesting that nature exists for humans to observe and understand assumes a distinction between nature and how human beings construe it for legal purposes, as if nature stands outside the process of human legal reasoning. Furthermore, it assumes that one can use nature as an independent source of critique against the results of human reasoning.

The idea that nature is an objective entity separate from the person who observes it reflects a scientific orientation in the human sciences and prioritizes natural science models of knowledge despite the often unscientific, indeterminate vicissitudes of human existence.[13] Even some, such as premodern soft naturalist al-Ghazali, recognized that a person who attempts to determine values such as the good and the bad cannot formalistically "find" or "discover" them. Such values are so embedded in who we are that we cannot escape our own context to find an objective position outside ourselves. Ideas of the good and the bad, according to al-Ghazali, are ideas to which we are conditioned at a young age. We accept something as good or bad as a result of various factors (*asbab kathira*) that we cannot fully estimate. To assert the value as true with *objective certainty* would entail disassociating the truth claim from any contextuality in order to discover the essence of the thing. But such disassociation is impossible, he suggested: "It is possible that extensive investigation may fashion a sense of truth about [these moral values]. And perhaps they are true determinations. But [they can be known as objectively true] only through minute [analysis] (*shart daqiqa*), which the mind cannot satisfy" (al-Ghazali n.d.:1:117). For al-Ghazali, the hard naturalists assume a type of rational certainty that is impossible given the role of our subjective perception that contributes to whether we deem something to be true.

However, al-Ghazali is not immune from his own critique. The soft naturalists' resort to God's grace to fuse fact and value in nature also presumes the objectivity of the natural order. Al-Ghazali may rely on source texts to justify a rational analysis of nature and erect a juridical method to limit his claim to objective certainty. But if we are so embedded in our context, our ability to assert the truth or falsity of something as God's law is limited by our own subjectivity. Both soft and hard naturalists objectify nature to firmly anchor their jurisprudence and justify reasoning in the law where source texts are otherwise silent. But is nature truly as objective as hard and soft naturalists suggest?

The premodern Islamic legal tradition is not alone in presuming an objectivity to nature and meaning. Whether we look to critiques of late-nineteenth- and early-twentieth-century U.S. legal formalism or more recent critiques of using the natural sciences as a model for knowledge in the human sciences, we find parallels across religious and legal traditions concerning the anxiety of objectivity.

For instance, Charles Taylor emphatically asserts that what he calls our moral framework is an unavoidable part of human existence, and it enables us to understand and order our world as moral agents. He denies that we can ever do without such frameworks. Indeed, he states in no uncertain terms "that living within such strongly qualified horizons is constitutive of human agency, that stepping outside these limits would be tantamount to stepping outside what we would recognize as integral, that is, undamaged human personhood" (Taylor 1989:27).

Likewise, Hans-Georg Gadamer (1994:284) reminds us that we are always historically embedded and thus unable to adopt a decontextualized position of analysis outside our own tradition: "In the human sciences, the particular research questions concerning tradition that we are interested in pursuing are motivated in a special way by the present and its interest." To interpret a text for its meaning involves engaging the past of the text *and* the reader's present values that drive his analysis. However, the reader's interpretation is an assertion of neither objective fact nor idiosyncratic value. It is an interpretation in which his prior commitments or prejudice bear on his analysis (Gadamer 1994:270). To ignore or assume away our prejudice "makes us deaf to what speaks to us in tradition" (Gadamer 1994:270). Gadamer argues that when we interpret, we do so as historical subjects embedded in our own traditions; therefore, any claim about knowledge or truth we make will always be vulnerable to the contingencies that constitute the human condition. As Gadamer (1994:276) states, "Is not, rather, all human existence, even the freest, limited and qualified in various ways? If this is true, the idea of an absolute reason is not a possibility for historical humanity."

Taylor's and Gadamer's theories reflect a parallel critique of objectivity that can apply to the objectivist assumptions of hard and soft naturalist theories of Islamic law.[14] Both hard and soft naturalists assumed nature is sufficiently objective to guide jurists to determine Shari'a doctrines in a contingent context. But the presumption of an objective nature may presume too much determinacy in a process that is fraught with nuance and contingency. Yet to suggest as much would be to insert an indeterminacy in Shari'a-based meaning that can and often does contribute to moral anxiety.

HERMENEUTICS, MEANING, AND ISLAMIC LAW

When writing about the purely reasoned conceptions of the good and the bad, premodern soft naturalist theologian and jurist al-Baqillani (d. 403/1013) said that one can rely on the dispositional traits embedded in human nature to make judgments about the good and the bad. As an example, he concluded that one can know without reference to a source text the goodness of the believer striking the unbeliever and the evil of the unbeliever striking the believer (al-Baqillani 1998:1:284). He asserted the good of one and the evil of another on soft naturalistic grounds. To assume the truth of this conclusion without questioning its objectivity, though, will render the reader oblivious to how al-Baqillani's conception of the good and the bad may be informed by a framework of moral meaning.

We can safely assume, given the nature of premodern Islamic education and the qualifications for a scholar of Islam, that al-Baqillani was familiar with the Qur'an. The Qur'an states in various places that Muslims are to fight the unbeliever. But famously, it also provides that when dealing with the "People of the Book" (*ahl al-kitab*) Muslims should fight them until the People of the Book pay a poll tax and submit to Muslim rule. Specifically, Q. 9:29 states, "Fight those who do not believe in God or the final day, do not prohibit what God and His prophet have prohibited, do not believe in the religion of truth, from among those who are given revelatory books, until they pay the poll-tax (*jizya*) from their hands in a state of submission (*saghirun*)."

One issue raised by this verse concerns what it means to pay the *jizya* in a state of submission. The term *jizya* refers to the poll tax that non-Muslims would pay to live in peace in Muslim territory. This particular tax has been the subject of much debate and discussion. For the purpose of this article, the analysis will concentrate on what it means to pay the *jizya* in a state of submission.

Some Muslim jurists suggested that the *jizya* was a form of humiliation. By paying the *jizya*, the *dhimmis* effectively acknowledge their humiliated, submissive, and subservient social position as second-class citizens, as compared with Muslims.[15] This ethos of subservience was further made manifest by procedural rules for paying the *jizya*: The *dhimmi* must come to pay the *jizya* walking and standing before the magistrate, who must sit when collecting the tax. The standing–sitting distinction is meant to remind the *dhimmi* that he is submissive in relation to the Muslim magistrate, who does not get up to greet the *dhimmi* as an equal (al-Mawardi n.d.:2:351–352; al-Razi 1999:6:25; al-Suyuti 2000:3:411; al-Tabari 1994:4:98–99; al-Tabarsi n.d.:3:44–45; al-Tusi n.d.:5:203).

Others, such as theologian and jurist Fakhr al-Din al-Razi (d. 1209), suggested that the *jizya* is an incentive to convert. Taking the *jizya*, he said, is not intended to preserve the existence of disbelief (*kufr*) in the world. Rather, the *jizya* allows the non-Muslim to live among Muslims and experience the goodness of Islam in the hope that the non-Muslim will convert to Islam (al-Razi 1999:6:27; see also McAuliffe 1990).

And yet other jurists held that the reference to submission means that non-Muslims are subjected to the Shari'a rule of law in the same fashion as

Muslims. Paying *jizya* is a form of contracting into the social fabric of a polity governed by a Shari'a rule of law system (Dallal 1996:189).[16] Indeed, this agreement to live under the rule of law is so important that al-Shafi'i (d. 820) rejected the validity of any agreement in which the non-Muslims offer to provide the *jizya* without being subjected to the law of Islam. The Qur'anic phrase therefore may be construed as ensuring that all who live in the Muslim polity accede to its rule of law.

If we reject the natural science model of objectivity in law and instead adopt a jurisprudence sensitive both to history and to the conceptual framework and tradition of Shari'a, we can understand how the Qur'anic verse on *jizya* begs a question about the "prejudice" or "moral framework" of those such as al-Baqillani who assert the good and the bad on what they consider to be purely rational terms.

A critical theory would raise questions today about the meaning and significance of values such as equal human dignity for both al-Baqillani and modern readers and how those values can result in different legal manifestations, whether in premodern Islamic law or in the modern liberal state. Concerning the Shari'a rules, we might ask whether *dhimmis* participate in a Muslim polity as second-class citizens or as participants in a Shari'a-based social order whose authority and sovereignty they recognize. Is the *jizya* intended to humiliate and even punish non-Muslims for their disbelief,[17] to enable them to live their lives in peace, or to give them an opportunity to experience the bounties of Islam and consider conversion? Does the *jizya* verse amount to a type of divine evidence of the non-Muslim's inherently, perhaps even naturally, inferior position?

Importantly, although the *dhimmi* personifies the challenge that comes with governing amid pluralism, this challenge is not unique to the Islamic tradition. For instance, in France in 2008, a veiled Moroccan Muslim woman was denied citizenship because the Conseil d'Etat deemed her insufficiently assimilated into French culture. Although she had good command of the French language, the Conseil d'Etat found that she "adopted radical religious practices that are incompatible with the essential values of French society, and particularly with the principle of gender equality."[18] This decision does not run afoul of the applicant's religious freedoms under French law. Rather, the relevant legislation allows the government to deny the grant of citizenship for failure to "assimilate in a manner other than linguistically." Although the Conseil d'Etat had held in prior cases that wearing the veil is not grounds for denying sufficient assimilation into French society, the government commissioner in this case emphasized the petitioner's veiling and *niqab* in arguments to the Conseil.[19] In France, the immigrant Muslim woman (veiled or not), not unlike the *dhimmi* in Islamic law, personifies the challenge of accommodating minorities amid a universal, albeit ambiguous, claim of French core values.

As long as the *dhimmi* or the "immigrant" is considered an objective, natural category of persons, the historical contingencies that contribute to the ways in which both are treated under the law will continue to influence debates on governing pluralism, without being subject to critique. Objective assumptions about nature and knowledge hide the prejudices and frameworks that seem to operate below the surface of normative pronouncements, such as those arising out of law. By acknowledging the inevitability of thinking and communicating within a thick tradition, we can better appreciate how a critical approach to law generally, and Shari'a particularly, will not only avoid reification but also renew scholarship on the law as a site of reasoned deliberation about ordering the world.

CONCLUSION

If we begin with Benjamin Berger's critique of liberal rule of law, we may find ourselves inclined to revisit our conception of religion and thereby investigate the potential for reasoned deliberation within a religious framework. Using the Islamic legal tradition as a focal point, I have shown that premodern Muslim jurists debated the scope of such deliberation within the law, coming to similar positions on the authority of naturalistic reasoning, although premised on competing theological presuppositions. But just as Berger problematized liberal rule of law, I also problematize Islamic naturalistic reasoning for its objectivist presuppositions that can have an overdetermining effect. Indeed, just as liberal rule of law can overdetermine the religious, so can an uncritical embrace of premodern Islamic legal theory have the same effect on the Other, whoever that may be.

The parallel in this regard has various implications that can contribute to the further study of rule of law and pluralism. First, the more we engage a religious tradition, the more we may find it suitably open to the kind of reasoned deliberation that those of us in the West associate with liberal secularism. Second, once we open both liberal rule of law and a religious framework such as Islamic law to critical inquiry, we will find that both manifest similar essentializing tendencies with regard to the Other. The significance of those tendencies will depend on whom each system considers the Other. For liberal secular rule of law, the religious is the Other for reasons that Berger and others have explored in this volume. In the Islamic legal context, we have seen how the non-Muslim is Othered. The Othering of the non-Muslim instrumentally contributes to the centering of an Islamic ethos to a Shari'a rule of law, just as the Othering of the religious contributes to the centering of a secular ethos in liberal rule of law.

A critical engagement of Islamic law, though, has an implication that will require a high degree of sensitivity to those of us seeking to understand and engage the religiously minded. The minute we open Islamic law to critical scrutiny is the minute we render the tradition potentially so indeterminate as to incite anxieties in those requiring determinacy in the law to anchor their identity-based claims. As I have argued elsewhere, to view Shari'a as rarefied rules offers Islamists a firm platform from which to assert identity-based claims. Likewise, Muslim reformists often rely on a rarefied view of Shari'a in order to castigate it as antiquated, nonresponsive to historical change, and oppressive (Emon 2006:352). To suggest to both of these camps that their perspective on Shari'a is unduly overdeterminate would require them to rethink their claims, which may not be in their interest.

One last implication to consider is that once Islamic law is rendered open to reasoned deliberation, we will need to be mindful of who gets to deliberate. The history of Islamic law since the late nineteenth century illustrates how European colonial powers attempted to define Islamic law for Muslims in a way that often had more to do with imposing European modes of law and governance (Emon 2006; Powers 1989). The history of academic study of Islamic law is not one that necessarily evokes trust among Muslims, who may be concerned about repeating the legacy of Orientalism. Indeed, if there is an "after" to the debate on pluralism, it is not about moving beyond the fact of pluralism or difference. Rather, it is about how, after gaining a conceptual appreciation of pluralism, we will contend with the political and intersubject problems that arise when we live with and for difference.

NOTES

1. For a discussion of competing approaches to Islamic natural law theory, see Emon (2004–2005, forthcoming).

2. For a general discussion of Islamic jurisprudence, including the role of source texts in the law, see Kamali (2003).

3. Scholarly works that address this issue, either directly or indirectly, with varying degrees of depth, include Crone (2004:263–264), Ezzati (2002), Frank (1983), Hourani (1960), Jackson (1999), and Reinhart (1995).

4. For a general discussion of these naturalist theories, see Emon (2004–2005).

5. He provided two other designations of bad acts: those that are best to avoid and others for which no consequence arises.

6. These legal values reflect the way in which all acts present varying degrees of good and bad and imply appropriate sanctions or rewards. Some acts are obligatory,

whereby one is rewarded for committing the act and punished for omitting it. Others are prohibited, such that one is punished for committing it and rewarded for omitting it. Between these two poles of legal valuation are acts that are recommended, reprehensible, and permitted, each of which has distinct consequences for the actor. For a discussion of these categories of legal value, see Kamali (2003:44–46).

7. For hard naturalist sources relying on this assumption, see al-Jassas (2000:2:100) and al-Basri (n.d.:2:320).

8. See the discussion on human epistemic weakness in al-Isfahani (1998:1:370–371).

9. Ibn al-Farikan (2001:347–350) stated that this position was adopted by the majority of Ash'arites.

10. For other voluntarists who resort to a similar purposive analysis of the law, see al-Razi (1997:5:160) and al-Shatibi (n.d.:1:26). Shihab al-Din al-Qarafi (1973:391, 392; 2000:4:170) held that dignity (*'ird*) either was a sixth value or took the place of religion among the values noted earlier.

11. In this sentence, al-Ghazali seems to refer implicitly to the Mu'tazilites and their rationalist argument about the good and the bad.

12. The technical term *fadl* or *tafaddul* is the key term of art that voluntarists used to erect their naturalist theory in a manner distinct from that of the Mu'tazilites. For other voluntarists relying on this same argument, see al-Qarafi (2000:4:642), al-Razi (1997:5:176), and al-Tufi (1964:213). Al-Shatibi (n.d.:2:131) makes reference to this same argument and endorses it as against the Mu'tazilite position.

13. Notably, even historians of science would contend with the idea of natural science as an objective discipline (Kuhn 1996).

14. The reference to Gadamer and Taylor is not meant to suggest that we should hold one tradition to the standards of critique of another. Indeed, those who write about Islam and Islamic law often include such qualifying statements when they rely on contemporary developments in philosophy as springboards for critiques of Islamic law. I offer a similar qualification here, although I recognize that doing so unduly relies on provenance and geography to limit the free flow of ideas across such geopolitical boundaries. Gadamer and Taylor may be "Western" theorists, but their geopolitical provenance as human beings does not (and should not) qualify the meaningfulness of their work as we cross cultures and traditions to investigate the meaning of other works. If we rely too heavily on geopolitical provenance to limit the free flow of ideas, we implicitly adopt a version of the Huntingtonian thesis, which I find unduly reductive and essentialistic.

15. See al-Muqatil (2000:2:166–167) (by giving the *jizya*, the *dhimmis* are made lowly [*madhallun*]), al-Nisaburi (1994:2:489) (payment of *jizya* renders *dhimmis* lowly and vanquished [*dhalilun muqahharun*]), and al-Tabari (1994:4:98–99). See also Ahmad (1975), Ayoub (1990), Bosworth (1982), Haddad (1996), and Izzi Dien (1997:51–52).

16. For this position, see also Haddad (1996:172–173). As an example, see al-Mawardi (n.d.:2:351–352) and Rida (1999:10:266).

17. Some argued that the *jizya* tax was a form of punishment (*'uquba*) for the *dhimmis'* ongoing disbelief (al-Tusi n.d.:5:203).

18. For news accounts of the case, see Chrisafis (2008:23). See also Bennhold (2008:4) and Sokol (2008:9).

19. For a statement of the case, the relevant legislation, and the conclusions of the government commissioner, see the decision of the Council of State, Case no. 286798 at http://www.conseil-etat.fr/ce/jurispd/index_ac_1d0820.shtml (accessed September 23, 2008).

WORKS CITED

'Abd al-Jabbar, Qadi Abu al-Hasan. n.d. *Al-Mughni fi Abwab al-Tawhid wa'l 'Adl*. Ed. Taha Husayn. Cairo: Wizarat al-Thaqafa wa-al-Irshad al-Qawmi, al-Idarah al-'Amma lil-Thaqafa (volumes on *Taklif* and *Lutf*).

Ahmad, Ziauddin. 1975. The Concept of Jizya in Early Islam. *Islamic Studies* 14, no. 4:293–305.

Ayoub, Mahmoud M. 1990. The Islamic Context of Muslim–Christian Relations. In *Conversion and Continuity: Indigenous Christian Communities in Islamic Lands, Eighth to Eighteenth Centuries*, ed. Michael Gervers and Ramzi Jibran Bikhazi, 461–477. Toronto: Pontifical Institute of Mediaeval Studies.

al-Baji, Abu al-Walid. 1995. *Ihkam al-Fusul fi Ahkam al-Usul*. 2nd ed. Ed. 'Abd al-Majid Turki. Beirut: Dar al-Gharb al-Islami.

al-Baqillani, Abu Bakr. 1998. *Al-Taqrib wa al-Irshad*. Ed. 'Abd al-Majid b. 'Ali Abu Zunayd. Beirut: Mu'assasat al-Risala.

al-Basri. n.d. *Al-Mu'tamad fi Usul al-Fiqh*. Beirut: Dar al-Kutub al-'Ilmiyya.

Bennhold, Katrin. 2008. A Muslim Woman Too Orthodox for France; It Bars Citizenship over Her Strict Garb. *International Herald Tribune*, July 19, p. 4.

Berger, Benjamin. 2007. Law's Religion: Rendering Culture. *Osgoode Hall Law Journal* 45, no. 2:277–314.

Bosworth, C. E. 1982. The Concept of *Dhimma* in Early Islam. In *Christians and Jews in the Ottoman Empire: The Functioning of a Plural Society*, ed. Benjamin Braude and Bernard Lewis, 37–54. New York: Holmes & Meier.

Brown, Wendy. 2006. *Regulating Aversion: Tolerance in the Age of Identity and Empire*. Princeton, N.J.: Princeton University Press.

Chrisafis, Angelique. 2008. France Rejects Muslim Woman over Radical Practice of Islam. *Guardian*, July 12, p. 23.

Crone, Patricia. 2004. *God's Rule: Government and Islam: Six Centuries of Medieval Islamic Political Thought*. New York: Columbia University Press.

Dallal, Ahmad. 1996. Yemeni Debates on the Status of Non-Muslims in Islamic Law. *Islam and Christian–Muslim Relations* 7, no. 2:181–192.

Emon, Anver M. 2004–2005. Natural Law and Natural Rights in Islamic Law. *Journal of Law and Religion* 20, no. 2:351–395.

Emon, Anver M. 2006. Conceiving Islamic Law in a Pluralist Society: History, Politics and Multicultural Jurisprudence. *Singapore Journal of Legal Studies* (December):331–355.

Emon, Anver M. Forthcoming. *Islamic Natural Law Theories*. New York: Oxford University Press.

Euben, Roxanne. 1999. *Enemy in the Mirror: Islamic Fundamentalism and the Limits of Modern Rationalism*. Princeton, N.J.: Princeton University Press.

Ezzati, A. 2002. *Islam and Natural Law*. London: ICAS Press.

Frank, Richard M. 1983. Moral Obligation in Classical Muslim Theology. *Journal of Religious Ethics* 11, no. 2:204–223.

Gadamer, Hans-Georg. 1994. *Truth and Method*. 2nd ed. New York: Continuum.

al-Ghazali, Abu Hamid. n.d. *Al-Mustasfa min 'Ilm al-Usul*. Ed. Ibrahim Muhammad Ramadan. Beirut: Dar al-Arqam.

al-Ghazali, Abu Hamid. 1971. *Shifa' al-Ghalil fi Bayan al-Shabh wa al-Mukhil wa Masalik al-Ta'lil*. Ed. Muhammad al-Kubaysi. Baghdad: Ra'asa Diwan al-Awqaf.

Haddad, Wadi Zaidan. 1996. *Ahl al-Dhimma* in an Islamic State: The Teaching of Abu al-Hasan al-Mawardi's *Al-Ahkam al-'ultaniyya*. *Islam and Christian–Muslim Relations* 7, no. 2:169–180.

Hourani, George F. 1960. Two Theories of Value in Medieval Islam. *Muslim World* 50, no. 4:269–278.

Ibn al-Farikan, Taj al-Din 'Abd al-Rahman b. Ibrahim. 2001. *Sharh al-Waraqat*. Ed. Sarah Shafi al-Hajiri. Beirut: Dar al-Basha'ir al-Islamiyya.

Ibn Hazm. 1984. *Al-Ihkam fi Usul al-Ahkam*. Cairo: Dar al-Hadith.

al-Isfahani, Abu 'Abd Allah. 1998. *Al-Kashif 'an al-Mahsul fi 'Ilm al-Usul*. Ed. 'Adil Ahmad 'Abd al-Mawjud and 'Ali Muhammad Mu'awwad. Beirut: Dar al-Kutub al-'Ilmiyya.

Izzi Dien, M. 1997. *The Theory and the Practice of Market Law in Medieval Islam: A Study of* Kitab Nisab al-Ihtisab. Cambridge: E. J. W. Gibb Memorial Trust.

Jackson, Sherman A. 1999. The Alchemy of Domination? Some Ash'arite Responses to Mu'tazilite Ethics. *International Journal of Middle East Studies* 31:185–201.

al-Jassas. 2000. *Usul al-Jassas: Al-Fusul fi al-Usul*. Ed. Muhammad Muhammad Tamir. Beirut: Dar al-Kutub al-'Ilmiyya.

al-Juwayni, Abu al-Ma'ali. 1997. *Al-Burhan fi Usul al-Fiqh*. Ed. Salah b. Muhammad b. 'Awida. Beirut: Dar al-Kutub al-'Ilmiyya.

Kamali, Mohammad Hashim. 2003. *Principles of Islamic Jurisprudence*. 3rd ed. Cambridge: Islamic Texts Society.

al-Khatib al-Baghdadi. 1977. *Kitab al-Faqih wa al-Mutafaqqih*. n.p.: Matba'at al-Imtiyaz.

Kuhn, Thomas S. 1996. *The Structure of Scientific Revolutions*. 3rd ed. Chicago: University of Chicago Press.

al-Mawardi. n.d. *Al-Nukat wa al-'Uyun*. Ed. Al-Sayyid b. 'Abd al-Rahim. Beirut: Dar al-Kutub al-'Ilmiyya.

McAuliffe, Jane Dammen. 1990. Fakhr al-Din al-Razi on Ayat al-Jizya and Ayat al-Sayf. In *Conversion and Continuity: Indigenous Christian Communities in Islamic*

Lands, Eighth to Eighteenth Centuries, ed. Michael Gervers and Ramzi Jibran Bikhazi, 103–119. Toronto: Pontifical Institute of Mediaeval Studies.

al-Muqatil b. Sulayman. 2002. *Tafsir Muqatil b. Sulayman*. Ed. 'Abd Allah Mahmud Shahatah. Beirut: Dar Ihya' al-Turath al-'Arabi.

al-Nisaburi. 1994. *Al-Wasit fi Tafsir al-Qur'an al-Majid*. Ed. 'Adil Ahmed 'Abd al-Mawjud et al. Beirut: Dar al-Kutub al-'Ilmiyya.

Powers, David. 1989. Orientalism, Colonialism, and Legal History: The Attack on Muslim Family Endowments in Algeria and India. *Comparative Studies in Society and History* 31:535–571.

al-Qarafi, Shihab al-Din. 1973. *Sharh Tanqih al-Fusul fi Ikhtisar al-Mahsul fi al-Usul*. Ed. Taha 'Abd al-Ra'uf Sa'id. Cairo: Dar al-Fikr.

al-Qarafi, Shihab al-Din. 2000. *Nafa'is al-Usul fi Sharh al-Mahsul*. Ed. Muhammad 'Abd al-Qadir 'Ata. Beirut: Dar al-Kutub al-'Ilmiyya.

al-Razi, Fakhr al-Din. 1997. *Al-Mahsul fi 'Ilm al-Usul al-Fiqh*. 3rd ed. Ed. Taha Jabir al-'Alwani. Beirut: Mu'assasat al-Risala.

al-Razi, Fakhr al-Din. 1999. *Al-Tafsir al-Kabir*. 3rd ed. Beirut: Dar Ihya' al-Turath al-'Arabi.

Reinhart, Kevin. 1995. *Before Revelation: The Boundaries of Muslim Moral Thought*. Albany: State University of New York Press.

Rida, Rashid. 1999. *Tafsir al-Manar*. Ed. Ibrahim Shams al-Din. Beirut: Dar al-Kutub al-'Ilmiyya.

al-Sam'ani. 1997. *Qawati' al-Adilla fi al-Usul*. Ed. Muhammad Hasan Muhammad Hasan Isma'il al-Shafi'i. Beirut: Dar al-Kutub al-'Ilmiyya.

al-Shatibi. n.d. *Al-Muwafaqat fi Usul al-Shari'a*. 2 vols. Ed. 'Abd Allah Daraz et al. Beirut: Dar al-Kutub al-'Ilmiyya.

al-Shirazi, Abu Ishaq. 1988. *Sharh al-Lum'a*. Ed. 'Abd al-Majid Turki. Beirut: Dar al-Gharb al-Islami.

Sokol, Ronald P. 2008. Why France Can't See Past the Burqa. *Christian Science Monitor*, July 21, p. 9.

al-Suyuti, Jalal al-Din. 2000. *Al-Durr al-Manthur fi al-Tafsir al-Ma'thur*. Beirut: Dar al-Kutub al-'Ilmiyya.

al-Tabari, Muhammad b. Jarir. 1994. *Tafsir al-Tabari*. Beirut: Mu'assasat al-Risala.

al-Tabarsi. n.d. *Majma' al-Bayan fi Tafsir al-Qur'an*. Beirut: Manshurat Dar Maktabat al-Hayah.

Taylor, Charles. 1989. *Sources of the Self: The Making of the Modern Identity*. Cambridge, Mass.: Harvard University Press.

al-Tufi, Najm al-Din. 1964. Al-Hadith al-Thani wa'l-Thalathun. In *Al-Maslaha fi al-Tashri' a-Islami wa Najm al-Din al-Tufi*. 2nd ed. Ed. Mustafa Zayd. Cairo: Dar al-Fikr al-'Arabi.

al-Tusi. n.d. *Al-Tibyan fi Tafsir al-Qur'an*. Ed. Ahmad Habib Qasir al-'Amili. Beirut: Dar Ihya' al-Turath al-'Arabi.

al-Zabidi, Muhibb. 1994. *Taj al-'Arus min Jawahir al-Qamus*. 20 vols. Ed. 'Ali Shiri. Beirut: Dar al-Fikr.

3. RELIGION NATURALIZED

The New Establishment

WINNIFRED FALLERS SULLIVAN

In Anglo-American legal studies, the study of religion has been traditionally marginalized, as has been the study of law within religious studies. Religion has been confined in the study of law largely to what has been called church–state studies, a subdiscipline that combined attention to the history of institutional relations in Europe and its colonies with an elaboration of the evolving jurisprudence of legal protection for religious freedom as a feature of human rights. For the most part, those studies have assumed as normative the modern state as secular and the relevant religious communities as the Protestant churches, now privatized. Other religions have gradually been legally accommodated in various ways, mostly to the extent that they have reinvented themselves as free church Protestant in ecclesiastical form. Religious law was simply not law, and its study was not part of legal studies (Huxley 2002). Indeed, the realization of religion, true religion, was understood by many to obviate law, particularly for Christians. Within religious studies the study of religious law was confined largely to the study of Judaism and Islam, traditions understood to be legalistic by nature, with all the negative connotations that ensued.

In the last thirty years or so, the combined effect of legal realism and critical legal studies, multiculturalism and globalization, theological and ecclesial changes within the Christian churches, international human rights movements, an expanded notion of what counts as religion in academic and political contexts, and larger social shifts toward egalitarian and horizontal relations has resulted in a new set of questions for law and legal studies and for religion and religious studies—questions about the religiousness (or cultural nature, as Benjamin Berger calls it in chap. 4, this volume) of law and the legal or regulatory nature of religion. In this chapter, I will offer some thoughts on emerging trends in U.S. constitutional jurisprudence about religion, with a view to exploring possible religio-legal implications of this new situation.

In U.S. constitutional terms, the borders of religious freedom—and therefore the terms on which religious pluralism has operated, practically speaking—since the mid-twentieth-century incorporation of the First Amendment religion clauses into the Fourteenth Amendment have been policed in two overt ways. First, the expansive declaration in the First Amendment that "Congress shall make no law . . . prohibiting the free exercise of religion" has been qualified by a rule of interpretation limiting the full guarantee to religious opinions. Religious acts usually may be legally regulated in the United States, as they are in other countries, according to prevailing social standards. Second, the First Amendment declaration that "Congress shall make no law respecting an establishment of religion" has been interpreted to prohibit direct government funding or endorsement of religious worship and proselytization, as well as any intentional discrimination between religions—or between religion and nonreligion—but not to prohibit other more indirect forms of government support for or accommodation of religion. Thus, constitutionally speaking, your particular religious exercise may be found to be legally unacceptable because your activities are uncivilized and therefore illegal (e.g., polygamy or the use of prohibited substances), or they may be found legally unacceptable because they are a threat to national security (e.g., wearing dreadlocks or a yarmulke if you are in the military) or even because they are simply too expensive to accommodate (e.g., the erection of awkward monuments in cemeteries). Your religious practice might also be regarded as legally unacceptable because it has government patronage, such as certain forms of in-school prayer or the teaching of intelligent design, or the public display of religious symbols. U.S. religion today happens in spaces constructed, in large part, by interpretations of the Constitution—mostly interpretations by members of the Supreme Court—and of state and local laws, but those spaces are also made by popular understandings of what law permits.

The permissible bounds of religious pluralism have also been enforced in the United States through legislative and judicial implementation of what are arguably secularized religious norms and practices, as in the regulation of marriage, sexual reproduction, and sexual practices but also in many less obvious ways in the administration of law at every level, local, state, and federal, including tax, zoning, and various licensing regimes, an administration of law that assumes often unmarked religious anthropologies and cosmologies. In all these ways, law has been deeply implicated in the structuring of U.S. religious practice, and that has increasingly become the case as government regulation has expanded into more aspects of the lives of Americans.

Ironically, perhaps, and notwithstanding this tight relationship, religion and the state in the United States have long been imagined as autonomous and separate, and necessarily so; religion and government functions have been largely understood to be distinct. Each has been said to be better off without explicit dependence on the other. Indeed, separation is often said to be the single most important factor responsible for the flourishing of American religion. Monitoring the border has been seen as important. But both legal and popular ways of imagining religion are changing. There is a sense among those who are watching that the ground is shifting in U.S. constitutional jurisprudence with respect to religion, particularly with respect to what is known as the establishment clause.

Disestablishment is coming to mean less privatized pluralism through the separation of religion from public life and more a permeable and inclusive public accommodation of religion, religion in general. Government funding *and* government endorsement of religion, heretofore spoken of as taboo, notwithstanding the irrefutable evidence of such support over the whole of U.S. history, are becoming constitutionally plausible in overt terms. Separationist ideology no longer has the purchase it once did in the United States. In part, this is so because it was founded in an anti-Catholic bias that has largely lost its relevance (Hamburger 2004). It is also so because of the troubling acceptability of a majoritarian ideology and the political strength of conservative Christianity in the United States. Yet something more fundamental is at work, in my view, a shift in what religion is understood to be—a shift in religious anthropology. Religion is being naturalized. As it is being naturalized it is becoming an accepted part of the domain of government.

There has been a remarkably broad embrace in the United States of the value of what are called faith-based initiatives, at their most inclusively understood, notwithstanding the taint of being associated with the Bush White House and its friends. Indeed, as president-elect, Barack Obama, already hailed as the most theologically astute president since Abraham Lincoln, promptly announced his intention to confirm and extend the executive's commitment to the support of faith-based social services by creating a new Council on Faith-Based and Neighborhood Partnerships. But it is not just in the executive branch. One finds a new openness to the formal recognition of the religious, or what is often called the spiritual, dimension of every human being, across the spectrum of government activity. The widely attested increase among Americans of interest in and identification with spirituality as a way of being in the world is receiving legal definition and institutionalization.

In some senses, the embrace both of the universality of spirituality and of the awkwardly named faith-based initiative can be seen as the continuation of older forms of American religious practice, gathered together historically under ever-expanding forms of nondenominational para-church Christianity, the acceptance and integration of various immigrant religious practices, and a persistent interest in natural religion and its various exotic relations. But universal religion is also taking new forms. The new openness to seeing people as naturally "faith-based" is enabled by a newly intense convergence between humanistic critiques of what are perceived to be overly scientistic understandings of the human person, social scientific and biological, and a contemporaneous shift in religious authority and anthropology from the clergy to the individual. The exclusivity of materialist understandings of the entire range of human capabilities and experience, and the ecclesiastical capacity to insist on orthodoxy and particularity, are both fast eroding in the face of this change, as are the grounds of secular opposition.

A legal division between the church and the state, or between people "of faith" and people *not* "of faith," on which separation law depends, no longer makes sense (if it ever did) to most Americans. Such a division can be made only on a doctrinal basis by established religious or legal authorities who define insiders and outsiders. Such authorities no longer exist in the United States. Most Americans, however orthodox their asserted religious identities, claim the right to associate themselves with religious communities—and religious ideas and practices—as they see fit, to change their religious identities and associations at will, and to "mix and match" religious traditions. That right is understood to be authorized by political, legal, and theological narratives and texts.

In theory, the high value placed today in the United States on choice includes the choice to be nonreligious. But as a political matter, it is not understood as entirely optional simply to exempt oneself from what many across the ideological spectrum see as a necessary correction to the Enlightenment. Atheists feel threatened. Religion today in the United States is a fragmented, fissiparous affair, highly resistant to fixed identities and associations, but it is also remarkably resilient. To be American is no longer to be Protestant, but hard-edged atheism is not acceptable (Edgell et al. 2006). You must be religious, but your religion can be "whatever." *Really* whatever, not just Protestant, Catholic, or Jewish, as long as you do not espouse terrorism or child abuse. Eisenhower's famous open embrace of all religion has been both realized and radicalized. Law is playing a part in these social changes.

Let me illustrate.

FREEDOM FROM RELIGION FOUNDATION V. NICHOLSON

A recent district court decision in the Western District of Wisconsin suggests the contours of this shift (*Freedom from Religion Foundation v. Nicholson*, 469 F. Supp. 2d 609 [W.D. Wisc. 2007]). The suit challenged the constitutionality of a program of the chaplaincy of the U.S. Veterans Administration (VA). According to the court's opinion, the VA operates 154 medical centers, 1,300 other "sites of care," 136 nursing homes, 43 residential rehabilitation treatment programs, and 88 comprehensive home care programs in the United States. More than 5 million people received health care in VA facilities in 2005. The Iraq and Afghanistan wars have produced a new wave of military personnel and veterans with serious medical and mental health needs, and there has been much media attention on the many asserted deficiencies in the efficiency and quality of medical and mental health care provided by the VA.

The VA also provides spiritual care. Although, as I have said, governments in the United States are not understood constitutionally to be permitted directly to fund or provide religious services, a limited exception has been made in the case of chaplaincies that serve people such as military personnel and prisoners, in other words, those who are in the care or custody of the government and have restricted access to the ideal: a free market in religious options. In fact, in this time of endless war and crisis, one could argue that the exception may be becoming the rule as the citizen is increasingly seen as a pastoral care client, and the exception is expanding to include most Americans receiving services from the government, both routine social services and those provided to the victims of natural disasters and ordinary street crime (Dolan 2008). Religious services for patients in VA facilities, inpatient and outpatient, have been explicitly included in this constitutional exception.

The VA chaplaincy traces its beginnings to the Homes for Disabled Soldiers established by President Abraham Lincoln during the Civil War, although its formal existence as a fully institutionalized national service begins after World War II. According to the district court findings in the *Nicholson* case, the VA chaplaincy has evolved since its founding from a focus that was once what the court calls "sacramental" to a focus that it calls "clinical." These terms have very specific meanings in this context. According to the VA's official online history, "The national Chaplaincy was [originally] organizationally assigned to the Office of Special Services, which also included the departments of Recreation, Canteen, Athletics and Patient Welfare."[1] What the court refers to as "sacramental," what we might call a private pluralist model, apparently refers to the supplying of opportunities to access religious services on a piecemeal demand basis, as an auxiliary to medical care, by analogy with the supplying of sports activities and snacks.

The new "clinical" chaplaincy, on the other hand, has a different role and a different purpose. The Wisconsin court states that in order "to effectively implement its clinical chaplaincy program, the VA Chaplain Service was recently reorganized under the Medicine and Surgery Strategic Healthcare Group. The purpose of this reorganization was to recognize VA's chaplaincy as a clinical, direct patient care discipline," no longer akin to recreation and athletics. The change, which was challenged in the *Nicholson* case, apparently sees religion not as an optional auxiliary to the medical mission—the supply of religious products as demanded for those who may need it—but as intrinsic to a holistic understanding of good health care. Although all VA chaplains today must commit themselves explicitly to respect the patient's constitutional religious free exercise rights and to protect patients from having religion imposed on them, chaplains are now fully integrated into the medical team in a new way. As a patient you must now opt out of religion rather than opting in. We might call this a post-pluralist model. In the words of the plaintiffs in the *Nicholson* case, religion has become a "health benefit" (*Nicholson*, Brief of Appellants at 17).

Every VA patient must now be given an initial spiritual assessment upon admission, and recommendations must be made concerning his or her spiritual care. The administration of VA facilities is somewhat decentralized so that the details of the actual practices of spiritual assessment vary from place to place, but the district court described three assessment tools commonly used by VA facilities:

> A Computer Assessment Program (hereinafter CAP) which was a religiously based in-depth spiritual assessment. The CAP was intended to better understand the role religious faith plays in the maintenance of health, healing of diseases, and coping with chronic illness and losses in people's lives. Accordingly, the CAP asked questions such as: (1) How often do you attend religious services during the year? (2) How much is religion (and/or God) a source of strength and comfort to you? (3) How often do you privately pray? and (4) How often do you read the Bible or other religious literature?
>
> The Spiritual Assessment Inventory. Said inventory contains questions that are broken down into four categories. These categories are as follows: (1) Organized Religious Activity Scale, (2) Subjective Religious Scale, (3) Non-organized Religious Activity Scale, and (4) Spiritual Injury Scale. Additionally, the Spiritual Assessment Inventory includes a Religious Resource Index and a score of fifteen or lower on this index indicates that the patient should be referred to chaplain services.
>
> The Spiritual Needs Assessment for the VA Healthcare Network of Upstate New York. This assessment asks questions such as: (1) What is your religious preference?

> (2) How often do you attend church, synagogue, or other religious meetings? (3) Do you consider religious or spiritual beliefs to be important in your life? (4) Does your faith or beliefs influence the way you think about your health or the way you take care of yourself? (5) Would you like to receive any devotional materials while you are hospitalized? and (6) Would you like to address any religious or spiritual issues with a chaplain? Additionally, the assessment contains the following language: "Completing this assessment questionnaire will help us to better understand your spiritual care needs. We believe that faith plays an important role in a person's sense of health and wellness."

These computerized information tools are, the court says, "structured to measure information about Organized Religious Activity, Non-organized religious activity, and Intrinsic Religious Values, which together provide . . . a Total Religious Index." The court concluded its description of the various assessment tools with the comment that "defendants admit that some VA assessments can be conducted on a very in-depth basis." A low Total Religious Index or spiritual assessment score results in referral to a chaplain.

Spiritual healing is integrated into VA treatment in a variety of ways. "The Dayton VA Medical Center," for example, "has incorporated the use of 'lament as prayer' and Fowler's Stages of Faith Development as part of the medical protocol for treating post-traumatic stress disorder patients" (*Nicholson*, Brief of Appellants at 12, citing Fowler 1981). As the court explained, this integration includes outpatients:

> The [VA's] goal is to provide [spiritual] care from a veteran's initial visit that continues as he or she receives any VA services necessary to sustain his or her spiritual health. The VA believes that it is imperative for veterans living outside the local daily distances to major VA health care facilities to have access to professional spiritual and pastoral care because research studies have shown that "when outpatients have access to quality spiritual and pastoral care, significant improvement in quality of life, reduced inpatient admissions, and cost savings result." Additionally, the VA believes that holistic health care and spiritual and religious needs go "hand-in-hand."

These practices are not peculiar to VA hospitals. Spiritual assessment and care are mandated by the Joint Commission on Accreditation of Healthcare Organizations, the accrediting agency for the VA facilities and for many other hospitals. Deficiencies in spiritual health can thus presumably threaten hospital accreditation, as well as, by extension, eventually, insurability, as might other poor health indicators such as overeating and smoking.

Although the VA argues that such government-funded "faith-based" treatment is constitutionally permissible as long as it is noncoercive (and no one argues that the program is formally coercive; you can refuse spiritual care, as you can any kind of care), the plaintiffs in the *Nicholson* case, the avowedly atheist Freedom from Religion Foundation (FFRF),[2] argue that routinely to assess every VA patient's spirituality is to establish religion, in the forbidden U.S. constitutional sense. To assume that every patient's health necessarily has a spiritual aspect is, they say, to promote religion over nonreligion, something the Supreme Court has repeatedly spoken of as prohibited over the last seventy years (see, e.g., *Board of Education of Kiryas Joel Village School District v. Grumet*, 512 U.S. 687 [1994]). The VA, FFRF complains, has "undertaken to diagnose spiritual injury and to offer religious cures" (*Nicholson*, Brief of Appellants at 16). To do so is to discriminate against atheists and to suggest that religion is a positively good—or natural—thing, FFRF says, rather than being simply an optional or "recreational" thing. They say the VA has crossed the constitutional line by incorporating religion into the delivery of all VA health care services.

The VA itself distinguishes spiritual care from religious exercise. As the *Nicholson* court said, "According to VA definition, spirituality is not necessarily religious because it concerns the meaning of life on a more general level." Spirituality is universal, whereas religion may not be. Universality licenses government attention. At the oral argument in the U.S. Court of Appeals for the Seventh Circuit, some of the judges pressed FFRF as to whether the VA might not have an affirmative obligation to provide spiritual care, given studies showing the effectiveness of such interventions.[3] If all people are spiritual and spiritual health is related to physical health, then, the judges seem to imply, attention to those facts might not be optional for a government medical facility (or for any medical facility under a system of universal health care).

The Wisconsin district court granted a motion for summary judgment in favor of the VA. (A summary judgment is a decision on the law with no hearing on the facts.) The court concluded that no constitutional violation had occurred because all VA religious activity, at both the assessment and treatment stages, was formally voluntary on the part of the patient. Distinguishing other court decisions, including those invalidating government-sponsored school prayer as involving a vulnerable population, the court found no establishment clause violation because, in the case of the newly styled VA chaplaincy, there was no government-sponsored "indoctrination." I found this decision surprising, even shocking, at first. The shift at the VA from what is called a "sacramental" to a "clinical" chaplaincy, one that is fully integrated into the medical team, and the VA's apparent presumptive view that every patient is a spiritual person, flies in the face of much judicial language insisting that the Constitution be interpreted to prohibit such a comprehensive government acknowledgment of people as religious. One would think that at the very least a hearing on the facts was needed.

Beyond the alleged constitutional difficulty posed simply by the formal incorporation of spiritual care into the treatment of all patients in government-owned and -run hospitals, there are other traditional, establishment-type problems with the actual design and administration of the VA program and, by extension, of all such government chaplaincies. All VA chaplains must hold a master of divinity (M.Div.) degree, have two years of clinical pastoral education credits, and be recommended by their "ecclesiastical endorser."[4] All three of these requirements have their origins in Protestant institutions and have historically been controlled by mainstream Protestant churches. Limiting employment of chaplains through the use of these private licensing procedures may arguably work its own establishment of religion, discriminating against both patients and applicants for chaplaincy positions who belong to less favored or less well-known religious communities, or those that do not have a specialized clergy.

There is also the possibility of abuse in one-on-one chaplain–patient situations such that spiritual care could de facto be administered in a way that is not voluntary. There is much anecdotal evidence of efforts by hospital personnel to evangelize at patient bedsides. Indeed, the VA's repeated insistence that it is vigilant in policing such proselytizing suggests that the risk is real. Moreover, as a recent scholarly review of spiritual assessment tools explains, however carefully and neutrally administered, all such tools imply a theology (Fitchett 2002). Yet the district court's opinion is replete with generalized approval of a broad effort merely to accommodate what is viewed as universal, that is, the spiritual.

It is not just the VA, as I have mentioned. National accrediting agencies for all medical facilities in the United States, responding to decades of criticism of patient care and of indifference to culturally inflected understandings of illness and health, now require them, as a condition of accreditation, to incorporate spiritual care into treatment plans. Yet despite these reforming motives, these moves are being seen by some in the rights community as an establishment of positive religion, coincident in a sinister way with what they understand to be a political campaign for greater public participation by conservative religious groups in the design and provision of social welfare services. To speak of religion at all is understood by this group to speak of an aggressively proselytizing, authoritarian, and superstitious fundamentalism. And not entirely without reason. The new political clout of religion has unquestionably given rise to zealotry in some places. Yet the *Nicholson* case, when seen in the context of recent Supreme Court First Amendment jurisprudence, represents a larger change, in my view, one not narrowly the result of partisan politics. Obscured by the culture wars rhetoric around the faith-based initiative is a wider cultural shift to greater public acknowledgment of religion, an acknowledgment that is moving away from determination by established Protestant models of religious life. Indeed, from the perspective of many conservative religious communities, aspects of these pastoral care regimes may seem a troubling demystifying and naturalization of revealed religion.

Given recent decisions approving school vouchers, as well as both judicial and public approval of faith-based social services more generally, the United States may be moving toward an acknowledgment of religious universality that has more in common with countries in which the state, despite secularization and the deprivileging of state churches, continues to assume responsibility for the religious well-being of citizens. Religious freedom and nondiscrimination are often understood there to be possible, even if not always realized, without separation in the austere American sense. As Grace Davie (2002) says of Europe, in contrast to the United States, religion is there more often regarded as a "public utility" than as an active personal commitment by an individual. It is not necessarily about belief in a Protestant evangelical sense. It is about getting the work of the public done, in orphanages, schools, hospitals, and other charitable institutions, as well as about providing ritual and comfort for significant times in people's lives. This kind of religion depends on a different religious anthropology. And it is no less committed to religious freedom. Such an approach is feared by the left and the right in the United States, for different reasons, but I think it may be happening nonetheless.

Let us consider another case and another legal route to universal religion, one that suggests that the ending of an earlier cultural war, the Protestant–Catholic one, can also explain what is not entirely a new acceptance of religion but a return, in some sense, to an earlier American religious universalism.

HEIN V. FREEDOM FROM RELIGION FOUNDATION

While the *Nicholson* decision was on appeal, and after oral argument in the case, consideration on the merits of that appeal was obviated by a decision of the U.S. Supreme Court. In response, the U.S. Court of Appeals for the Seventh Circuit remanded the *Nicholson* case to the district court, ordering that court to enter an order dismissing the complaint in conformity with the then brand-new decision of the U.S. Supreme Court: *Hein v. FFRF*, 127 S. Ct. 2553 (2007). *Hein* was another case brought by the FFRF, another complaint that unsuccessfully argued that government preference for social services that are founded in a religious anthropology is unconstitutional.

The *Hein* decision was the only religion clause case decided by the U.S. Supreme Court in its October 2006 term and is increasingly understood to be the most significant decision on the establishment clause in many years. FFRF alleged in *Hein* that expenditures by the director of the White House Office on Faith-Based and Community Initiatives for conferences promoting and facilitating participation by religious groups in government contracting with private social service agencies constituted an unlawful establishment of religion. As with *Nicholson*, FFRF's concern was the government favoring of religion over nonreligion. *Hein* was an exceptional form of legal action known as a taxpayer suit. The plaintiffs alleged that the government was making unconstitutional use of their taxes. A majority of the justices found that FFRF had no standing to bring the action. In other words, FFRF and its members were the wrong plaintiffs for the case. Although standing questions may seem to be the kind of question that only a lawyer could love, this seemingly dry procedural ruling further illustrates what I am suggesting is a significant change in the U.S. courts' attitude toward religion.[5]

The vote in *Hein* was 5 to 4, and there were four different opinions. The three opinions authored by justices in the majority differ on whether they should overrule a key religion clause precedent, *Flast v. Cohen*, 392 U.S. 83 (1968), but what unites them is their suggestion that the danger of religious establishment no longer requires special constitutional vigilance. All three assert that such special treatment is the legacy of an earlier, now anachronistic U.S. anti-Catholicism and therefore ought to be abandoned. The Catholic Church has been domesticated. The president can promote religion, they say, just as he can promote any other social policy, limited only by electoral politics. And taxpayers—as taxpayers—no longer have standing to complain in federal court.

Article III of the U.S. Constitution, which establishes the judicial branch of the federal government, provides that the jurisdiction of the federal courts is limited to "cases and controversies." These words have been interpreted to mean that U.S. courts may rule only in what are known as justiciable controversies. They cannot give advisory opinions, that is, decide essentially political questions, or rule on issues that are moot. To do these things would be to invade the provinces of the other two branches of government and thus violate the doctrine of the separation of powers. In *Frothingham v. Mellon*, 262 U.S. 447 (1923), the Supreme Court held that lawsuits initiated by federal taxpayers, simply in their capacity as taxpayers, to challenge the constitutionality of congressional statutes are not constitutionally justiciable because individual taxpayers, solely on the basis of their individual tax burden, lack a sufficient personal financial stake in such cases to make them real cases or controversies. Taxpayers can sue the government over issues specific to their own tax bills, but they cannot sue the government, in the role of what would be that of private attorneys general, to challenge how the government spends the general funds it raises through taxes.

Only one exception has been made since the *Frothingham* decision to this rule against taxpayer suits. In *Flast v. Cohen*, 392 U.S. 83 (1968), the Court allowed such taxpayer cases specifically in order to challenge the constitutionality of congressional acts alleged to be in violation of the establishment clause. Religion is special, the Court said in 1968, and it is especially dangerous. The *Flast* taxpayers had challenged a federal grant of assistance to local schools, including religious schools, to purchase textbooks and other instructional materials for disadvantaged students. In an 8 to 1 decision, the Supreme Court held in *Flast* that the foundational and structural importance of the principle of church–state separation to the U.S. government demanded an exception to the rule in *Frothingham*.

Special emphasis was placed by the majority in *Flast* on the evil of using any government funds whatsoever, however small, to support religion. Authority for this proposition was found in James Madison's *Memorial and Remonstrance*: "The same authority which can force a citizen to contribute three pence only of his property for the support of any one establishment, may force him to conform to any other establishment in all other cases whatsoever." In his concurring opinion in *Flast*, Justice William Douglas, in anti-Catholic language characteristic of the time, warned of the "notorious" and "mounting federal aid to schools" and of the risk that any money given to parents of parochial school children would be given directly to "the priest."

In a prophetic dissent to the *Flast* decision, Justice John Harlan wrote,

> We have recently been reminded that the historical purposes of the religious clauses of the First Amendment are significantly more obscure and complex than this Court has heretofore acknowledged. Careful students of the history of the Establishment Clause have found that "it is impossible to give a dogmatic interpretation of the First Amendment, and to state with any accuracy the intention of the men who framed it. . . . " Above all, the evidence seems clear that the First Amendment was not intended simply to enact the terms of Madison's *Memorial and Remonstrance against Religious Assessments*.[6]

Anticipating, one might say, the decline of anti-Catholicism and the return to religious universalism that was to occur some thirty or forty years later, Harlan insisted that "the difficulty with which the Court never comes to grips, is that taxpayers' suits under the Establishment Clause are not . . . meaningfully different from other public actions" (*Flast* at 128). Rejecting the majority's conclusion that the establishment clause is, in some sense, more "structural" than other constitutional limitations on congressional spending, Harlan's dissent significantly foreshadows both the recent reworking of establishment clause jurisprudence in general and the Court's decision in *Hein* in particular.

The full reach of the 2007 *Hein* precedent is still unclear. The decision did not explicitly overrule *Flast* but formally only limited *Flast* to taxpayer establishment clause challenges to acts of Congress, distinguishing the White House Office as a part of the executive branch. But as Justice Scalia wrote in his concurrence in *Hein*, *Flast*'s days are numbered. Souter's opinion on behalf of the four dissenting justices in *Hein* responds to that implied rejection of the reasoning in *Flast*, and though long and impassioned, it sounds anachronistic, relying as it does on a social understanding of the dangers of religious establishment more characteristic of the *Flast* era. Souter insists that religion is special, that individual conscience must be protected by a high wall of separation, and that James Madison ought still to rule. "Favoritism for religion," says Souter, citing multiple Supreme Court precedents, "'sends the . . . message to . . . nonadherents' that they are outsiders, not full members of the political community." This position, the position that religion is different—and dangerously authoritarian—is increasingly a minority voice in the United States. We are all religious now. As a leading architect of integrating spirituality into medicine says, "Our belief [is] that there is a spiritual dimension in every person's life, even in those who deny that there is" (Fitchett 2002:97).

CONCLUSION

Nicholson and *Hein* fit into a series of recent U.S. court cases interpreting the establishment clause, including the school voucher decisions, that move away from the high separationism of the mid-twentieth century toward what we might call a post-pluralistic acknowledgment of religion as natural or universal. Although this move is seen as establishmentarian by some, by others it is seen as benignly so, permissible because no longer tainted by religious bigotry. More accurately perhaps, these new cases recognize that "establishment" and "disestablishment" as structuring ideas for organizing religious life are no longer relevant. Religious life is so entirely disaggregated and religious authority so thoroughly shifted to the individual that both establishment and disestablishment are functionally impossible. There are no churches left to establish or to disestablish. In the terms of this volume, this new recognition significantly challenges the normative assumptions underlying recent discussions of pluralism as a political project.

One way of reading the two clauses of the First Amendment to the U.S. Constitution has been to understand the free exercise clause as protecting individual conscience and the establishment clause as protecting citizens from a government dictated by clerics. Historically in the United States that understanding was founded in a particularly Protestant understanding of what kind of religion was desirable. Religion that is internal, chosen, and believed—religion that is about conscience—could and should be free without threat to the public order. Indeed, religion as conscience is understood to make public order possible. Other kinds of religion—in the United States, this has meant primarily Mormonism, Jehovah's Witness, Native American religions, Judaism, and Catholicism—as well as various forms of folk religion—but also now Islam—have often been regarded as unacceptable and policed as illegal acts or as presenting a threat of theocracy. But an ideology of equality combined with a pan-religious alliance against the imagined aridity of secularism has made such a crabbed anthropology progressively less credible. Now religion includes everybody, even those without religion, and the First Amendment religion clauses have themselves arguably become an anachronism, at least as usually understood.

The response of the Supreme Court in recent years has been to get itself out of the business of deciding what religion is. With the free exercise clause, U.S. laws must be neutral and universal, not discriminatory. Laws may not target particular religious groups, but no judicial exemptions to laws of general application will be given to those with religious motivations for their actions. With respect to the establishment clause, no particular disability is laid on religious institutions in their dealings with the government just because they are religious, and increasingly the acknowledgment of the citizen as spiritual is seen as unexceptional. A new abstraction of religion is developing to accommodate this new situation, one that is particularly evident in the delivery of health care. But it is also present in prisons (Sullivan 2009a) and in the armed services (Banerjee 2008). It is dependent on the belief that, in the words of a leading scholar of pastoral theology, "both the symbolic truth of traditional religious language and the truth of philosophical and scientific critiques of religious language [can] be held together in a conjunctive style of faith" (Fitchett 2002:110). The Court seems to be in the mood to countenance such an approach, notwithstanding the insistent demand from those such as FFRF, echoing many critics in religious studies, who see such a position as covertly theological and coercive in unacknowledged ways (Sullivan 2009a).

There still are, and will be, excluded disfavored religions under this new legal regime, of course, but the arbiter will no longer be the courts. Religion is being neutralized and naturalized—deconstitutionalized, formally. It is the individual chaplain who will determine what constitutes spiritual health. And it will be politics, not the Constitution, that determines whether he should be given a job.

Charles Taylor (2007) says that we live in a secular age and that naiveté is no longer available to anyone. That is a brave statement to make about the United States. We also live in a religious age. The new post-pluralist universalism is no more innocent than the old versions and no less naive.

NOTES

Versions of parts of this chapter have been published on the SSRC blog "The Immanent Frame" (http://www.ssrc.org/blogs/immanent_frame/), in an essay forum on religion and politics (Sullivan 2008), and in an essay for *Social Research* (Sullivan 2009b).

1. U.S. Department of Veterans Affairs, http://www1.va.gov/chaplain/page.cfm?pg=1 (accessed June 27, 2008).

2. Freedom from Religion Foundation, http://www.ffrf.org (accessed June 27, 2008).

3. An MP3 file of the argument is available on the Seventh Circuit Web site: http://www.ca7.uscourts.gov/ (accessed June 27, 2008).

4. Employment information is available on the Web site of the VA chaplaincy: http://www1.va.gov/chaplain/page.cfm?pg=7 (accessed June 27, 2008). A master of divinity degree is a terminal master's in ministry. Clinical pastoral education was invented in the 1920s and institutionalized in the 1940s. "The clinical chaplain draws from both the behavioral sciences and theological reflection in understanding the human condition." http://www.acpe.edu/ (accessed August 12, 2008). A list of approved ecclesiastical endorsers is available on the U.S. Army Web site. http://www.defenselink.mil/prhome/mppchaplain.html (accessed August 12, 2008).

5. Hughes (2008), an article on the Web site of the Roundtable on Religion and Social Welfare Policy, a forum funded by the Rockefeller Institute, analyzes the significance of the *Hein* decision.

6. For the proposition that the First Amendment is more complicated in origins than the majority justices suggest, Harlan cites Mark deWolfe Howe's classic work, *The Garden and the Wilderness* (1965).

WORKS CITED

Banerjee, Neela. 2008. Religion and Its Role Are in Dispute at the Service Academies. *New York Times*, June 25, p. A14.

Davie, Grace. 2002. *Europe: The Exceptional Case: Parameters of Faith in the Modern World*. London: Darton, Longman, and Todd.

Dolan, Mary Jean. 2008. Government-Sponsored Chaplains and Crisis: Walking the Fine Line in Disaster Response and Daily Life. *Hastings Constitutional Quarterly* 35:505–546.

Edgell, Penny, Joseph Gerteis, and Douglas Hartmann. 2006. Atheists as "Other": Moral Boundaries and Cultural Membership in American Society. *American Sociological Review* 71:211–234.

Fitchett, George. 2002. *Assessing Spiritual Needs: A Guide for Caregivers*. Lima, Ohio: Academic Renewal Press.

Fowler, James W. 1981. *Stages of Faith: The Psychology of Human Development and the Quest for Meaning*. San Francisco: HarperCollins.

Hamburger, Philip. 2004. *Separation of Church and State*. Cambridge, Mass.: Harvard University Press.

Howe, Mark deWolfe. 1965. *The Garden and the Wilderness: Religion and Government in American Constitutional History*. Chicago: University of Chicago Press.

Hughes, Claire. 2008. One-Year-Old Supreme Court Decision Ripples Through Church–State Lawsuits. The Roundtable on Religion & Social Welfare Policy. http://www.religionandsocialpolicy.org/homepage/article.cfm?id=8463 (accessed June 27, 2008).

Huxley, Andrew, ed. 2002. *Religion, Law and Tradition: Comparative Studies in Religious Law*. London: RoutledgeCurzon.

Sullivan, Winnifred Fallers. 2008. The New Disestablishment. *Religion and American Culture: A Journal of Interpretation* 18:21–26.

Sullivan, Winnifred Fallers. 2009a. *Prison Religion: Faith-Based Reform and the Constitution*. Princeton, N.J.: Princeton University Press.

Sullivan, Winnifred Fallers. 2009b. We Are All Religious Now. Again. *Social Research* 76:PAGES.

Taylor, Charles. 2007. *A Secular Age*. Cambridge, Mass.: Harvard University Press.

4. THE CULTURAL LIMITS OF LEGAL TOLERANCE

BENJAMIN L. BERGER

The success of the rhetoric of legal multiculturalism has clouded our capacity to see clearly the true nature of the relationship between religious diversity and the constitutional rule of law. Legal multiculturalism has held that, in a society characterized by deep cultural pluralism, the role of the law is to operationalize a political commitment to multiculturalism by serving as custodian and wielder of the twin key tools of tolerance and accommodation. In the context of religious difference, this commitment has translated into a prevailing juridical wisdom that freedom of religion is a hallmark of the liberal constitutional order and that the mechanism by which religious culture can be harmonized with the state is through the rights-based use of these legal tools.

In the context of many questions of difference, a similar role for law has, from a juridical perspective, proven not only laudable but essential: In Canada we have seen that the judicious use of principles of tolerance and accommodation of difference inspired by constitutional rights has produced certain positive legal outcomes in matters concerning sexual orientation, disability, political dissent, and, in some instances, religion.[1] Undoubtedly, these practical legal achievements of tolerance and accommodation—aspects of the triumph of law—have cemented in our imagination the role of a tolerantly implemented set of constitutionalized rights and freedoms as the framework within which to address such issues.

But when this approach is applied to instances in which the law comes face to face with pronounced cultural difference, it also creates a deeply flawed story about the relationship between religious difference and the constitutional rule of law. This relationship repeatedly proves to be far more conflictual, far more agonal, and far more durable than the language of legal tolerance conventionally suggests. In particular, conflicts between religious freedom/equality and other constitutional rights, rather than tolerant accommodation, seem to be the principal manifestation of religious pluralism in contemporary Canadian public life. What's more, some religious communities and commentators express dissatisfaction with what they feel to be the oppressive force of secular law (Sullivan 2005:153). Yet the story that the law tells about its encounter with religion—and, indeed, the story told by most liberal theory that treats this issue—seems ill equipped to account for these features of modern religious life in Western constitutional democracies. The purpose of this chapter is to explain why this is so. Why does "legal multiculturalism" seem so dissonant both with our observations of the relationship between religious pluralism and the law and with the experience of religiously committed groups living within the secular rule of law?

In their introduction to this volume, Pamela Klassen and Courtney Bender foreground the question of the descriptive and analytic adequacy of the public story about religious pluralism; in chapter 1 of this volume, Janet Jakobsen forcefully adds the dimension of the ethical to this critical questioning of this framing narrative. In this chapter, I take the adequacy of this account in all three dimensions—the descriptive, the analytic, and the ethical—as it manifests in a crucial modern site for the negotiation of religious pluralism, the constitutional rule of law. My principal argument is that using the lens of rights and the tools of legal tolerance and accommodation to manage deep religious diversity hides the fact that the meeting of law and religion is not a juridical or technical problem but rather an instance of cross-cultural encounter. This being so, the use of the explanatory and managerial tools of legal multiculturalism—and, in particular, the device of legal tolerance—is an instance of and a contributor to, not a solution for, the growing tensions we see in a contemporary condition of deep religious diversity in modern secular constitutional democracies. Nor do most influential theories of law and religious pluralism offer relief from this tension.

Both juridical and academic approaches to addressing religious diversity in the modern legal setting are afflicted by a double blindness. First, they fail to see that the constitutional rule of law is itself a cultural system, that is, an interpretive horizon, composed of sets of symbols, categories of thought, and particular practices that lend meaning to experience. The tacit starting proposition of legal multiculturalism is that law is a means of managing or adjudicating cultural difference but enjoys a strong form of autonomy from culture, a claim of autonomy that Wendy Brown (2006:166ff) characterizes as a central "conceit" of modern liberal orders. The cultural pluralism imagined by legal multiculturalism never includes the constitutional rule of law itself; rather, law sits in a managerial role above the realm of culture. Law is the curator, rather than a component, of cultural pluralism. Putting law above culture in this way means that the tools used by the law in this managerial endeavor—principally the tools of tolerance and accommodation but also certain structural commitments and adjudicative values—are themselves seen as distinct from any particular cultural system and hence not exerting cultural force.

A second, correlative blindness is in place once this distance between law and culture is established: a failure to appreciate the culturally specific way in which law constructs and imagines the value of the object of its attention, religion, and the extent to which this honors or does violence to the realities of and diversity among forms of religious life (Berger 2008b). The invisibility of law's cultural force enables an easy passage over the category "religion," which is merely tagged as a culture in need of law's managerial attention; no significant thought is given to the experience and meaning of inhabiting an "other" culture within the culture of law, nor to the way in which law's understanding of religion is a salient aspect of this intercultural encounter and the challenges it poses. As Winnifred Fallers Sullivan (2005:153) argues, the "tendency to accept modern law's representation of itself as autonomous, universal, and transparent . . . makes religion, not law, the problem."

Appreciating these hidden cultural dimensions of law's interaction with religion is important because if the cultural nature of the assumptions and tools of legal multiculturalism is not assessed, it is difficult to take meaningful account of either the tenacity with which the law protects its symbolic, structural and normative commitments or the experience of inhabiting a religious culture that faces the force of the culture of Canadian constitutionalism. Without such an appreciation, one can have only limited sensitivity for what is at stake for both the law and religious cultures in this interaction, and absent a sense of the stakes, it is impossible to really understand the game.

In short, the lens of legal multiculturalism—the lens applied by juridical and most academic accounts alike—obscures the fact that the contemporary encounter between religion and the constitutional rule of law is a cross-cultural encounter. As a result, when religious groups find themselves before the bar of the law, the terms of the debate are, in important ways, always already settled. This "bounded openness," whereby the core assumptions of the law are bracketed even as space is left open to assess the just, is an intrinsic feature of law's rule. In the context of interactions between law and religion, this means that certain commitments and assumptions of the culture of constitutionalism are not up for grabs or open to debate because they are seen as solutions to or terms of analysis for, not aspects of, the underlying tension. When this is the case, the rhetoric of pluralism, tolerance, and accommodation can be experienced as a language of power, coercion, and enforced transformation. This is the felt cultural force of law's rule, of which our public stories about law and religious pluralism must take account.

Before turning to explore and analyze the nature of the cross-cultural encounter between law and religion, a word on the framing of the questions in this piece is apropos. Formulating the issue as one of the encounter of the culture of constitutionalism with religious culture may appear to cast the two cultural forms as utterly distinct and fundamentally at odds, inappropriately reifying both in the process. In this way, my framing of the analysis in this chapter could seem to be in tension with much of the work in this volume, which seeks to contest a "billiard ball" model of pluralism, emphasizing and embracing the complexity, overlap, and messiness inherent in pluralism. I concur in the call to wrestle with the shifting, porous, and internally contested nature of culture when thinking about pluralism, and of course law and religion have a particularly rich history of mutual interpenetration and influence, a genealogy that interests me elsewhere in my work. My more Manichean casting of the issue in this chapter is a product of seeking to understand what is truly going on at the points at which a given religious culture becomes the object of the adjudicative scrutiny of constitutional law, points at which the story about legal tolerance is deployed. At such points, the constitutional rule of law is commonly experienced in something like the autonomous and reified form in which I present it here. Furthermore, at these moments the law understands itself in this way and, as I have argued elsewhere, renders religion in an equally stylized fashion (Berger 2008b). Approaching law and religion in the way that I do in this chapter is therefore a reflection of something real about the modern institutionalized encounter of constitutional law and religious difference and a heuristic move in service of generating a more satisfying account of the relationship between law and religion that is taking place under the rubric of legal tolerance and multiculturalism.

LOOKING THROUGH THE LENS OF CROSS-CULTURAL ENCOUNTER

Multiculturalism, in the first instance, is a description of a state of affairs, referring to the fact of a number of cultures existing in relationship to one another. In Canada, the language of multiculturalism is also something more; it is the name of a policy adopted by the federal government in 1971, a policy that took a normative position on this descriptive state of affairs—that multiculturalism was a good to be cultivated.[2] In neither the descriptive nor the aspirational use, however, does this language tell us much of practical interest. It says nothing in itself about the quality or nature of the interactions between the multiple cultures embraced by its meaning. It says nothing about the details about how this state is to be achieved or worked out. Furthermore, it says nothing about the experience of this interaction for those living within it, nor about the possibilities and room for commensurability of strong cultural difference within this encounter. To begin to assess with detail and sensitivity the engagement between law and religion, one must move beyond the merely descriptive or aspirational language of multiculturalism and set in place lenses appropriate to cross-cultural interaction; we need an idiom for analyzing the essential character of cross-cultural encounters.

Fred Dallmayr offers one such idiom in his book *Beyond Orientalism* (1996). Although his particular focus is on the cross-cultural encounter that began in the Americas in 1492, Dallmayr offers a taxonomy of modes of cross-cultural encounter. These modes are descriptive of various postures of engagement between cultures and, most critically for present purposes, the attitudes with which each approaches difference and understands the relation between the self and other. His taxonomy offers a helpful starting point for talking about law and religion as the meeting of two cultural systems and, ultimately, assessing the nature of this meeting and the adequacy of contemporary accounts.

Dallmayr's historically informed taxonomy can be divided into three broad categories. The first comprises modes of encounter that, in one way or another, ultimately deny difference. Here we find three closely related and often, though not always or necessarily, linked modes: conquest, conversion, and assimilation or acculturation (Dallmayr 1996:9). Colonialism is the quintessential modern form of conquest, involving the subjugation, complete assimilation, or even extermination of the encountered culture. As has been all too apparent in the context of European "engagement" with various indigenous populations, encounter through conquest is informed by a particular ideological posture and predicated on a particular way of conceiving of other cultures. Specifically, conquest entails a rigid confidence in one's own cultural assumptions and a matching conviction that the dissemination of this way of being is not only permitted but justified. When the dominant feature of a cross-cultural meeting informed by this mindset is the forced cultural assimilation of the alien population, the mode is best described as conversion. Whereas conquest operationalizes a denial of difference in a "radical-hierarchical way" that inscribes a schism between the two cultures, in the case of conversion, "difference is denied through the insistence on a common or identical human nature" (Dallmayr

1996:9–10) that marks the encountered population as a target for proselytization. Any instance of cultural encounter in which one culture, operating on the basis of an assumed identity of human nature, seeks to transform the other to its own way of being can thus be described as a practice of conversion. Closely related to conversion is the idea of assimilation or acculturation, which is best thought of as a domestic form of conversion that involves "the spreading of diffuse cultural patterns or ways of life (of religious and/or secular vintage)" (Dallmayr 1996:14), usually targeted at marginalized ethnic, linguistic, and national groups within a given country.

These first three modes of cross-cultural encounter are cut from the same cloth. They share a universalist ethic that translates into a dedication to the preservation of a single cultural form at the expense of others. Whether by violence and force of arms (conquest) or by ideological means either abroad (conversion) or at home (assimilation), each shares a core characteristic: a commitment to asserting the dominance of one's own culture, including its basic ways of knowing, its symbolic and normative commitments, and its ways of life.

A second category in this way of thinking about the varieties of cross-cultural encounter reacts against the universalism and ideological violence of the first set of modes and instead counsels minimal engagement. This is the familiar response of modus vivendi liberalism in which the hope is to stave off conflict by adopting a posture of indifference to cultural diversity and using procedural mechanisms to buffer interactions between cultures. Animated by "relative mutual disinterest and aloofness" (Dallmayr 1996:24), liberalism seeks a stable division between public procedures and institutions that we share and private culturally specific aspects of life, which are owed hands-off tolerance. The cultural violence found in the conquest, conversion, and assimilation modes is thought to be forestalled by minimizing substantive engagement, which is seen as inherently risky.

But perhaps engagement need not take this universalistic and potentially violent form. Dallmayr (1996:18) outlines a final category of modes of encounter that, like liberal minimal engagement, rejects the first category of modes as unjust but finds its solution in a different attitude or ethic informing cross-cultural engagement, one in which "the respective cultures must face each other on a more nearly equal or roughly comparable basis." Once the rigid hierarchy assumed in the first three forms is softened and the cultures in question begin to borrow from one another, anything from cultural incorporation to genuine cultural self-transformation can take place. Cultural borrowing is a form of engagement that "involves a prolonged, sometimes arduous process of engagement in alien life-forms, a process yielding at least a partial transformation of native habits due to a sustained learning experience" (Dallmayr 1996:24). More ambitious yet is the mode of encounter that Dallmayr (1996:31) views as the "normatively most commendable": dialogical engagement. This form of encounter also relies on a nonhierarchical view of cultures but goes further, demanding a kind of "caring respect" and "agonistic mutuality" in which both cultures are willing "to undergo a mutual learning process while simultaneously preserving the distinctiveness of difference of their traditions" (Dallmayr 1996:36). In stark contrast to the monism at the core of conquest, conversion, and assimilation, a dialogic mode of cross-cultural encounter actively encourages pluralism and diversity, and does so expecting to have one's own way of being changed through the influence of the other.

All these models proceed from the proposition that a culture sits on both sides of every encounter. Each mode describes a different posture informed by a very different set of assumptions and attitudes regarding the nature and possibilities of self–other relations in the context of cross-cultural encounters. Viewed through the lens of this taxonomy, how can we best characterize and understand the interaction between the culture of the constitutional rule of law and religious cultures, guided by the terms of legal tolerance?

LAW'S APPROACH

Focusing on the Canadian case, one can discern the particular mode of encounter that law assumes in its interaction with religion by looking to the Charter jurisprudence governing the management of strong claims of religious freedom. One could legitimately look to other institutional sites to examine law's interaction with religion, but judicial decisions are a particularly rich and helpful source, for as George Grant (1998) put it, "Theories of justice are inescapably defined in the necessities of a legal decision."

The starting point for understanding law's posture when it encounters religion is the fountainhead case on religious liberties in Canada, *R. v. Big M. Drug Mart*, [1985] 1 S.C.R. 295. *Big M.* involved an early Charter challenge to a piece of Sunday closing legislation, called the Lord's Day Act, on the basis that it offended the constitutional protection of religious freedom. In holding the legislation unconstitutional, Justice Dickson linked the notion of religious freedom to the very nature of a free society, stating that such a society "is one which can accommodate a wide variety of beliefs, diversity of tastes and pursuits, customs and codes of conduct" (*Big M.* at 336). The concept of freedom of religion, then, is centrally concerned with permitting the free and unconstrained expression of religious belief and conduct. Freedom of religion is, in the jurisprudence, an ideal that revolves around the notion of tolerance. In *Syndicat Northcrest v.*

Amselem, [2004] 2 S.C.R. 551, the Supreme Court of Canada explained that "respect for and tolerance of the rights and practices of religious minorities is one of the hallmarks of an enlightened democracy" (*Amselem*, para. 1), going so far as to declare that "mutual tolerance is one of the cornerstones of all democratic societies" (*Amselem*, para. 87). The Court has characterized Canada as "a diverse and multicultural society, bound together by the values of accommodation, tolerance and respect for diversity" (*Chamberlain v. Surrey School District No. 36*, [2002] 4 S.C.R. 710, para. 21). The story that law tells about its encounter with religion is shot through with the language of tolerance.

The Court explains that this commitment to tolerance is directly linked to the fact of living in a "multiethnic and multicultural country such as ours, which accentuates and advertises its modern record of respecting cultural diversity and human rights and of promoting tolerance of religious and ethnic minorities" (*Amselem*, para. 87). Our policy of multiculturalism produces the commitment to religious tolerance, and the constitutional manifestation of this commitment is the protection of religious freedom in section 2(a) of the Charter. This, then, is the first plank in law's approach to religion: Given the multicultural character of the state, tolerance is the guiding feature of law's engagement with religion, affording a healthy margin of freedom for a broad diversity of pursuits, tastes, beliefs, and practices.

The picture is rather more complex, of course. The Supreme Court of Canada has explained that "respect for religious minorities is not a stand-alone absolute right; like other rights, freedom of religion exists in a matrix of other correspondingly important rights that attach to individuals" (*Amselem*, para. 1). The issue is not solely one of the parallel individual rights of others. The tolerance of religious difference takes place within a society with its own concerns, needs, and imperatives. Therefore, "respect for minority rights must also coexist alongside societal values that are central to the make-up and functioning of a free and democratic society" (*Amselem*, para. 1). In recognition of this embeddedness in a context of other rights and other pressing societal interests and needs, the Canadian legal story adds to its aspiration of tolerance a second feature: Limits on freedom of religion may be justified in order to protect broad social interests or preserve the rights of others. In its recent jurisprudence the Supreme Court of Canada has explained that the most appropriate means of dealing with tensions between religious freedom and other rights or other social interests is to balance them under the rubric of section 1 of the Charter, which states that a right can be limited when such limitation is "demonstrably justified in a free and democratic society." The analysis under section 1 is, in essence, a form of means–ends proportionality review exemplary of contemporary liberal constitutional logic (Barak 2006; Beatty 2004). The toleration of religious difference suggested by the guarantee of freedom of religion is circumscribed by a constitutional limiting apparatus that looks to law's view of the socially reasonable in order to decide on the justifiable boundaries of legal toleration.

This doctrinal framework serves as the rules of engagement for law's cross-cultural encounter with religion in Canada, shaping the posture that the Canadian constitutional rule of law assumes in its encounter with religion. In light of the modes of cross-cultural encounter described in the last section, how is law's approach, conditioned as it is by these rules, best understood? On the surface, law begins firmly in the posture of liberal minimal engagement. The law claims that our society is strongly dedicated to multiculturalism, and this commitment demands tolerance of the ways in which people choose to live their lives, including the free expression and manifestation of cultural beliefs and practices. However, there is no assumption that religious cultures might offer something valuable from which the legal culture might borrow. Law and religion are certainly not engaging in a conversation as relative equals, one that may result in the transformation of either. Law's formal encounter with religion is an instance of neither cultural borrowing nor dialogic engagement. Nor is there an attempt—at this point—to subordinate difference by means of the kind of ideological force that characterizes conversion or assimilation. Instead, the law affirms diversity, but at arm's length. Religious cultures are entitled to the benefit of a liberal modus vivendi tolerance.

The difficulty with tolerance, as Bernard Williams (1999:65) has argued, "is that it seems to be at once necessary and impossible." Tolerance takes its place as a robust virtue at the points at which the tolerating group "thinks that the other is blasphemously, disastrously, obscenely wrong" (Williams 1999:65; see also Forst 2004:314). A virtuous toleration that will "accommodate a wide variety of beliefs, diversity of tastes and pursuits, customs and codes of conduct" (*Big M.* at 336) must be one that finds it difficult to accept these practices and beliefs within its own system of meaning and commitments. As Williams (1999:65) explains, "We need to tolerate other people and their ways of life only in situations that make it really difficult to do so. Toleration, we may say, is required only for the intolerable. That is its basic problem." Otherwise put, "when tolerance is contextually possible, it is untenable; tolerance, I want to suggest, is paradoxical" (Halberstam 1982–1983:190). The doctrinal structure of Canadian constitutional law as I have described it reflects this "basic problem" or "paradox" and in so doing points to important characteristics of law's mode of cross-cultural engagement with religion.

The easy language of toleration exhausts itself juridically at the section 2(a) freedom of religion stage of the analysis in which a court must decide whether a given belief or practice attracts the prima facie protection of the Constitution. The capaciousness of the court's definition of religion and subjective sincerity test for religious freedom means that little is disentitled to this initial protection

(*Amselem*; Berger 2008b). That which has come before the law is nominally "religion," and religious difference should be tolerated. Yet if the religious conduct or beliefs in question are arguably "intolerable," the law moves to a means–end proportionality analysis that asks whether the limit on legal tolerance is justified. With this move, the law quickly collapses into a conversionary mode of cross-cultural encounter. A particular instance of religious pluralism has been deemed problematic, and the law now asks whether the limit imposed on the tolerance of this religious culture is justified. When asking whether a limit on religious freedom is justified, the question is assessed within the values, assumptions, and symbolic commitments of the rule of law itself (*R. v. Oakes*, [1986] 1 S.C.R. 103, 136; *Gosselin v. Quebec (Attorney General)*, [2002] 4 S.C.R. 429, para. 353). In particular, law's conception of religion comes strongly into play: Law never really meets religion; rather, it engages its own projected image of religion's nature and value, one that may make it more accepting of certain forms of religion than others (Berger 2008b).[3] The law assesses whether the religious expression in question has deviated—and if so, how much—from "acceptable religion." Here, the relevant questions include whether the controverted practice is closely linked to individual flourishing, whether it was merely private or encroached on the public, and whether it limited the autonomy or equality of another. These are the criteria that determine whether this instance of cultural difference will be tolerated. Crucially, these criteria are drawn from inside the culture of Canadian constitutionalism itself. The more that a given religious culture or practice accords with law's understanding of religion, the less abrasive and challenging to law's commitments it will be and hence the more likely it is that it will fall within the limits of legal tolerance. However, when a claim to religious freedom begins to grate or put pressure on the law, it appears legally intolerable. The deeming of a particular manifestation of religion as intolerable—and hence the limitation of religious freedom as justified—can always be read as the product of a misfit between the claimant's religion or religious practice and what law understands as tolerable religion (Berger 2008b:285; Sullivan 2005:7–8).

Note the analytic upshot of this juridical posture: If the limit on tolerance is justified, it is justified by its fidelity to the commitments, values, and overarching objectives of the rule of law. Importantly, however, if the limit on tolerance is not justified, *the reason is the same*. It is not justified because we erred in thinking that the practice actually offended the basic commitments of law's rule. The limitation was unduly onerous, or we did not appreciate that, in fact, the religious practice or belief in question could be viewed as or rendered consonant with these commitments—commitments such as autonomy, the protection of individuals, and the maintenance of a private sphere characterized by personal values and a public sphere cleansed of the influences of choice and taste. Within this analytic structure, law always vindicates its own cultural understandings.

With this, law's encounter with religion takes on salient features of the conversionary/assimilationist mode of cross-cultural encounter.[4] Characteristic of conversionary/assimilationist modes of cross-cultural encounter, there is an underlying denial of difference, a repudiation of the diversity recognized, from a distance, in the minimal engagement posture. Law tolerates that which is different only as long as it is not so different that it challenges the organizing norms, commitments, practices, and symbols of the Canadian constitutional rule of law. The conversionary move has both a universalist and a culturally specific dimension: the assertion that there is a single and indissoluble package of criteria that is appropriate to judging the result of such conflicts of rights and the fact that these criteria are all drawn from within the culture of the rule of law itself. Once this move has taken place, there are only two possibilities: The courts will either deem the conduct intolerable and require the religious group or individual to conform to the norms and commitments of the rule of law, or the courts will conclude that the state was wrong in limiting this instance of religious diversity because this instance of cultural pluralism is itself consistent with the values and commitments of the rule of law. In the final analysis, you are either required to conform your way of life to the symbols, values, and meanings of the rule of law or permitted to carry on without interference because the law recasts the meaning of your practices and beliefs as already consistent with those cultural commitments. In either instance, the law spreads a cultural pattern or way of life that has, at its base, "the insistence on a common or identical human nature" (Dallmayr 1996:9–10). In either instance, the religionist is sent the message that, despite the values at stake for him or her at this analytic moment, what *really* matters is the set of values and commitments held by the rule of law, and, whether by proscribing certain behavior or by recasting the meaning of that behavior, you will be made to conform to the culture of law's rule. This is one juridical manifestation of what James Tully (1995:7) calls an "imperial culture embodied in most liberal constitutions."

Consider two examples drawn from the jurisprudence, one in which religion "wins" and one in which religion "loses." What is the message about the nature of legal tolerance expressed in each of these cases? The case of *Multani v. Commission Scolaire Marguerite-Bourgeoys*, [2006] 1 S.C.R. 256, is an interesting example of apparent legal tolerance, in part because it also contains a passionate plea by the Court for the importance of religious tolerance in Canadian society and the need to teach this value to Canadian youth. *Multani* involved an Orthodox Sikh boy who felt that his faith required him to wear a *kirpan*, a small ceremonial dagger, at all times. His school's governing board held that he was prohibited from wearing the *kirpan* at school on the basis of its policy that prohibited students from carrying any "weapons and dangerous objects." Given that it was the product of a sincerely held religious belief, the Court had no difficulty finding that the policy offended Multani's section 2(a) right. The bulk of the analysis turned on section 1. Although the school authority argued that the prohibition was justified as a safety measure and that the *kirpan*'s presence could have an adverse impact on the school environment, the Court concluded that this absolute prohibition was not a proportional limit on Multani's religious right. Dismissing the safety concern as ill-founded, the Court noted that there was no history of *kirpan*-related violence and that Multani had already agreed to wear the *kirpan* under his clothes and in a wooden sheath, itself wrapped and sewn in a cloth envelope. Contrary to the argument that the presence of a *kirpan* would damage the school environment, the Court explained that it was, in fact, the absolute prohibition that would have this effect, by sending "the message that some religious practices do not merit the same protection as others." "On the other hand, accommodating Gurbaj Singh and allowing him to wear his kirpan under certain conditions demonstrates the importance that our society attaches to protecting freedom of religion and to showing respect for its minorities" (*Multani*, 79).

So this religious practice is entitled to legal tolerance. But note that before arriving at this conclusion, the Court cast the meaning of Multani's religious expression in a form consistent with law's understanding of religion, whether that comports with his understanding or not. The logic of the section 2(a) analysis says that Multani's religious expression is constitutionally cognizable because it is an aspect of an "individual's self-definition and fulfilment and is a function of personal autonomy and choice" (*Amselem*, para. 42). Although it takes place at school, this religious practice is an expression of individual difference, does not touch the domain of public reason, and does not threaten the autonomy, choice, or equality of any others. Sheathed, sealed, and tucked away inside the folds of young Multani's clothing, religion does not threaten any of the values or structural commitments of the rule of law. *Multani* holds that this religious difference will be "tolerated," but the underlying message is that it will be tolerated because it conforms to law's understanding of religion and does not meaningfully grate on any of the central cultural commitments of the culture of Canadian constitutionalism. In this way, even as it tolerates, law asserts its cultural superiority and performs the dominance of public norms. The message sent is that Multani's religion should be tolerated because it ought not to be of genuine public concern.

On the other hand, what message is sent when the law trumps religious freedom? In *B.(R.) v. Children's Aid Society of Metropolitan Toronto*, [1995] 1 S.C.R. 315, the religious freedom issue was whether the government of Ontario had interfered with the religious liberties of Jehovah's Witness parents by overriding their decision not to permit a blood transfusion for their infant child. The majority of the Court accepted that this decision was an expression of the parents' religious freedom as protected by section 2(a). However, when the judges turned to the section 1 analysis, they reasoned that the state's actions were justified limitations on this religious freedom. The judges explained that the child had "never expressed any agreement with the Jehovah's Witness faith" and that respect for the child's autonomy demanded that she be allowed to "live long enough to make [her] own reasoned choice about the religion [she] wishes to follow" (*B.(R.)* at 437), if any. The parents had found the limit of legal tolerance at the border of individual autonomy and choice. There was simply no way that the Canadian constitutional rule of law would cede the necessary territory to make room for the parents' sincerely held ethical and epistemological commitments. The message sent in *B.(R.)* is that, in the presence of a religious difference that actually challenges the fundamental commitments of the Canadian constitutional rule of law, tolerance is at an end.

Many further examples can be drawn from the case law. There are the cases of *Trinity Western University v. College of Teachers*, [2001] 1 S.C.R. 772, and *Chamberlain*, both of which concerned the relationship between religious views and the provision of public education. In the first, the religious group in question "won," and in the second, religion "lost"; the operative conceptual difference in the two cases is the degree to which the law could view the religion in question as sufficiently private. Read together, the underlying message of the decisions is that tolerance is in order inasmuch as religious beliefs comply with law's understanding of religion as dominantly a private issue and can be contained within law's structural commitment to the public–private divide.[5] A pattern appears in these cases: To the extent that religion can be contained within the structural commitments of the rule of law, interpreted as comporting with its values, and read as consistent with its understanding of religion, tolerance is the mode of cross-cultural engagement. The grant of tolerance is based on the implicit judgment that the cultural differences found in the "tolerated" really ought not to bother the law. The point at which religion transgresses these commitments and defies these conceptions is the point at which tolerance gives way to the forceful imposition of the culture of Canadian constitutionalism.

In his essay "Tolerating the Intolerable," Bernard Williams refers to an apparent form of tolerance in the history of the relationship between various churches and denominations within the Christian world. One means of managing this pluralism was to assert that, despite seeming differences, all these brands of Christianity were, in essence, the same. Given that all were ultimately concerned with the same goals, one need not care much about the details of what the other believed. Although he acknowledges that this solution produces certain practical political goods, Williams (1999:67) cautions against an excessively sanguine evaluation of this state of affairs, stating that "as an attitude, it is less than toleration. If you do not care all that much what anyone believes, you do not need the attitude of toleration, any more than you do with regard to other people's tastes in food." The attitude being relied on beneath the language of toleration is, in truth, indifference.

As I have described it, Canadian constitutionalism treats religious culture with just such a tolerance of indifference. This kind of tolerance ends at the point at which the religious culture genuinely begins to grate on the values, practices, and ways of knowing of Canadian constitutionalism. When religious practice actually starts to *matter* to the law by challenging something central to the culture of law's rule, we begin to see the depth and force of law's commitments. Legal tolerance of religion reenacts the public–private divide that is so central to law's culture. The law is able to tolerate religious beliefs and practices that exert little pressure on the public norms and commitments of Canadian constitutionalism. There is an irony in this point. The rhetoric of multiculturalism is usually levied against a vision of religious and cultural difference as a purely private matter. I am suggesting that, although in certain ways resisting the easy relegation of difference to the private sphere, the invocation of legal tolerance has the simultaneous effect of, in other ways, shoring up that border between the public and private. As Wendy Brown writes, "Tolerance of diverse beliefs in a community becomes possible to the extent that those beliefs are phrased . . . as being constitutive of a private individual whose private beliefs and commitments have minimal bearing on the structure and pursuits of political, social, or economic life" (Brown 2006:32; see also Asad 2003:199). When the law can no longer be indifferent—when the religious belief or practice begins to trouble the law—we encounter the cultural limits of legal toleration.

This designation of a religious belief or practice as something that "troubles the law" triggers an interesting symbolic economy. Sometimes these issues crystallize around practices about which the symbolic stakes are, *ex ante*, symmetrically high for both law and religion. Law's tolerance may run out precisely at the point where it matters most to the religious culture. *B.R.*, the Jehovah's Witness blood transfusion case discussed earlier, is an example. Yet even if the religious expression is less central to the culture in question, the symbolic stakes are not, in the result, so different. Once marked as a matter of cultural significance to the law, the religious practice assumes deep importance to the religious culture because the practice has become a site for negotiating the relationship between cultures. For this reason, we sometimes see practices not at the self-understood core of a religious tradition suddenly embraced as uniquely definitional of a given religious culture. In such a case, the practice or principle in question has become the emblem of something larger than itself: the power and politics of engagement with the culture of the Canadian constitutional rule of law. At these points there is felt to be genuine difference, yet at these points toleration as indifference runs out and the structural and cultural reticence of law to give up anything of significance takes shape.

Law's tolerance as indifference is neither simple nor without virtue. Recall the constitutional logic used in analyzing whether an aspect of religious culture that might appear to chafe on the commitments of the liberal rule of law ought to be tolerated: Before limiting the right, the courts should carefully consider whether the religious expression that is producing the apparent conflict can be satisfyingly digested within the values and commitments of the rule of law. This reflective process demands a continual refinement and perhaps even expansion of the realm of indifference. Law asks itself to reconsider and reconfigure the geography of indifference using its own categories, such as the private and public, and its own values, such as autonomy and choice. Perhaps what we thought on first glance was objectionable is actually something that we can convince ourselves we shouldn't really mind after all. Seen in this way, modern legal tolerance takes place within the margins set by culturally conditioned points of incommensurability between law and religion at which law will move to a posture of enforcement or "conversion." This is a more modest practice than suggested in the conventional story about legal tolerance and multiculturalism. But in imposing the reflective demand to learn about the nature and contours of the religious practice or commitment appearing before it and asking whether it should really matter that much to the law, there is the abiding prospect that the law will stay its violent hand in more cases than it might absent this demand for the refinement of indifference. Alexander Bickel (1986:129) famously described the political importance of a court's declaration that legislation is "not unconstitutional." The tacit or express declaration that a particular religious expression is "not intolerable" is, similarly, a kind of political intervention with virtues and significance that it would be a mistake to ignore. There is real liberty within this margin created by an expanded and continually refined indifference.

Nevertheless, when toleration of a given religious commitment would require the law to actually cede normative or symbolic territory, law trumps it in the name of procedural fairness, choice, autonomy, or the integrity of the public sphere; with this, tolerance gives way to conversion. Dallmayr describes conversion as a form of universalism of ideals, and perhaps this description provides some insight into why religion and law have been locked in this form of cross-cultural encounter for so long. Like religion, the rule of law is concerned with shaping meaning, and it is not modest in its claims. Living within the Canadian constitutional rule of law is living within a culture that makes claims about the relevance of space and time, about the source and nature of authority, and about what is of value about the human subject. So, too, does religion. Law and religion are homologous in this sense; through norm, ritual, and symbol both constitute meaningful worlds (Réaume 2001:196; Sullivan 2005:153). This homology means that religious claims and practices can come into direct competition with those of the law. And within a liberal democratic rule of law the tacit but powerful assumption is that law's understandings and commitments must prevail. Perhaps this instinct is natural enough. Every culture assumes that its way of seeing is basically correct; however, in the modern liberal state, law is uniquely privileged and equipped to enforce its sense of its own centrality. As a result, at such points of strong cultural difference, law asserts its dominance, and law's asserted dominance is experienced as a conversionary effort for those committed to the religious culture's way of being in the world. These are the unacknowledged cultural stakes of law's encounter with religion.

"Once we see that the rule of law is a way of being in the world that must compete with other forms of social and political perception, a range of questions about the actual forms and character of this competition open up. We need to study the places at which conflict emerges and the ways in which law has succeeded or failed in these conflicts" (Kahn 1999:84–85). Studying the points of conflict between the culture of law's rule and religious forms of being in the world has revealed an unacknowledged complexity. Law's self-understanding speaks of multiculturalism, toleration, and accommodation as the key principles. Yet, as I have shown, this brand of toleration depends on a kind of indifference (no matter how cultivated), and at precisely the points at which the law can no longer be indifferent—tellingly, often at the points at which the stakes for the religious culture concerned have themselves become the highest—its conversionary aspirations appear. The conventional story we tell about the nature of tolerance and accommodation in a multicultural society is far more comforting but far less satisfying.

THE LIMITS OF THEORY

Modern theories of multiculturalism have tended to offer approaches that suffer from the same blindness as the legal account. These theories also suffer from the explanatory failure I have described, giving neither a strong account for the realities and difficulties of the conflict of legal and religious cultures nor a meaningful sense of the stakes of this encounter for these cultures. Although there has been no dearth of theoretical ink spilled on the question of the just means of approaching the interaction of law and religious culture, this explanatory shortfall and its conceptual root can be seen by turning to consider two accounts that have been influential in the Canadian scholarly debate in recent years.

In *Multicultural Citizenship*, Will Kymlicka (1995) takes up the project of developing a liberally defensible theory of minority rights. Kymlicka's theory is based largely on the distinction between internal and external restrictions: Minority cultures should be afforded external protections that enhance the equality of these groups within broader society, but they should not be afforded support for internal restrictions that limit the autonomy and freedom of members. Based as it is in liberalism, Kymlicka's idea of tolerance is bounded by the goods of equality, autonomy, and freedom and guided by the categories of the inside and outside, private and public. He offers a theory of legal multiculturalism that is different in its details from the conventional legal approach but one that similarly affords tolerance only to the extent that the given culture comports with the values, symbols, and practices of the law, which is itself set apart from the multicultural fray. As with the legal approach, the boundaries of toleration are always already set, and set in a fashion that structurally insulates the norms and assumptions of legal culture from meaningful engagement and contestation. Thus, "liberals can only endorse minority rights insofar as they are consistent with respect for the freedom or autonomy of individuals" (Kymlicka 1995:75). Beyond this point of tolerance as indifference, when faced with illiberal cultures, the general rule is that the ultimate goal of liberals should be "to seek to liberalize them" (Kymlicka 1995:75). Kymlicka offers a full working out of a liberal theory of multiculturalism, demonstrating how far liberalism can go while working within its own categories. In so doing, he exposes in the realm of liberal theory the same limits of toleration that I have identified in liberal legal discourse.

As is the case with legal multiculturalism, Kymlicka's brand of tolerance as indifference flows from his initial conception of culture. Kymlicka states that, for his purposes, a "culture" is understood as "an intergenerational community, more or less institutionally complete, occupying a given territory or homeland, sharing a distinct language and history." A state is multicultural if its members belong to or have emigrated from different nations "and if this fact is an important aspect of personal identity and political life" (Kymlicka 1995:18). Two features of this conception of culture are of particular salience. First, it is thin in the sense that there is no ideological, symbolic, or belief-based component. In this respect, religious minorities might well find themselves fitting awkwardly within this understanding of culture, just as I have argued they might struggle to fit themselves within law's understanding of religion. Second, law does not figure in as a culture. The law oversees and moderates, but does not itself engage as a cultural actor in, the multicultural terrain that he imagines. By locating culture only on one side of the issue, Kymlicka obscures the dominance and power at play in the cross-cultural encounter between law and religion, even as his theory performs it.

Another influential Canadian theorist of multiculturalism, Ayelet Shachar, takes a critical stance toward Kymlicka's liberal theory of multiculturalism, arguing that his external–internal binary is inadequate inasmuch as it "fails to provide a workable solution in practice for certain real-life situations involving accommodated groups" (Shachar 2001:18; see also Modood 2007:79). She rightly notes that his approach could exacerbate the invidious position of historically disadvantaged or vulnerable members "where the external protections that promote justice between groups uphold the very cultural traditions that sanction the routine in-group maltreatment" (Shachar 2001:18). Yet in attending to these concerns, Shachar's theory of "transformative accommodation" ultimately replicates the mode of cross-cultural engagement between law and religious pluralism found in Kymlicka's work and Canadian jurisprudence alike.

Shachar's laudable goal is to find an approach to multiculturalism that shows a concern for cultural integrity but that is also sensitive to the distributional social costs borne primarily by women when such cultures are afforded too much autonomy from the influence of public norms. She wants to add the individual to the normally dyadic debate about multiculturalism that focuses on the interaction of the state and the group. Shachar is critical of the "unavoidable costs" approach to multiculturalism, which holds that if you want to take multiculturalism seriously you must simply bear the costs of possible in-group rights violations. Yet she is equally critical of the "reuniversalized citizen option," which says that the only way to resolve this tension is to pick the primacy of individual rights over group cultural integrity. Shachar's preferred approach leans heavily on the concept of jurisdiction to achieve a form of balance that she calls transformative accommodation. In this vision of multiculturalism, there are overlapping, nonexclusive jurisdictions shared between the state and the group, leading both to compete for the loyalties of citizens and thus creating incentives for both to speak to the needs of individuals within minority groups. Yet as she unfolds her theory of transformative accommodation through "joint governance," we see that the transformation envisioned is really one whereby religion is forced to change to take better account of the normative commitments of Canadian constitutional culture. On one hand, she claims that "the objective of harnessing this individual–group–state dynamic is not to strip communities of their distinctive *nomos*" (Shachar 2001:126). This claim is important to her because she wants to respect group and individual commitment to traditional cultures. Yet she argues that the very goal of this model of transformative accommodation—a goal reflected in her chosen label itself—is to make in-group practices that are inconsistent with the equality and autonomy norms of the constitutional rule of law very costly and thus to "create incentives for the group to transform the more oppressive elements of its tradition" (Shachar 2001:126). The goal is to "lead to the internal transformation of the group's *nomos*" (Shachar 2001:124). Ultimately, Shachar's is a conversionary model of encounter.

Shachar's is an imaginative and legally crafty alternative model of multiculturalism that admirably seeks to ameliorate the in-group social costs too often borne by women. But it is also a good example of a theory that concerns itself with *nomoi* that are "over there" while failing to account for the extent to which the manipulation of concepts of jurisdiction and authority is a project firmly embedded in a *nomos*, this time law's *nomos*. Throughout, Shachar presents law in an overwhelmingly functional light—as a tool for managing culture—and in so doing elides the presence and influence of law's culture in her analysis. Indeed, Shachar's controlling concept—jurisdiction—is itself a history- and meaning-laden way of understanding the intersection of authority and space that is specifically tied to the culture of law's rule (Cover 1983:8; Ford 2001; Raustiala 2005). In effect, she imposes law's symbolic categories in service of enforcing values that are themselves internal to the culture of Canadian constitutionalism. Shachar's theory is fairly described, in Dallmayr's terms of cross-cultural encounter, as a model of gradual or "soft" conversion. She assumes certain boundaries regarding the tolerable beyond which cultural transformation is the goal. Her means of protecting these boundaries is simply more nuanced and gradual than a direct imposition or outright demand for change. Yet whether the product of "toleration," "internal versus external restrictions," or the hypercultural legal concept or symbol of jurisdiction, the process of being forced to change to comply with a given cultural system can be experienced as a dynamic of power characteristic of conquest, conversion, or assimilation.

Despite their differences, these two models are both exemplary of conventional theorizing about legal tolerance as it relates to religious difference. Both amount to theoretical reconfigurations of the geography of legal tolerance, preserving the cultural dynamics I have described. The efforts of those such as Kymlicka and Shachar to soften law's force and to expand and refine the margins of indifference are important. Nevertheless, these accounts essentially replicate the pattern of engagement found beneath law's story about religious pluralism. Each views law as something quite apart from the cultures it is overseeing. Accordingly, each assumes limits to tolerance and means of managing difference that do not force law to critically examine its own symbolic and normative assumptions or seek cross-cultural understanding; as a result, toleration tends to expire at precisely the point where these assumptions are threatened. This produces a strong tendency to collapse into assimilationist modes of engagement with religious and cultural groups. Herein lies the source of the durable and protracted tensions between religious communities and the constitutional rule of law, tensions we have seen build in recent years. If, under the banner of multicultural tolerance, religious diversity is being subject to conversionary force at precisely those points of meaningful cultural difference, the experience of those minority cultures is not one of respect for pluralism and accommodation of diversity but rather of coercion at the hands of the law.

What other forms of legal tolerance of religious difference can be imagined? An apparently promising candidate would be an approach to constitutionalism based on theories of dialogical engagement. A constitutional order dedicated to the ethics of dialogic cross-cultural engagement would be more than an attempt at normative agreement. Rather, it would manifest "a willingness to enter the border zone or interstices between self and other, thus placing oneself before the open 'court' of dialogue and mutual questioning" (Dallmayr 1996:47). "Wedged between surrender and triumph, dialogical exchange has an 'agonal' or tensional quality which cannot be fully stabilized" (Dallmayr 1996:xviii). In this form of dialogic encounter, "'one must seek to understand the other' even at the risk of self-critique and self-decentering, which entails that 'one has to believe that one could be wrong'" (Dallmayr 1996:48–49). For theorists such as Dallmayr, Tzvetan Todorov, Hans-Georg Gadamer, and William Connolly, it is this kind of cross-cultural encounter that could navigate the "precarious course between (or beyond) assimilation and atomism" (Dallmayr 1996:33).

Taken from the heights of political and hermeneutic theory, this approach to the encounter between cultures seems both to offer a more satisfying recognition of the stakes for law and religion and to chart a possible new path. So can the answer to the cultural limits of legal toleration nevertheless be found in these contemporary dialogic theories of cross-cultural interaction? I argue that it cannot. The distinctive character of the culture of contemporary constitutionalism limits the possible modes of cross-cultural encounter and precludes the kind of dialogical engagement imagined in these theories.

One of the common features of dialogic theories of cross-cultural encounter is the demand that each culture face a degree of risk in the encounter with the other. For example, Dallmayr describes dialogic encounter as requiring that both cultures open themselves to mutual questioning and manifest a "willingness to risk oneself" (Dallmayr 1996:xviii). Connolly (2005:125) requires that "something in the faith, identity, or philosophy of the engaged parties is placed at risk." Otherwise put, and as noted earlier, a precondition to this form of cross-cultural understanding is the "risk of self-critique and self-decentering, which entails that 'one has to believe that one could be wrong'" (Dallmayr 1996:48–49).

One of the distinctive features of law's rule is that, in a very particular and practical respect, it is never wrong. This is not to say that law never admits error and makes changes accordingly; it surely does this. Rather, the point is that the ultimate authority or correctness of the law is never in question for itself. Even when it accepts that the application of its principles were misguided in a given case or that certain rules should adjust to account for changes in society, there is a permanent conservation of law's authority and, contrary to the dialogic demand to be open to the risk of self-decentering, a structurally permanent affirmation of its place at the center of the management of all public dispute. As Paul Kahn (1997:167) explains, "Law does not win localized victories over action; it cannot tolerate defeats as long as they are balanced by victories. Law never explicitly concedes defeat; it never admits powerlessness." Thus, although it might, in a given case, concede that the line between the private and public was incorrectly drawn in the past, we cannot imagine Canadian constitutional rule of law disavowing the organizing significance of this conceptual trope. Similarly, although the legal configurations necessary to protect individual autonomy and choice might be hotly debated in the law, the normative primacy of these values is never itself at stake. If this is true, it leaves little room for dialogic engagement.

When religious cultures claim the protection of rights that are a part of modern legal multiculturalism, there is no openness to the possibility that the law might not be the ultimate arbiter of the terms and conditions that will settle this dispute. Another way of seeing this very particular feature of the culture of contemporary Canadian constitutionalism is in linguistic terms. In his plea for a form of dialogic constitutionalism that can better serve the needs of deep diversity, Tully (1995:24) concludes that

> if there is to be a post-imperial dialogue on the just constitution of culturally diverse societies, the dialogue must be one in which the participants are recognized and speak in their own language and customary ways. They do not wish either to be silenced or to be recognized and constrained to speak within the institutions and traditions of interpretation of the imperial constitutions that have been imposed over them.

My argument is that, once cast as a claim about legal tolerance or accommodation within contemporary Canadian constitutional culture, the possibility of the use of a language other than law's own is foreclosed. The language becomes the language of rights constitutionalism, privileging the terms *autonomy*, *equality*, and *choice*. The salient concepts are those of the public and the private, jurisdiction, and standing. The ways become the way of legal process, and the matter is firmly set within the institutions and traditions of interpretation of the culture of law's rule. It is little wonder that, as Tracy Leavelle cogently explains in chapter 6, for many cultural groups (including indigenous North Americans) dialogue with the law under the rubric of legal multiculturalism can be so deeply unappealing.[6] As Tully (1995:56) himself concludes, "A just dialogue is precluded by the conventions of modern constitutionalism," including the assumption that understanding the other inheres in translating cultural claims "into a conceptual framework in which it can then be adjudicated." Indeed, it is this conclusion that impels Tully's search for a means of entirely reconceiving and reconstructing modern constitutionalism.

The meaningful form that law gives to experience is not the only form imaginable; indeed, law's meanings are always and essentially in competition with other ways of imagining the world—other cultures. This is what makes the dialogic form of cross-cultural encounter so attractive. But in a liberal constitutional democracy, the law is privileged among such possible interpretations, and it is this feature of legal culture that seems to put this more promising form of cross-cultural encounter out of reach. Once cultural conflict is embedded in the language of rights and legal accommodation, by its very nature the rule of law exerts a kind of structural dominance immiscible with dialogic forms of cross-cultural encounter. So, in the end, whereas blindness to the fact of the culture of contemporary Canadian constitutionalism consigns legal multiculturalism to a form of cultural assimilation, seeing the precise nature of this contemporary legal culture forecloses the possibility of the promising dialogic form of cross-cultural engagement.

CONCLUSION: THE CHALLENGES OF SEEING CULTURE

The challenging cultural dynamics of legal tolerance I have explored in this chapter can be found wherever the orthodox understanding of legal multiculturalism is invoked as a tool for the management of religious pluralism. In a recent Supreme Court of Canada decision, Justice Abella set the tone and context for the majority decision with the following introductory paragraph:

> Canada rightly prides itself on its evolutionary tolerance for diversity and pluralism. This journey has included a growing appreciation for multiculturalism, including the recognition that ethnic, religious or cultural differences will be acknowledged and respected. Endorsed in legal instruments ranging from the statutory protections found in human rights codes to their constitutional enshrinement in the Canadian Charter of Rights and Freedoms, the right to integrate into Canada's mainstream based on and notwithstanding these differences has become a defining part of our national character. (*Bruker v. Marcovitz*, [2007] 3 S.C.R. 607, para. 1)

One sees here the extent to which contemporary legal debate about the interaction of law and religion remains very much in thrall to the conventional account of legal multiculturalism. Justice Abella paints a picture that reflects the familiar and comforting story about the management of religious pluralism by means of legal tolerance. Yet her words also betray the way in which this story fails to adequately reflect the deeper and more complex reality of the interaction between law and religion. With the suggestion that the constitutional protections for religious, cultural, and ethnic differences exist to facilitate integration into a Canadian mainstream "based on and notwithstanding" these elements of pluralism, Justice Abella gestures—perhaps unwittingly—toward the true character of legal tolerance. The posture of dominance and indifference that I have argued characterizes the cross-cultural encounter of law and religion shows itself in the midst of the official rhetoric of legal tolerance.

The conceptual core of this chapter is the suggestion that the conventional story about the relationship between the rule of law and religious cultures depends on the conceit of law's autonomy from culture, a conceit that hides the fact that law is not merely an overseer or instrumental force in the politics of multiculturalism. When it is analyzed as a cultural force in its own right, the boundaries of legal doctrines of tolerance and the nature of the cross-cultural encounter between religion and law become more transparent. Yet what is thereby revealed is that legal tolerance is a more modest posture toward religious pluralism than the rhetoric of multiculturalism suggests. In the end, law's tolerance is a form of cultivated and continually refined indifference toward religious cultures, and when the boundaries of this indifference are found—when religious belief and practice begin to push on the law in a way that would force contemporary constitutionalism to cede, reconsider, or revise its core cultural commitments—this posture of tolerance collapses into one that is assimilationist or conversionary. Understood in terms of cross-cultural encounter, the stakes of this interaction are high, and it becomes clear that the culture of law's rule is structurally positioned and very much prepared to assert its dominance.

Understanding the meeting of law and religion as a cross-cultural encounter breaks down our complacencies about what it means for law to accommodate strong forms of religious pluralism and exposes the cultural limits of legal toleration. It is a more honest account of what is occurring between law and religion under the rubric of legal multiculturalism, one that goes some way toward heeding Janet Jakobsen's resonant call in this volume that the norms of secular liberalism, powerfully expressed in the culture of the constitutional rule of law, "must be seen as a party to the conflict." Yet with the limits exposed by this more satisfying account of the cross-cultural nature of law's interaction with religion in clear view, the horizon is somewhat bleak when we turn to look for other, more satisfying modes of engagement. It may be that Tully is correct that the only way of properly attending to deep cultural diversity is by reconstructing another form of constitutionalism. Such a form would have to differ fundamentally in its basic assumptions and self-understanding from that which we currently possess. Or perhaps we can do no better than to work to expand the borders of our indifference. If so, we are also faced with the continuing challenge of explaining why, at points of genuine friction, the culture of law's rule is entitled to dominance over other forms of culture. Irrespectively, if viewing—with detail and precision—the interaction of law and religion as a cross-cultural encounter causes us to see this interaction as decidedly fraught and durable, then it is an account that has served us well because it has helped us to see better.

NOTES

This chapter was published in a more elaborated article form in Berger (2008a). It was greatly enriched by discussions with participants in the After Pluralism workshops. Particular thanks are owed to Tomoko Masuzawa and Natalie Zemon Davis for their kind encouragement and incisive responses to an early version of this chapter. I am also grateful to Paul Kahn, Robert Leckey, Andrew Petter, and the participants in the Spring 2008 Legal Theory Workshop at McGill University for their comments and suggestions. Finally, many thanks to Lyndsay Watson and Micah Weintraub for their editorial assistance.

1. Whether these legal successes have translated into political gains for these groups is another question. I suspect that the nature and concomitant political effects of legal tolerance described in this chapter apply in analogous ways to these groups as well.

2. For the history of the development of the policy of official multiculturalism in Canada, see Jedwab (2003), Kymlicka (2003), and Magnet (2005).

3. Michael McNally (chap. 9, this volume) demonstrates some of the ways in which Native American religion is ill fitted to the conception of religion found in U.S. constitutional law, impelling a search for other legal means to protect indigenous religion. John Borrows (2008) comes to analogous conclusions in his analysis of indigenous religions in the Canadian constitutional context. By contrast, I note elsewhere the close affinities between Canadian constitutional law's conception of religion and certain Protestant understandings of religiosity (Berger 2008b:284–285).

4. This experience of an encounter with law as an experience of cultural imperialism or as conversion/assimilation is something all too familiar for the aboriginal peoples of Canada. For a reflection on the assimilationist policies concerning aboriginal communities in Canada as part of the story of Canadian constitutional engagement with cultural diversity, see Sheppard (2006:466–467).

5. For further examples and analysis on this point, see Berger (2008a).

6. As Leavelle so powerfully puts it in chapter 6, "Pluralism, with its demands for explanation and engagement, looks to many Native peoples like a peculiarly modern form of colonialism."

WORKS CITED

Asad, Talal. 2003. *Formations of the Secular: Christianity, Islam, Modernity*. Stanford, Calif.: Stanford University Press.

Barak, Aharon. 2006. *The Judge in a Democracy*. Princeton, N.J.: Princeton University Press.

Beatty, David M. 2004. *The Ultimate Rule of Law*. Oxford: Oxford University Press.

Berger, Benjamin L. 2008a. The Cultural Limits of Legal Tolerance. *Canadian Journal of Law and Jurisprudence* 21, no. 2:245–277.

Berger, Benjamin L. 2008b. Law's Religion: Rendering Culture. In *Law and Religious Pluralism in Canada*, ed. Richard Moon, 264–296. Vancouver: UBC Press.

Bickel, Alexander M. 1986. *The Least Dangerous Branch: The Supreme Court at the Bar of Politics*. 2nd ed. New Haven, Conn.: Yale University Press.

Borrows, John. 2008. Living Law on a Living Earth: Aboriginal Religion, Law, and the Constitution. In *Law and Religious Pluralism in Canada*, ed. Richard Moon, 161–191. {{Pages different in selected bibl}} Vancouver: UBC Press.

Brown, Wendy. 2006. *Regulating Aversion: Tolerance in the Age of Identity and Empire*. Princeton, N.J.: Princeton University Press.

Connolly, William E. 2005. *Pluralism*. Durham, N.C.: Duke University Press.

Cover, Robert M. 1983. The Supreme Court 1982 Term—Foreword: Nomos and Narrative. *Harvard Law Review* 97:4–68.

Dallmayr, Fred. 1996. *Beyond Orientalism: Essays on Cross-Cultural Encounter*. Albany: State University of New York Press.

Ford, Richard T. 2001. Law's Territory (A History of Jurisdiction). In *The Legal Geographies Reader: Law, Power, and Space*, ed. Nicholas Blomley, David Delaney, and Richard T. Ford, 200–217. Oxford: Blackwell.

Forst, Rainer. 2004. The Limits of Toleration. *Constellations* 11:312–325.

Grant, George. 1974/1998. *English-Speaking Justice*. Toronto: House of Anansi Press.

Halberstam, Joshua. 1982–1983. The Paradox of Tolerance. *Philosophical Forum* 14, no. 2:190–207.

Jedwab, Jack. 2003. To Preserve and Enhance: Canadian Multiculturalism Before and After the Charter. *S.C.L.R. (2d)* 19:309–344.

Kahn, Paul W. 1997. *The Reign of Law:* Marbury v. Madison *and the Construction of America*. New Haven, Conn.: Yale University Press.

Kahn, Paul W. 1999. *The Cultural Study of Law: Reconstructing Legal Scholarship*. Chicago: University of Chicago Press.

Kymlicka, Will. 1995. *Multicultural Citizenship: A Liberal Theory of Minority Rights*. Oxford: Clarendon Press.

Kymlicka, Will. 2003. Canadian Multiculturalism in Historical and Comparative Perspective: Is Canada Unique? *Constitutional Forum* 13, no. 1:1–8.

Magnet, Joseph Eliot. 2005. Multiculturalism and Collective Rights. *S.C.L.R. (2d)* 27:431–497.

Modood, Tariq. 2007. *Multiculturalism: A Civic Idea*. Cambridge: Polity.

Raustiala, Kai. 2005. The Geography of Justice. *Fordham Law Review* 73:2501–2560.

Réaume, Denise G. 2001. Legal Multiculturalism from the Bottom Up. In *Canadian Political Philosophy: Contemporary Reflections*, ed. Ronald Beiner and Wayne Norman, 194–206. Oxford: Oxford University Press.

Shachar, Ayelet. 2001. *Multicultural Jurisdictions: Cultural Differences and Women's Rights*. Cambridge: Cambridge University Press.

Sheppard, Colleen. 2006. Constitutional Recognition of Diversity in Canada. *Vermont Law Review* 30:463–487.

Sullivan, Winnifred Fallers. 2005. *The Impossibility of Religious Freedom*. Princeton, N.J.: Princeton University Press.

Tully, James. 1995. *Strange Multiplicity: Constitutionalism in an Age of Diversity*. Cambridge: Cambridge University Press.

Williams, Bernard. 1999. Tolerating the Intolerable. In *The Politics of Toleration in Modern Life*, ed. Susan Mendes, 65–75. Durham, N.C.: Duke University Press.

PART II

Performing Religion After Pluralism

5. THE BIRTH OF THEATRICAL LIBERALISM

ANDREA MOST

> It may be that being a Jew satisfied the frustrated actress in me. It may be that I have dramatized myself as a Jew.
>
> —Edna Ferber, *A Peculiar Treasure*

On Armistice Day, November 11, 1938, Kate Smith sang "God Bless America" for the first time on her CBS radio program, recorded live at the New York World's Fair. The song was instantly popular. Smith continued to sing it on every one of her radio broadcasts for the next year, she recorded it with RCA in 1939, the lyrics were introduced into the *Congressional Record*, and it has long been considered an alternative national anthem.[1] The song remains central to American popular culture today and experienced a renewed burst of popularity after September 11, 2001, when congressmen, Broadway performers, baseball players, and stock traders all sang the song as a way of asserting their patriotic commitment (Corliss 2001). "God Bless America" was originally written for the musical revue *Yip, Yip, Yaphank*, by Irving Berlin, a Russian-Jewish immigrant to America at the turn of the twentieth century, the son of a cantor, and one of the most successful writers of popular theater music in American history. Berlin's choice to become a secular American songwriter rather than a cantor like his father has long been the stuff of American immigrant legend (Bergreen 1990:12, 410; Freedland 1986; Furia 1998:11).[2] Indeed, "God Bless America" is one of the songs that has solidified the narrative of the transformation of religious Jew into secular American. But let's take a close look at the lyrics to the song:

While the storm clouds gather
Far across the sea,
Let us swear allegiance
To a land that's free;
Let us all be grateful
For a land so fair,
As we raise our voices
In a solemn prayer.

God bless America,
Land that I love,
Stand beside her and guide her
Through the night with a light from above.
From the mountains, to the prairies,
To the oceans white with foam,
God bless America,
My home sweet home.

What about those bits about the "solemn prayer" and about God blessing America? How can a song that is clearly a prayer be connected unproblematically with a writer who insisted on a secular identity? Or with a public sphere that is considered secular? What exactly does *secular* mean in this context?

As we can see in the ongoing national embrace of "God Bless America" (and of its composer), American popular culture is the closest thing we have to an established national culture. The central values of this culture are expressed in songs, plays, and movies, most of them not about God and blessings but about the theater itself. As we will see, however, in Jewish-created American popular culture, the distance between God and the theater is far shorter than current scholarship on religion might assume. As numerous chapters in this volume make clear, the American public sphere has always been heavily shaped by its various religious cultures. Major developments in American popular culture therefore need to be understood in light of America's volatile, creative, and expansive religious energy. First- and second-generation American Jews created a popular theatrical realm that is commonly understood as secular yet on closer examination reveals itself to be far more Jewish than the word *secular* indicates. In this world of popular entertainment, Judaic values about freedom, performance, action, and communal obligation exist in productive tension with Protestant liberal ideals. Grounding the history of American popular culture in the multiple religious traditions that informed the worldviews of its practitioners allows us to understand more clearly why Jews were and are so deeply involved in American popular entertainment, how Jews successfully acculturated to

America in the twentieth century, and how American liberalism developed and changed in response to the arrival of millions of immigrants from many different religious backgrounds.

It is well known that throughout the twentieth century, American Jews were deeply involved in the creation of American popular entertainment. Never much more than 3 percent of the population, Jews were nonetheless instrumental in the development of the major industries and entertainment forms that provided mass culture to a majority of Americans through much of the twentieth century: Broadway, Hollywood, the television and radio industries, stand-up comedy, and the popular music industry have all been deeply influenced by the activity of Jews.[3] If we look beyond America's shores, we find the same story, although not quite to the same extent, in many centers of European culture.[4] This connection between Jews and popular performance has perplexed and inspired cultural historians for decades. Among the most popular explanations for this persistent relationship is an identity-based argument that contends that Jews who created Broadway musicals, Hollywood films, superhero comics, or Tin Pan Alley songs were, above all, interested in leaving behind their (or their parents' or grandparents') immigrant roots and traditional religious observance and assimilating into mainstream American society and that the theater and other forms of popular culture offered a clear escape route. In my own work on Broadway musicals, I have argued that the Jewish creation of popular entertainment is one important way, if not *the* most important way, in which Jews acculturated to America, by creating a fantasy America that is distinctly open to and tolerant of people like them (Most 2004). But this fantasy version of America—and the analyses that explicate it—posit the existence of a secular space outside of and untouched by religious ritual and values. As Pamela Klassen and Courtney Bender note in the introduction to this volume, this American secular space is seen as a kind of level playing field on which various ethnic groups encounter one another and reshape the secular field to accommodate various forms of difference. This model of an American public sphere fails to take into account the deep-seated religious underpinnings of this form of secularism, the multiple and complex ways in which religious communities express values and beliefs, and the unexpected venues in which those expressions appear. Put simply, Judaism has always existed for Jews beyond the reaches of the synagogue and organized religious practice, and in the early and mid-twentieth century, Judaism continued to shape the worldview of so-called assimilated or secular Jews, albeit in ways that were not as obviously "religious" or "Jewish" as the observance of holidays or the maintenance of dietary laws. The films, plays, and novels I discuss in this chapter offer complex visions of imagined communities, individual desire, communal responsibility, and sacred space that emerge from the encounter of Judaic and Protestant worldviews that characterized the early- and mid-twentieth-century American Jewish experience. Furthermore, the Jewish worldview that permeates much of American theatrical culture of the twentieth century did not speak only to the Jews who created it. Its enormous popularity demonstrates the power of these ideas for many Americans, and offers a highly complex picture of the ways in which religious communities intersect and transform themselves within a pluralist national context.[5] As we will see, first- and second-generation American Jewish writers and directors negotiated a position for themselves within and alongside Protestant American liberalism by reimagining key aspects of traditional Jewish culture as theatrical.[6] In an extraordinary outpouring of artistic, cultural, and commercial energy, these artists of the 1920s, 1930s, and 1940s created a popular culture that offered one of the best expressions of what it might mean to be a modern American Jew. I call this worldview theatrical liberalism.

AMERICAN JEWISH SECULARISM AND AMERICAN LIBERALISM

The *Oxford American Dictionary of Current English* (1999:728) defines *secular* as "concerned with the affairs of this world; not spiritual or sacred," and the *New Oxford American Dictionary* defines it as "denoting attitudes, activities, or other things that have no religious or spiritual basis" (McKean 2005). Theatrical liberalism begins from an assumption shared by many of the essays in this volume: that the terms *religion* and *secular* cannot be understood as universal categories. Both terms share a distinct history that situates them firmly within the Protestant Reformation and Enlightenment. The phrase "Jewish secular culture" furthermore implies a complex history of the relationship between Jews and their host cultures. Jewish secular culture is no more universal than "secular" and "Jewish" are, and to understand how and why particular Jewish cultural expressions took root in twentieth-century America, we first need to understand more generally what we mean when we talk about secular culture in America.

In the face of advances in science and the rise of liberal political systems in Europe and America in the late nineteenth century, scholars began to describe what became known as the secularization thesis, which argued that with the advent of modernity, the world was becoming progressively less religious.[7] In the past few decades, religious studies scholars have taken issue both with the thesis itself (it turns out that modern societies have not followed the neat arc defined by the thesis; religion has survived and been transformed in the modern age) and with the universalizing assumptions on which the secularization thesis relies. As Janet R. Jakobsen makes clear in chapter 1 of this volume, secularism cannot be understood as a general category; indeed, she argues, American secularism can be understood only in relation to the Protestant values that shaped so much of U.S. history. Recognizing the Protestant basis for the idea of the universal secular, she asserts, will allow us to begin to distinguish between different responses to Protestantism and different types of secularisms.

This rethinking of the secular is rooted in a reconsideration of the meaning of religion itself (Asad 1993). For example, both Tomoko Masuzawa (2005) and Robert J. Baird (2000) argue in their recent work that religion is a modern and Protestant construction. The notion of religion as a particular aspect of social life rather than the organizing principle of a civilization, Masuzawa argues, is a uniquely Protestant and modern idea, and the idea of "world religions" is closely linked to the rise of a particular nationalist and imperialist ideology (as Todd also shows in chap. 8, this volume). Baird pushes this further, arguing that "world religions" have long been understood in terms of their resemblance to or difference from Protestantism. Pointing to David Hume's eighteenth-century tract, *The Natural History of Religion*, Baird (2000:128) argues that Hume and other Protestant enlightenment thinkers grouped together those aspects of a culture's social life that, like Protestantism, emphasized private, individual confessions of faith and called them religion: "For both Hume and his polemical targets, the Deists and rationalizers, *religion consists solely of a set of coherent propositions, and religious faith is reconceived fundamentally as an assent to the truth of these propositions*." Janet Jakobsen and Ann Pellegrini (2000:8) have argued that this new classification system not only created a set of practices called religions but also created pressure on non-Protestant groups to reinvent themselves as religions in order to achieve rights, freedoms, or social powers. If certain private, individual acts are labeled as religion, then the rest of a culture becomes secular. American secularism therefore is built on a Protestant model that divides aspects of culture into public and private spheres and relegates religion to the private sphere.

How does Judaism, which has never neatly conformed to this public–private model, fit into this picture? Whereas nineteenth-century liberal Jewish movements in both Central Europe and America incorporated many of these Protestant ideas about religion, a number of Jewish thinkers in early-twentieth-century America were self-consciously critical of Jewish movements modeled along Protestant lines. Rabbi Israel Friedlaender, an important figure in the early days of the Jewish Theological Seminary, wrote in 1919,

> It was a fatal mistake of the period of emancipation, a mistake which is the real source of all the subsequent disasters in modern Jewish life, that, in order to facilitate the fight for political equality, Judaism was put forward not as a culture, as the full

expression of the inner life of the Jewish people, but as a creed, as the summary of a few abstract articles of faith, similar in character to the religion of the surrounding nations. (quoted in Kaplan 1934:vii)

Mordecai Kaplan, the founder of the Reconstructionist movement in Judaism, likewise argued in his manifesto *Judaism as a Civilization* (1934) that Judaism can survive in the face of science and skepticism only if it reembraces the concept of Jewishness as a complete way of life, not simply a matter of private faith. Contemporary religion scholar Laura Levitt reinforces these early thinkers, picking up on Baird's argument to show how many Jewish communities in Western and Central Europe, which up until emancipation were "self-governing corporate bod[ies]," were transformed in the nineteenth century into collections of voluntary individual adherents to a particular faith:

> What religion offered to Jews in the liberal West was a Protestant version of religious community that they could apply to themselves as Jews. . . . Although political emancipation was the product of the age of reason, the end of the rule of religion, for Jews in the West, this version of the rule of reason brought with it, ironically, a reaffirmation of religion, and specifically of religion as a kind of faith. (Levitt 2007:811–812)

In other words, in order to achieve civil rights, these liberalizing Jews redefined themselves as members of a religion, Judaism, which much more closely resembled Protestantism. Levitt historicizes liberal Judaism in this way in order to draw connections between this transformation of Judaism and the varieties of Jewish secularism that emerged in its wake, in particular to draw a distinction between the secularism of Central European Jewish immigrants to America and that of Eastern European immigrants, who, because they were not in constant contact with a liberal, Protestant state, did not share the same early pressure to transform Judaism into a faith-based religion. Levitt (2007:828) argues that Yiddish secular culture in America offered a means to resist the faith-based idea of community largely embraced by Central European Jewish immigrants.

Levitt's genealogy of American Jewish resistance to a Protestantized version of Judaism is echoed in Naomi Seidman's (2007) recent work on Jewish secularization. A pioneering attempt at what she calls "a Jewish secularization thesis," Seidman's essay demonstrates the ways in which the Jewish case never neatly fit into the secularization thesis. Jewish secularization, Seidman argues, occurred largely in response to the particular political and cultural position of Jews in European society rather than as a response to an internal crisis of faith, as was the case for Protestants. And Jewish secularization is commonly characterized as a change in practice rather than belief—

the disintegration of religious practice among modernizing Jews and the assimilation of those same Jews, via new practices, habits, and modes of self-presentation, into the surrounding Christian community. Seidman shows how these differences in Jewish secularization led to a dialectical process of modernization, one shaped by both the Europeanization of Judaism and the almost simultaneous resistance to that Europeanization through what Seidman (2007:15) calls "post-secularization": "The Haskalah served both as the ideological platform for secularization and a brake on the process; at different moments and in different contexts, the maskilim were either the avant-garde of secularization or a rear-guard insisting on some maintenance of Jewish affiliation in the wake of its disappearance."[8] Both Seidman and Levitt argue that many Jews resisted (or at least were ambivalent about) a secularization that so acutely circumscribed religious identity, and they point to aspects of Eastern European Jewish literary and political culture—Hebraic, Zionist, Yiddish, socialist—as sites of this resistance.

American Jewish responses to liberal Protestant ideas about the role of faith and religion in the public sphere were likewise complex and multifaceted. Many, especially Jews of Central European descent, gladly embraced a new identity in America that defined them as members of a particular faith, with all the religious and political freedoms granted to such faith groups; the Reform movement modeled many of its practices on mainline American Protestant behaviors. As Levitt shows, a portion of Eastern European Jewish immigrants turned to another model, that of secular Yiddish culture—theater, literature, politics, and art—as a means of achieving the rights and religious freedoms promised by American law while still resisting self-definition as a faith group.[9] In Jewish-created popular culture in the non-Jewish public sphere—the Hollywood films, Broadway plays, and popular novels written by secular American Jews—we find yet another distinctively Jewish response to the pressures of Protestant secularization. These secular Jews can be understood not simply as Jews who have given up religion but as Jews who inhabit a public space shaped by a liberal Protestant conception of the private nature of faith. The quality of this American and English-language version of Jewish secularization is more elusive than its Yiddish counterpart not only because it is embedded directly in Protestant secular culture but because it is designed expressly to appeal to members of that culture. At the same time, this form of Jewish secular culture has turned out to be the most resilient, perhaps because it is the most organically American. Although these writers and artists come from a wide variety of Jewish backgrounds, they are united by a liberal Jewish perspective that insists on the potential compatibility of Judaism with American liberalism. Rather than creating alternative secular spaces in which to inhabit a Jewish cosmos, therefore, these artists worked within the existing mainline Protestant secular culture and found ways to reshape it to better reflect their own values, practices, and larger world-view. They wanted to be Americans, so they created works of American popular culture that not only would allow them to participate in that culture but would allow them to do so on their own terms.

These secular Jews dove headfirst into the raucous, vulgar, chaotic world of American performance in the early twentieth century, passionately embraced it, and celebrated it without shame. Within the elastic boundaries of this popular culture, they reimagined familiar Jewish values, practices, and attitudes in theatrical terms, simultaneously easing their own acculturation and creating enormously successful works that tapped into early-twentieth-century America's inherent theatricality. The new genres that emerged to express this secular and theatrical Judaism—backstage musicals, fast-talking comedies, musical plays—are both Jewish and American. To identify this elusive American Jewish secular culture is not, for the most part, to look for overtly religious or ethnic representations on stage and screen. Rather, this project explores more subtle affinities between Judaism and the theater. These works of secular American Jewish culture combine familiar Jewish rhetorical structures, attitudes, and behaviors with more typically American characters and settings, creating a truly hybrid American Jewish culture that speaks to a broad American public. The very impulses that made these works so popular also make them the best examples of the dynamics of theatrical liberalism.

Four key features define works of theatrical liberalism. First, these works reconstruct the theater as a sacred space, a venue for religious expression and the performance of acts of devotion, thereby raising the status of theatricality, actors, and the theater to levels never before achieved in American culture. Second, in celebrating theatricality, these plays and films privilege a particularly Jewish attitude toward action and acting in the world, stressing the external over the internal, public over private. Third, these works strenuously resist essentialized identity categories, promoting a particular kind of individual freedom based on self-fashioning. Theatrical liberalism guaranteed secular Jews the freedom to perform the self, a freedom particularly cherished by a people so often denied the right to self-definition, whether by Christian dogma or racial science. And fourth, that individual freedom is circumscribed by a set of incontrovertible obligations to the theatrical community. In these plays and movies, there is a palpable tension between the liberal rhetoric of rights and the Judaic rhetoric of obligation (mitzvot), and the moral weight of these stories turns on the fulfilling of theatrical obligations, even at the expense of individual rights. "The show must go on" becomes the new dogma of the theatrical liberal. I discuss all four of these features in depth in the work from which this chapter is extracted. For the purposes of this chapter, I will focus on the first two: the theater as sacred space and the privileging of action over faith.

FROM THE SACRED TO THE PROFANE: THEATRICALITY AND THE JEWISH PERFORMANCE OF MODERNITY

One of the most Jewish and most successful theatrical works of the 1920s, *The Jazz Singer*, by Samson Raphaelson, performed on Broadway in 1926 and made into the first talking picture, starring Al Jolson in 1927, explicitly depicts the theater as the place where religion goes in secular America.[10] In this play and film, Jakie Rabinowitz becomes the American Jack Robin by performing on the vaudeville stage. This causes a rift between him and his immigrant father, an orthodox cantor on the Lower East Side. Jack tries to convince his father that his choice to be a jazz singer is not so different from being a cantor:

> *Cantor*: I taught you to sing to please God, but you sang to please yourself. One minute you were singing in the synagogue and the next minute singing in the street. . . .
>
> *Jack*: You're right, Papa. I am the same. You did teach me to sing songs of prayer. And I sang them here for you. But when I got out on the street with the other kids, I found myself singing the same songs they sang. And they're very much alike—our songs—and the street songs [*He sings "Ain Kelohenu," a Hebrew prayer tune. And then, suddenly, to exactly the same tune and with exactly the same plaintiveness but with a new rhythm . . . he sings a popular song.*] (Raphaelson 1925:51)

When asked to replace his father in the synagogue instead of performing on Broadway, however, Jack at first argues for the higher calling of the stage: "Show business is different from anything else," he says, "The finest actors keep right on working, even if there's a death in the family. The show must go on. . . . It's like a religion" (Raphaelson 1925:96). Although Jack does agree to grant his father's wish, it is his ultimate conversion to the stage that is most typical of plays and movies of the time. There is a distinctly religious quality to these secular narratives; the theater is described as an all-consuming passion, a tradition, heritage, and way of life to which its adherents owe undying allegiance. Countless rituals and myths shape this religion, and a complex value system determines the morality of those who operate within it.

We have come to accept this theatrical religion as commonplace, even clichéd. Some might toss it off as yet another example of bowing to the "temple of art." But there is nothing particularly sacred about the art here; in fact, the vaudeville show Jack appears in is a distinctly commercial enterprise, and even the producer acknowledges that, aside from Jack's powerful rendering of his blackface "mammy" songs, the show isn't much good. But Jack argues not for his individual performance but for the theater itself as a new object of devotion. The religious content in stories about the theater tends to be overlooked or underplayed because the stories are treated as unequivocally secular works of popular culture, not to mention ephemeral, trivial, and undeserving of serious intellectual attention. Furthermore, these early backstage musicals undermine the conventional moral standards of religious Americans of the time: all those scantily clad women, young people leaving their families to go on the stage, showgirls in dubious relationships with wealthy men, actors pretending to be something they are not. Indeed, many battles were fought, between self-appointed antitheatrical censors and the producers and writers of these shows and films, over the apparently immoral and irreligious nature of theatricality. But although the battles were often framed as a struggle between moral, religious folk and secular, immoral, and money-hungry businessmen and artists (which, in their ugliest characterizations, were represented simply as a battle of Christians vs. Jews), they may be more productively imagined as a battle between competing worldviews, differing visions of what constitutes religion and its corresponding secular culture.[11]

Antitheatricality in Western culture can be traced all the way back to Plato, who was famously hostile to impersonation. As Jonas Barish (1981:2) notes, Plato's hostility to the theater became the cornerstone of an anti-theatrical edifice that has shown remarkable resilience in two millennia of European culture. Whereas epithets from other art forms tend to be used in a positive manner (e.g., an "epic" struggle, "lyrical" beauty, a "musical" voice), he notes, "terms borrowed from the theatre—theatrical, operatic, melodramatic, stagey, etc.—tend to be hostile or belittling. And so do a wide range of expressions drawn from theatrical activity expressly to convey disapproval: *acting, play acting, playing up to, putting on an act, putting on a performance, making a scene, making a spectacle of oneself*" (Barish 1981:1).

For many centuries, the Catholic church tolerated theatrical spectacle that emerged from religious activity (medieval church drama and passion plays), but with the rise of Calvinism in the sixteenth century, religiously based antitheatrical movements gained momentum in many parts of Western Europe. The legitimization of the secular Elizabethan stage created a Puritan backlash that ultimately led to the brief closing of the British theaters in 1642. Various Puritan pamphleteers labeled actors hypocrites, considered the creation of an alternative world on the stage tantamount to idolatry (competing with God for the gift of creation), fulminated against cross-dressing on the stage, and generally accused the theater of encouraging lewd and lascivious behavior (Barish 1981). According to Puritan pamphleteer William Prynne, God determined the character of each person, and it would be sinful and hypocritical to attempt to alter one's character through play-acting: "He enjoy[n]es all men at all times, *to be such in shew, as they are in truth: to seeme that outwardly which they are inwardly*; to act themselves, not others" (Barish 1981:92). Absolute sincerity is the mandate of every good Christian, and the stage was seen as a sinful impediment to that goal. Lingering Puritanical influence, combined with the fact that the British theater was connected to the monarchy, led to highly ambivalent reactions to theatrical activity in the newly formed American republic. In 1778, the Continental Congress passed an edict condemning the stage and demanding the dismissal of any government official "who shall act, promote, encourage, or attend such plays" (Gilmore 1994:577). Massachusetts banned plays of any kind until 1792, and even supporters of the stage, who prized the democratic social encounters it made possible, condemned the moral laxity of actors and associated the theater with prostitution (Gilmore 1994:578).

This bias against actors continued even when other prejudices against the theater began to soften. In nineteenth-century America, although high-society theater audiences often enjoyed stage spectacles, they rarely consented to admit professional performers into their ranks. An overview of popular plays and melodramas of the period reveals a persistent sense that performing on the stage is seductive, sinful, and vulgar and that those who practice the theatrical arts are neither respectable nor trustworthy. The theater is represented in countless nineteenth- and early-twentieth-century plays as an especially dangerous place for young women, whose virtue would be sullied by the very act of appearing on the stage.[12] Interestingly, Jews were often implicated in this antitheatricality; Jewish rootlessness was conflated with theatricality in the works of countless European and American novelists of the nineteenth and early twentieth centuries, and both were viewed with suspicion by many nineteenth-century dramatists as well.[13] In *The Gay Science*, Friedrich Nietzsche identifies what he sees as a peculiar and insistent relationship between Jews and performance, claiming that the Jews are "a people possessing the art of adaptability par excellence" and equating acting with the condition of being a Jew: "What good actor today is *not*—a Jew?" he asks (2001:226). In late-eighteenth-century France, the questions of Jewish citizenship and of the rights of actors were debated simultaneously. As Jonas Barish (1981:467) argues, anti-Semitism and antitheatricalism share many common features. One example (among many) of the many popular antitheatrical melodramas of the late nineteenth century that makes use of anti-Semitism to make its point is *Trilby*, adapted by American playwright Paul M. Potter from George du Maurier's novel of the same name. This play centers on the actions of the evil Svengali, a Jewish maestro who snatches a young, innocent French girl from her fiancé and forces her, through the powers of hypnosis, to perform as a singer on the stage.

Although early modern traditional European Jewish communities were equally antitheatrical, theater held a carefully circumscribed place within the culture, bursting forth on Purim, when role-playing, pageantry, costumes, and general hilarity were mandated by Jewish law and in wedding celebrations, where the *badkhn*, or wedding-jester, told stories and jokes, and his accompanying *klezmorim* (musicians) performed musical numbers for the bride and groom and their guests. Nonreligious theatrical activity was constrained by a number of factors: biblical prohibitions against cross-dressing, rabbinic prohibitions against a woman singing (or, by extension, performing) in public, and the general resistance to any form of intellectual or artistic pursuit that fell outside of the study of Torah (Sandrow 1995).[14] At the same time, traditional European Jewish communities, with a few exceptions, did not subscribe to Puritanical notions about sincerity and constancy. Although lying is certainly not sanctioned in traditional Jewish life, certain allowances are made for acting that leads to righteous behavior or the furthering of God's will, such as Jacob pretending to be Esau, Tamar pretending to be a prostitute, and Esther hiding her identity in the king's palace. Furthermore, because of the particular historical circumstances Jews faced, it was understood that one might have to "pretend to be what one was not" in order to survive in a hostile world.[15]

In both Europe and America, the emergence of Jewish culture from this traditional religious context was nearly always accompanied by significant Jewish production of secular theater and, in particular, plays that explored the ambivalence Jews felt about the shifting identity boundaries characteristic of modern life. In eighteenth-century Berlin, for example, Jewish playwrights used characters speaking multiple languages (French, German, Yiddish, Hebrew) to signify particular attitudes toward religious and public life and to express complicated ideas about enlightenment, class, and assimilation (Feiner 2002).[16] In late-nineteenth-century Eastern Europe, Jews founded a Yiddish-language secular theater that was equally obsessed with modernity and assimilation. Indeed, Jewish modernity itself can be understood as a kind of theatrical endeavor. Wherever Jews were forced, by historical circumstances, to adopt double roles, to use performance as a survival strategy, there we see the twin roots of Jewish modernity and Jewish theatricality. For example, Gershom Scholem (1971: 78–141) argues that we can locate the beginning of modern Jewish self-consciousness in the experiences of the Spanish Jews of the fifteenth and sixteenth centuries forced to live as Marranos: Christians in public, Jews in private. This distinction between inner and outer selves was later turned into a more general maxim for Jewish modernization by poet Judah Leib

Gordon (1980:313) when he exhorted Russian Jews to be a "man abroad and a Jew in your tent." That theatrical sense of playing a role in public increasingly pervaded the writing of modernizing Jews and indeed became its defining feature.

The theatricality of Jewish modernity reached an apotheosis in early-twentieth-century America, when Jewish writers and artists entered a culture already shifting in favor of what Warren Susman called "the culture of personality" and began to create popular works that aggressively countered Calvinist antitheatrical bias, works that lifted up the actor and the theatrical arts to a level never before imagined in American culture (Susman 2003:271–285).[17] With the entrance en masse of first- and second-generation Jewish writers, directors, and producers into the world of American entertainment, the theater underwent a radical shift. Theatrical life was transformed from the "wicked stage" to the most celebrated, most American, and most desirable way to live. An enormously successful new form, the backstage drama (or backstage musical), emerged to articulate this new ethos, and plays about actors or about putting on a show became an extremely popular and long-lasting feature of American popular culture.[18] In the musical number "Life Upon the Wicked Stage," from the Hammerstein and Kern operetta *Show Boat*, for example, a show boat actress comically bemoans the fact that the antitheatrical connection between stage performance and sexual immorality is, alas, mistaken. "The wicked stage," it turns out, is not so wicked after all. Ellie laments that, contrary to what a girl supposes, although one may depict vice in the theater (she tells us later that she can "play a hussy or a paramour"), the actress retains her virtue, much to her chagrin. Although life on the stage does not necessarily lead to a better sex life off stage, it does offer something else that more than compensates for this lack:

I admit it's fun to smear my face with paint,
Causing ev'ryone to think I'm what I ain't,
And I like to play a demi-mondy role, with soul!

Here *role* is rhymed with *soul*, implicitly connecting the internal with the external performance. For Ellie, the reward of acting is the soulful pleasure of performance itself. At the end of the song, she claims,

If some gentleman would talk with reason
I would cancel all next season.
Life upon the wicked stage
Ain't nothin' for a girl!

But her chorus immediately disputes this, responding, "You'd be back the season after!" The theater may not offer Ellie the life of decadence and glamour she desires and the nineteenth-century guardians of moral virtue abhorred, but it does offer something even more powerful. The freedom to "cause everyone to think you're what you ain't" is not dispensed with lightly.

Whereas for centuries the theater was seen by most American Protestants as opposed to the values of good Christians, plays and films of the early twentieth century began to feature positive comparisons between the theater (or "show business") and a moral life. Conversion to the ethos of the stage was a staple of the backstage musical in the 1930s. A typical Warner Brothers musical of the era, *Dames* (1934), for example, features the Puritanical and antitheatrical Ezra Ounce, who leads a crusade against the very theater in which his nephew and niece are performing, only to be converted to the delights of the stage by the end.[19] In George S. Kaufman and Edna Ferber's comedy *Stage Door* (1936), the central character, Terry, describes her commitment to the stage: "It was almost a spiritual thing, like being dedicated to the church" (Ferber and Kaufman 2004:626).[20] Similarly, in both Ben Hecht and Charles MacArthur's movie *Twentieth Century* and Ferber and Kaufman's play *Royal Family*, wavering converts are convinced to return to the stage when given the opportunity to perform in explicitly religious (albeit Christian) passion plays. Richard Rodgers and Lorenz Hart's hit musical *Babes in Arms* (1937) proposes the theater as the route to a more Emersonian-style salvation: Putting on a successful show is a sign of self-reliance that will prevent the kids of Seaport, Long Island, from being sent away to a work camp, where they will be "public charges."[21]

Show Boat, in all its various incarnations—the novel by Edna Ferber (1926), the fabulously successful stage musical with music and lyrics by Jerome Kern and Oscar Hammerstein (1927, as well as four Broadway revivals), and the two Hollywood films—retells American history, from the 1870s to the 1920s, as a story about the theater and in doing so reinvents theatricality as a respectable mode of American national and spiritual expression.[22] Just as in the backstage film musicals, the battle between the forces of Protestant antitheatricality and the more liberal, freedom-loving, and tolerant world of stage actors is foregrounded in the story. In Ferber's novel, the mother, Parthenia Ann Hawks (Parthy), is described as belonging to "the tribe of Knitting Women; of the Salem Witch Burners; of all fanatics who count nature as an enemy to be suppressed; and in whose veins the wine of life runs vinegar" (Ferber 1994:25). When her husband, Andy, presented her with the idea of living on a show boat, "the Puritan in her ran rampant. He would disgrace her before the community. He was ruining the life of his child" (Ferber 1994:47). Likewise, in one of Parthy's first scenes in the play, she makes clear her feelings about the theater in a tirade to her husband, now Captain Andy, the director of the show boat:

> An' you—you think more of your show boat troupe than you do of your own daughter's upbringing. . . . Well, thank God, her mother had a good Christian bringin' up in Massachusetts. Where I come from, no decent body'd touch this show boat riff-raff with a ten foot pole—let alone have their daughters mixed up with them. (*Show Boat* [1927], act 1, scene 1, p. 12)

Parthy makes it clear that despite the fact that the family lives on the boat, she does not want her daughter becoming an actress: "You stick to the pianner, young lady—no play-actin' for you." And yet, despite her apparent reliance on long-established American moral codes, in the context of *Show Boat* Parthy's "religion" represents an immoral obstacle not only to the freedom of the characters to live, work, and love as they choose but to the very liberal ideals on which America is founded. Parthy's views are mocked in the novel, and she is given no songs in the musical. Instead, audience and reader sympathy is quickly won by the theatrical characters, including the two stars in Parthy's own family: her husband, Captain Andy, and their daughter, Magnolia. It is ultimately Captain Andy, a firm believer in the moral and spiritual power of theatricality, whose values lead the show boat, Magnolia, and the nation into a new age.

The end of the Warner Brothers film version of *The Jazz Singer* (1927) makes a more direct comparison between the theater and the synagogue, and both are acknowledged as spiritually edifying. Furthermore, the progression from one to the other is represented not as a fall from a higher moral position but as a natural development of Old World Jewish values. Torn between replacing his father at services on the eve of Yom Kippur and performing opening night in his first Broadway show, Jakie finally decides to honor his father and return to the Lower East Side. He passionately chants the Kol Nidre service as his father dies. At the same time, his producer and costar girlfriend listen through a window. The girlfriend directly compares his chanting to his stage performances. The intertitle reads, "A jazz singer—singing to his God." Jakie sings the final climactic note of Kol Nidre, and the film cuts immediately to an intertitle that reads, "The season passes—and time heals—and the show goes on," and then it cuts immediately to Jolson's famous star turn as Jack Robin in blackface singing "Mammy." "The show goes on" is an ambiguous intertitle here: Which show? Is the synagogue service "going on" in Jakie's plaintive mammy-songs? Or vice versa? As the film ends, with a shot of Jakie's beaming mother in the front row of the audience, it becomes clear that in America, the best possible answer is *both*.

ACTION AND ACTING: THE ART OF DEEDS

> A Jew is asked to take a *leap of action* rather than a *leap of thought*. He is asked to surpass his needs, to do more than he understands in order to understand more than he does. . . . Right living is a way to right thinking.
>
> —Abraham Joshua Heschel, *God in Search of Man*

> Acting is the most exact and exacting of arts. In it nothing can ever be left to chance—to an inspiration of the moment. . . . To wait, in acting, for inspiration to flash upon you is about as sensible as to wait until your house is in flames before looking for a fire escape. Night after night, often for many months, the same words must be spoken, the same actions be performed in the same way. . . . It is, I believe, safe to say that no actor ever produced a truly great effect in acting except as a result of long study, close thought, deliberate purpose and careful preparation.
>
> —David Belasco, "Acting as a Science"

In the opening scene of the Hecht–MacArthur film *Twentieth Century*, star director Oscar Jaffe (John Barrymore) teaches a lingerie model, Lily Garland (née Mildred Plotka, and played by Carole Lombard, née Jane Alice Peters) to act. The process is slow, methodical, and painful. First, she must learn to enter a room with the proper bearing and composure. She must speak with the right accent and tone. Then she must walk across the stage in the correct manner, and stop in a particular place before speaking her next line. Lily has difficulty remembering when and where to walk and to speak, and so Jaffe demands chalk and begins to draw lines on the stage indicating exactly where she should be at each moment in the play. Near the end of the scene, a shot from above reveals a stage completely covered by white chalk lines. Lily must also learn how to scream in agony when her character learns that her lover is dead. She can't do it. Finally, Jaffe helps her along by sticking a pin into her backside at the appropriate moment. It works, Lily screams convincingly, and is soon on her way to becoming a Broadway star. This method of building character involves little discussion of emotion and certainly no discussion of the actor's own internal psychological motivations. The acting philosophy of *Twentieth Century*, and of countless similar representations of acting, is simple and straightforward: Walk here, say this, a little louder, now walk there, look behind you, sit down, moan softly. Do it over and over again until you feel it, understand it, and can convey it to those sitting in the very back row of the balcony.

Glancing through a prayer book in my synagogue one Shabbat morning, I found a set of penciled-in notes, a reminder a congregant or perhaps a nervous bar mitzvah boy or novice prayer leader had jotted down, indicating how one should recite the *musaf amidah*, the set of prayers that conclude the morning Shabbat service. To paraphrase the instructions (a set of behaviors that are regular practice in any traditional synagogue), "Rise. Take three steps forward, then three back. Bow slightly. Sing altogether. Say this part to yourself. Mumble aloud. Repeat. Rise up on toes three times. Bend knees and bow slightly. Say this part only between Sukkot and Passover. Step backward and forward, sway to the right, the left and bow forward. Sit down." Similarly detailed instructions can be found in the Passover Haggadah: "Distribute pieces of the bottom matzah. Take a piece of matzah and break it into two pieces. Add the bitter herbs, dip it into the charoset, and eat it while reclining to the left." How do you light candles on Hanukkah? First, be sure your head is covered. Put the candles into the menorah from right to left, and light them from left to right, using not a match but a separate candle, called a *shamash*. There are two blessings to say each night and an additional blessing to say on the first night. This kind of detailed instruction about how to act Jewishly is not limited to rituals related to praying in synagogue and observing holidays. One can find explicit, detailed instructions for daily behaviors of all sorts. How does a Jew wash hands before eating? Use a cup, not the faucet. Pour water on each hand three times, alternating hands each time. Then say the blessing while drying your hands. If you are washing as part of the Friday evening Shabbat dinner, bless the wine first, then wash, then bless and cut the bread. No one should speak until the bread is blessed, but humming is permitted. An observant Jew can find in the Talmud instructions on just about any action a Jew might do in the course of everyday life, including having sex: "There must be close bodily contact during sex. This means that a husband must not treat his wife in the manner of the Persians, who perform their marital duties in their clothes" (Babylonian Talmud, Ketubot 48a).

For Oscar Jaffe, acting in the theater demands, above all, close and careful attention to the details of everyday behavior. So does Judaism. Like David Belasco,[23] whose statements on acting opened this section and on whom the character of Oscar Jaffe was based, Jaffe knows that if Lily practices enough, and does so with the proper spirit and attitude, eventually she will be a great actor. For Abraham Joshua Heschel (1955:345), one of the most important American Jewish theologians of the twentieth century, practicing is also key: "A good person is not he who does the right thing, but he who is in the habit of doing the right thing." Heschel (1955:403) argued for the importance of *acting* Jewishly, even if one doesn't understand exactly why or doesn't feel spiritually moved to do so: "Judaism insists upon the deed and hopes for the intention." Action is the first step to spiritual illumination, not the last. Inverting a famous line of Proverbs, Heschel insists, "The way to pure intention is paved with good deeds." From doing will eventually come understanding: "It is the act that teaches us the meaning of the act" (Heschel 1955:404). Acting on the stage and acting Jewishly clearly have many affinities, and this common ground provided a space for secularizing Jews to maintain a familiar stance toward everyday behavior while dispensing with the overtly religious rituals that formed obstacles to acculturation to the American way of life. In the self-consciously theatrical world of many early-twentieth-century plays and films, a good performance was the measure of a good actor. What an actor did on the stage is what mattered; what an actor believed—who an actor *really was*—was of little interest. Theatrical liberalism privileged this external and public version of a self, the acting self. Americans have long wrestled with questions about where the "truth" of a self lies, and although action in the world has often been seen as a sign of good internal character, for most Protestants, internal, private faith is the driving force that animates action (rather than the other way around); faith, and the kinds of character traits that allow for and support Christian faith, determine one's chances of salvation and move one to act morally in the world. This Protestant divide between action in the world and private faith deeply influenced early liberal thinkers and helped to shape American attitudes toward freedom of religion. For John Locke, for example, religion was largely a matter of faith, and faith is a private, not a state, matter. Separating church from civil government in this way allowed Locke (2003:240) to argue for civil rights not only for Catholics and Protestants but also for Jews, because a Jew's faith was not—in his liberal philosophy—the concern of the civil sphere.

When Jewish thinkers began to engage with liberal ideas, they revealed the ways in which Protestant Enlightenment notions of religious toleration imperfectly fit the lives Jews actually lived. Eighteenth-century Jewish philosopher Moses Mendelssohn responded to Locke by exploring the tension in Judaism between action and faith. In *Jerusalem* (1783), he wrote, "Among all the prescriptions and ordinances of the Mosaic law, there is not a single one which says: *You shall believe or not believe*. They all say: *You shall do or not do*. . . . Nowhere does it say: *Believe, O Israel, and you will be blessed; do not doubt, O Israel, or this or that punishment will befall you*" (100). Mendelssohn acknowledges that faith is needed for one to accept the obligations of a Jewish life but points out that professions of faith are not needed in and of themselves.[24] He points to one of the key defining moments for Judaism when Moses, after receiving the Ten Commandments on Mt. Sinai, recited them aloud to the assembled Israelites at the foot of the mountain. The people then agreed to the terms of the covenant with God, saying, "Na'aseh v'nishma," the exact Hebrew translation of which is "We will do and we will hear" (Exodus 24:7). This phrase has been the source of centuries of discussion among Jews because of the apparently reversed order of the verbs. Shouldn't we hear first and do afterward? On the contrary, argue Jewish thinkers across the ages (Abraham Joshua Heschel among them). "Na'aseh v'nishma," we will do and we will hear, argues for the importance of following laws, of acting, of living a life according to Jewish law, *in order to* learn or "hear" why, in order to develop greater understanding of the divine, and in order to bring the world closer to redemption (Heschel 1955:281).[25]

Up until the modern period, to be a Jew therefore was not primarily to profess a particular set of beliefs but to act Jewishly in everything one does, from the foods one eats, to the clothes one wears, to the ways in which one interacts with other members of the community, to the role one takes in caring for one's house, crops, livestock, or the earth itself. As Tevye says at the beginning of *Fiddler on the Roof*, "Here in Anatevka we have traditions for everything, how to eat, how to sleep, even how to wear clothes" (Harnick 2000:2). Thousands of Jewish immigrants arrived on America's shores with direct, lived experience of a traditional society deeply concerned with the ethical and spiritual implications of everyday behavior. As John Dewey (1934:60) noted in *A Common Faith*, Jewish immigrants were among the few Americans who, in the early twentieth century, had a self-conscious connection to a religious civilization that permeated all aspects of daily life and that was not limited to private, interior confessions of faith: "There are a few persons, especially those brought up in Jewish communities in Russia, who can understand without the use of imagination what a religion means socially when it permeates all the customs and activities of group life. To most of us in the United States such a situation is only a remote historic episode."

Accustomed to a culture that asserted the primacy of ritual and deed over declarations of faith, these immigrants confronted in early-twentieth-century America the oppositional force (and seductive energy) of a liberal political and social model that granted them freedom of belief and freedom of speech but not necessarily the cultural freedom to act in accordance with those beliefs. For the most part, no civil law in America circumscribed the practice of Jewish rituals such as kashrut, Sabbath observance, and the covering of heads. But the overtly secular, tacitly Protestant cultural and social sphere shaped all the contours of modern American life, from the calendar and daily cycle, to the proper place and time for religious practice, to the forms and content of public education, to attitudes toward social life, eating, fashion, and relations between the sexes and between parents and children. This transparent overlay of Christian social practice in America made it almost impossible to become fully accepted Americans without giving up public signs of religious difference.[26] Most American Jewish writers and thinkers of this generation departed from orthodox

Jewish practice, but even the most assimilated of them did not completely embrace a worldview that relegated religious action to the private sphere.[27] Rather, Jewish writers and performers shaped a new kind of American public sphere, one that relocated the Jewish spiritual obligation to act in the world from an Old World religious context to a legitimately American arena, the world of popular entertainment.

Just as Heschel insists that "we do not have faith because of deeds; we may attain faith through sacred deeds," the plays, films, and novels of theatrical liberalism argue for the power of acting to shape belief and feeling. In Rodgers and Hammerstein's *The King and I*, for example, the female lead, Anna, teaches her son to banish fear by whistling. In the song "I Whistle a Happy Tune," the external performance of bravery actually effects an internal change from fear to confidence:

I whistle a happy tune,
And ev'ry single time
The happiness in the tune
Convinces me that I'm
Not afraid. (Rodgers and Hammerstein 1955:373)[28]

Show Boat similarly dramatizes the power of acting in one of its opening songs, "Make Believe." Gaylord Ravenal, a dashing gambler, and Magnolia, Andy and Parthy's daughter, have just seen one another on the dock. Magnolia insists they should not be speaking because they have not been introduced. Ravenal, an experienced gambler, is well versed in the theatrical arts. He suggests that they "make believe [they] know each other," arguing in song:

If the things we dream about
Don't happen to be so,
That's just an unimportant technicality.

Ravenal dismisses any antitheatrical prejudice against play-acting as "an unimportant technicality" and wholeheartedly engages in a serious game of acting. When Magnolia, eager to be an actress, jumps into the game, he pushes further, suggesting they pretend that they have "fallen in love at first sight." Gaylord sings,

Only make believe I love you,
Only make believe that you love me.
Others find peace of mind in pretending—
Couldn't you? Couldn't I? Couldn't we?

Magnolia responds eagerly and innocently, but she has not yet fully come to understand the power of acting to shape her world. They are, after all, just pretending:

If we put our thoughts in practice
We can banish all regret
Imagining most anything we choose.
We could make believe I love you,
We could make believe that you love me.

Magnolia's interior world is driving the game (she "put[s] [her] thoughts in practice"), and she therefore believes she remains in control. She assumes that external acting is far less important than internal motivations. The phrase "make believe" is a telling one, however. To act in a play is to "make" a belief that did not previously exist. Acting the part of lovers quickly leads to a change in their thoughts and feelings:

Magnolia and *Ravenal*: Might as well make believe I love you,
Ravenal: For to tell the truth, I do . . .
(*Ravenal* reaches up and kisses *Magnolia*'s hand. They stand and gaze at each other.)

In "make believe," acting creates faith, not the other way around. In countless similar songs and scenes in backstage musicals, lovers, aspiring performers, and eager idealists are encouraged to act, and from this acting emerge new visions, new love, new worlds.[29]

CONCLUSION: THERE'S NO BUSINESS LIKE SHOW BUSINESS

To conclude, let us return briefly to the work of Irving Berlin. Nearly thirty years after penning "God Bless America," Berlin wrote a rousing anthem that neatly expressed all the values of theatrical liberalism. Introduced in the musical *Annie Get Your Gun* in 1946, "There's No Business Like Show Business" is sung by a couple of theater producers aiming to convert the backwoods Annie Oakley into the world, and worldview, of the theater. Here we see the America on which Berlin asked that God rain blessings. "What's show business?" Annie asks. Her producers respond with a rousing celebration of theatrical liberalism. They describe the many roles available: "The cowboys, the tumblers, the wrestlers, the clowns, / The roustabouts who move the show at dawn." They note that this is a world that is actively self-fashioned—"the costumes, the scenery, the makeup, the props"—a world in which acting takes precedence over truth: "There's no people like show people / They smile when they are low." A world that is meritocratic, with success dependent on good acting:

> *Yesterday they told you you would not go far,*
> *That night you open and there you are,*
> *Next day on your dressing room they've hung a star—*
> *Let's go on with the show.*

The rewards of good acting? "*Ev'rything* about it is appealing." The commitment to acting:

> *You get word before the show has started*
> *That your fav'rite uncle died at dawn.*
> *Top of that your ma and pa have parted,*
> *You're brokenhearted, but you go on.*

And even in a capitalist culture, the obligation to the theater comes first:

> *Even with a turkey that you know will fold,*
> *You may be stranded out in the cold,*
> *Still you wouldn't change it for a sack of gold –*
> *Let's go on with the show.* (Berlin 1949:22–25)

For Berlin, and for the characters in *Annie Get Your Gun*, the theater is "show business." And yet this business differs from most in its ambivalent relationship to profit. In refusing to exchange one's commitment to the stage for a "sack of gold," Berlin's devotees of "show business" revise Max Weber's Protestant work ethic in a manner typical of theatrical liberalism. To stick with the theater, even when it does not generate a profit, does not make rational sense in the world of business. Although success in the theater certainly depends on talent and dedication, for Annie and her colleagues, "show business" is not exactly a calling in the Weberian sense—a God-given vocation through which she can generate profit (Weber 1992:chap. 3). Rather, it is an entire worldview. Individual plays may run forever or fold overnight, but the theater itself is not up for sale. To trade the theater for a sack of gold would be to place oneself outside the theatrical liberal system altogether. Insisting on a vision of America that is theatrical at its core, Irving Berlin's "show business" shows that to be American is to be a theatrical liberal and vice versa. In turning the "wicked stage" into a site for American virtue, theatrical liberalism transformed assimilationist American ideology from an either–or choice between religious Judaism and secular liberalism into a remarkable synthesis of the two, a new American ethos for the twentieth century.

NOTES

1. On "God Bless America," see Library of Congress, http://lcweb2.loc.gov/diglib/ihas/loc.natlib.ihas.200000007/default.html.

2. Dimont (1978:353–373) and Howe (1976) offer examples of the rags-to-riches legends of Jewish popular entertainers.

3. This ground has been well covered in the past twenty years. See Bial (2005), Brooks (2006), Buhle (2007), Gabler (1989), Hoberman and Shandler (2003), Melnick (1999), Most (2004), Rogin (1996), Weber (2005), and Whitfield (1999).

4. The influence of Jews in European popular culture has been less studied than the American context. One important work in this area is Otte (2006).

5. This chapter focuses on the Jewish case and the particular relationship between Jewish-created popular culture and Judaism. But equally fascinating narratives could be told about the Catholic secularism of Irish American drama and the relationship between the black Baptist church, African cultures, and the development of jazz, ragtime, and tap dancing.

6. I am defining as Jewish writers those with a clear connection to traditional Judaism, through their own education, through contact with the Jewish habitus (in Bourdieu's usage) and belief systems of parents or grandparents, or through close enough proximity to a traditional Jewish community to have learned clear messages about what constitutes Jewish values and practices. But the evidence for this Jewish sensibility lies not in the biographies of the writers but in the texts they wrote. As these cultural ideas become part of the popular culture, they take on a life of their own. The Judaic nature of these ideas is by no means the exclusive property of Jews, and many are later adopted by those who have no particular connection to traditional Jewish life. Regarding *habitus*, see Bourdieu (1984:chap. 3).

7. For a nuanced history of the rise and fall of this thesis, see Casanova (1994:chap. 1).

8.. The *Haskalah* is the name for the Jewish Enlightenment, and *maskilim* refers to those who subscribed to the principles of the Haskalah.

9. Some secular Jews also turned to Zionism and Hebrew language as a means of establishing identity. And of course, some American Jews retained their orthodox practices and resisted secularization altogether, whereas others severed all ties to the Jewish community, intermarried with Protestants, and fully assimilated into the mainstream culture.

10. The film has been the subject of intense scholarly interest in the last decade or so because of its use of blackface and the connections it draws between blacks and immigrant Jews. Although that is not the subject of my analysis here, I have written about it elsewhere (Most 2004:32–39). See also Jacobson (1998), Lhamon (1998), and Rogin (1996).

11. On theater censorship battles and religious involvement in the establishment of the Production Code, see Black (1994), Couvares (2006), Johnston (2006), Skinner (1993), and Walsh (1996). On anti-Semitism and censorship, see Carr (2001).

12. For example, *Rollo's Wild Oats* (1920), by Clare Beecher Kummer; *The Chorus Lady* (1907), by James Forbes; *The Torch Bearers* (1922), by George Kelly; and *The Little Clown* (1918), by Avery Hopwood. Also Louisa May Alcott's *Work: A Story of Experience* (1873) and Anna Cora Mowatt's *Autobiography of an Actress; or, Eight Years on the Stage* (1853).

13. See *Oliver Twist* (1838), by Charles Dickens; *The Tragic Muse* (1890), by Henry James; *Daniel Deronda* (1876), by George Eliot; and *Ulysses* (1922), by James Joyce.

14. On the *Purim-spiel*, see Horowitz (2006:chap. 9).

15. See Mary Antin's (1985:18, 20) comments in her memoir *The Promised Land*: "In your father's parlor hung a large colored portrait of Alexander III. The Czar was a cruel tyrant,—oh, it was whispered when doors were locked and shutters tightly barred, at night,—he was a Titus, a Haman, a sworn foe of all Jews,—and yet his portrait was seen in a place of honor in your father's house. You knew why. It looked well when police or government officers came on business. . . . 'It is a false world,' you heard, and you knew it was so, looking at the Czar's portrait. . . . 'Never tell a police officer the truth,' was another saying, and you knew it was good advice."

16. For specific examples, see Isaac Euchel's "A Family Portrait" and Aaron Wolfsohn's "Frivolity and Bigotry," both described in Zinberg (1972–1978:8:chap. 5).

17. Warren Susman (2003) is one of a number of historians who have noted a shift in definitions of the American self in this period from "character" to "personality." See also Halttunen (1982), Rabinowitz (1989), and Trachtenberg (1982).

18. The sheer number of "backstage" titles from the 1920s, 1930s, and 1940s is staggering. Think of *The Jazz Singer, Show Boat, The Royal Family, Stage Door, 42nd Street, Twentieth Century, On Your Toes, Babes in Arms, Annie Get Your Gun*, A *Night at the Opera, Jumbo, Pal Joey, Shall We Dance*, and *Holiday Inn*, to name only a few of the most successful and memorable ones.

19. *Dames* was also produced by Warner Brothers, directed by Ray Enright, with musical numbers by Busby Berkeley, and it starred Warner regulars Ruby Keeler, Dick Powell, and Joan Blondell.

20. *Stage Door* opened at the Musix Box Theatre in New York in October 1936, produced by Sam H. Harris and directed by George S. Kaufman. George S. Kaufman was one of the preeminent writers of Broadway and Hollywood comedies in the late 1920s and 1930s. He wrote satirical musicals with the Gershwins and madcap screenplays for the Marx Brothers as well as important collaborations with Edna Ferber and Moss Hart. His many successful plays were nearly always about actors, the theater, or theatricality. Edna Ferber, likewise, was one of the most popular writers of her day,

with numerous short stories, popular novels, and plays to her name (including her most successful, *Show Boat*).

21. *Babes in Arms* was written by Richard Rodgers and Lorenz Hart, who had already been an extremely successful musical comedy team for more than ten years when this play was produced in 1937 and ran for 289 performances. Both Rodgers and Hart were second-generation Jews of German background.

22. Like Rodgers and Hart, both Jerome Kern and Oscar Hammerstein were of second-generation German Jewish descent (although Hammerstein was only half-Jewish).

23. David Belasco (1853–1931) was a prolific and highly influential Jewish-American playwright, director, and producer. Two of his plays, *Madame Butterfly* and *The Girl of the Golden West*, were adapted by Puccini into operas, and more than forty of Belasco's other stage works were made into films.

24. Heschel does take exception to Mendelssohn's rather single-minded focus on action. For Heschel, intention does matter, and he cautions against interpreting Judaism as exclusively devoted to law. But the relationship of faith (or intention) to action is the issue here. For Mendelssohn and Heschel both, action is a key to understanding (and for Heschel, achieving) Jewish faith. See Heschel (1955:320).

25. Other relevant commentaries on this text include a compilation of well-known midrashim on Exodus 24:7, detailed in Ginzberg (2003:593). See also *Talmud Bavli*, Tractate Shabbat, 88a; *Talmud Bavli*, Tractate Kiddushin, 40b; and on the meaning of *sh'ma* (hearing), see also the section of *Sefer Abudarham* (1340) on kriat sh'ma.

26. The American religious landscape that Jewish immigrants encountered on their arrival in America was—as it has always been—complex and varied. But for most Jewish immigrants, the most relevant distinction was between Christian and Jewish, with Christian further broken down into Protestant and Catholic. Although Jewish immigrants may not have been fully aware of the differences between the many Protestant sects and churches that dotted the American landscape, it was clear that a certain mainline Protestant majority enjoyed political, financial, and cultural power in American society and were therefore the obvious model for those assimilating to American culture. American Catholics such as the Poles, Irish, and Italians, who also shared outsider status for much of the early twentieth century, would not have provided such a model, and neither did the emerging Pentecostal churches, which, though highly theatrical, appealed to a rural population that was also seen to be nativist. Most of the first- and second-generation Jewish writers and composers I study were shaped by the values of the Protestant social gospel that were present in the discourse of American public schools, settlement houses, and social welfare movements located in the major cities of New York and Chicago. See Kraut (1998).

27. This is not to say that Jews were not also extremely protective of the privacy rights guaranteed by the First Amendment. Indeed, to recent immigrants, the freedoms promised by the Constitution appeared to far outweigh the sacrifices inherent in them. The Supreme Court justice to coin the phrase "right to privacy" was also the first Jewish justice, Louis D. Brandeis.

28. See my analysis of this musical in Most (2004:183–196).

29. As I discuss in the longer version of this chapter, the relationship between action and faith varies in Protestant and Jewish theology and at different historical moments.

Versions of Protestant evangelicalism and Jewish Hasidism shift the emphasis between the two and even sometimes reverse them. But the popular moral language of mainline Protestantism that most American Jews encountered was one that dwelt more on conviction in statements of faith rather than ritual practice, whereas the traditional Judaism of most Central and Eastern European Jewish immigrants emphasized the importance of action and ritual. The longer version of this discussion also includes an exploration of different kinds of action and different acting styles using relevant examples from Rodgers and Hart's *Babes in Arms* and Ernst Lubitsch's films *The Love Parade*, *The Smiling Lieutenant*, *Trouble in Paradise*, and *To Be or Not to Be*.

WORKS CITED

Antin, Mary. 1985. *The Promised Land*. Princeton, N.J.: Princeton University Press.

Asad, Talal. 1993. *Genealogies of Religion: Discipline and Reasons of Power in Christianity and Islam*. Baltimore: Johns Hopkins University Press.

Baird, Robert J. 2000. Late Secularism. *Social Text* 18, no. 3:123–136.

Barish, Jonas. 1981. *The Antitheatrical Prejudice*. Berkeley: University of California Press.

Belasco, David. 1970. Acting as a Science. In *Actors on Acting*, ed. Toby Cole and Helen Krich Chinoy, 576–583. New York: Crown.

Bergreen, Laurence. 1990. *As Thousands Cheer*. New York: Viking.

Berlin, Irving. 1949. *Annie Get Your Gun*. New York: Irving Berlin Music Corporation.

Bial, Henry. 2005. *Acting Jewish: Negotiating Ethnicity on the American Stage and Screen*. Ann Arbor: University of Michigan Press.

Black, Gregory D. 1994. *Hollywood Censored*. Cambridge: Cambridge University Press.

Bourdieu, Pierre. 1984. *Distinction: A Social Critique of the Judgement of Taste*. Cambridge, Mass.: Harvard University Press.

Brooks, Vincent. 2006. *You Should See Yourself: Jewish Identity in Post-Modern American Culture*. New Brunswick, N.J.: Rutgers University Press.

Buhle, Paul, ed. 2007. *Jews and American Popular Culture*. Westport, Conn.: Praeger.

Carr, Steven Alan. 2001. *Hollywood and Anti-Semitism*. New York: Cambridge University Press.

Casanova, José. 1994. *Public Religions in the Modern World*. Chicago: University of Chicago Press.

Corliss, Richard. 2001. That Old Christmas Feeling: Irving America. *Time*, December 24. http://www.time.com/time/sampler/article/0,8599,189846,00.html (accessed January 9, 2010).

Couvares, Francis G., ed. 2006. *Movie Censorship and American Culture*. Amherst: University of Massachusetts Press.

Dewey, John. 1934. *A Common Faith*. New Haven, Conn.: Yale University Press.
Dimont, Max I. 1978. *The Jews in America: The Roots, History and Destiny of American Jews*. New York: Simon & Schuster.
Feiner, Shmuel. 2002. *The Jewish Enlightenment*. Philadelphia: University of Pennsylvania Press.
Ferber, Edna. 1926/1994. *Show Boat*. New York: Penguin.
Ferber, Edna. 1927. *Show Boat*. New York: Billy Rose Theater Collection, New York Public Library.
Ferber, Edna. 1938/1961. *A Peculiar Treasure*. New York: Lancer.
Ferber, Edna, and George S. Kaufman. 2004. *Stage Door*. In *Kaufman & Co: Broadway Comedies*, 591–685. New York: Library of America [Penguin].
Freedland, Michael. 1986. *A Salute to Irving Berlin*. London: Allen.
Friedlaender, Israel. 1919. *Past and Present*. Cincinnati: Arkansas Publication Co.
Furia, Philip. 1998. *Irving Berlin*. New York: Schirmer.
Gabler, Neal. 1989. *An Empire of Their Own: How the Jews Invented Hollywood*. New York: Doubleday.
Gilmore, Michael T. 1994. The Literature of the Revolutionary and Early National Periods. In *Cambridge History of American Literature*. Vol. 1, 1590–1820, ed. Sacvan Bercovitch, 539–693. Cambridge: Cambridge University Press.
Ginzberg, Louis. 2003. *Legends of the Jews*. 2nd ed. Trans. Henrietta Szold, 1909–1938. Philadelphia: Jewish Publication Society.
Gordon, Judah Leib. 1980. "Awake, My People." In *The Jew in the Modern World: A Documentary History*, ed. Paul Mendes-Flohr and Jehuda Reinharz, 312–313. New York: Oxford University Press.
Halttunen, Karen. 1982. *Confidence Men and Painted Women: A Study of Middle-Class Culture in America, 1830–1870*. New Haven, Conn.: Yale University Press.
Harnick, Sheldon. 2000. Tradition in *Fiddler on the Roof*. New York: Limelight Editions.
Heschel, Abraham Joshua. 1955. *God in Search of Man*. New York: Farrar, Straus and Giroux.
Hoberman, J., and Jeffrey Shandler. 2003. *Entertaining America: Jews, Movies, and Broadcasting*. Princeton, N.J.: Princeton University Press.
Horowitz, Elliott. 2006. *Reckless Rites: Purim and the Legacy of Jewish Violence*. Princeton, N.J.: Princeton University Press.
Howe, Irving. 1976. *World of Our Fathers*. New York: Schocken.
Jacobson, Matthew Frye. 1998. *Whiteness of a Different Color*. Cambridge, Mass.: Harvard University Press.
Jakobsen, Janet R., and Ann Pellegrini. 2000. World Secularisms at the Millennium: Introduction. *Social Text* 18, no. 3:1–27.
Johnston, Robert K. 2006. *Reel Spirituality*. Grand Rapids, Mich.: Baker Academic.
Kaplan, Mordecai. 1934. *Judaism as a Civilization*. New York: Macmillan.
Kraut, Benny. 1998. Jewish Survival in Protestant America. In *Minority Faiths and the American Protestant Mainstream*, ed. Jonathan D. Sarna, 15–60. Urbana: University of Illinois Press.

Levitt, Laura. 2007. Impossible Assimilations, American Liberalism, and Jewish Difference: Revisiting Jewish Secularism. *American Quarterly* 59, no. 3:807–832.

Lhamon, W. T. 1998. *Raising Cain*. Cambridge, Mass.: Harvard University Press.

Locke, John. 2003. *Two Treatises of Government and A Letter Concerning Toleration*. New Haven, Conn.: Yale University Press.

Masuzawa, Tomoko. 2005. *The Invention of World Religions: Or, How European Universalism Was Preserved in the Language of Pluralism and Diversity*. Chicago: University of Chicago Press.

McKean, Erin, ed. 2005. *The New Oxford American Dictionary*. 2nd ed. Oxford University Press. http://www.oxfordreference.com/views/ENTRY.html?subview=Main&entry=t183.e69266 (accessed January 10, 2008).

Melnick, Jeffrey. 1999. *A Right to Sing the Blues: African Americans, Jews, and American Popular Song*. Cambridge, Mass.: Harvard University Press.

Mendelssohn, Moses. 1783/1983. *Jerusalem, or, On Religious Power and Judaism*. Trans. Allan Arkush. Hanover, N.H.: University Press of New England.

Most, Andrea. 2004. *Making Americans: Jews and the Broadway Musical*. Cambridge, Mass.: Harvard University Press.

Nietzsche, Friedrich. 2001. *The Gay Science*. Ed. Bernard Williams. Trans. Josefine Nauckhoff. Cambridge: Cambridge University Press.

Otte, Marline. 2006. *Jewish Identities in German Popular Entertainment, 1890–1933*. Cambridge: Cambridge University Press.

The Oxford American Dictionary of Current English. 1999. Oxford University Press. http://www.oxfordreference.com/views/ENTRY.html?subview=Main&entry=t21.e27622 (accessed January 10, 2008).

Rabinowitz, Richard. 1989. *The Spiritual Self in Everyday Life*. Boston: Northeastern University Press.

Raphaelson, Samson. 1925. *The Jazz Singer*. New York: Brentano.

Rodgers, Richard, and Oscar Hammerstein. 1955. *The King and I*. In *Six Plays by Rodgers and Hammerstein*, 371–449. New York: Random House.

Rogin, Michael. 1996. *Blackface, White Noise: Jewish Immigrants in the Hollywood Melting Pot*. Berkeley: University of California Press.

Sandrow, Nahma. 1995. *Vagabond Stars: World History of Yiddish Theater*. Syracuse, N.Y.: Syracuse University Press.

Scholem, Gershom. 1971. Redemption Through Sin. In *The Messianic Idea in Judaism*, 78–141. New York: Schocken.

Seidman, Naomi. 2007. Secularization and Sexuality: Theorizing the Erotic Transformation of Ashkenaz. A pre-circulated paper for a session at the annual meeting of the Association for Jewish Studies, December 17.

Skinner, James M. 1993. *The Cross and the Cinema*. Westport, Conn.: Praeger.

Susman, Warren. 2003. "Personality" and the Making of Twentieth-Century Culture. In *Culture as History*, 271–285. Washington, D.C.: Smithsonian Institution Press.

Trachtenberg, Alan. 1982. *The Incorporation of America: Culture and Society in the Gilded Age*. New York: Hill & Wang.

Walsh, Frank. 1996. *Sin and Censorship*. New Haven, Conn.: Yale University Press.

Weber, Donald. 2005. *Haunted in the New World: Jewish American Culture from Cahan to the Goldbergs*. Bloomington: Indiana University Press.

Weber, Max. 1930/1992. *The Protestant Ethic and the Spirit of Capitalism*. Trans. Talcott Parsons. London: Routledge.

Whitfield, Stephen. 1999. *In Search of American Jewish Culture*. Hanover, N.H.: Brandeis University Press.

Zinberg, Israel. 1972–1978. *History of Jewish Literature*. Cleveland: Case Western University Press.

6. THE PERILS OF PLURALISM

Colonization and Decolonization in American Indian Religious History

TRACY LEAVELLE

In *Spirit and Resistance: Political Theology and American Indian Liberation*, Osage theologian George E. Tinker (2004:4) argues with bitter realism as well as a sense of hope for a theology of American Indian liberation that "remember[s] the past in order to dream the future." The process of creating such a theology must originate from within Indian communities, Tinker claims, guided by Indian people. "Our past and our future," he writes, "have been consistently signified for us—by missionaries, by anthropologists and other university academics, by government bureaucrats." Remembering and engaging the history and legacy of colonialism is a necessary part of any potentially effective attempt to create the conditions for sovereignty and self-determination in economic, in political, and even in religious affairs. "After all this time," Tinker (2004:4) suggests, "it should be abundantly clear, to Indian and non-Indian, that Indian people can count on neither the U.S. government, nor the churches of the United States, nor the private-sector institutions of free enterprise to solve any of the problems that these institutions have invested so much time in creating." Even in the supposedly more pluralistic era of our own time, the heavy weight of these institutional structures and histories of oppression has not disappeared. There is no postcolonial category in Native American history (Wilson and Yellowbird 2005:1–7). And religious pluralism, with its demands for explanation and engagement, looks to many Native peoples like a peculiarly modern form of colonialism.

Tinker recognizes that coercive pressures have failed to disappear in the modern American context, even as religious pluralism has emerged as a widely accepted model for more positive and less destructive forms of interreligious engagement. Tinker (2004:55–72) seems most concerned in the present at least with the appropriation of Native religious practices by non-Native religious seekers and profiteers—a very real and well-documented threat. Yet the prescriptive demands of pluralistic practice also contain a noticeable and lingering element of colonial ideologies, displaying a clear expectation of a certain level of conformity.

For example, Tracy Fessenden notes that "an implicitly Christian culture puts pressure on all who make claims on American institutions to constitute themselves as religious on a recognizably Protestant model." Fessenden (2007:1–6) argues that Protestantism is an "unmarked category" that supports narratives of American religious history that celebrate the nation's progressive acceptance of religious difference (see also Jakobsen, chap. 1, this volume). However, the presumably secular arena for discussion, dialogue, and adjudication of conflicts continues to enforce religious norms that fail to account adequately for the significant differences between "Western" religion—primarily Christianity—and indigenous spiritual practices. The influence of these colonial concepts and institutional structures has prompted a kind of convergence in which Native peoples adopt, out of necessity, the category of religion as a form of resistance to ongoing colonial processes. There are dangers associated with such a strategy, however, for it makes indigenous spiritual practices and sacred places available for neocolonial enterprises that classify, judge, appropriate, and sometimes destroy Native cultures.

The practice of pluralism insists on a kind of public revelation of Native religion that can be incorporated into existing legal regimes and adapted to interreligious dialogues that rely on concepts that originated within the religions and applied anthropologies of the colonizers. The problem reflects the ongoing tension between the prevailing pattern of marking indigenous peoples as eternal others and the desire to absorb them bodily and culturally into the larger nation-state.

In an anthology of contemporary American Indian writing about home and place, poet Joy Harjo presents in only a few compact lines of verse a profound statement on the nature and significance of home that confirms the ongoing challenge of survival and the corresponding value of obscurity. She writes,

> *My house is the red earth; it could be the center of the world. I've heard New York, Paris, or Tokyo called the center of the world, but I say it is magnificently humble. You could drive by and miss it. Radio waves can obscure it. Words cannot construct it for there are some sounds left to sacred wordless form.* (Harjo 1995:49)

Harjo suggests that the mindful person sheltered in this gloriously inconspicuous place might locate there the very center of the world, the *axis mundi* around which all else turns. In this view the house also appears to exist independently of human creation. So unlike the fantastic metropolitan cities of the world is this place that an automobile, a map, and a highway may not provide sufficient means to travel there. Indeed, the invisible waves of sound that pass silently through the air may present too much of a disturbance for appreciation and understanding of this place. Harjo even acknowledges that the words people speak, the language of her own poem, cannot shape a true expression of its essential character. Rather, only living and listening in the presence of this place will guide one to it. Harjo's (1995:49) red earth and other places like it survived colonization and its consequences in part because they were hidden in plain sight.

FINDING RELIGION: EPISODIC HISTORIES FROM EARLY AMERICA

Since the beginning of colonization in the Americas, observers have claimed that they could identify nothing in American Indian societies that resembled religion. As Harjo's poem suggests, they failed to see what was actually there. Cultural blindness made more effective the process of analysis that supported colonial enterprises, which were constructed out of the fierce desire to possess and transform the world. French trader and colonial official Pierre Deliette (1934:361–371) declared confidently in the early eighteenth century that "[the Illinois] nation, as well as the Miami, has no religion. Some have the buffalo, the bear, others the cat, the buck, the lynx, for their Manitou [or spirit]. Almost all the old men are medicine men and consequently healers." This dismissive statement could have appeared in any number of assessments offered by colonial authors in North America. In this particular case Deliette presented his conclusions in an otherwise invaluable memoir of his stay in the Illinois country in the late seventeenth century. The manuscript reveals his deep knowledge of the Miami and Illinois peoples, containing abundant information on subsistence practices, social organization, sexuality and gender relations, ceremonial performances, and the impact of colonization.

Not unexpectedly, his descriptions also reveal the limits of his understanding. In his view the Miamis and Illinois practiced superstition, not religion, and the healers were merely jugglers, *jongleurs* in French, who performed tricks to take advantage of suffering victims. Deliette noted that when these healers successfully drew an illness out of the body, "the people [are] filled with amazement . . . and chant: 'Medicine is the science of sciences.'" According to this European observer, the charade worked, and the people even confused performance with science. Deliette's use of concepts unavailable in the Miami–Illinois language—"science of sciences"—reflected the difficult problems of cultural and linguistic translation that have always plagued attempts to locate American Indian religious or spiritual practices within a colonial framework (Deliette 1934:361–371; Leavelle 2007).

Although commentators such as Deliette typically argued that Native spiritual practices reflected at best an incomplete and superstitious understanding of the world and its ultimate destiny, they were in at least one sense correct. The highly personal, relational, localized spiritual practices of many Native communities were totally unlike the large hierarchical, bureaucratic, doctrine-defending institutions Europeans and their descendents associated with the category of religion (Morrison 2002). Missionaries and other colonial officials thus labored to establish in Native communities the beliefs, practices, and institutions that they could recognize as truly religious in nature. A common method they used was the identification and exploitation of perceived convergences, cultural concepts and practices that seemed to contain buried elements of Christianity or the prospect of translation into a more acceptable orthodox idiom. The missionary project involved in part the excavation and rehabilitation of artifacts of the original revelation and the infusion of new meaning into disordered and dangerous spiritual practices. Although Native peoples also discovered productive cultural convergences in these religious encounters, the long-term effect of colonization has been to encourage comparative analyses that enforce categories reflecting the standards and practices of colonial religions.

Deliette engaged in descriptive practices that have remained frustratingly persistent over time and that also illuminate the program of transformation that supports colonial regimes. These practices follow a pattern that historian Robert Berkhofer (1979:25–26) has identified and explained well. In Berkhofer's words, commentators such as Deliette "[conceive] of Indians in terms of their deficiencies according to White ideals . . . and [use] moral evaluation as description of Indians." Deliette not only believed that the Illinois and Miamis had no religion but also considered existing practices to be evidence of cultural and social corruption. Missionaries arrived in the country to address the problem, attempting to separate people from prior customs and to replace manitous with the Christian God. "Although this nation is much given to debauchery, especially the men," Deliette wrote, "the reverend Jesuit fathers . . . manage (if one may say so) to impose some check on this by instructing a number of girls in Christianity." The presence of missionaries created conflict in the community. According to Deliette (1934:361–362) (and other sources agree), the girls "mock at the superstitions of their nation . . . , which greatly incenses the old men and daily exposes these fathers to ill-treatment." People threw stones, pieces of wood, and corn husks at the missionaries as they tried to preach.

While dodging projectiles and pleading with the people to listen well to their teachings, the missionaries appealed to familiar indigenous concepts. They searched for likenesses and stressed differences at the same time. "The stones which are sometimes thrown at them do not dismay them," Deliette (1934:362) recorded, "they continue their discourse, contenting themselves with saying that it is the master of life who orders them to do what they are doing." The Jesuits offered Jesus as the new master of life, the only manitou the Illinois and other Indians would ever need. In making such claims the missionaries appealed to apparent convergences between cultures. French Jesuits in particular accepted some indigenous practices and cultural forms as long as they absorbed and then reexpressed essential Christian content.

Jesuit missionary Joseph François Lafitau explained some of the reasoning behind this approach in his *Moeurs des sauvages américains comparées aux moeurs des premiers temps* (*Customs of the American Indians Compared with the Customs of Primitive Times*, 1724). Lafitau (1974:28) wrote, "I have seen, with extreme distress, in most of the travel narratives, that those who have written of the customs of primitive peoples have depicted them to us as people without any sentiment of religion. . . . This is a mistake made even by missionaries and honest men," he concluded. Lafitau argued that this initial impression obscured the truth. "The Indian disputes little on matters of religion," Lafitau asserted, "he agrees easily with everything based on reason" (1974:88–91, 94).

Lafitau believed that cultural diversity arose from the degeneration of the one pure culture and religion bestowed by God. Lafitau (1974:93) traced the original revelation to Adam and Eve, arguing that "the author of nature, when he created man in his own image and likeness, at that time imprinted the idea of his existence indelibly on the most ferocious hearts and basest minds." He suggested further that ignorance was the penalty for original sin and that human passions distorted this natural religion, leading ultimately to idolatry, magic, and superstition. Lafitau discovered vestiges of natural religion in the customs of American Indians and ancient peoples. As evidence Lafitau (1974:29) pointed to "the unanimous consent of all peoples in recognizing a Supreme Being and honouring him in some way, a unanimity which shows that people feel his superiority and the need of turning to him."

His own experiences as a missionary in North America and his intensive study of numerous descriptions of Native cultures led him to the conclusion that "generally all the people of America, whether nomadic or sedentary, have strong and forceful expressions which can only designate a God. They call him the Great Spirit, sometimes the Master and Author of Life" (Lafitau 1974:101). To Lafitau and numerous other European observers, American Indians were not irreligious; they were merely idolaters who had fallen from grace. The role of the missionary was to recover and restore the remains of the true faith buried in their hearts and minds, to refocus worship from the Great Spirit to the Trinitarian God. In this way missionaries tried to correct what they believed was a critical cultural and spiritual deficiency (Lafitau 1974:29–36, 92–116, 229–259; see also Jaenen 1976; Pagden 1986).

Many Jesuit missionaries had been working on these assumptions for a while. To share only one example, missionary Claude Allouez (1959:47–51) reported in the 1660s that after only a little instruction some Illinois representatives had started to "honor our Lord among themselves in their own way, putting his Image, which I have given them, in the most honored place on the occasion of any important feast, while the Master of the banquet addresses it as follows: 'In thy honor, O Man-God, do we hold this feast; to thee do we offer these viands.'"

The inclusion of an image of Jesus Christ in Illinois feasts during these initial contacts represented a crucial intersection of two very different worldviews and spiritual traditions. A product of culturally aggressive colonization, the intersection nevertheless created a point of exchange that produced opportunities for dynamic cross-cultural dialogue and negotiation. The imagery and ritual of the feasts were flexible cultural symbols open to a variety of interpretations. As Deliette noted, the Illinois maintained reciprocal relationships with their manitous, offering them gifts in return for power and protection. Allouez admitted that they paid tribute to Jesus "in their own way." Nonetheless, he welcomed the opportunity to establish the cultural connections that might eventually grow into something more traditionally Christian.

For their part, the Illinois explored the potential of Jesus Christ to bring abundance and success to a people troubled by the regional disruptions caused by European imperial competition and intertribal conflict. Not surprisingly, even while the Illinois and other Native peoples recognized the missionaries and their teachings as something new, they also initially interpreted them from within a familiar cultural context. An early-eighteenth-century manuscript dictionary produced by the Jesuits shows that in the Miami–Illinois language, God became "kichemanet8a" or "missimanet8a," meaning "great spirit." The Holy Spirit was "pekisita manet8a," beautiful or sacred spirit (Le Boullenger n.d.:63). Indeed, one scholar has commented that in this early period of missionization "Indians were not so much being converted to Christianity as Christ was being converted into a manitou" (White 1991:25–27). As in so many other situations of encounter, hybridity—and not distinctly bounded systems—turns out to have been the normal state of things (Klassen and Bender, introduction, this volume).

Evangelization was not as important to the English colonial enterprise in North America as it was for the French, although English missionaries made several high-profile efforts to bring Native peoples to Christ. The English concentrated more on building profitable agricultural and commercial colonies than on planting the seeds of the gospel among Indians. Yet English observers had much to say about indigenous religions, and they debated intently the fundamental issue of whether Indians had any true religious life at all.

New England colonist Thomas Morton argued in a 1637 book that the Massachusetts Indians had no religion, even as he offered a detailed description of their spiritual beliefs and practices. Morton's somewhat contradictory assessment was much like Deliette's in that he judged Massachusetts culture by what it lacked in relation to his own. Morton acknowledged that the Massachusetts retained a faint memory of the biblical God, noting for instance that they shared stories of the creation of a single man and woman directed by a supreme being to live together as stewards of the land and its animal inhabitants. According to Morton, the Massachusetts also remembered a great deluge that wiped the world clean of wicked people sometime in the distant past. The vagueness with which they addressed this supreme being and the collection of disordered practices that had emerged since the flood did not in Morton's opinion rise to the level of religion. Indians had fallen too far, and only the Bible could save them (Kupperman 2000:117–118; Salisbury 1982:162).

English religious dissident Roger Williams, founder of Rhode Island, documented in his *Key into the Language of America* in 1643 the connections he discovered between Indians and the history recorded in the Bible. He accepted the common origins of the Narragansett Indians and the English, commenting that "from *Adam* and *Noah* that they spring, it is granted on all hands" (Williams 2002). Williams struggled to understand what had happened in the many generations since, however. "But for their later *Descent*, and whence they came into these parts," he wondered, "it seems as hard to finde, as to finde the *Wellhead* of some fresh *Streame* . . . [that] hath met with many mixing *Streames* by the way. They say themselves," he continued, "that they have *sprung* and *growne* up in that very place, like the very *trees* of the *Wildernesse*." Williams searched for clues in the language and cultural practices of the Narragansetts. He believed that he had found a relationship between the Narragansett and the Hebrew and Greek languages. Furthermore, Williams (2002:179) concluded that some of their cultural practices matched biblical descriptions of Jewish rites and that their oral traditions contained a miracle-working figure "with some kind of broken Resemblance to the *Sonne of God*" (see also Kupperman 2000:119).

In the same era of early English colonization, Edward Winslow of Plymouth examined the beliefs and practices of local Indians and made feeble attempts to educate them in the basic tenets of Puritan Christianity. Winslow at first concluded that Indians had no religion and no real connection to God, but he later changed his views as he discovered what he thought were parallels between the Christian God and Native deities. He suggested that Indians recognized a particular deity as the creator of all things, including human beings. Even as Indians worshipped this supreme being, according to Winslow, they also relied on a spiritual figure for healing and visions that he equated with Satan. The Plymouth man did not notice or learn, as Williams later did, that the creator being he described had in Native oral tradition destroyed all of humanity, including the first man and woman, and started over. The second couple became the ancestors of the people Winslow encountered. Winslow's haphazard missionary work targeted disordered understandings and evil practices associated with the devil. He was particularly concerned with the influence of Native healers or powwows. His solution to the problem of creating Puritan Indians was to attack these representatives of Satan and inspire recognition and worship of the true God that was obscured by centuries of unorthodox faith (Kupperman 2000; Salisbury 1982).

One of the first to adopt this approach was Thomas Mayhew Jr., missionary to the Indians of Martha's Vineyard. Like their French competitors, English missionaries also used apparent convergences to guide their evangelical practice. Mayhew uncovered what he thought was a remnant of the notion of a supreme being in the manitou concept, just as the Jesuits did in New France. Mayhew explained with concern that "this diabolical way [the Indians] were in, giving heed to a multitude of heathen traditions of their gods, . . . they with much slavery were held, and abounding with sins, having only an obscure notion of a god greater than all, which they call Mannit [or Manitou], but they knew not what he was, and therefore had no way to worship him." According to the missionary, the apparent degeneration of Native religious practices had produced not simply superstition and false knowledge but rather a much more serious decline into enslavement by the devil. As he put it, "The devil also with his angels had his kingdom among them [and] in them" (Hall 2004:258–259).

Mayhew's equation of Native religious practices with diabolical possession forced him to confront directly the alleged evil he witnessed. Given the dire situation, Mayhew found less in the indigenous culture that he was willing to work with than the Jesuits. The cultural reconstruction effort had to be broader and deeper, involving a more complete transformation of targeted Indian communities. Theological imperatives required submission to English civilization. In the language of the time, the Indians needed to be "reduced" to civility and Christianity. "Reduction" referred both to the colonial project to impose English-style civilization on Native communities and to the desire to lead Indians back to the religious truths they had distorted and abandoned in the distant past. On Martha's Vineyard acceptance into the kingdom of Christ involved a complete rejection of the old ways tainted by association with Satan (Axtell 1985:131–178; Bowden 1981:111–133; Kupperman 2000:120).

Mayhew reported some success in his endeavors in 1653, claiming that "since it hath pleased God to send his Word to these poor captivated men (bondslaves to sin and Satan) he hath through mercy brought two hundred eighty three Indians (not counting young children in the number) to renounce their false gods, devils, and powwows" (Hall 2004:258–259). As David Silverman (2005) demonstrated in his recent work, over time the Martha's Vineyard Indians created vibrant Christian communities that actually reflected a number of indigenous practices, particularly in the way in which congregations and communities were organized. They shaped Protestant Christianity to meet their needs as they struggled to survive in a difficult colonial environment. In this case, Indians discovered and exploited convergences even more readily than their ministers.

These patterns of inquiry, analysis, classification, and judgment remained strong as European empires labored to establish viable colonies in North America. Religious and cultural transformation of Indian individuals and communities was a key component of this process. Whereas some idealistic missionaries dreamed of a time when all Indians would become Christians and live peacefully with and among their European neighbors, more pragmatic colonial officials simply hoped to develop and maintain healthy alliances or at least avoid unnecessarily bloody conflicts. The missionary vision of a multicultural religious utopia never came to pass, however, and the alliances often failed. When relationships came apart and violence spread across the land, not even the most ardently Christian Indian communities could avoid the terrible consequences. During the conflagration known as King Philip's War in 1675 and 1676, fearful colonial leaders exiled the Praying Indians of Massachusetts Bay to a cold, windswept island in Boston Harbor, where all suffered and many died in miserable conditions. Catholic Indians allied with France fled their homelands in such conflicts to live in mission villages along the St. Lawrence. The eighteenth-century imperial wars for control of the continent produced similar dilemmas for Native peoples, Christian and non-Christian, as military and political exigencies forced them to take sides or seek protection (Axtell 1985:247–267; Lepore 1999:138–145; Richter 2001:151–236).

Effective colonization relied in part on the power to collect and classify information and to impose clear structures of knowledge and meaning. Europeans (and Americans) acted as if such categories as "religion" and "superstition," "savagery" and "civilization" were natural and enduring. Even early historical approaches to the study of difference were assimilationist and hierarchical. In these works the Native peoples of North America stood outside of history or at least remained marginal to the major movements that shaped the world. They entered history only in their relations with Europeans. However, Native peoples showed, in both rejecting and adapting colonial Christianities, that these encounters occurred within robust indigenous intellectual, social, cultural, and historical frameworks.

PEACE POLICIES AND RELIGIOUS CRIMES: ASSIMILATIONIST PROGRAMS AND INDIAN CRITICS IN THE UNITED STATES

The tension between the desire to remake Indians in the European image and, simultaneously, to guard vigilantly the cultural, social, and spatial boundaries that separated them from the colonists reemerged in a particularly divisive and destructive manner in the Indian policies of the United States. Well into the twentieth century federal Indian policy stressed assimilation but did so in such a way that it led to further marginalization of Native peoples. The ideologies of Manifest Destiny, including Christian nationalism, supported the displacement of Indian nations through armed conflict and enforcement of treaties, the allotment of Indian lands and subsequent pressure to adopt American citizenship, and the boarding school system that separated children from parents, communities, and Native traditions. Reservations isolated Indian communities and made them available for comprehensive programs of "civilization." Elected officials, military officers, missionaries, local Indian agents, and reform-minded citizens failed to recognize the legitimacy or authenticity of Indian religious practices and targeted them relentlessly for permanent eradication. Assimilationists viewed Indian religions as superstitious and potentially dangerous practices that interfered with "progress" toward civilization. Giving them up was simply the painful yet necessary cost of becoming an American citizen and decent Christian.

In 1870, for example, President Grant announced his "Peace Policy" to reduce corruption in the Indian service and to strengthen assimilation efforts on the reservations. He transferred control of the reservations from the military to a number of different religious denominations. In a message to Congress, Grant explained that "the [religious] societies selected are allowed to name their own agents . . . and are expected to watch over them and aid them as missionaries, to Christianize and civilize the Indian, and to train him in the arts of peace." The president looked forward to a time when the policy would "bring all the Indians upon reservations, where they will live in houses, and have schoolhouses and churches, and will be pursuing peaceful and self-sustaining avocations." Missionaries from religious denominations as diverse as the Society of Friends, Methodists, Congregationalists, Episcopalians, Catholics, and several others fanned out across the West to implement the new policy (Prucha 1990:135, 141–143).

The next decade the federal government developed the Indian Religious Crimes Code, which prohibited dances, healing rituals, and other ceremonies. Secretary of the interior Henry M. Teller argued that "many of the agencies are without law of any kind, and the necessity for some rule of government on the reservations grows more apparent each day. If it is the purpose of the Government to civilize the Indians, they must be compelled to desist from the savage and barbarous practices that are calculated to continue them in savagery." Teller instructed the commissioner of Indian affairs to set up Courts of Indian Offenses to police reservations and punish those who persisted in "the continuance of the old heathenish dances." The secretary believed that ceremonies "are not social gatherings for the amusement of these people, but, on the contrary, are intended and calculated to stimulate the warlike passions of the young warriors of the tribe." Teller refused to accept feasts and dances as religious in any sense. He did not even classify them as social events intended to bring communities together. They remained for him merely an example of "all the debauchery, diabolism, and savagery of the worst state of the Indian race" (Prucha 1990:160–162; see also Irwin 2000:295–296).

The Office of Indian Affairs set up Indian tribunals on reservations to enforce the policy. In a classic display of colonial power, the government employed indigenous peoples to implement its policies, further dividing already fractured communities. Instructions for the Indian Courts issued in 1892 explained that "the judges must be men of intelligence, integrity, and good moral character, and preference shall be given to Indians who read and write English readily, wear citizens' dress, and engage in civilized pursuits." Dances appeared first on the list of offenses and the practices of medicine men third. Conviction for participating in dances or providing services as a healer could result in the withholding of rations and in imprisonment (Prucha 1990:186–189).

Indian communities resisted these oppressive policies in a number of ways. They moved important rituals to hidden valleys, high hills, and private homes, places that became, as Harjo suggests, the "magnificently humble" center of the world. Others they masked with gatherings and feasts that Indian agents supported, such as Fourth of July celebrations. New religious movements also appeared as prophetic voices called adherents to renew their commitments to core values of communal obligation and proper living. Inspired by tradition and responding creatively to change, religious leaders offered hopeful visions and innovative practices to people struggling against the consequences of conquest and colonization. The Ghost Dance movement promised to restore the land to its Native inhabitants and reunite the living with treasured ancestors. Ceremonialists carried peyote rites north from Mexico, often combining the sacramental use of the cactus with Christian concepts and symbols. Oklahoma practitioners incorporated the Native American Church in 1918 to protect their ceremonies from interference, explicitly identifying the peyote movement with Christianity. Government officials and Christian leaders were equally concerned about the growing appeal of such movements, concluding that they represented a reemergence of the old ways that prevented assimilation. Indian agents and the U.S. Army responded to the Ghost Dance movement on the Plains with fear and violence, most infamously at Wounded Knee in 1890. Possession and use of peyote remained a crime in many places (Irwin 2000:297–302; Martin 2001:84–110).

The education that was intended to create pliable citizens who would avoid such practices unexpectedly produced Indian intellectuals who could comment effectively on religious concerns, turning the language of the colonizer against the colonizers themselves. Zitkala-Ša (Gertrude Bonnin), a Yankton Sioux writer who attended a Quaker boarding school and taught at the Carlisle Indian School in Pennsylvania, defended "paganism" in a story she published in the *Atlantic Monthly* in 1902. Recalling her encounters with "the pale-faced missionary," Zitkala-Ša proclaimed, "I prefer to their dogma my excursions into the natural gardens where the voice of the Great Spirit is heard in the twittering of birds, the rippling of mighty waters, and the sweet breathing of flowers. If this is Paganism," she wrote, "then, at present, at least, I am a Pagan." Still, to make her case, Zitkala-Ša adopted accepted categories of religious classification and judgment (Zitkala-Ša 2001:69–73).

Charles Eastman seemed to be the highest and best example of an assimilated Indian, having graduated from Dartmouth College and Boston University Medical School. He worked as a physician at the Pine Ridge reservation in the early 1890s and later in private practice. He also served as a field organizer for the YMCA. A committed Christian, Eastman (2001:78) still "wondered much that Christianity is not practised by the very people who vouch for that wonderful conception of exemplary living. It appears that they are anxious to pass on their religion to all races of men, but keep very little of it themselves." Accommodation could be a form of resistance as well. In these cases, Charles Eastman and Zitkala-Ša converged toward American ideals without giving up their Indian identities. Both writers labored in the early decades of the twentieth century to protect the rights of Native peoples. Eastman (2001:73–79) withdrew from the modern world late in his life, passing his time in an Ontario cabin.

The Indian New Deal in the 1930s relaxed some of the most severe restrictions on indigenous religious practices, but the damage was done and government paternalism continued. The dramatic change in policies did not represent a process of decolonization. Allotment of reservation lands to Native individuals and the sale of "surplus" land resulted in widespread dispossession. Indian lands in the United States were reduced from around 138 million acres in 1887 to about 48 million in 1934, when the government finally ended the disastrous policy of allotment. Confinement to reservations and the loss of land separated Native communities from homelands and places of origin, traditional locations for ceremonial gatherings, and important religious sites. The educational assault on Native cultures made the transmission of languages, oral traditions, and ceremonies more difficult. Resistance and innovation could not halt all the effects of the long ban on religious practices. These policies of detribalization weakened communities culturally, socially, and economically without achieving the stated objective of assimilation. Marginalization made Native nations more easily available for continued colonization of land and resources, including cultural resources, for the remainder of the twentieth century (Calloway 2004:339–344).

Indian critics such as Zitkala-Ša, Charles Eastman, and many others before and since created a vibrant intellectual tradition of cultural commentary and political resistance. They documented the effects of colonization, identified key mechanisms in systems of oppression, and developed ideological perspectives that support continued claims for Indian sovereignty and Native nationalism (Vizenor 1994; Warrior 1994; Weaver et al. 2006). Indian intellectuals, from cultural critics and philosophers to writers of poetry and prose, helped initiate the modern movement for decolonization.

"WE DON'T WANT TO TALK TO THE GOVERNMENT FENCE": THE PERILS OF PLURALISM

Acoma Pueblo poet Simon Ortiz describes in verse a conversation with a Paiute elder that illustrates the ongoing effects of colonialism, reveals the strength of religious attachments to place, and expresses the intense pain and alienation caused by separation. Coso Hot Springs is a place of great healing power enclosed in the China Lake Naval Air Weapons Station in the Mojave Desert of California. In the poem "That's the Place Indians Talk About," Ortiz writes from the point of view of the elder:

The Coso Hot Springs would talk to us.
And we would talk to it.
The People have to talk to it.

That's the place Indians talk about. That's the place.
Children, women, men,
we would all go up there.
You drink that water, it makes you well.
You put it on your hands, face, all over,
and you get well, all well.
That's the place Indians talk about,
the Coso Hot Springs the People go to.

For this Paiute community Coso Hot Springs is a powerful place that contains healing waters. The bubbling springs have inspired conversations between people and place for generations, and the site needs attentive care and regular ritual (Ortiz 1995:1–2).

But now the springs have been absorbed by a government agency dedicated to military violence. This source of healing has become a site for the expression of communal loss and mourning. "And now," Ortiz continues,

They have a fence around the Coso Hot Springs.
We go up there, but they have a fence around.
. . .
We don't want to talk to the government fence,
the government Navy.
That's the place the Indian people are talking about now.

Colonization did not end for the Paiutes, or many other Native nations, at the end of the nineteenth or early in the twentieth century. The Navy arrived during World War II and put a fence around the springs. The community has to seek permission to visit its place of power and healing, the place that speaks to them most strongly. As Ortiz explains through his narrator, "We don't like to talk to the fence and the Navy / but for a while we will and pretty soon / we will talk to the hot springs power again." They will do so because they must. The conversation cannot end unless there are no people left to listen (Ortiz 1995:3–4).

Connections to place have been an essential part of American Indian religious traditions through time, but these strong attachments have often been the source of bitter conflicts. David Chidester and Edward Linenthal contend that sacred space is by its very nature contested space. They suggest that often "the most significant levels of reality are not 'mythological' categories, such as heaven, earth, and hell, but hierarchical power relations of domination and subordination, inclusion and exclusion, appropriation and dispossession" (Chidester and Linenthal 1995:17). The contest over sacred spaces in America—the numerous battles over possession and use of American Indian sacred lands—is one of the most significant and lasting legacies of American colonialism. Conflicts such as the one at Coso Hot Springs also vividly illustrate some of the fundamental problems with contemporary approaches to religious pluralism (Chidester and Linenthal 1995:15–20).

Diana Eck argues in her influential descriptive and prescriptive account of religious pluralism in America that "today all of us are challenged to claim for a new age the very principles of religious freedom that shaped our nation. . . . We must embrace the religious diversity that comes with our commitment to religious freedom." She suggests that this contentious process "will require moving beyond laissez-faire inattention to religion to a vigorous attempt to understand the religions of our neighbors. And it will require the engagement of our religious traditions in the common tasks of our civil society" (Eck 2002:25). But what of communities that do not desire such attention or that maintain a healthy skepticism toward the civil society that has so consistently marginalized them? What happens when there is nothing to see, as in Harjo's red earth?

Tinker warns against any reliance on the institutions that emerged out the conquest of Native peoples. He writes, "Our liberation, our healing, depends on our not allowing someone else to remember or dream on our behalf." The context for remembering is "five hundred years of memories of genocide and oppression that have left Indian peoples with emotional, spiritual, and social wounds that continue to fester" (Tinker 2004:4). It is worth noting here that the primary example Eck shares of Native American participation in religious dialogue is the National Day of Mourning, held each Thanksgiving at Plymouth Rock (Eck 2002:32–36). Plymouth is surely a place of intense symbolism for the indigenous peoples of North America, connected as it is to a long history of colonization and survival, but Plymouth Rock has more to do with Wounded Knee than with places such as Coso Hot Springs and other sacred sites. Confronting these broader issues may be an important and even necessary step toward liberation, but Eck's model of engagement seems insufficient for the many problems associated with preservation of American Indian religious traditions and sacred sites.

For two centuries government policy in the United States reflected active hostility or, sometimes, indifference toward Native American religious practices. The protections of the First Amendment to the Constitution have not applied to Native peoples (McNally, chap. 9, this volume). Congress passed the American Indian Religious Freedom Act (AIRFA) in 1978 to close the distance between the American ideal of religious freedom and the absence of recognition and respect Native religions had received in the past. The language of the act acknowledged that "the lack of a clear, comprehensive, and consistent Federal policy has often resulted in the abridgment of religious freedom for traditional American Indians . . . [and that] traditional American Indian ceremonies have been intruded upon, interfered with, and in a few instances banned." Supporters of the legislation hoped to correct these persistent problems. The act reads, "It shall be the policy of the United States to protect and preserve for American Indians their inherent right of freedom to believe, express, and exercise [their] traditional religions . . . including but not limited to access to sites, use and possession of sacred objects, and the freedom to worship through ceremonials and traditional rites" (Prucha 1990:288–289).

Unfortunately, the law never lived up to its potential. Land owners, employers, government officials, and judges have had trouble understanding religious systems based on practices rather than creeds and sacred texts and on access to land rather than buildings and bureaucratic institutions. The biggest blow to AIRFA came in the Supreme Court ruling in *Lyng v. Northwest Indian Cemetery Protective Association*, 485 U.S. 439 (1988). In this pivotal case, known also as the GO Road case, the U.S. Forest Service decided to build a road through the Chimney Rock area of the Six Rivers National Forest in northern California. The Yurok, Karok, and Tolowa peoples had historically used and continued to use this area high in the mountains for religious ceremonies. The Court admitted that "the threat to the efficacy of at least some religious practices is extremely grave." Yet the majority ruled in favor of government property rights, concluding that "no disrespect for these practices is implied when one notes that such beliefs could easily require de facto beneficial ownership of some rather spacious tracts of public property. Even without anticipating future cases, the diminution of the Government's property rights, and the concomitant subsidy of the Indian religion, would in this case be far from trivial." Pragmatism and public property rights superseded principle. The Court explained that "the Constitution does not, and courts cannot, offer to reconcile the various competing demands on government, many of them rooted in sincere religious belief, that inevitably arise in so diverse a society as ours." The Forest Service never completed the road, but the legal damage was done.

AIRFA has been amended, and President Clinton signed an executive order instructing federal agencies to accommodate American Indian religious practices on public lands, but the existing legal landscape has created steep hills to climb. Property rights in the United States remain sacred American values. As the *Lyng* decision demonstrates, federal law still prioritizes natural resource issues and the protection of property rights over Native cultural values. Moreover, colonization of Indian lands and cultures continues in the extraction of natural resources and the commodification, appropriation, distortion, and theft of Native culture and religious traditions (Gulliford 2000:101–102, 119–120; Martin 2001:123–124; Page 2001:131–132).

There are serious problems with the trend toward inquiry, engagement, and negotiation, the expectation that Native peoples should participate in a pluralistic dialogue. The official and unofficial spaces that have opened up are still not all that welcoming, and many Native people do not want to participate. Legal scholar Charles Wilkinson understands the dilemma. In a 2001 forum on sacred lands, he noted that AIRFA provides direction to federal land managers to accommodate access to sacred sites and that the *Lyng* case also acknowledged that the Forest Service had the discretion *not* to build the road and therefore to preserve the high-country site. Wilkinson suggested that it is imperative that Native spiritual and political leaders appear in person before federal officials and judges to argue their positions and force decision makers to recognize their fundamental humanity. Wilkinson is probably right when he claims that lifeless paper records are not enough to sway the people with the power to decide. However, court cases and dialogue force Indian participants to reveal sensitive information about sites and ceremonies. Publicity endangers sacred sites, invites visitation, and increases the risk of vandalism. Native peoples also wonder why they must submit evidence of their beliefs and practices. They ask why they must justify themselves and their sacred histories, unlike so many other religious groups in the United States. They want to know why they have to talk to the government fence (Sacred Land Film Project 2001).

DECOLONIZING RELIGION

Native philosopher Vine Deloria Jr. (Standing Rock Sioux) had much to say about these contentious issues before his death in 2005. In one of his strongest statements on the contemporary situation, Deloria (1999:211–212) asserted that the "courts will protect a religion if it shows every symptom of being dead but will severely restrict it if it appears to be alive." Deloria's family connections and intellectual training prepared him well to comment. His great-grandfather was a medicine man and his grandfather a convert to Christianity who became an Episcopal priest and missionary. His father was also a priest and missionary, and Deloria himself completed a degree in theology at a Lutheran seminary. Like those of Charles Eastman and Zitkala-Ša long before him, Deloria's educational achievements prepared him to present a serious and at times devastating critique of Christianity and American society.

In an essay on sacred lands and religious freedom, Deloria identified a serious problem in the perception of American Indian religions that has made protection of free exercise difficult. "In denying the possibility of the continuing revelation of the sacred in our lives," Deloria complained, "federal courts, scholars, and state and federal agencies refuse to accord credibility to the testimony of religious leaders, demand evidence that a ceremony or location has *always* been central to the belief and practices of the tribe, and impose exceedingly rigorous standards on Indians who appear before them." Deloria (1999:211–212) concluded bitterly that "at least for the federal courts, God is dead."

This attitude is a reflection of well-developed colonial attitudes that relegate authentic Indian religion only to the past. From this perspective modern Native religious practices seem like quaint performances that bear little resemblance to the great ceremonies of the idealized Indian past. Contact and combination have tainted them, leaving them in limbo somewhere between the old ways of long dead elders and expectations for mainstream religions and religious practices in the present. Sacred sites have become places where non-Native pilgrims can view the remains of ancient practices in the form of a stone medicine wheel, a spring, or a high mountain peak. Museums display collections of ritual objects in static poses behind protective glass, separating the items from the people and ceremonies that make them live. The language of the AIRFA relies on the notion of "the authentic," ostensibly protecting the free exercise of "traditional religions." There is an inherent contradiction in this attitude that on one hand acknowledges the long history of colonization and conquest and on the other expects Native religions to maintain perfect purity and easily identifiable links to the past (Gulliford 2000:41–66).

Deloria used concepts of revelation to illuminate major differences between Christianity and indigenous religions. "Presumably," he wrote, "God authored the books of the Bible, [but] with the closing of the canon there has been no public message or revelation from the deity for nearly two thousand years." By contrast, tribal religions maintain "an open expectation that revelations can and will be received." Deloria explained that religious experiences in the Native context have little to do with doctrine or faith. Rather, revelations offer essential guidance to an authentic life in a specific community and access to healing powers and potentially important prophetic announcements. American Indian religious practices often acknowledge the connection of the extraordinary and the ordinary. There is a correspondence between the transcendent and imminent domains of life. "Everything," Deloria argued, "exists in the ceremonies and powers which are a part of the human experience" (1999:157).

Deloria's analysis might be overly general, even simplistic, particularly in its characterization of Christianity, but he was trying to send a clear message about real religious differences. His writing, always political and often polemical, effectively contrasted competing worldviews and questioned basic assumptions of the most influential American ideologies of religion and cultural superiority. Deloria was not interested in identifying or celebrating convergences, although he often engaged in a kind of interreligious dialogue. In the pieces cited here, he developed a critique of colonialism and its consequences. Still, the "Western" Christian framework structured many of the comparisons and the debates that followed. Deloria used the likeness of categories to explain critical differences between Christianity and indigenous religions and to defend American Indian religious freedom. Other Indian intellectuals have done the same (Kidwell et al. 2001).

Central to the case Deloria and other commentators make is the living, growing, evolving, revelatory nature of American Indian religions. The Paiutes must return to Coso Hot Springs despite the presence of the fence. They will speak to the Navy and make arrangements so that they can conduct appropriate ceremonies and continue the long conversation with the water. Yet they look forward to a day in the future when there will be no mediator, and they will listen only to the voice of the spring. In northern California, Native religious practitioners will climb into the Chimney Rock area to renew the entire world, not just their own. They will seek wisdom in the high peaks. These ceremonies must take place at these sites and no others. They are irreplaceable.

One of the fundamental problems here is that there has been no process of decolonization in the United States. Native communities have survived a long history of colonization and conquest, but neocolonial forces remain a serious problem to this day. A convergence toward the acceptance of common religious categories and participation in active forms of interreligious dialogue is a solution that many Native people find unattractive at best. It is true that Indian communities want recognition and respect for their religious practices and sacred sites. Pawnee attorney Walter Echo-Hawk described his reasons for attending the Third Parliament of World Religions in Cape Town, South Africa, in 1999: "[Native religions] have survived, but they are overlooked and unprotected by the laws of their countries. . . . Our delegation came here to try to get a 'seat at the table' with the recognized religions on the planet. . . . We want a seat at the table to make this gathering real and complete" (quoted in Cousineau 2006:27–28).

However, there is also reasonable skepticism toward processes that have demanded so much in the past. A participant in the 2001 Native sacred lands forum asked, "Is consultation to be preferred over conquest? You bet. Can consultation just pick itself up, declare a new era, and detach itself from conquest? No way." Another participant commented, "Accommodation. We hear accommodation a lot today. Is that the current disposition—that the religious rights of the first Americans have been reduced to an accommodation?" (Sacred Land Film Project 2001:15, 48). In *For Indigenous Eyes Only: A Decolonization Handbook*, editors Waziyatawin Angela Wilson and Michael Yellowbird (2005:4) argue that "decolonization ultimately requires the overturning of the colonial structure. It is not about tweaking the existing colonial system to make it more Indigenous-friendly or a little less oppressive."

Pluralism (and secularism for that matter) enacts definitions of acceptable difference. Pluralism in its current form is not ahistorical, nor is it apolitical. As a descriptive act and prescriptive practice, it is clearly implicated in the long history of colonization. In a diverse post-pluralistic world of contact, combination, and conflict, there must be room for divergence—for incommensurability, nonparticipation, dissonance, and misunderstanding—of a whole range of religious and political practices that may or may not include engagement and dialogue. George Tinker calls for a "theology of resistance" that is fundamentally political. This Native American liberation theology rests on the protection and expansion of indigenous sovereignty (Tinker 2004). And, sometimes, discussion and dialogue are simply not possible. Like Harjo's (1995:49) red earth, the center of the world, "Words cannot construct it for there are some sounds left to sacred wordless form."

WORKS CITED

Allouez, Claude. 1959. Relation of 1666–1667. In *The Jesuit Relations and Allied Documents*, ed. Reuben Gold Thwaites, 51:47–52. New York: Pageant.

Axtell, James. 1985. *The Invasion Within: The Contest of Cultures in Colonial North America*. New York: Oxford University Press.

Berkhofer, Robert F., Jr. 1979. *The White Man's Indian: Images of the American Indian from Columbus to the Present*. New York: Vintage.

Bowden, Henry Warner. 1981. *American Indians and Christian Missions*. Chicago: University of Chicago Press.

Calloway, Colin. 2004. *First Peoples: A Documentary Survey of American Indian History*. 2nd ed. Boston: Bedford/St. Martin's.

Chidester, David, and Edward T. Linenthal, eds. 1995. *American Sacred Space*. Bloomington: Indiana University Press.

Cousineau, Phil, ed. 2006. *A Seat at the Table: Huston Smith in Conversation with Native Americans on Religious Freedom*. Berkeley: University of California Press.

Deliette, Pierre. 1934. Memoir of De Gannes Concerning the Illinois Country. In *Collections of the Illinois State Historical Library*. Vol. 23, *The French Foundations, 1680–1693*, ed. Theodore Calvin Pease and Raymond C. Werner, 302–396. Springfield: Illinois State Historical Library.

Deloria, Vine, Jr. 1999. *For This Land: Writings on Religion in America*. Ed. James Treat. New York: Routledge.

Eastman, Charles. 2001. Charles Eastman Compares the Morality of Indians and Modern Christians, 1916. In *Talking Back to Civilization: Indian Voices from the Progressive Era*, ed. Frederick E. Hoxie, 73–79. Boston: Bedford/St. Martin's.

Eck, Diana L. 2002. A *New Religious America: How a "Christian Country" Has Become the World's Most Religiously Diverse Nation*. San Francisco: HarperSanFrancisco.

Fessenden, Tracy. 2007. *Culture and Redemption: Religion, the Secular, and American Literature*. Princeton, N.J.: Princeton University Press.

Gulliford, Andrew. 2000. *Sacred Objects and Sacred Places: Preserving Tribal Traditions*. Boulder: University Press of Colorado.

Hall, David D., ed. 2004. *Puritans in the New World: A Critical Anthology*. Princeton, N.J.: Princeton University Press.

Harjo, Joy. 1995. My House Is the Red Earth. In *Home Places: Contemporary Native American Writing from Sun Tracks*, ed. Larry Evers and Ofelia Zepeda, 49. Tucson: University of Arizona Press.

Irwin, Lee. 2000. Freedom, Law, and Prophecy: A Brief History of Native American Religious Resistance. In *Native American Spirituality: A Critical Reader*, ed. Lee Irwin, 295–316. Lincoln: University of Nebraska Press.

Jaenen, Cornelius. 1976. *Friend and Foe: Aspects of French–Amerindian Cultural Contact in the Sixteenth and Seventeenth Centuries*. New York: Columbia University Press.

Kidwell, Clara Sue, Homer Noley, and George E. Tinker. 2001. A *Native American Theology*. Maryknoll, N.Y.: Orbis.

Kupperman, Karen Ordahl. 2000. *Indians and English: Facing Off in Early America*. Ithaca, N.Y.: Cornell University Press.

Lafitau, Joseph François. 1974. *Customs of the American Indians Compared with the Customs of Primitive Times*. Trans. and ed. William N. Fenton and Elizabeth L. Moore. Toronto: Champlain Society.

Le Boullenger, Jean. n.d. Miami–Illinois Dictionary. Manuscript (microfilm copy). John Carter Brown Library, Providence, R.I.

Leavelle, Tracy. 2007. "Bad Things" and "Good Hearts": Mediation, Meaning, and the Language of Illinois Christianity. *Church History* 76 (June):363–394.

Lepore, Jill. 1999. *The Name of War: King Philip's War and the Origins of American Identity*. New York: Vintage.

Martin, Joel W. 2001. *The Land Looks After Us: A History of Native American Religion*. New York: Oxford University Press.

Morrison, Kenneth M. 2002. *The Solidarity of Kin: Ethnohistory, Religious Studies, and the Algonkian–French Religious Encounter*. Albany: State University of New York Press.

Ortiz, Simon J. 1995. That's the Place Indians Talk About. In *Home Places: Contemporary Native American Writing from Sun Tracks*, ed. Larry Evers and Ofelia Zepeda, 1–5. Tucson: University of Arizona Press.

Pagden, Anthony. 1986. *The Fall of Natural Man: The American Indian and the Origins of Comparative Ethnology*. New York: Cambridge University Press.

Page, Jack, ed. 2001. *Sacred Lands of Indian America*. New York: Abrams.

Prucha, Francis Paul, ed. 1990. *Documents of United States Indian Policy*. 2nd ed. Lincoln: University of Nebraska Press.

Richter, Daniel. 2001. *Facing East from Indian Country: A Native History of Early America*. Cambridge, Mass.: Harvard University Press.

The Sacred Land Film Project. 2001. *Report of the Native American Sacred Lands Forum, Boulder/Denver, October 9–10, 2001*. http://www.sacredland.org/PDFs/SL_Forum.final.pdf.

Salisbury, Neal. 1982. *Manitou and Providence: Indians, Europeans, and the Making of New England, 1500–1643*. New York: Oxford University Press.

Silverman, David J. 2005. *Faith and Boundaries: Colonists, Christianity, and Community Among the Wampanoag Indians of Martha's Vineyard, 1600–1871*. New York: Cambridge University Press.

Tinker, George E. 2004. *Spirit and Resistance: Political Theology and American Indian Liberation*. Minneapolis: Fortress Press.

Vizenor, Gerald. 1994. *Manifest Manners: Postindian Warriors of Survivance*. Hanover, N.H.: University Press of New England.

Warrior, Robert. 1994. *Tribal Secrets: Recovering American Indian Intellectual Traditions*. Minneapolis: University of Minnesota Press.

Weaver, Jace, Craig S. Womack, and Robert Warrior. 2006. *American Indian Literary Nationalism*. Albuquerque: University of New Mexico Press.

White, Richard. 1991. *The Middle Ground: Indians, Empires, and Republics in the Great Lakes Region, 1650–1815*. Cambridge: Cambridge University Press.

Williams, Roger. 2002. *A Key into the Language of America*. In *American Religious History*, ed. Amanda Porterfield, 178–180. Oxford: Blackwell.

Wilson, Waziyatawin Angela, and Michael Yellowbird, eds. 2005. *For Indigenous Eyes Only: A Decolonization Handbook*. Santa Fe, N.M.: School of American Research.

Zitkala-Ša. 2001. Zitkala-Ša (Gertrude Bonnin) Defends Paganism, 1902. In *Talking Back to Civilization: Indian Voices from the Progressive Era*, ed. Frederick E. Hoxie, 69–73. Boston: Bedford/St. Martin's.

7. A MATTER OF INTERPRETATION

Dreams, Islam, and Psychology in Egypt

AMIRA MITTERMAIER

Al-Hagg Ahmad, an Egyptian in his eighties, once told me about his encounter with a group of German doctors who insisted that dreams are meaningless. "You in the West are the children of Freud and of Nietzsche!" al-Hagg Ahmad responded to them. "But we as Muslims *have* to believe in dreams. If you don't believe in dreams, you're not a Muslim." I heard such claims frequently in Egypt, where many assert that Western and Islamic epistemes are entirely incompatible. In the case of dreams, such claims at first sight seem to make sense. Reviving the Aristotelian verdict that dreams have little to do with the Divine, Freud (1900:608) famously hailed the interpretation of dreams as a "royal road to a knowledge of the unconscious activities of the mind." By contrast, classical and contemporary Islamic dream manuals contend that not all dreams originate in the unconscious. Rather, some dreams come *to* the dreamer, not *from* her. They are prophetic and provide ethical guidance. Underlying the two dream models are divergent views not only on the nature of dreams but also on human nature and on reality itself. Therefore, according to al-Hagg Ahmad, it is *either* Freud and Nietzsche *or* Islam. There is no space for Muslims who are also informed by Freud and Nietzsche or for interspaces that might be opened up when Freud's and Nietzsche's legacies come into play with other beliefs and practices.

In this chapter I critically engage with the either–or that underlies al-Hagg Ahmad's claim. By tracing the dynamic interplay between two discursive traditions, I hope to complicate the ahistorical notion of a sealed Islamic tradition that continues to prevail in media and public discourses—in Egypt and the "West" alike. The image of a sealed tradition, ironically, figures both in discourses that speak of a clash of civilizations and in those that prescribe a dialogue between them. Besides offering ethnographic insight into actual interplays, this chapter calls for a conceptualization of interplay that draws on models of in-betweenness that are not tied to a prescriptive project of pluralism. Alternative models can emerge from the very acts of crossing over that occur in places rarely called pluralistic—places such as Egypt.

Al-Hagg Ahmad's attempt to sort out the proper relationship between Nietzsche, Freud, and Islam does not speak to an exclusively modern dilemma. The question of how the Islamic tradition is to deal with non-Islamic knowledges has a long history. At the time of the revelation, the Prophet Muhammad had to distinguish his message from pre-Islamic thought systems, and Muslim scholars in the Abbasid period tried to negotiate the proper place for Greek philosophy within their tradition. The challenge of seemingly incompatible worldviews was posed in new ways with the rise of the natural sciences and preoccupied many Muslim reformers in the nineteenth and twentieth centuries. The reformer al-Afghānī, for instance, wrote a response to Orientalist Ernest Renan, who had argued at the Sorbonne in 1883 that a scientific outlook and Islam are entirely incompatible. While trying to refute Renan's claim, al-Afghānī (2002:108) conceded that "the Muslim religion has tried to stifle science and stop its progress."[1] The fact that Muslims still have not freed themselves from the yoke of tradition, in al-Afghānī's view, was ultimately the masses' fault because they dislike reason and fail to see the beauty of science. An alternative response to the challenge posed by modern science is the widespread Muslim reformist claim that "that's what we've been saying all along." According to some reformist interpretations, the nature of microbes, the ozone layer, the shape of the moon's orbit around the earth, and human embryonic development are all already prefigured in the Qur'an. Not surprisingly, then, a modern Islamic psychology was also developed in the later half of the twentieth century that equates Qur'anic concepts with their Freudian counterparts: *al-nafs al-amāra* becomes the id, *al-nafs al-lawāma* the superego, and *al-nafs al-mutma'inna* the ego.[2] Mustafa Mahmūd, a prominent religious figure in Egypt, developed a "Qur'anic psychology,"[3] and Muslim scholars in the Gulf States and Malaysia have also been active in working toward an Islamization of psychology, taking writings by medieval scholars such al-Kindī (d. 873), al-Tabarī (d. 923), al-Rāzī (d. 925), Ibn Sīnā (d. 1037), al-Ghazālī (d. 1111), Ibn Bajjah (d. 1138), and Ibn Tufayl (d. 1185) as possible starting points (Haquem 1997). With regard to the Islamization of medicine in Egypt, Soheir Morsy (1988) has argued that such attempts might best be read as a particular manifestation of biomedical hegemony and not as a revival of Islamic medical traditions.[4] A similar argument could easily be made with regard to the Islamization of psychology. The very attempt to prove that the Qur'an already prefigures all the achievements of modern science ultimately concedes to and reinscribes the hegemony of the latter.

Regardless of whether Islam and modern science are described as incompatible or as fully compatible, they are in both cases conceptualized as distinct entities. Yet, as Stefania Pandolfo (2000:123) notes in her work on spirit healers and psychiatrists in Morocco, concepts of cultural authenticity that are embraced by Orientalists and nationalists alike "obliterate the long history of exchanges and transformations in the shaping of those entities that are today called the Arab world and the West." Not only "Egypt" and the "Arab world" need to be problematized as geographic frames of analysis, but, as anthropologists such as Talal Asad have repeatedly argued, the Islamic tradition must also be reconceived as neither static nor sealed. It is a set of beliefs and practices that is continuously made and remade within particular power relations.[5] In tracing the ongoing remaking of the Muslim tradition of dream interpretation in conjuncture with Western scientific concepts, this chapter draws on fifteen months of fieldwork in Cairo (2003–2004). Interested in the roles that dreams and visions play in Egyptians' everyday lives, and in both the contestation and the revival of Muslim dream interpretation, I spoke with Sufis, psychologists, dream interpreters, intellectuals, and many laypeople, observed dream tellings and dream interpretations, bought dream booklets, and watched dream interpretation programs on television. As I talked to people about the meaning of dreams, it quickly became clear to me that, far from subscribing to one fixed field of knowledge, my interlocutors often juggled different authoritative discourses, drawing on the Qur'anic text, hadiths, psychoanalytic interpretations, and modernist paradigms alike. For many, Islam does not stand in opposition to modern science, nor does it function as the predecessor of science or as its mirror image. Islam rather is articulated with, and through, modern science, just as science is articulated through religion.

Diverging from al-Hagg Ahmad's claim about an inherent incompatibility and bracketing reformist attempts at harmonization, in this chapter I want to draw attention to interspaces, ambiguities, and the messiness that comes into play when actual dreams are told and interpreted in Egypt today. After a brief excursion into pluralism and into Muslim dream interpretation, I examine the interpretive work performed by two Egyptian men of roughly the same age: a psychoanalyst and a Muslim dream interpreter. As we will see, for Muslim dream interpreters the line between classical texts and imported psychological dream models can be highly porous. At the same time, skeptical psychoanalysts sometimes unwillingly get caught in religious idioms. The epistemes offered by the Islamic tradition and the secular sciences continuously inform and inflect one another. They might be incommensurable, but their contradictions can persist comfortably side by side without any need to be resolved.[6]

In highlighting interplays between different epistemes, I do not mean to imply that all Egyptians find ambiguities and fluid boundaries politically or theologically desirable. Al-Hagg Ahmad insists on the either–or, and, like him, many are critical of interplays between religious and secular knowledges. Nevertheless, the shifts, borrowings, and unexpected alliances that occur in everyday interactions complicate notions of sealed monolithic traditions also—and maybe especially—in places that do not explicitly embrace the political project of pluralism. Simple acts of dream telling and dream interpretation therefore can alert us to openings that are not already framed within familiar political vocabularies celebrating diversity. Precisely for that reason, these practices of dream interpretation might also open up the concept of pluralism to new readings.

BEYOND PLURALISM

Although I am interested in the interplay between different discursive traditions, I do not propose that Egypt is pluralistic. Before turning to the question of how one might ethnographically think beyond a prescriptive model of interaction, I want to briefly address some of the ways in which the concept of pluralism obscures the assumptions on which it is based. Without disavowing the desirability of the peaceful coexistence of different projects of being in the world, a number of contributors to this volume show that the concept of pluralism is not politically innocent. Whether equated with tolerance or the active pursuit of dialogue, *pluralism* often plays a similar discursive role as terms such as *democracy, human rights,* or *liberty*. While seeming to embrace humanity as a whole, such discourses often demarcate otherness. The United States, Canada, and Western European countries thus praise themselves for being multireligious, whereas countries such as Egypt are reproached for failing to protect the rights of religious minorities.[7] Arguments about *us* needing to safeguard pluralism and multiculturalism have also become prominent in Europe, especially since Dutch filmmaker Theo van Gogh was murdered in 2004 and since the Danish cartoon controversy in 2005. In Europe and North America today it is often the Muslim Other who somehow fails to live up to the demands of multiculturalism and pluralism. Just as nineteenth-century reformer al-Afghānī reproached the Muslim masses for failing to grasp the beauty of science, Muslims at the beginning of the twenty-first century are reproached for failing to grasp the beauty of diversity. The term *pluralism*, while seeming to be all-inclusive, ultimately reinforces the boundaries between the (supposedly) tolerant West and the (supposedly) intolerant rest of the world. As Tomoko Masuzwa (2005) notes, although religious pluralism and diversity are conceptualized as central achievements of the Enlightenment ethos, such discourses do not displace the logic of European hegemony but ultimately reinscribe it.

A related problem with the ethos of pluralism is that even the "West" is not as pluralistic as it likes to present itself. An eminent proponent of nonviolence and tolerance recently quoted Thomas Mann at a public lecture at the University of Toronto: "Tolerance becomes a crime when applied to evil." Considering that "evil" is not a self-evident label, this quote epitomizes the inherent limitations of "pluralism" and "tolerance."[8]

Pluralism is limited in that only those whose values are not *too* different are invited into the circle of toleration. John Locke, a passionate proponent of tolerance in the seventeenth century, did not believe that tolerance should be extended to Jews, Papists, and atheists. Still today, the public sphere in the modern West is not an open playing field but a space of both inclusions and exclusions (Asad 1993, 2003; see also Todd, chap. 8, and Hicks, chap. 10, this volume). Taking this critique even further, Wendy Brown (2006) draws our attention to the fact that the very concept of tolerance ultimately implies disapproval. Jürgen Habermas's (2005) recent call for a more sincere dialogue in which one not only lets the Other speak but also *listens* and William E. Connolly's (2005) attention to a "politics of becoming"[9] are attempts to find ways out of these limitations, yet so far they seem to have found little resonance in dominant political discourses.

More importantly, as our editors point out, even well-intended calls for a more sincere dialogue continue to prescribe an engagement across difference instead of trying to understand interactions as they unfold in the world. As noted earlier, something that al-Hagg Ahmad, Orientalists, nationalists, and proponents of pluralism have in common is the tendency to construct sealed, bounded entities. These sealed entities and claims to authenticity must be understood as discursive effects and should not lead us to overlook the ways in which these entities are already engaged, intertwined, and mutually constitutive. Just as anthropologists' critiques of a homogenizing culture concept have troubled the paradigm of multiculturalism,[10] attempts to rethink the very category of the religious can destabilize and complicate calls for religious pluralism that assume that religious traditions are bounded entities in the first place.

Whereas this volume calls for a skeptical look at normative and prescriptive discourses around pluralism, I want to draw our attention to spaces of interplay as they exist in places rarely called pluralistic. My focus on such spaces is an interpretive choice—one that, critical readers might say, is itself enabled by the privileged subject position of a cosmopolitan anthropologist able to cross multiple boundaries and borders. Yet, although not all my Egyptian interlocutors would approve of my focus on in-betweenness, explorations of emergent sites of interplay can undermine the notion that only in Western, democratic, "multicultural" societies do multiple paradigms coexist and interact. More importantly, attention to interplay and in-betweenness inevitably complicates the notion of firm and fixed boundaries. My examples accordingly aim at deconstructing notions of clash-like oppositional encounters or unambiguous displacements that presuppose two hermetically sealed, unchanging belief systems. Close attention to the ongoing, messy, and often ambiguous remaking of meaning in everyday life can help us think beyond religion versus science and tradition versus modernity paradigms.

Instead of positing pluralism as a prescriptive framework, I thus explore the actual interplay between, and within, different discursive traditions and epistemes in Egypt. To understand this interplay and the ensuing messiness and complexity, we do well to think beyond al-Hagg Ahmad's insistence on the either–or and to consider instead what makes particular idioms meaningful and compelling in particular social contexts. In my opinion this can best be done through an ethnographic tracing of ambiguities and of what lies between multiple discourses, such as those associated with Islam and Western psychology. Again, my point is not to prove that Egyptians too are (unintentionally) pluralistic, but I want to suggest that ethnographies that attend to the messiness of social life inevitably reveal the ways in which traditions are embedded in continuous interplays, exchanges, negotiations, contestations, and appropriations. This does not mean that everyday life is best understood as a free flow and intermingling of ideas and practices. Muslim dream interpretation as a practice is itself continuously reshaped through various forms of power and difference, and religious authorities often attempt to constrain acts of the imagination that spill over the boundaries of "orthodox" Islam. Close ethnographic attention will inevitably alert us to the power relations that pervade, shape, and delimit all interchanges and interplays, whether within a religious tradition or between "religious" and "secular" paradigms.

CROSSING OVER

Not only is dream interpretation in Egypt situated between different discursive traditions, but *taʿbīr*, dream interpretation in classical Arabic, itself also literally means "taking across, making something pass over." In Islamic traditions, the dream interpreter is a mediator between the divine and the human realm. Muslim dream interpretation goes back to the time of the Prophet Muhammad, who supposedly interpreted his followers' dreams and assured them that the only form of prophecy left after his death would come in the form of truthful dream-visions.[11] The dream-vision (*ru'yā*) is considered to be a divine gift, and classical dream manuals and contemporary dream interpreters distinguish it from two other kinds of dreams: those inspired by the Devil or evil spirits (*hulm*) and dreams that reflect the dreamer's wishes and worries (*hadīth nafsī*). Because of their close relationship to prophecy, dream-visions were highly valued in the Islamic tradition, and dream interpretation emerged as an orthodox practice.[12] Though considered fully Islamic, the Muslim tradition of dream interpretation did not evolve in isolation but was greatly affected by Artemidorus's famous dream book, which was translated from Greek into Arabic in the ninth century. More than a thousand years later another dream model entered into dialogue with the continuously reimagined Muslim tradition of dream interpretation. Around 1950 the Freudian legacy crossed over into Egypt, making it the first country in the Middle East to actively engage with psychoanalysis.[13]

The importation of psychoanalysis was part of a larger endeavor concerned with enabling Egypt to "catch up" with Europe. Since the early nineteenth century, Egyptian students had been traveling to Europe to seek knowledge, spurred by the urgently felt and constantly re-created need to help Egypt overcome its supposed backwardness. One of the many students who went to Paris in the early twentieth century was Mustafa Ziwer. Born in 1907, Ziwer had been among the first philosophy students at what is now Cairo University, and after graduating in 1927, he left for France, where he studied philosophy, medicine, chemistry, biology, and applied psychology, and he also underwent psychoanalysis. On his return to Egypt, he was appointed by Taha Hussain, then minister of education, to found the first psychology department in Cairo in 1950, and he came to be praised as the first Egyptian, or even first Arab, psychoanalyst. Whereas most of the people seeking out Ziwer's help as an analyst came from elite backgrounds, Freudian theories traveled into Egyptian households by way of Ziwer's radio programs, and on Cairo's campuses, as an elderly Egyptian psychologist told me, "Freud was like the Qur'an at that time."

Referring to India, Ashis Nandy (1995:82, 138) has noted that psychoanalysis, after having become a "positive science, an exportable technology, and an index of progress," was imported "into the [so-called] savage world in the high noon of imperialism." In Egypt, too, the importation of Freud's theories can be understood as part of a larger modernization movement. Freudian psychology arrived infused with claims to truth, authority, and expertise. It was a form of modern science that, in Foucault's (1988:106) words, is a "power that forces you to say certain things, if you are not to be disqualified not only as being wrong, but, more seriously than that, as being a charlatan." Whereas the relevance of Freud continues to be debated in the West (not to mention within and between various schools of psychoanalysis) and whereas the rise of pharmaceuticals and biomedical models have undermined psychoanalytic explanatory models (Luhrmann 2001), many of my interlocutors in Egypt refer to Freud's model as *'ilmī* (scientific).[14] By contrast, Muslim dream interpretation is called *fulklūrī* (folkloristic), *sha'bī* (popular), or *usūlī* (traditional).

Contemporary Egyptians have a basic familiarity with Freudian concepts, but this does not mean that his theories are simply accepted as true or even relevant. During my fieldwork I was repeatedly struck by the ambiguous place Western psychology holds in Egyptians' everyday dream talk. Just like the Muslim reformers, laypeople sometimes claim that what Islam says ultimately coincides with what modern science says. Others draw on Western psychology to prove that Muslim dream interpretation is backward, outdated, unscientific, and ultimately un-Islamic. In addition, al-Azhar, the authoritative institution of Sunni Islam, and key figures of the Islamic Revival movement have decried dream interpretation as charlatanry in recent years,[15] and the Egyptian Ministry of Religious Affairs has claimed that "there is nothing in the Islamic religion that confirms the idea of dream interpretation."[16] Azharite and state-aligned critics sometimes reject both Muslim dream interpretation and Western psychological models. Still others, such as al-Hagg Ahmad, defend the Islamic interpretive tradition while claiming that Freud is mistaken or irrelevant for Muslim dreams. "Freud is wrong," an imam told me, "because he relates everything back to sex." In any case, the imam continued, none of the people who go to the mosque and pray regularly will ever need a psychologist.

Freudian psychology and Muslim reformism have by no means marginalized religious dream discourses in Egypt. On the contrary, there seems to have been a revival of interest in dream interpretation in wake of the larger Islamic Revival since the 1970s.[17] Muslim dream interpretation is marketed today by way of cheap paperback booklets, newspaper and magazine columns, TV programs, Web sites, and CD-ROMs. This renewed, mass-mediated interest in dreams does not exclude Freudian psychology but often incorporates it. Next to the many new editions of standard dream manuals, one finds in Cairo's street stalls booklets featuring titles such as *Dreams and Nightmares: Scientific and Religious Interpretation*, *Dreams Between Science and Belief*, and *The Foundations and Principles of Dream Interpretation Between Freud and the Muslim Scholars*.[18]

The very distinction between "science" and "belief," which gets recycled in these titles, is itself the outcome of a specific understanding of science that finds its roots in the Enlightenment. Yet on Cairo's streets, in everyday dream talk, and on Egyptian television this distinction often becomes blurry. A prophetic or divine sign in the eyes of some can be a hallucinatory projection according to others. Importantly, these debates are not necessarily predictable along the lines of who is inside and who outside which tradition or who considers herself more closely aligned to it. Neither the Islamic nor the psychological dream episteme should be treated as homogeneous, unchanging entities. Far from the Freudian legacy simply displacing the religious interpretive model, the two dream epistemes have come to mutually constitute each other in ways that are not always predictable.

To illustrate this process, I next turn to two interpretive moments that center on terms many Egyptians would associate primarily with Freud: *desire* and the *unconscious*. Though seemingly Freudian, these terms are characterized by a textual and lived heteroglossia, carrying within them multiple layers and possibilities of meaning.[19]

As Bakhtin (1981:272) puts it, "every concrete utterance of a speaking subject serves as a point where centrifugal as well as centripetal forces are brought to bear." Forces work toward ideological unification, but "each word [also] tastes of the context and contexts in which it has lived its socially charged life" (Bakhtin 1981:293). Although Bakhtin is attentive to the nature of authoritative discourses and thus to asymmetrical power relations, the concept of heteroglossia directs our attention to spaces of ambiguity that do not insist on exclusive, stable meanings.

HUNGRY PEOPLE DREAM OF BREAD

Dr. Hakim is an Egyptian Lacanian psychoanalyst and one of Mustafa Ziwer's former students. At the time of my fieldwork he was retired, and I visited him a number of times because I enjoyed his profound knowledge of European and Egyptian literatures and his detailed memories of the early years of psychology in Egypt. However, he seemed somewhat ambivalent about our meetings and my research. Although he was generally welcoming, he was critical of popular dream beliefs and seemed annoyed by my interest in the work of Muslim dream interpreters. "They're all charlatans," he said whenever I told him about the shaykhs I worked with. "Dreams are not about prophecy at all; they're about desire (*raghba*)."

During one of our conversations I brought up a popular dream interpretation program on Egyptian television that used to feature a shaykh and a psychologist. On this show viewers called in to tell of their dreams, and the shaykh would discern what kind of dream they were recounting and, accordingly, who should interpret it. The shaykh took on all divinely inspired dream-visions; the rest he left to the psychologist. For many Egyptians this show was a perfect example of how "science" and "religion" could harmoniously be brought together. When I mentioned the program, Dr. Hakim told me that he once was invited to participate but declined the offer because he disliked the fact that the shaykh always had the last word on the show. He then added in passing that he used to run his own dream program on a Saudi Arabian satellite television station in the late 1990s. Together with a colleague he would interpret dreams of viewers who called in to the show. Curious about the program, I borrowed a stack of videotapes from Dr. Hakim and watched them at home. Besides the décor, which featured the two psychologists on black leather seats placed on top of clouds—godlike, one might say—what intrigued me most about the program was the complex interpretive field the psychologists were required to navigate. They had to respond to dreams such as the following, related by a woman calling from Qatar: "I have recurrent dreams, spiritual dreams; I'm in contact with people. I'm afraid when I wake up. After my father died, I used to still communicate with him. The Prophet also comes to me in my dreams. At first I was not sure whether it was him, but then I prayed *istikhāra* to find out and I saw him again. . . . Does that mean I'm clairvoyant?"[20]

While only saying a few sentences, the woman evokes a range of potentially meaningful dreams. She refers to dreams of the dead, dreams of the Prophet, and *istikhāra* dreams. The latter are dreams seen after a nonobligatory prayer through which one can seek advice when feeling unable to decide between two permissible alternatives. A dream seen after this prayer is generally taken to be a divinely sent answer, a dream-vision, a *ru'yā*.

Knowing Dr. Hakim, one would expect a triple negation in response to the woman's questions: No, it's not really the Prophet you see; you only want to see him. No, *istikhāra* does not provide God-sent answers. And no, you're not clairvoyant. Wanting to see the Prophet and truly seeing the Prophet are separated by an insurmountable gap from Dr. Hakim's customary point of view.

Yet the religious coloring of the dreams (and the fact that the program is broadcast on a channel based in Saudi Arabia)[21] makes such a bluntly negative answer impossible. Dr. Hakim diplomatically responds by quoting the well-known hadith that affirms that whoever sees the Prophet in a dream-vision has truly seen him. Then he refers to another prophetic tradition that defines the dream-vision as one of forty-six parts of prophecy (e.g., Sahih Bukhari, 9:104–106, 119). Though not a Muslim dream interpreter, Dr. Hakim seems to be caught in an authoritative discourse, which, as Bakhtin (1981:342) has noted, "demands that we acknowledge it, that we make it our own; it binds us, quite independent of any power it might have to persuade us internally; we encounter it with its authority already fused to it." Though most probably not persuaded internally, Dr. Hakim gives a religious response to what has been framed as a series of religious dreams. He adopts a religious discursive rationale to make himself heard and to authorize his discourse. Thus, not only modern science can force people to say certain things if they are not to be disqualified as being wrong or as being a charlatan, but, depending on the context, so can religious traditions.

Dr. Hakim's colleague, another Egyptian psychoanalyst, jumps in to suggest that the dreams of the deceased father are clearly related to the woman's longing. This allows Dr. Hakim to switch his interpretive mode and to emphasize that the woman's dreams are indeed a form of wish fulfillment. Before moving on to the next caller, the colleague adds a final word of psychological wisdom: "Hungry people dream of bread."

Yet the woman's own framing of her dreams as religiously significant and the psychoanalyst's initial reference to the prophetic tradition have already destabilized the universalistic explanatory power of psychology. Even introducing the concept of desire does not unambiguously close this opening because desire is itself an overdetermined term that is at home in multiple interpretive traditions and that can index very different conceptions of the real. Although the Islamic dream model recognizes the role of longing in evoking visions of the Prophet, the fact that dream encounters with the Prophet can be evoked does not mean that they are hallucinatory. In the Islamic model, rather, desire can pave the road for a divinely sent dream-vision. The heteroglossia that infuses the term *desire* complicates and undermines the psychoanalysts' final verdict. Whereas the hungry fantasize about bread in their dreams but still wake up hungry, the religious dreamer might use her longing to invite a real visit of the Prophet or encounters with the dead.

The interchange between the Qatari woman and the two psychoanalysts problematizes the assumption that the secular sciences will always be the authoritative way to explain natural phenomena in today's world. It shows that, along with social contexts, the authority of interpretive approaches can shift, and that the same terms can underline the truth of very different conceptions of the real. Interpretations do not take place in empty space, but they are shaped by the social contexts in which they occur. What Dr. Hakim says on television is very different from what he told me in his living room. Yet the fact that the psychoanalyst gives in to a religious authoritative discourse should not simply be understood as resulting from the necessity of hiding his "true" views because he lives in a repressive society. This kind of playing into context occurs around the world, including in North America and Europe. Dr. Hakim's invocation of a religious discourse on television is just one instance of how he uses different discourses in different contexts. In doing so, he changes the way he engages with his profession and, probably unwillingly, expands the meaning of *desire*.

The picture could be complicated even further were one to study the reception of Dr. Hakim's dream interpretation program. As in Lila Abu-Lughod's (2005) work on Egyptian soap operas, television messages are deflected and offset in multiple ways by their viewers' own everyday realities. Michel de Certeau (2002) invites us in more general terms to think of consumption as a kind of production. In his view, everyday life is about navigating and creatively using imposed products, spaces, and languages. I do not know how Dr. Hakim's program was received, but I next turn to an instance of such creative redeployment, of what de Certeau would call reading-as-poaching, or what Claude Lévi-Strauss (1966) might call bricolage, the creative drawing together of different things out of which something new emerges. As this example shows, terms do not simply index different traditions, but they can be borrowed from one and invested with new meanings in another. The meaning of dreams, Islam, and reality is constantly renegotiated and remade—by dreamers, interpreters, psychologists, and the occasional anthropologist.

THE UNCONSCIOUS RESIGNIFIED

Along with the practice of psychoanalysis, Mustafa Ziwer imported the distinct Freudian notion of the unconscious into Egypt.[22] Although Freud (1900:143) acknowledged that "there is at least one spot in every dream at which it is unplumbable—a navel, as it were, that is its point of contact with the unknown," dominant understandings of his theory take the origin of dreams to be limited to a faculty located inside the human subject. Adopting the belief that all dreams originate in this particular faculty, Egyptian psychologists tend to deny the possibility that dreams might offer insight into a metaphysical world. Rather than refute the existence of this metaphysical realm altogether, they often refer to Qur'anic verses that state that only God has keys to the unknown.[23] Although psychologists insist that dreams offer access only to the personal but not to a metaphysical unknown, psychological tropes can be picked up and resignified by religious dream interpreters. Like the concept of desire, the unconscious is heavy with cultural baggage, but it is never a stable term. Far from being the sole and mechanistic source of dreams, it might become a medium of communication with a supernatural Elsewhere. This ongoing resignification of religious and psychological dream concepts can be illustrated through an interpretation offered by Shaykh Nabil, a Muslim dream interpreter in Cairo.

Dr. Hakim and Shaykh Nabil are roughly of the same age but belong to different socioeconomic classes. Shaykh Nabil lives in a working-class neighborhood and Dr. Hakim in an upper-middle-class one. Although both men interpret dreams, they draw on different interpretive traditions. Whereas Dr. Hakim's intellectual trajectory was shaped by his engagement with Freud, Lacan, and Ziwer, Shaykh Nabil is the guardian of the shrine of Ibn Sīrīn, an eighth-century scholar who has long been considered the father of Muslim dream interpretation. The majority of dream booklets sold on Cairo's streets are ascribed to Ibn Sīrīn, usually offering updated and abridged versions of his classic manual. Shaykh Nabil spends most of his time at Ibn Sīrīn's small shrine, reading the Qur'an, praying, sleeping, smoking *shisha*, receiving visitors, and interpreting dreams. He likes to refer to himself as the "little Ibn Sīrīn" or the "modern Ibn Sīrīn." Whereas other Muslim dream interpreters are dismissive of Freud, Shaykh Nabil has no problem with evoking Freud when interpreting dreams because he believes that Freud can help bring the tradition up to date. His understanding of Freud's theory is admittedly reductive, yet it is simultaneously expansive as he applies Freudian concepts to divinely inspired dream-visions as well.

Shaykh Nabil also interprets dreams online but without actually ever touching a computer. A journalist prints out the dream texts that are sent to a Web site and drops them off at the shrine on a weekly basis. In a stack of papers that the journalist brought to the shrine one day in November 2003 was the dream of a twenty-two-year-old Egyptian woman named Huda who had written the following: "I saw in my sleep one of my dear friends, and he was dead. In truth he's not dead. Twice a month I have this dream, and every time I wake up and find myself crying. I also cry in the dream."

Other dreams in the stack were longer, others even shorter; some more vivid or more dramatic. Huda's dream was not exceptional in any way. Without a moment of hesitation Shaykh Nabil jotted down his response on the lower half of the page: "The message is from the unconscious (*al-lā wa'y*) and it points to a happy future. It is a glad tiding (*bushra*) of the death of the past, of the beginning of the future, and of leaving behind hardships. The symbol of death in the dream is the death of the past. We die in the dream and wake up to new life. [The dream] directs you to a happy future."

The effect apparently intended by Shaykh Nabil's interpretation was to dispel Huda's worries. According to his response, she had nothing to be concerned about. The dream that had troubled her turned out to be a foretelling of a not clearly defined yet happy future. That death symbolizes life and crying means release from hardship resonates with standard Muslim dream manuals. What is unusual in the shaykh's interpretation, however, is his use of the term *unconscious*. The exact word he uses is the Arabic word *al-lā wa'y*, a term borrowed from modern psychology and generally associated with Freud in Egypt.[24] Shaykh Nabil's terminology is perplexing because it erases the line between a meaningful dream-vision and a dream that merely reflects the dreamer's concerns and wishes. Many of my Egyptian interlocutors hold that dream-visions are seen by the dreamer's heart (*qalb*) or by her spirit (*rūh*), which leaves the sleeping body and roams in an intermediary realm called the *barzakh* where it can communicate with the spirits of the dead. Others relate dream-visions to a heightened perceptiveness of one's inner gaze (*basīra*), or they told me that dream angels transmit dream-visions to the dreamer. The term *unconscious* seems out of place when speaking of a dream-vision.

I visited Shaykh Nabil a few days later to ask him to explain his interpretation of Huda's dream. How can a dream that comes from the unconscious tell Huda something about the future? How can it be a *bushra*, a glad tiding, which according to the Prophet Muhammad would come only in the form of divinely sent dreams?[25] Would not a dream that springs from the unconscious simply index Huda's wishes and worries? Where then does her dream originate: in her unconscious or in an Elsewhere?

Shaykh Nabil seemed slightly irritated by my questions, which implied that his practices should submit to the logic of either–or. Nevertheless, he ordered tea for both of us from the street café facing the shrine, sat down with me, and explained, once again, that things do not have to be so black and white. The "unconscious" (*al-lā wa'y*) and the "inner mind" (*al-'aql al-bātin*), he told me, refer to the same thing. As he phrased it, "It's like the sun that shines here and there but that is felt differently in different places and called by different names." He explained that the inner mind is located in the heart and that it is much stronger than the conscious mind because it has the capacity to read from the Eternal Tablet in heaven. The Eternal Tablet (*al-lawh al-mahfūz*) generally refers to an archetypical repository of the Qur'an, or more broadly to a heavenly tablet on which all human destinies are inscribed. The dream angels who transmit dream images to the dreamer are sometimes said to read the dream-vision on the Eternal Tablet and to then deliver it to the dreamer, either by showing it to her inner gaze or by telling her the dream-vision. In claiming that the unconscious has access to this Eternal Tablet, Shaykh Nabil turns the unconscious into a medium that offers insight not into the depths of the human mind but into a metaphysical Elsewhere. His interpretation contrasts sharply with that of Orientalists, who referred to the unconscious to suggest that the Prophet Muhammad wrongly believed that his revelation experiences originated outside himself. Deferring to the authority of "modern advances in psychology and psychiatry," Maxime Rodinson (1980:77) argued that the concept of the unconscious has enabled us to understand the true nature of the Prophet's so-called revelation. Similarly, Montgomery Watt (1974:17) remarked that the "modern Westerner" realizes that what seems to the Prophet to come from "outside himself" can really come from the unconscious and that Muhammad might have simply been a man with a strong "creative imagination." For Shaykh Nabil the imagination encompasses a much broader range of possibilities (including prophetic ones), and evoking the unconscious does not make the dream experience any less real or relevant. A dream that is received by the unconscious in his view can reveal a timeless truth and future events. The unconscious here is a prophetic medium.

Shaykh Nabil only seemingly locates the origin of the dream within the dreamer. Although he is familiar with Freud's notion that unconscious wishes motivate dreams, he subsumes the term under his own dream theory, which implies a less sealed model of the self than that underlying the Freudian paradigm. He agrees that most dreams arise from what one is preoccupied with, but according to his semi-Freudian interpretation, a dream can be a hope and a manifestation from God even at the same time. Thus, although modernity did not introduce subjective interiority to Islam,[26] one might say that Freudian psychology has provided Shaykh Nabil and other interpreters with a new vocabulary for talking about the relationship between the religious self and an Elsewhere.

One could read Shaykh Nabil's use of Freudian terms as falling within a broader practical concept of the Freudian tradition that is just as legitimate as a professional psychoanalyst's use of the terms. Instead, I choose to look at the shaykh's engagement with these terms as constituting an in-between space of its own. This does not mean that Shaykh Nabil is "naturally" syncretic whereas Dr. Hakim is the authentic bearer of Freud's legacy. Rather, the example of Shaykh Nabil's use of Freudian terms highlights that every citation is also an interpretation. For Freud the concept of the unconscious served as evidence that dreams *cannot* come from a metaphysical Elsewhere; Shaykh Nabil (maybe unknowingly) challenges these assumptions. For him the unconscious is the immediate source of the dream, but it ultimately belongs to God and is operated by His will.

CONCLUSION

The notion of sealed traditions that underlies the language of pluralism and of clashing civilizations diverts our attention from the ways in which many traditions are already mutually constitutive. Taking dream interpretation as an example, I have aimed to show in what ways religious and secular epistemes are intertwined and engaged in Egypt. They stand in tension to one another, but each is understood in conjunction with the other. Simplistic accounts of psychology displacing Muslim dream interpretation—or of the latter puristically defying and rebuffing the former—fail to do justice to the complexities of their interplay. The relationship between Freudian and Islamic idioms is never static, but it can change even within the view of individuals, depending on the context in which they speak. Instead of insisting on simple narratives of resistance or acceptance, I therefore argued for attention to the ways in which particular knowledges are made meaningful in concrete social contexts by looking at subtle interplays and processes of resignification.

At times attention to interplay might run the risk of overlooking the power relations that frame, delimit, and shape this very interplay. I opened my discussion with al-Hagg Ahmad's assertion that one is *either* a follower of Freud and Nietzsche *or* a Muslim and suggested that such claims to incompatibility can be made purposefully, not only by Orientalists or nationalist purists but also in the context of everyday, mundane encounters. Al-Hagg Ahmad makes his claim to make a particular point in a particular context and while talking to particular people: German doctors at first, and later me, a German-Egyptian anthropologist associated with a U.S. institution at the time. In the current political climate it is easily understandable why al-Hagg Ahmad would want to construct a sealed Muslim identity and to assert its superiority. His utterance subverts claims to the inherent superiority of Western knowledge systems. Yet, although power and politics certainly should not be written out of ethnographic accounts, attention to interplays also shows that power relations are themselves not static. "Lived hegemony," as Raymond Williams (1977:112) has put it, "is always a process. . . . It has continually to be renewed, re-created, defended, and modified. It is also continually resisted, limited, altered, challenged by pressures not at all its own."[27] A static model of hegemony overlooks the complex processes through which authority is claimed and enacted in concrete contexts.

My ethnographic examples illustrate the fluidity of lived hegemonies. In the case of Dr. Hakim, the disciplinary power of the Islamic tradition traps a skeptical psychoanalyst. In the case of Shaykh Nabil, a Muslim dream interpreter resignifies psychoanalytic vocabularies. This does not mean that only Islamic traditions are disciplinary, whereas the adoption of the Western psychological model is voluntaristic. Rather, by juxtaposing these examples, I hope to have complicated the notion that the secular sciences are necessarily hegemonic. Islamic *and* secular discursive traditions can force people to say certain things if they want to be taken seriously, and only close attention to context can allow us to trace the shifting terrains of hegemony.

Ultimately, which dreams are projections and which the result of divine inspiration often remains ambiguous in Egypt. The origin of Huda's dream is suspended between the unconscious and an Elsewhere, and whether or not the woman from Qatar truly saw the Prophet or whether she only wanted to see him is left an open question in the psychoanalyst's dream show. Ethnographic attention to interplays challenges us to move beyond a focus on what is and invites us to think instead about what lies between. In-betweenness offers an alternative conceptual framework to focusing on the various entities that make up the *plural* in *pluralism*. Finding a language for the in-between can be difficult, but as Vincent Crapanzano (2003:64) has pointed out, despite its universalist pretension, our "insistent ontology of presence" is not universally shared. Directing our attention to silences, absences, and spaces in between, Crapanzano draws on concepts such as the Japanese *ma* and the Arabic *barzakh*. Similarly, Stefania Pandolfo (1997), in her work on postcolonial Morocco, evokes the *barzakh* to refer to the elusive space that she elsewhere calls the "Thin Line, an entre-deux, an interstitial zone, an emergent beyond, in between classificatory terms" (Pandolfo 2000:120). Central to Sufi cosmologies, *barzakh* refers to the space that lies between the spiritual and the material, between the visible and the invisible, between being and not-being. The *barzakh* is the in-between space in which the spirits of the dead and the living mingle, and it is the imaginary space in which dream-visions originate. Following Crapanzano and Pandolfo, I find the *barzakh* to be a provocative concept for thinking about in-betweenness and about that which exceeds dichotomous orders of reality. Although certainly not all Egyptians embrace or celebrate in-betweenness, and although crossing cultural or religious boundaries can result in retribution or deprivation, I believe that vocabularies such as the *barzakh* pose a productive challenge to concepts of pluralism, which tend to reinscribe bounded entities. In my larger work I accordingly take the *barzakh* not only as an object of ethnographic description but also as an analytical space that evades an insistence on the either–or (Mittermaier 2011).

A focus on the in-between can also alert us to the fact that the West is just as full of ambiguities and internal debates and contests for intellectual legitimacy as is Egypt. Even Freudian psychology itself is not a closed system. Through his rereading of Freud, Jacques Lacan (2002) has opened a space for alterity within Freud's theory, and James DiCenso (1998) argues that, besides the more widely known tendency toward closure in Freud's work, one can detect conflicting qualities that resist totalization. According to such readings, dream interpretation even in Freud's writings can be seen as a paradigm for an opening to alterity that has profound ethical implications. Maybe this openness and excess in Freud is more tangible in Egypt, where his theories are subverted, resignified, and opened up not necessarily through a conscious act of resistance on the part of traditionalists but rather through an ongoing reimagining of what dreams are and where they come from. Ethnographic attention to interplays, heteroglossias, and the *barzakh* thus not only complicates straightforward accounts of displacement but also requires us to move beyond our tendency to focus on what is as opposed to allowing for unscripted futures.[28] One might find such futures arising not only in elections, revolutions, scholarly forums, or abstract debates but also in seemingly apolitical practices, in the cyberworld, on television, and in everyday talk of dreams.

NOTES

Many thanks to Pamela Klassen and Courtney Bender for organizing the After Pluralism workshop and for editing this volume, to the workshop participants and Natalie Zemon Davis for their helpful comments, and to Alejandra Gonzalez Jimenez, Jess Bier, Nadia Fadil, Michael Lambek, and two anonymous reviewers for their comments on earlier drafts of this chapter.

1. Jamāl al-Dīn al-Afghānī (1838–1897) is considered a founding figure of Salafi modernism. Despite his name, he was not from Afghanistan but most probably from Iran, and he was active in a number of places, including Egypt and France. He was a proponent of political reform and argued that only greater unity within the Muslim world would enable it to resist European rule. *Salafism* more broadly refers to a Sunni reform movement intent on purifying Islam and highlighting its compatibility with modern reason.

2. In the Qur'an, *nafs* refers to the soul or human self. It moves through three stages. *Al-nafs al-amāra* (the commanding self) is controlled by passion and impulses; it commands evil (e.g., Qur'an 12:53). *Al-nafs al-lawāma* (the reproaching self) is torn between good and evil (e.g., 75:2). *Al-nafs al-mutma'inna* (the trusting self), which is the highest stage, is the self at peace (e.g., 89:27).

3. Mustafa Mahmūd (1921–2009) was trained as a medical doctor, and after an initial attraction to Marxism, he became a popular preacher and launched a TV series called *al-'ilm wa-l-imān* (*Science and Faith*). On his trajectory, see Salvatore (2000).

4. On the Islamization of the sciences more broadly, see Abaza (2002). On the complex negotiation of different Muslim ethical positions on organ transplantation in Egypt, see Hamdy (2009).

5. For a related conceptualization of an anthropology of Islam, see Asad (1986).

6. I draw here on Michael Lambek's use of the term *incommensurable*. In his book on local knowledges in Mayotte, Lambek traces how three different traditions are articulated in practice. He argues not simply that these traditions are incommensurable but that "incommensurability is a critical feature of most forms of knowledge (including science)" (Lambek 1993:8). He thus draws attention to tensions not only *between* but also *within* discursive traditions.

7. Egypt's constitution provides for equal rights without regard to religion, but human rights organizations often criticize Egypt for discriminatory treatment (e.g., of Copts and even more so of Baha'is). I am not trying to gloss over such discrimination but am simply concerned here with the ways in which the language of pluralism functions. In this context it is telling that U.S. president Barack Obama's speech at Cairo University in June 2009 was a balancing act between upholding universal human

rights and insisting that no system of government should ever be imposed on one nation by another. Skeptical Egyptians commented that, even in disavowing America's presumed world leadership, Obama's speech ultimately reinscribed it.

8. It is telling and ironic that the quotation from Thomas Mann's *Der Zauberberg* not only figured in this lecture on nonviolence and tolerance but also appears on the Web site of Daniel Pipes, the founder of Campus Watch, a neoconservative think tank dedicated to the surveillance of Middle East studies at North American colleges. See http://www.danielpipes.org/comments/49479 (accessed February 10, 2008).

9. William E. Connolly (2000, 2005) points out that pluralism is often limited to acceptance of what *is*, as opposed to allowing spaces for what is *arising*.

10. Whereas early anthropologists such as E. B. Tylor and Franz Boas used the term *culture* to refer to the totality of beliefs and institutions within a given society, the concept has been criticized since the 1980s for creating the false notion of homogeneous, neatly bounded, internally coherent entities. For attempts to write "against culture," see Clifford and Marcus (1986), Clifford (1988), and Abu-Lughod (1991). Lee and LiPuma (2002) argue that, instead of thinking of cultures as bounded entities, we should account for "cultures of circulation" in their own right: ones that are unsealed, unbounded or differently bounded, and not locally specific but no less real.

11. I use the term *dream-vision* to maintain some of the ambiguity that surrounds the term *ru'yā*. According to classical sources, a *ru'yā* can come in the form of a truthful dream or a waking vision. My Egyptian interlocutors sometimes did not specify whether they were awake or asleep when seeing a *ru'yā*.

12. For more details on the history of Muslim dream interpretation, see Fahd (1966), Kinberg (1994), Lamoreaux (2002), and Schimmel (1998).

13. Earlier in the twentieth century, psychology had been sporadically evoked in lectures at Egypt's newly founded secular universities, for example, to characterize the "psychology of women" or to explain mental disorders to law students (Soueif and Ahmed 2001). In the 1950s and 1960s, Egypt was pioneering in the Middle East in its engagement with psychoanalysis. Today Lebanon and Morocco are leading in the institutionalization of psychoanalysis.

14. The dichotomy between Islam and modern science is a discursive one, related to a reconfiguration of *'ilm*, an Arabic term that now largely refers to the natural and empirical sciences. Historically, *'ilm* referred to religious spontaneous knowledge of God, as opposed to *ma'rifa*, which stood for knowledge acquired through reflection. See entry on *'ilm* in the *Encyclopedia of Islam*.

15. The Arabic term that I translate as "charlatan" is *dajjāl*, which also means "swindler, cheat, or imposter." I choose "charlatan(ry)" to make the term resonate with Foucault's remark on modern science.

16. When Muslim dream interpretation today gets labeled "un-Islamic" and "superstitious," this has to do not only with Western psychology but also with Muslim reformism and larger political issues that exceed the scope of this chapter. The position of the Ministry of Religious Affairs was quoted widely after a debate erupted in 2003 over the legitimacy of dream interpretation on Egyptian national television.

For this precise statement, see the newspaper article "Ba'da waqf birnāmij Ru'a bi-sabab shā'i'at mawlid al-mahdī al-muntazar," *al-Khāmis,* March 20, 2003, p. 10 (my translation).

17. The Islamic Revival (*al-sahwa al-islāmiyya*) is marked by visible transformations such as an increasing number of mosques, religious study circles, Islamic books sold on Cairo's streets, sermon tapes played in cabs and at juice stands, and bodily religious signifiers, such as beards and hijabs. The revival is also related to what has been referred to as a democratization of religious knowledge. On the role of the mass media (particularly tapes) in the revival, see Hirschkind (2006). On the continuing (or increasing) popularity of Islamic dream models in Egypt, see Hoffman (1997) and Gilsenan (2000).

18. The titles in Arabic are *Al-ahlām wa-l-kawābīs: Tafsīr 'ilmī wa dīnī, Al-ahlām bayna al-'ilm wa-l-'aqīda,* and *Usus wa Usūl fī tafsīr al-ahlām bayna Frūyid wa ulamā' al-muslimīn.*

19. Heteroglossia is a concept central to Bakhtin's discussion of the genre of the novel and refers to the novel's incorporation of various languages and to its complex intertextuality. Although the heteroglossic mode is privileged in the novel, Bakhtin notes that language as a whole unites within it a plurality of socio-ideological contradictions.

20. Video recording of Allāhumma Aja'lu Khayr, A.R.T., May 1, 1998 (my translation).

21. Wahhabism, an eighteenth-century reform movement and today the official doctrine of Saudi Arabia, aims at purging Islam of all "superstitions." Yet Wahhabi scholars often are ambiguous with regard to dream interpretation. Often they call the practice un-Islamic while acknowledging the possibility of divinely inspired dream-visions. This partially explains why dreams and dream interpretations are not simply erased from Saudi-based TV programs.

22. The history of the "unconscious" is complex. See Lacan (1978), who highlights the historical particularity of Freud's concept of the unconscious, and Ellenberger (1970), who emphasizes the continuity between exorcism, magnetism, hypnotism, and dynamic psychiatry.

23. For example, 6:59: "For, with Him are the keys to the things that are beyond the reach of a created being's perception: none knows them but He" (Muhammad Asad's translation).

24. When the first book on psychology appeared in Egypt in 1895, the Arabic term *al-sarīra* (secret thought) was used to refer to the unconscious. The term was then replaced by *al-'aql al-bātin* (inner mind) and subsequently by *al-lā shu'ūr* (un-feeling), which is also used in the 1958 translation of Freud's *Traumdeutung*. In everyday conversations, Freud's concept of the unconscious is most often called *al-lā wa'y* (the un-consciousness).

25. The term *bushra* is derived from the same root as *mubashshirāt* (glad tidings), which the Prophet Muhammad announced to be the only thing that would be left of prophecy after his death. When asked what glad tidings are, the Prophet answered, "truthful dream-visions" (*al-ru'yā al-sādiqa*).

26. As Talal Asad (2003:225) points out, Sufism, in its early ascetic renderings, placed emphasis on the importance of *muhāsaba*, psychological introspection, and the Sufi al-Hallāj (d. 922) at times is revered as the first individualistic Muslim. Describing precolonial notions of interiority, Brinkley Messick (2001) has argued that Islamic legal conceptions of intent are predicated on a historically specific inwardness: Intent is located in the heart (*qalb*), which is part of a larger interior realm of the self (*nafs*). As noted earlier, classical Islamic dream models also speak of dreams that originate within the self (*hadīth nafsī*).

27. Raymond Williams largely draws on Gramsci's definition of hegemony. The latter defines hegemony as a form of control exercised by the dominant class that works through consent rather than brute force.

28. I borrow this term from Joseph A. Massad's recent work, *Desiring Arabs* (2007:417).

WORKS CITED

Abaza, Mona. 2002. *Debates on Islam and Knowledge in Malaysia and Islam: Shifting Worlds*. New York: Routledge.

Abu-Lughod, Lila. 1991. Writing Against Culture. In *Recapturing Anthropology: Working in the Present*, ed. Richard Fox, 137–162. Santa Fe, N.M.: School of American Research.

Abu-Lughod, Lila. 2005. *Dramas of Nationhood: The Politics of Television in Egypt*. Chicago: University of Chicago Press.

al-Afghani, Jamal al-Din. 2002. Answer to Renan. In *Modernist Islam, 1840–1940: A Sourcebook*, ed. Charles Kurzman, 103–110. Oxford: Oxford University Press.

Asad, Talal. 1986. *The Idea of an Anthropology of Islam*. Occasional paper. Washington, D.C.: Center for Contemporary Arab Studies, Georgetown University.

Asad, Talal. 1993. *Genealogies of Religion: Discipline and Reasons of Power in Christianity and Islam*. Baltimore: Johns Hopkins University Press.

Asad, Talal. 2003. *Formations of the Secular: Christianity, Islam, Modernity*. Stanford, Calif.: Stanford University Press.

Bakhtin, M. M. 1981. *The Dialogic Imagination: Four Essays*. Ed. Michael Holquist. Trans. Caryl Emerson and Michael Holquist. Austin: University of Texas Press.

Brown, Wendy. 2006. *Regulating Aversion: Tolerance in the Age of Identity and Empire*. Princeton, N.J.: Princeton University Press.

Certeau, Michel de. 2002. *The Practice of Everyday Life*. Trans. Steven F. Rendall. Berkeley: University of California Press.

Clifford, James. 1988. *The Predicament of Culture: Twentieth Century Ethnography, Literature, and Art*. Cambridge, Mass.: Harvard University Press.

Clifford, James, and George E. Marcus, eds. 1986. *Writing Culture: The Poetics and Politics of Ethnography*. Berkeley: University of California Press.

Connolly, William E. 2000. *Why I Am Not a Secularist*. Minneapolis: University of Minnesota Press.

Connolly, William E. 2005. *Pluralism*. Durham, N.C.: Duke University Press.

Crapanzano, Vincent. 2003. *Imaginative Horizons: An Essay in Literary-Philosophical Anthropology*. Chicago: University of Chicago Press.

DiCenso, James. 1998. *The Other Freud: Religion, Culture and Psychoanalysis*. New York: Routledge.

Ellenberger, Henri. 1970. *The Discovery of the Unconscious: The History and Evolution of Dynamic Psychiatry*. New York: Basic Books.

Fahd, Taoufiq. 1966. *La Divination arabe: Études religieuses, sociologiques et folkloriques sur le milieu natif de l'Islam*. Leiden: Brill.

Foucault, Michel. 1988. *Politics, Philosophy, Culture: Interviews and Other Writings, 1977–1984*. Ed. Lawrence D. Kritzman. New York: Routledge.

Freud, Sigmund. 1900. The Interpretation of Dreams. In *The Standard Edition of the Complete Psychological Works of Sigmund Freud*. Vols. 4 and 5. Ed. James Strachey. London: Hogarth.

Gilsenan, Michael. 2000. Signs of Truth: Enchantment, Modernity, and the Dreams of Peasant Women. *Journal of the Royal Anthropological Society* 6, no. 4:597–615.

Habermas, Jürgen. 2005. *Zwischen Naturalismus und Religion: Philosophische Aufsätze*. Frankfurt am Main: Suhrkamp Verlag.

Hamdy, Sherine F. 2009. Islam, Fatalism, and Medical Intervention: Lessons from Egypt on the Cultivation of Forbearance (*Sabr*) and Reliance on God (*Tawakkul*). *Anthropological Quarterly* 82, no. 1:173–196.

Haquem, Amber. 1997. Psychology and Religion: Their Relationship and Integration from an Islamic Perspective. *American Journal of Islamic Social Sciences* 15, no. 4:97–115.

Hirschkind, Charles. 2006. *The Ethical Soundscape: Cassette Sermons and Islamic Counterpublics*. New York: Columbia University Press.

Hoffman, Valerie J.. 1997. The Role of Visions in Contemporary Egyptian Religious Life. *Religion* 27:45–64.

Kinberg, Leah. 1994. *Ibn Abī al-Dunyā: Morality in the Guise of Dreams*. Leiden: Brill.

Lacan, Jacques. 1978. *The Four Fundamental Concepts of Psychoanalysis*. Ed. Jacques-Alain Miller. Trans. Alan Sheridan. New York: Norton.

Lacan, Jacques. 2002. *Ecrits: A Selection*. Trans. Alan Sheridan. New York: Norton.

Lambek, Michael. 1993. *Knowledge and Practice in Mayotte: Local Discourses of Islam, Sorcery, and Spirit Possession*. Toronto: University of Toronto Press.

Lamoreaux, John C. 2002. *The Early Muslim Tradition of Dream Interpretation*. Albany: State University of New York Press.

Lee, Benjamin, and Edward LiPuma. 2002. Cultures of Circulation: The Imaginations of Modernity. *Public Culture* 14, no. 1:191–213.

Lévi-Strauss, Claude. 1966. *The Savage Mind*. Chicago: University of Chicago Press.

Luhrmann, Tanya. 2001. *Of Two Minds: An Anthropologist Looks at American Psychiatry*. New York: Vintage.

Massad, A. Joseph. 2007. *Desiring Arabs*. Chicago: University of Chicago Press.

Masuzwa, Tomoko. 2005. *The Invention of World Religions: Or, How European Universalism Was Preserved in the Language of Pluralism*. Chicago: University of Chicago Press.

Messick, Brinkley. 2001. Indexing the Self: Expression and Intent in Islamic Legal Acts. *Islamic Law & Society* 8, no. 2:151–178.

Mittermaier, Amira. 2011. *Dreams That Matter: Egyptian Landscapes of the Imagination*. Berkeley: University of California Press.

Morsy, Soheir. 1988. Islamic Clinics in Egypt: The Cultural Elaboration of Biomedical Hegemony. *Medical Anthropology Quarterly* 2, no. 4:355–369.

Nandy, Ashis. 1995. *The Savage Freud and Other Essays on Possible and Retrievable Selves*. Princeton, N.J.: Princeton University Press.

Pandolfo, Stefania. 1997. *Impasse of the Angels: Scenes from a Moroccan Space of Memory*. Chicago: University of Chicago Press.

Pandolfo, Stefania. 2000. The Thin Line of Modernity: Some Moroccan Debates on Subjectivity. In *Questions of Modernity*, ed. Timothy Mitchell, 115–147. Minneapolis: University of Minnesota Press.

Rodinson, Maxime. 1980. *Muhammad*. New York: Pantheon.

Salvatore, Armando. 2000. Social Differentiation, Moral Authority, and Public Islam in Egypt. The Path of Mustafa Mahmud. *Anthropology Today* 16, no. 2:12–15.

Schimmel, Annemarie. 1998. *Die Träume des Kalifen: Träume und ihre Deutung in der islamischen Kultur*. Munich: Verlag C.H. Beck.

Soueif, Moustafa, and Ramadan A. Ahmed. 2001. Psychology in the Arab World: Past, Present, and Future. *International Journal of Group Tensions* 30, no. 2:211–240.

Watt, W. Montgomery. 1974. *Muhammad: Prophet and Statesman*. London: Oxford University Press.

Williams, Raymond. 1977. *Marxism and Literature*. Oxford: Oxford University Press.

8. THE TEMPLE OF RELIGION AND THE POLITICS OF RELIGIOUS PLURALISM

Judeo-Christian America at the 1939–1940 New York World's Fair

J. TERRY TODD

On the last Sunday in April 1939, opening day of the New York World's Fair, many of New York's civic and religious leaders gathered in the exposition's Temple of Religion to herald their vision of an America where religion would become a force for tolerance and mutual respect. The spirit of inclusion and collaboration was captured in the temple's motto, "For All Who Worship God and Prize Religious Freedom," engraved on the temple's entablature, visible to guests as they ascended a flight of stairs and into a building that one prominent supporter dubbed "The Cathedral of the American People." The temple was the exposition's official religion exhibit, set within a lush garden and walled off from the bustle of the fairgrounds. During the fair's spring and summer seasons in 1939 and 1940, an estimated 4.5 million fairgoers attended events designed to promote "the Fatherhood of God and the Brotherhood of Man," a principle the temple's organizers insisted formed the core of American Protestant, Catholic, and Jewish traditions. As a cooperative project supported by many of New York's leading citizens, the temple seemed like a bold venture for the 1930s, a time of intense religious and ethnic tensions in New York (Bayor 1988). The comments left by visitors in the leather-bound autograph books that lay on a table near the entrance attest to the temple's ability to inspire. "Remarkable," Jessie Reichel commented, "to find Jew, Catholic, and Protestant united under one roof." Ruth Besen declared the temple "Beautiful. Combination of religion shows the peace & good will in America." Arnold Cook believed the temple "should do much to bring unity of faith."[1]

A study of the fair's religion project reveals much about the early formation of what is arguably the twentieth century's most powerful model of framing religious pluralism in the United States: the idea of a Judeo-Christian America. Wendy Wall tell us that the term *Judeo-Christian* first began to take on political meanings in the context of struggles against communism and fascism in the 1920s and 1930s, when it came to signify a common well of values—respect for individual freedom and democratic political processes—supposedly shared by America's Protestants, Catholics, and Jews. The campaign to bridge religious differences through appeals to a mutually shared American Judeo-Christian tradition had been building since at least 1927, with the founding of the National Conference of Christians and Jews (NCCJ). This was the flagship organization of the goodwill movement, as this interfaith campaign came to be known. The movement drew strong support from many American intellectuals and religious and business leaders who argued that spiritual values rather than secular Enlightenment principles lay at the core of the American democratic project. They tagged Jewish, Catholic, and Protestant traditions as the "religions of democracy" and declared the commonalities between American Jews, Catholics, and Protestants more important than the differences (Kraut 1990; Silk 1989; Wall 2008).

In subsequent decades the idea of the United States as a Judeo-Christian nation gained more and more currency. The tri-faith military classification of religious identity during World War II and the camaraderie between Jewish, Catholic, and Protestant soldiers furthered its development (Moore 1998, 2004). During the Cold War years, the idea blossomed. Will Herberg, in his now-classic study of postwar religious life, *Protestant–Catholic–Jew: An Essay in American Religious Sociology* (1955), coined the phrase "triple-melting pot" to highlight the influence of the tri-faith model. There were now three ways to be American and religious, Herberg recognized: Protestant, Catholic, and Jewish. Well into the 1970s and even beyond, civic ceremonies in many cities and towns in the United States drove home the point. Minister, priest, and rabbi often stood together on the same dais in a patriotic tri-faith tableau, embodying the idea of a Judeo-Christian America committed to the values of democracy and tolerance. It all looked very much like what had been staged at New York's Temple of Religion in the summers of 1939 and 1940.

The chapters in this volume call into question many of the assumptions underlying current academic and popular discourses on religious pluralism. As Pamela Klassen and Courtney Bender remind us in the introduction to this volume, notions of religious pluralism are often prescriptive rather than descriptive and imagine a well-ordered body politic where dialogue across religious traditions is not only possible but also expected for the sake of a stable civic order. Amira Mittermaier (chap. 7, this volume) calls attention to the unexamined political implications of these discussions. Discourses on religious pluralism tend to appropriate terms such as *democracy* and *liberty*, implying that the United States, Canada, and Western Europe are exceptional cases in their support of those values. Mittermaier also argues that the West is not as pluralistic as it claims to be. "Pluralism is limited in that only those whose values are not *too* different are invited into the circle of toleration." This observation underscores the asymmetry of power relations within and outside that circle of toleration, a point also argued by Tracy Leavelle in his chapter on the "problem" of American Indian religion (chap. 6, this volume).

My chapter joins this questioning of current discussions about pluralism through its historical focus on the United States and, in particular, New York City in the late 1930s. The organizers of the temple hoped to present a prescriptive picture of religious harmony, a veritable exhibit of the future of American religious pluralism. Yet this was made possible only through a series of exclusions that were sometimes ideologically driven and other times simply practical. While adopting the motto "For All Who Worship God and Prize Religious Freedom," the temple's managers banned from participation religious groups they deemed "not decidedly American." Requests for participation from Buddhists, Baha'is, and so-called cult groups were denied, and political views and dissident voices were suppressed. A close look at the project's development reveals how in one particular context the rhetoric of American religious pluralism was driven by a politics of exclusion that, among its other effects, rendered invisible the messy realities of religious life in order to present the illusion of a nation united.

Staged in Flushing Meadow in the borough of Queens, the New York World's Fair of 1939–1940 was designed to be unlike any other previous world exposition, "pregnant with educational, philosophical, and social significance," according to Frank Monaghan, the fair's Yale-trained public relations executive and official historian. "No other fair of the past has been able in the midst of a troubled and disturbed world, to give promise of promoting a message so significant in its social implications." With its theme, "Building the World of Tomorrow," the New York World's Fair would give the public "a renewing and a compelling cause for hope" (Monaghan 1938:45). The fair came at an important moment, sandwiched between the economic dislocations of the Great Depression and the onset of another world war. Its mixture of nostalgia and futurism offered the promise of escape from a present world that seemed to grow ever more dangerous and unpredictable (Duranti 2006).

The announcement of the fair drew proposals from a great number of religious organizations and assorted spiritual entrepreneurs, proposals that bear witness to a strikingly diverse religious scene in New York—indeed, in the United

States—in the late 1930s. Jockeying for a place in New York's "world of tomorrow" were Protestants of many sorts (fundamentalist revivalists and staid mainline churches), Catholics from many different Catholic organizations, Christian Scientists, Jews (Orthodox, Conservative, Reform, and secular Zionists), Mormons, Baha'is, and even an American who had ventured to Tibet to become a Buddhist monk. (Theos Bernard was his name, and he wanted to build a replica of Lhasa's Ganden monastery at the exposition, bringing Tibetan monks to New York to staff it.) World expositions had always provided opportunities for religious groups to present and perform their own varieties of faith to an audience of fairgoers. New York's futurist theme upped the ante, as potential exhibitors wanted to project themselves into the "tomorrow" imagined by the exposition.

Previous U.S. fairs, such as Chicago's 1893 Columbian Exposition and its World Parliament of Religions, defined the boundaries of American religion by staging narratives about tolerance, diversity, freedom, and friendly competition. Richard Seager argues that the Parliament of Religions was a turning point in the expansion of American models of religious pluralism, shifting the parameters of what might pass as American religion. After the parliament, "Krishna, the kami, the Buddha . . . and the Divine Mother had all been tucked into the nation's 'sacred canopy,' where they joined the Christian Father, Son and Holy Spirit; the extra-human power in the universe; Apollo and his Muses; and the Goddess of Liberty, too" (Seager 1995:175). Seager's assessment of a growing openness to other religious ideas and practices indeed might apply to subsequent American fairs, at least until New York's in 1939, when that expansive vision of American religious pluralism began to narrow.

American fairs generally held in creative tension the imperatives of displaying differences and commonalities between religious groups. At Philadelphia's 1926 Sesquicentennial Exposition, for example, in the fair's educational pavilion, an astonishing variety of religious exhibits stood side by side in a kind of spiritual bazaar. "Exhibiting in a group here," according to the exposition's official guidebook, "were the Gideons; the Church of the New Jerusalem; the Unitarian Churches; the Moody Bible Institute of Chicago; the *Progressive Thinker*, a paper devoted to Spiritualism; the Theosophical Society; and the Synagogue Council of America" (Austin and Hauser 1929:414). The arrangement of the galleries there and at many other American fairs provided a visual code for the diversity of religious paths, as long as they converged under the U.S. flag.

At Chicago's 1933–1934 Century of Progress Exposition, the exhibition galleries also reflected a multireligious diversity, focusing on social and civic contributions of American religious organizations. An ecumenical Protestant display, sponsored jointly by Presbyterians, Congregationalists, Methodists, and Baptists, cast Protestant ecumenism itself as a sign of civilization's advancement. Other exhibits highlighted the social welfare work of the Salvation Army, the

Volunteers of America, and various Jewish community organizations. Chicago's Hall of Religions proved to be a surprising hit. It drew more than a million people during its first season, according to its director, George W. Dixon, chair of the fair's Committee on Progress Through Religion, who noted, "The public is intensely interested in religious unity" (quoted in McDermott 1933:5).

With memories of Chicago's Hall of Religion fresh in their minds, religious organizations moved quickly to secure exhibition space in New York, only to discover that the balance in New York tilted away from displays of diversity. One influential member of the World's Fair Corporation Executive Committee wanted the exposition's religion exhibit to emphasize the commonalities of religion. William Church Osborn, who stepped forward to lead the planning of the religion project, was a man Calvin Tomkins (1989:219) has described as "Old New York, socially prominent, wealthy, and Protestant." Indeed he was. A lifelong Episcopalian, Osborn was one of New York's leading lawyers, who moved in a circle of wealth and privilege. Osborn's establishment pedigree made him a seemingly unlikely choice to lead religion's charge into the future imagined by the fair, but Osborn was also a threshold figure. He stood between the vanishing world of Gilded Age Protestant cultural power and the birth of a Judeo-Christian public sphere.

Osborn's New York was a place where Protestants (well-placed white Protestants, at least) shared power with influential Catholics and Jews—not always on equal footing, to be sure, but in culturally significant ways nonetheless. This new American reality had been dawning since the late nineteenth century, in New York and in other major cities, but the pace of change had accelerated in the early twentieth century. Protestant, Catholic, and Jewish elites increasingly met and mingled in Manhattan's marketplaces, if not in their respective social clubs. New York's elites shared a stake in maintaining a stable city, but they sensed tensions that threatened to disrupt civic life and business affairs. "Seldom has the future been more clouded with uncertainties," Osborn declared. "Our achievements toward a better and more satisfying life are seriously menaced. Insidious influences attempt to tear down the structure our fathers have erected, stone by stone, during the last 150 years."[2] Osborn saw the fair's religion exhibit as a way to ensure the persistence of moral values into the future projected by the fair. Yet he also recognized that those values must draw on a base of support broader than New York's old Protestant establishment, and so Osborn set about recruiting Jewish and Catholic as well as Protestant supporters from among his network of friends to plan an exhibit highlighting what he believed was the common ethical core of all religious traditions.

Meanwhile, in the winter of 1937, Michael Williams, editor of the influential Catholic journal *Commonweal*, began to lobby Osborn and other fair administrators to focus the religion exhibit on the American experience of religious and civic liberties. Williams quickly racked up endorsements for the proposed Temple of Religious Tolerance, including an early and important one from the NCCJ. He then pitched the temple idea in a major address to the women's division of the American Jewish Congress in March 1937. He told of his hope that the Temple of Religious Tolerance would contrast life in the United States with other parts of the world, where religious liberties were suppressed by communist and fascist regimes. Williams then turned to Fiorello La Guardia, who was also on the dais, to enlist the mayor's support. La Guardia enthusiastically embraced the idea but, never one to be upstaged, shifted the focus squarely onto Nazi Germany. The mayor suggested the temple include a "chamber of horrors" to "illustrate the abuses of European fascism," especially Hitler, "that brown-shirted fanatic who is now menacing the peace of the world."[3]

The mayor's remarks caused a storm of controversy that threatened to sink the project before it ever got off the ground. What originated as a proposal to encourage promotion of religious tolerance exposed some of the ethnic and religious fault lines that ran beneath New York City. Some German Americans accused the mayor of pandering to Jewish voters in an election year. Others denounced La Guardia as a communist sympathizer because his comments focused on Germany but ignored religious repression in the Soviet Union. The Reverend Edward Lodge Curran, a Brooklyn-based Catholic priest and president of the American Association Against Communism, known to his critics as the "Father Coughlin of the East," charged La Guardia with being "soft on communism" and proposed placing a wax figure of La Guardia himself in the temple's "chamber of horrors." Meanwhile, in Germany, La Guardia was vilified in the press as a "dirty Talmud Jew."[4]

These heated rhetorical outbursts further convinced Osborn, Williams, and other prominent promoters of the need to sidestep partisan controversy and focus instead on the common moral core and political values they assumed lay at the heart of Judaism and Christianity. After much back and forth, fair officials instated a ban on denominational exhibits and terminated lease negotiations with the many religious organizations that wanted to organize exhibits in the fair's Temple of Religious Tolerance. The decision was a radical departure from the tradition of world's fair religion exhibits, a direct affront to the many groups clamoring for display space, and predictably, it raised a storm of controversy. Lutheran officials interpreted the decision as a sign that "certain Semitic influences" in New York wanted to block their participation.[5] A Lutheran periodical went on to warn that the temple "will, of course, have no religious message or influence, and will be merely expressive of the days of religious indecisiveness and flabbiness on which religion in America has fallen."[6]

Exposition officials jumped to defend the decision to ban exhibits. Fair Corporation president Grover Whalen claimed that New Yorkers had learned from the mistakes of previous world expositions. The Fair Corporation would not permit "such a heterogeneous collection of exhibits that the whole would lose in dignity and effectiveness." There was also a deeper reason. Whalen hoped the religion exhibit would promote the "unity of religious belief," a goal to be achieved, in Whalen's mind, only through the evacuation of differences. Stripped of the visible markings provided by worship and exhibits, the temple would become a place where "all our people might unite in the spirit of worship, without distinction or difference."[7]

Right around this time, the title of the project also changed. The Temple of Religious Tolerance became the Temple of Religion, which meant the project now entered into the tricky business of putting the imprimatur *Religion* on whatever was to be found under the temple's roof, thus implicitly denying it to whatever was excluded. This move was of tremendous importance to the temple's projection of a new tri-faith model of American religious pluralism because it implicitly concealed the question, "What counts as religion, as American religion?" In the earliest planning stages the New York temple began with a rather expansive response to that question. Religious organizations of many different kinds assumed they would have the opportunity to represent themselves through exhibition and display, the general practice at world expositions in the United States. But soon the project narrowed to include what temple promoters called the nation's "three great historical traditions": Protestantism, Catholicism, and Judaism.

Although the roots of the idea of a Judeo-Christian America lie in the nineteenth century, in developments associated with the Jewish enlightenment and emancipation, the concept did not come of age until the 1920s and 1930s, in the period Michael Parrish (1994) has called "the anxious decades." It was during those two decades that the Anglo-American Protestant dominance of public religious life in the United States showed further signs of weakening, even as anti-Semitic, anti-Catholic, and anti-immigrant sentiment continued unabated and in many instances increased in intensity. These cultural turns gave birth to the goodwill movement, a loose association of organizations and individuals whose aspirations included the curtailment of ethnic and religious bigotry and the recognition of a common American civic tradition shared by Protestants, Catholics, and Jews. The movement promoted "mutual understanding" through university conferences, local roundtable discussions, parades, and civic events such as National Brotherhood Day. As Benny Kraut (1990:197) has written, "The term 'goodwill' served as a cultural cue in Protestant, Jewish and some Catholic circles, signaling new sociocultural and religious aspirations." Those aspirations included not only an end to interreligious and ethnic conflict but also a cultural mainstreaming of American Catholics and Jews. Yet as we will see, the move to create a tripartite center had other effects, including the marginalization of other religious groups that did not fit so neatly into the tri-faith mold.

The Temple of Religion needed to draw on a broad base of support, yet its officers, including its president, William Church Osborn, and its executive director, John Brunini, keenly understood the potential pitfalls of an interfaith project. Jews were often suspicious of Protestant motives, fearing that interfaith cooperation was really a cloak for proselytizing. Catholics were suspicious as well and had the added burden of Vatican directives forbidding engagements in interfaith dialogue (Dolan 2002; Hennessy 1981). As a way around these road-blocks, the temple was framed as a civic rather than a religious undertaking, a crucial shift in nuance that influenced every subsequent step of the temple's development and operation.

The new strategy involved securing the support of two major public figures: Fiorello La Guardia and John D. Rockefeller Jr. Mayor La Guardia's endorsement would lend an air of official civic sponsorship, and Rockefeller's would pump much-needed money into the temple. La Guardia's endorsement of the temple was hardly difficult to secure, because it fit well with his own campaign to overcome New York's reputation as indifferent if not hostile to religious values. Of course New York had once served as the capital of the Protestant Benevolent Empire, and far beyond the 1930s, the city remained the national headquarters of many religious bureaus and agencies. But New York was recognized more for Wall Street and Broadway and burlesque—more for its contributions to finance and entertainment—than for its contributions to the nation's piety. Serving as captain of a religious-cum-civic crusade, La Guardia could reclaim at least part of New York's heritage as a spiritual center. Then there were also the very real threats to public order that New York faced during La Guardia's mayoralty. Evidence from the street suggests that New Yorkers were anything but united in the late 1930s. Racial and ethnic tensions tugged at the fabric of public life, with Jewish boycotts of German goods, the growth of the Christian Front and other anti-Semitic organizations among the city's unemployed Irish, and charges of communists in the La Guardia administration launched by the always-vocal Father Edward Lodge Curran (Bayor 1988).

La Guardia jumped aboard as a temple supporter, regularly appearing at temple fundraisers throughout 1938 and 1939. On October 22, 1938, the mayor issued an official proclamation calling the temple "a symbol of the happy spiritual life of our country . . . where prayers murmured in various tongues would blanket out the noise and the turmoil and roar of cannons too often heard in the world today."[8] In subsequent appearances La Guardia toned down the internationalist rhetoric and began to speak the language of a tri-faith American tradition poised to vanquish the enemies of democracy. "The people of New York cannot afford to lose an opportunity to show the world that the Protestant, Catholic, and Jewish faiths in America believe in the Fatherhood of God and the Brotherhood of Man, that they are united as never before, and that in that union rests a challenge to the forces against democracy and religion."[9]

The second pillar of the civic campaign was John D. Rockefeller Jr., a devout Baptist and philanthropist who gave away roughly $1 billion between 1917 and his death in 1960. Rockefeller funneled much of that money to projects he hoped would build the kingdom of God in America. Christian (by which he meant Protestant) values were the source of America's greatness, Rockefeller believed, but increasingly in the 1920s and 1930s it became clear to him that Protestants must share the task of kingdom building with like-minded Catholics and Jews. Although Rockefeller continued to channel most of his religious philanthropy into Protestant projects, after 1920 he occasionally gave to Catholic, Jewish, and interfaith endeavors, and also began occasionally to adopt a tri-faith rhetoric that placed Protestants, Catholics, and Jews together under the U.S. flag. For instance, in announcing a 1929 gift to the Catholic Charities of the Archdiocese of New York, Rockefeller declared, "In trying to meet human needs and make life happier for our fellow men we are all of us—Catholic, Protestants, and Jews alike—serving a common cause" (quoted in Schenkel 1995:86).

Rockefeller joined Mayor La Guardia on stage at a major fundraising luncheon held at the Bankers Club in Manhattan in the fall of 1938. The audience was composed of 150 influential Protestant, Catholic, and Jewish businessmen—no women were invited—with names such as Lehman, Warburg, Morgan, Guggenheim, Baker, Harkness, Gillespie, and Andersen. (Many of these men were already capital investors in the fair itself.) Both La Guardia and Rockefeller spoke glowingly of the fair and its projections of the future. "Today we are able to touch the final item," the mayor said, "by giving the World's Fair a soul." Rockefeller then announced his $25,000 gift and blessed the project by linking the temple to America's historical legacy: "May it stand as a witness to the peoples of the world as they visit our fair that we hold religion to be the supreme authority and guide of life; that we have kept faith with the founders of our country and their God."[10]

A tri-faith team of architects—one Protestant, one Catholic, one Jew—worked for two years to translate this jumble of civic and religious ideas into visible form. To create a space intended to evoke religious and nationalist sentiment, but neutral enough to avoid giving offense, was a tricky assignment. Jewish representative and project leader Clarence Stein, the most prominent of the three architects, seemed at times flummoxed by the task. "We are of the opinion," Stein wrote early on in the process, "that the interior should have a really religious character, and the exterior will suggest a religious building without distinctly being a church."[11] What the team of architects finally developed was a mishmash of neoclassical, neo-Gothic, and modernist elements, something that looked vaguely like the façade of the Lincoln Memorial crossed with a Depression-era post office. Stripped of nearly all adornment, the interior featured whitewashed walls, blue stained glass clerestory windows with abstract designs, a pipe organ, and a stage set within a semicircular apse. A polychromatic reredos decorated the walls of the apse just above the platform. The temple included no cross, no crucifix, no Star of David, and no other obvious religious symbol. The lack of ornamentation in the temple suggested that its organizers' conception of American religion depended on the near-total erasure of visible religious differences.

In the spring and summer of 1939 and 1940, the temple hosted a variety of tri-faith programs, including its popular Twilight Hour, in effect an interfaith vespers service, perhaps the first regularly scheduled event ever to draw American Protestants, Catholics, and Jews together in a common space for something that resembled worship. Twilight Hour was held Monday through Saturday evenings at six o'clock and featured a clergy address on the subject of religious liberty followed by a musical presentation by a visiting choir. Realizing just how controversial the Twilight Hours might become—since when did Protestants, Catholics, and Jews pray together?—temple managers actively discouraged the use of the term *service* to describe the event and emphatically insisted that the events did not include prayer. "It may seem like splitting hairs," the temple's executive director, John Brunini, told a Protestant minister who continually referred to the Twilight Hour as a service, "but we know from experience that Catholics will not participate in an interdenominational service. The Temple of Religion in all its literature has stressed the fact that it is not promoting interdenominational services."[12] Perhaps Catholic clergy could see through Brunini's denials. Whereas Protestant ministers and rabbis from Orthodox, Reform, and Conservative branches of Judaism were often enthusiastic participants, very few priests signed up to speak at Twilight Hour, although Catholic choirs were well represented.

Most often the speaker and choir at a Twilight Hour hailed from the same congregation, but some events broke that pattern, cutting across religious and, at times, racial boundaries in ways that later became very important in the promotion of a Judeo-Christian America. On one August evening in 1940, Rabbi Arthur Neulander of Temple Beth Israel in Richmond Hill, Queens, teamed up with the Thomas Negro Composers Group, a professional chorus of fifty-five men's and women's voices. Neulander delivered an address on Jewish contributions to American notions of freedom and liberty while the choir sang spirituals, including "Go Down, Moses" and "We Are Climbing Jacob's Ladder."

The performance linked Jewish and African American experiences through a common focus on biblical exodus narratives—hardly a new theme, of course, yet one that became increasingly significant in the 1950s and 1960s, when some within the Civil Rights Movement evoked the American Judeo-Christian tradition in the cause of equality and freedom.

The tri-faith theme was reflected in other ways as well, such as the composition of its volunteer staff. Each day, three chaplains from the New York metropolitan region reported for duty at the temple. Each chaplain had his own office, and each wore a red chaplain's ribbon identifying him as a Protestant, a Catholic, or a Jew. Chaplains were to provide "counseling" to temple visitors, but in reality their presence was ornamental. They were the clerical symbols of this tri-faith model of American religion. If the three chaplains were the fathers of Judeo-Christian America, then the Protestant, Catholic, and Jewish women who served as "temple hostesses" were its mothers. Three women were on duty throughout the day "to give a courteous welcome to all visitors."[13]

This model of American religious pluralism allowed for a controlled display of religious diversity within strictly limited tri-faith categories, all under the canopy of the U.S. flag. During the fair's two-season run, the temple hosted hundreds of denominational meetings staged by Protestant, Catholic, and Jewish organizations. Jewish groups were the most enthusiastic participants—unsurprisingly, given the increasingly bad news arriving from Europe and fears of advancing anti-Semitism in the United States. Jews took the opportunity to stake their place in the United States. For instance, when the Union of Orthodox Jewish Congregations held its convention at the temple on May 29, 1939, the event opened with patriotic spectacle that seamlessly interweaved Hebrew and American traditions. One of orthodoxy's best-known rabbis, Herbert S. Goldstein of Manhattan's Institutional Synagogue, gave the keynote address, inviting his listeners to redefine the word *Americanism*, a term historically associated with anti-immigrant and even anti-Jewish sentiment. "In a world beset by isms as numerous as a nest of snakes," Goldstein declared, "I enjoy hearing the word 'Americanism.'" While recognizing that racists and nativists had long owned the term, Goldstein insisted that true Americanism signaled freedom, not intolerance. In what was no doubt intended as a slap at Father Coughlin and other American demagogues, Goldstein said, "Learn the meaning of Americanism—not from the deluded ranting of our contemporary 'broadcast philosophers' nor from the distorted frothing of the communistic or fascistic-minded. Learn it from the source, the Constitution of the United States."[14]

Similar themes were echoed by a number of Catholic speakers as well. Catholic officials seemed at times wary of the temple's tri-faith initiative, despite the fact that a Catholic layman, John Brunini, served as the temple's executive director. Yet some enthusiastically supported it. The most notable

Catholic to appear at the temple was radio personality Monsignor (later Bishop) Fulton J. Sheen, the headline speaker at the opening of the temple's second season in May 1940. While denouncing Soviet communism, Sheen offered his own reappropriation of the term *Americanism*, which had shadowed immigrant Catholics for decades. The right to freely worship and the right to hold private property, Sheen announced, were "the essence of Americanism," an understanding that he insisted was shared by American Catholics and Jews as well as Protestants—another indication of the developing ideological orientation of this tri-faith model.[15] Margaret Armstrong, president of the Ladies of Charity of the New York Archdiocese, was the featured Catholic speaker at many temple events, particularly those targeted to women. In a speech to the National Federation of Temple Sisterhoods, a Jewish group, Armstrong provided her own definition of religious tolerance, undoubtedly shaped by her class position and by years of involvement in charity initiatives that brought together New York's Jewish, Catholic, and Protestant society women. "Tolerance is benevolence, goodwill, affection for the poor, an understanding of the opinions of others and their beliefs, their practices different from one's own, and freedom from bigotry."[16]

Protestants of many different kinds used the temple for denominational meetings—indeed, the very variety underscored the absurdity of claiming Protestants as a coherent category within the tri-faith formula—yet unlike Catholics and Jews, most did not need to proclaim their identity as loyal Americans. Two exceptions were African Americans and German Lutherans. The most spectacular African American religious event at the fair involved a September 1939 rally sponsored by the largest black Baptist group in the United States, the National Baptist Convention (NBC). The meeting featured the Reverend Lacey Kirk Williams, NBC president and pastor of the denomination's mother church, Mount Olivet in Chicago. Williams, revered as one of the most rousing orators of his day, delivered an address that played themes of Americanism similar to those of other temple speakers, yet in a different key. The major contribution of black people to American culture, Williams claimed, was in the realm of religion. "It can be said that the genius of the Negro is his religion," Williams declared. The essentialist notion of black religiosity could be a useful hedge against other racial stereotypes, or it could be wielded, as Williams used it here, as an implicit critique of white forms of Christianity. Williams declared that Americans of African descent had exhibited abiding faithfulness in the face of adversity, a mark of true Christian devotion: "This disposition and the ability of this group to exist by faith in God anyhow has helped bring to America and back to Christian religion its supreme value" (quoted in Horace 1978:216–217). Williams then led a parade of black Baptists to the exposition's immense Court of Peace, where he presided over a "Patriotic Service" attended by fair president Grover Whalen and Mayor La Guardia.

Lutherans, particularly those of German ethnicity, were also on a focused mission to use the temple to proclaim their identity as loyal citizens—not surprisingly, given German American fears of what another U.S. war with Germany might mean for them. On an August Saturday in 1939 and again in 1940, thousands of Lutherans crowded the Temple of Religion for "the largest religious assembly the World's Fair has seen."[17] Some 7,000 visitors spilled from the temple's enclosed garden and into the streets of the fair's Community Interests Zone. They heard an address by Walter A. Meier, the radio voice of American Lutheranism, and then left the temple for a Lutheran parade into the "world of tomorrow." The message was clear: If the future did not quite belong to Lutherans, then Lutherans belonged to the future as loyal, powerful, and very visible Americans.

Although the temple's programs allowed for such limited displays of religious diversity under the banner of Americanism, project managers instated a strict set of rules to safeguard the project's tri-faith model. Temple directives disallowed worship, liturgical symbols, congregational singing, and appeals for conversion, but groups often ignored these restrictions and used the temple as they pleased. One Catholic choir hauled a crucifix into the temple with them for a choral event and installed it prominently before the audience. Lutherans and other Protestants routinely defied a ban on congregational singing. The guidelines further stressed that programs be positive and avoid attacks on others. But that ban, too, was often ignored. In May 1939, in the wake of Mayor La Guardia's appearance at the dedication of the fair's Soviet Pavilion, the Reverend Edward Curran Lodge, the Brooklyn priest dubbed the "Father Coughlin of the East" by his critics, launched an attack on La Guardia from the temple's podium, accusing the mayor of harboring communist sympathies.

It was just that kind of jab that temple managers had hoped to avoid by banning political advocacy from its platform, especially in this moment of sharpening disagreement about U.S. intervention in another European war. But the rage for consensus expressed by temple administrators could not paper over the very real antagonisms of the day. Several incidents at the temple revealed cracks in the wall of civic consensus the temple had hoped to embody. The rules of engagement did nothing to stop Florida state senator Claude Pepper from calling for America's entry into the war, in flourishes of rhetoric interweaving patriotic and religious zeal. Entertainer Eddie Cantor also caused a stir over comments delivered to a Hadassah conference meeting at the temple. Cantor, known in Hollywood for his outspoken denunciations of anti-Semitism, took President Roosevelt to task for turning his back on Europe's Jews, blaming anti-Jewish elements within the State Department. The temple's executive director, reminding Hadassah officers of the ban on political speech from the temple, warned against any other such transgressions.

New York's temple had hoped to encompass religious diversity and thereby define the boundaries of American religious pluralism, but opposition to the project points to a roaring debate about those boundaries in Depression-era New York. Critics of the temple included some evangelical Protestants, mostly of fundamentalist bent, who shunned the temple and its programs, judging interfaith initiatives a form of heresy requiring surrender of the Christian imperative to convert others, the sign of an apostate church and nation. Then there were those who found themselves—for one reason or another—excluded from the temple's model of religious pluralism. They ranged from Christians who did not fit the temple's tri-faith mold, to New Thought and proto–New Age adherents who were labeled "cultists" by fair administrators, to Baha'is, Buddhists, and an assortment of others whose entreaties to join the temple's program were denied or simply ignored. Vocal opposition to the project, and the exclusions required by the temple's carefully contrived tri-faith model, remind us of the suppression seemingly necessitated by the drive to find consensus and pluralism's "common ground."

The ban on proselytizing and the provision of a platform open to Jews and Catholics turned many Protestant evangelicals against the tri-faith temple. Perhaps the most sustained criticism from evangelical quarters came from William Ward Ayer, minister of Calvary Baptist Church, New York's renowned citadel of fundamentalism on West Fifty-seventh Street. Ayer pilloried the fair's interfaith initiatives, which he saw as the first step toward the surrender of Christian doctrine and creed. He went on to denounce those who, like temple patron John D. Rockefeller Jr., called for cooperation across denominational and other religious boundaries. "The objective is a world religion, a fellowship of all faiths," Ayer (1939:41) declared of the fair's religion project, an apostate church that he called in apocalyptic terms "Babylon, the Mother of Harlots."

Whereas some Protestant critics such as Ayer denounced the temple for challenging God's singular revelation in Christ and for promoting what they believed was apostasy, other critics complained that the temple's tri-faith model of American pluralism was simply too narrowly framed and argued for a more internationalist perspective. "People here in the western world, when they think of the unity of religious ideals, usually think of Protestants, Catholics, and Jews," a Norwegian-born American by the name of Ingeborg Barth declared, "not taking into consideration that a majority of people in the world belong to other faiths." Barth asked fair administrators to extend invitations to Hindus, Buddhists, Zoroastrians, and Muslims and even suggested that events in the temple feature scripture readings from the world's "great religions."[18]

Elizabeth Davidson, a volunteer member of the Women's Fundraising Committee, was even more emphatic. Davidson resigned her position to protest temple rules that shut out Hindus, Muslims, Buddhists, and others, accusing fair administrators of ignoring the global scope of world expositions and focusing too narrowly on national concerns. "It seemed quite incredible to me that religions still practiced by over three-fifths of the inhabitants of the globe should be so summarily dismissed from any part in the program and any voice in what was pronounced as an international event," Davidson told temple administrators, "I am sure you will understand that I am no longer interested in the success of your enterprise."[19]

A student of religion from Harvard who turned up at one of the temple's fundraising events smartly exposed the contradiction at the heart of the project. George Kaiser asked whether the New York fair could really claim to present a "Temple of Religion" if it shut out every tradition other than Judaism and Christianity. "I do not wish to hold a brief that such other great religions as Buddhism or Mohammedanism should be represented in a country where they are not entrenched," Kaiser said, in an astute analysis of the gap between the project's Judeo-Christian boundaries and its very name, "but unless the Temple were to be a haven for the people of such faiths as these also, then my suggestion would be to call it 'The Temple of the Established Religions of America.'"[20]

One of the most trenchant protests against the fair's religion project was launched by Mirza Ahmad Sohrab, an American Baha'i whose requests to participate in the temple's programs were repeatedly denied. Sohrab took the feud public in an impassioned letter published in the New York *Times*, where he demanded to know, "Is there an American religion?" Born in Iran and educated at Tehran's Imperial University and later at Harvard, Sohrab escaped religious persecution in Iran to live in exile in Bombay. In 1927, he moved to New York, where he became a tireless advocate for religious freedom and interfaith dialogue. Sohrab took the temple's tri-faith Judeo-Christian model of American religion as a slap in the face, declaring, "I was astonished to learn that, in this day and age, the spiritual leaders of America have lost sight of the fact that there are other religions besides those of Judaism and Christianity."

Sohrab invoked memories of a seemingly more inclusive gathering, Chicago's 1893 World Parliament of Religions. "Has America lost this vision of forty-five years ago? Or has it become totalitarian in its religious attitude and outlook?" By excluding Buddhists, Muslims, and Baha'is, Sohrab asked, "do the sponsors of the Temple of Religion imply that they are heathen?" Sohrab's flight from Iran reenacted one of the founding myths of the United States—America as an asylum from religious persecution—and thus uniquely positioned him to question the temple's exclusion of groups outside the emerging Judeo-Christian model of what it meant to be American and religious. As a final jab, Sohrab appropriated the futurist rhetoric of the fair itself, perhaps as an attempt to shame the exposition's administration into accepting an appeal for inclusion. "I should consider it nothing short of a calamity," Sohrab said, "if in the World's Fair, which calls itself the 'World of Tomorrow,' we offer a spectacle of religious isolation which can only belong to the World of Yesterday."[21]

Fair administrators, especially the temple's executive director, John Brunini, pushed back heavily against these and other critics, and in doing so they were forced to articulate more carefully their own vision of the project. Their defense is instructive, because it reveals details about just how carefully drawn were the boundaries of this tri-faith model. First, to evangelical Protestants who saw anti-Christian motives at work in the temple's rules restricting religious expression, Brunini gave assurances that the temple did not promote religious "amalgamation" but rather civic dialogue between Jews, Catholics, and Protestants. To those who believed the temple's focus was too narrow, Brunini declared, "The American tradition is the one we wish to follow," adding that there would be "no program sponsored by religious groups which, though numerous in other parts of the world, *are not decidedly American*."[22]

In justifying exclusions from the temple, Brunini drew heavily from a decade or more of interfaith—especially tri-faith—discourse involving Protestants, Catholics, and Jews. These narratives generally postulated a common ethical ground in scripture—or at least the Old Testament—and a shared historical experience in America. In a speech made at the temple, Brunini stated the criterion for an organization's admission to the temple: "a belief in God." But it didn't end there. He continued, in words worth quoting at length,

> We were asked, by those who prefer to quibble, "What God?" as though there were many. But lest confusion might arise, our answer was, "God the Father Almighty, Creator of Heaven and Earth," the God the Founding Fathers meant when they penned the bible of our government; the God of Whom Washington took his oath of office. . . . Our forefathers called on that God to bless this union of states one hundred and fifty years ago. It is that God which our people should keep before them and, through their devotion to him, before our statesmen—a God Who is not kept in an isolated niche but One Whose consciousness influences all our actions.[23]

Like Rockefeller before him, Brunini attempted to enfold the temple project within a national narrative stretching back to the founding fathers. This "God of Whom Washington took his oath of office," this god of "our forefathers," is the god that Protestants, Catholics, and Jews in the United States supposedly held in common. His explanation linking God and nation suggests why he insisted on excluding Baha'is, Buddhists, and others from the temple's projection of American religion. Christians and Jews share a tradition that others do not,

Brunini believed, and that tradition is uniquely related to an authoritative understanding of the Bible and of U.S. history and of their linkage. Biblical narratives give American Protestants, Catholics, and Jews a common language to understand and interpret the national experience, Brunini suggested. What excludes other traditions from this formation of American religious pluralism is their lack of access to biblical language, a lack that means they cannot directly share in the communion of national memory.

The Temple of Religion at the 1939–1940 New York World's Fair provided a platform for participating Protestants, Catholics, and Jews to play down the realities of their own internal divisions and their clashes with other religious groups while playing up their faith in American values and in "the Fatherhood of God and the brotherhood of man." The temple's planners and their supporters hoped to redefine what it meant to be American and religious by projecting a tri-faith image into the future imagined by the fair, a move that seemingly required the exclusion of religious groups that did not fit the emerging model. Yet New York's tri-faith model was not the only possible framing of American religious pluralism in those anxious years leading up to World War II, as a brief comparison with the Temple of Religion at San Francisco's 1939–1940 Golden Gate Exposition suggests.

Like New York's religion project, San Francisco's temple drew from the same well of contemporary discourse as the New York project, evoking a tradition linking American religious identity to democratic principles. "Freedom of religious worship, the Fatherhood of God and the Brotherhood of Man were the ideals which we wanted to raise in mortar and wood on Treasure Island," announced Rabbi Rudolph I. Coffee, a former local executive of the NCCJ who directed the project (quoted in Hunter 1940:xxiv). But San Francisco's temple nonetheless presented a different model of American religious pluralism. Whereas New York's project forged its tri-faith version through targeted exclusions, San Francisco's Temple of Religion and Tower of Peace included participation by Mormons, Seventh-Day Adventists, Baha'is, and Christian Scientists—groups that had been barred from New York's temple. Perhaps most remarkably, seen from the vantage of New York, was the observance of the Buddha's birthday held in the temple's plaza in the spring of 1939. As a crowd of 4,000 watched, Buddhist priests and monks conducted rites against the backdrop of an enormous American flag, a scene that would have been unthinkable at New York's temple.

Coffee was conscious of both the similarities and differences between the New York and San Francisco models. On a number of occasions, he tried unsuccessfully to forge ties between the projects, recognizing what he believed were common aspirations. "Why cannot we work in harmony," Coffee asked the managers of the New York temple in the spring of 1938, "since our objectives are the same—the union of religious forces for the strengthening of freedom and democracy in the United States!" But Coffee also recognized that San Francisco's model was indeed more expansive, and he tipped his hat to geography and history to explain the difference. "It is the American city nearest the Orient," Coffee said of San Francisco, evoking the city's frontier possibilities, "and as a new city it is less hidebound, theologically, than older ones. Things are possible here that might not be brought about elsewhere."[24] The extent to which the differences mark a distinction between East and West Coast models of American religious pluralism in the late 1930s warrants further investigation. Yet it wasn't the San Francisco temple's seemingly more liberal model but rather New York's narrower tri-faith formula that generally set the tone for future developments in the United States.

Many of the chapters in this volume point to how discourses of pluralism often emerge from a civic need to find ways of relating across religious differences. In this chapter, by taking the religion exhibit at the 1939–1940 New York World's Fair as a case study, I have examined efforts to deal with religious differences in the United States in the late 1930s, a particularly dangerous and challenging historical moment for many Americans. The efforts to build a tri-faith model of religious pluralism in the United States were driven by acute civic concerns and arose in the context of conflict involving ethnicity and religious identity both at home and abroad. The model proposed at the New York World's Fair imagined three traditions with impermeable boundaries: Protestantism, Catholicism, and Judaism. The tri-faith formulation itself required the erasure of differences within each of the traditions and the exclusion of religious expressions that fell outside those three categories. At the same time, this model of American religious pluralism required acknowledgment of the differences between each tradition while insisting on a common core of civic and political values within each tradition, including a respect for individual freedom and liberty and for the political system of democracy that would sustain those values.

The New York Temple of Religion packaged this model of religious pluralism and successfully propelled it into the very future imagined by the exposition. In the decades ahead, as the movement to create a civic culture of consensus fully flowered, the tri-faith model was hitched to the idea of a Judeo-Christian America, which in turn became the preeminent model of American religious pluralism during the Cold War. That move was well under way by 1947, with the release of the Oscar-winning film *Gentleman's Agreement*. In Elia Kazan's adaptation of Laura Hobson's novel, Gregory Peck's character, Phil Green, turned to the tri-faith model to answer his young son's confusion about religious difference in America. In one of the film's most memorable scenes, Phil Green tells Tommy, "You can be an American and a Catholic, or an American and a Protestant, or an American and a Jew." For many Americans of the period, that tri-faith formula represented an expansion of understanding, yet it also suggested that if you're anything other than a Protestant, Catholic, or Jew, then you're not an American.

I do not mean to say that New York's formulation of American religious pluralism was eventually embraced by the entire nation. The process of implementing the tri-faith model at the Temple of Religion met with stiff resistance, as we have seen, and that resistance took on multiple forms in subsequent decades, in the larger project of propagating the idea of a Judeo-Christian America. Some Protestants held onto the conviction that America was and always had been and should remain a Christian, even Protestant nation. Other critics of consensus protested that the formulation was too narrow. Yet the Judeo-Christian model of American religious pluralism gained traction, in some regions of the United States more so than others. Increasingly in the postwar years, moral appeals for nearly every civic concern from anticommunism to civil rights to curbing juvenile delinquency were often cast in the name of a Judeo-Christian body politic.

At some point the tri-faith Judeo-Christian model of American religious pluralism began to crack apart, although exactly how its prescriptive power declined warrants further investigation. The larger cultural movement for consensus bumped up against countervailing winds in the 1960s, and as dissenting voices grew louder and more insistent the illusion of consensus that had marked the postwar period simply could not hold up (Wall 2008). By the 1970s, some within the emerging Christian Right who once spoke of perils to the "Christian nation" began to warn of similar threats to the "Judeo-Christian nation," demonstrating that a liberal idea had begun its migration to the right side of the political spectrum. By the 1990s, scholars and religious progressives largely had abandoned the idea of a tri-faith Judeo-Christian America, exchanging it for a multifaith model of American religious pluralism that reflected the multicultural concerns of the period (Eck 1999, 2002). Hindus, Sikhs, Jains, Muslims—indeed, those of all religious persuasions—counted as Americans, these advocates declared, and their different ways enlarged and enriched the meaning of what it meant to be American and religious.

In the years since September 11, 2001, in a world where religion seemed to become suddenly more fractious and dangerous, conflicting models of American religious pluralism have tried to account for the divisiveness, manage it or move beyond it, or sometimes combat it. A new version of tri-faith imagined a so-called Abrahamic tradition that embraced Muslims, Jews, and Christians as children of the same Abraham and as equally and authentically American. Other, countervailing sentiments rejected such irenic trends, thereby giving the old civic notion of a Judeo-Christian tradition new life in the battle against a new specter, that of a resurgent Islam. "In order to win we cannot simply fight *against* the jihadists or terrorists or whatever the politically correct designation is for those who would destroy what remains of Western civilization," Robert Spencer (2007:9–10), founder of Jihad Watch.org, declared in a combative tone, "we must be contending for something, and in the Judeo-Christian tradition there is a great deal to defend."

As I have suggested in my study of the 1930s, periods of intense cultural anxiety tend to generate new strategies of understanding and managing religious diversity, and hence new models of religious pluralism. Those models are never innocent, as they carry undisclosed assumptions about what religion is and what the nation should be. Models of religious pluralism often hide asymmetric power relations as well. In our own anxious moment, attempts to rethink what it means to be American and religious must be examined for the political and religious assumptions they carry, a point this chapter has tried to underscore. What are the boundaries of American religious pluralism? How are those boundaries drawn, and by whom? What politics of exclusion are at work in the rhetoric of inclusion? Or perhaps more basically, as Mirza Ahmad Sohrab so pointedly and perceptively asked in 1938, is there an American religion?

NOTES

1. Visitor's Register, Book no. 3, July 1–July 21, 1939, Temple of Religion Records (hereafter TR), box 12. Manuscripts and Archives Division. The New York Public Library. Astor, Lenox and Tilden Foundations.

2. Undated fund-raising pamphlet, TR, box 15.

3. "Religious Center at Fair Proposed," *New York Times*, March 4, 1937, p. 25.

4. "At K of C Gathering, La Guardia Is Named for 'Hall of Horrors'—Reds Assailed," *New York Times*, March 22, 1937, p. 6; "Germany Protests 'Insult' by Mayor; Hull Voices Regret," *New York Times*, March 5, 1937, p. 1.

5. John Brunini to Leslie Baker, February 18, 1938, New York World's Fair 1939–1940 Records, box 208. Manuscripts and Archives Division. The New York Public Library. Astor, Lenox and Tilden Foundations.

6. "No Religious Exhibit at New York World's Fair," *American Lutheran*, May 1938, p. 6.

7. "Religion at the World's Fair," *Living Church*, April 17, 1938, p. 506.

8. Fiorello La Guardia, "Mayor's Proclamation," October 22, 1938, TR, box 15.

9. "Temple of Religion Called Key to Fair," *New York Times*, January 10, 1939, p. 16.

10. "Rockefeller Gift Aids Temple Drive," *New York Times*, November 10, 1938, p. 29.

11. Clarence Stein to William Osborn, August 30, 1938, TR, box 15.

12. John Brunini to William Hulbert, April 6, 1939, TR, box 7.

13. "Duties of a Hostess," undated, Hostess File, TR, box 1.

14. Herbert Goldstein, "Americanism and Religious Freedom," May 29, 1939, TR, box 7.

15. Fulton J. Sheen, "Americanism," May 11, 1940, TR, box 6.

16. Margaret Armstrong, "Tolerance in International Relations," October 6, 1939, TR, box 7.

17. "Religion at the World's Fair," *American Lutheran*, October 1938, p. 21.

18. Ingeborg Barth to John Brunini, December 7, 1938, TR, box 1.

19. Elizabeth Davidson to John Brunini, April 16, 1940, TR, box 1.

20. George Kaiser to William Osborn, May 26, 1938, TR, box 4.

21. Mirza Ahmad Sohrab, "Religion at the Fair," *New York Times*, June 3, 1938, p. 20.

22. John Brunini to Ingeborg Barth, December 10, 1938, TR, box 1 (italics added).

23. John Brunini, address to the Interfaith Movement, Inc., June 30, 1940, TR, box 7.

24. Rudolph Coffee to John Brunini, June 17, 1938, TR, box 1.

WORKS CITED

Austin, E. L., and O. Hauser. 1929. *The Sesqui-Centennial International Exposition*. Philadelphia: Current Publications.

Ayer, William W. 1939. *God's World of Tomorrow*. Grand Rapids, Mich.: Zondervan.

Bayor, Ronald H. 1988. *Neighbors in Conflict: The Irish, Germans, Jews, and Italians of New York City, 1929–1941*. 2nd ed. Urbana: University of Illinois Press.

Dolan, Jay. 2002. *In Search of an American Catholicism: A History of Religion and Culture in Tension*. New York: Oxford University Press.

Duranti, Marco. 2006. Utopia, Nostalgia, and World War at the 1939–40 New York World's Fair. *Journal of Contemporary History* 41:663–683.

Eck, Diana. 1999. The Multireligious Public Square. In *One Nation Under God? Religion and American Culture*, ed. Marjorie Garber and Rebecca Walkowitz, 3–20. New York: Routledge.

Eck, Diana. 2002. *A New Religious America: How a "Christian Country" Has Become the World's Most Religiously Diverse Nation*. San Francisco: HarperSanFrancisco.

Hennessy, James. 1981. *American Catholics*. New York: Oxford University Press.

Herberg, Will. 1955/1983. *Protestant–Catholic–Jew: An Essay in American Religious Sociology*. Chicago: University of Chicago Press.

Horace, Lillian B. 1978. *"Crowned with Glory and Honor": The Life of Rev. Lacey Kirk Williams*. Hicksville, N.Y.: Exposition Press.

Hunter, Stanley A. 1940. *Temple of Religion and Tower of Peace at the 1939 Golden Gate International Exposition.* San Francisco, Calif.: Temple of Religion and Tower of Peace.

Kazan, Elia, director. 1947. *Gentleman's Agreement* [film]. Los Angeles: Twentieth Century Fox.

Kraut, Benny. 1990. A Wary Collaboration: Jews, Catholics, and the Protestant Goodwill Movement. In *Between the Times: The Travail of the Protestant Establishment*, ed. W. R. Hutchison, 193–230. New York: Cambridge University Press.

McDermott, W. F. 1933. 750,000 Attend Hall of Religion. *Chicago Daily News*, July 29, p. 5.

Monaghan, Frank. 1938. *New York World's Fair 1939: The Fairs of the Past, the Fair of Tomorrow*. Chicago: Encyclopedia Britannica.

Moore, Deborah Dash. 1998. Jewish GIs and the Creation of the Judeo-Christian Tradition. *Religion and American Culture* 8:31–53.

Moore, Deborah Dash. 2004. *G.I. Jews: How World War II Changed a Generation.* Cambridge, Mass.: Belknap Press of Harvard University Press.

Parrish, Michael. 1994. *Anxious Decades: America in Prosperity and Depression, 1920–1941*. New York: Norton.

Rydell, Robert. 1993. *World of Fairs: The Century of Progress Expositions*. Chicago: University of Chicago Press.

Schenkel, Albert. 1995. *The Rich Man and the Kingdom: John D. Rockefeller, Jr., and the Protestant Establishment*. Minneapolis: Fortress Press.

Seager, Richard H. 1995. *The World's Parliament of Religions: The East/West Encounter, Chicago, 1893*. Bloomington: Indiana University Press.

Silk, Mark. 1989. *Spiritual Politics: Religion and America Since World War II*. New York: Touchstone.

Spencer, Robert. 2007. *Religion of Peace? Why Christianity Is and Islam Isn't*. Washington, D.C.: Regnery.

Tomkins, Calvin. 1989. *Merchants and Masterpieces: The Story of the Metropolitan Museum of Art*. Rev. ed. New York: Holt.

Wall, Wendy. 2008. *Inventing the "American Way": The Politics of Consensus from the New Deal to the Civil Rights Movement*. New York: Oxford University Press.

PART III

The Ghosts of Pluralism

Unintended Consequences of Institutional and Legal Constructions

9. NATIVE AMERICAN RELIGIOUS FREEDOM BEYOND THE FIRST AMENDMENT

MICHAEL D. MCNALLY

The concerns of this volume are particularly visible in contemporary efforts by Native American communities to secure freedom for sacred practices, beliefs, places, objects, and ancestors within the U.S. legal regime. Since the early twentieth century, as Native peoples were forcibly and legally assimilated into the polity and economy of the United States, and as their indigenous traditions were discouraged and in many cases criminalized, Native activists and leaders have made strategic efforts to render their traditions in the language of the law as religion in order to find protections for their continuation as distinctive peoples and cultures (Wenger 2009).

As Benjamin Berger, Winnifred Fallers Sullivan, and other contributors to this volume show, the language of the law, and in particular the construal of religion in that language, has had much to do with the establishment of a particular legal cultural system that, among other things, has naturalized the "religion" of religious freedom as a universal matter of individual conscience or of inner spirituality. My chapter shows an important series of instances in which this sociolegal discourse of pluralism has consistently foreclosed on religious freedom for Native peoples in the United States. In the early twentieth century, when Quanah Parker and other practitioners of the intertribal ethical and ceremonial complex of the Peyote Way formally incorporated as the Native American Church, they did so strategically, calling attention to the teachings that practitioners such as Parker shared with Christianity and organizing as a church to gain legal protection for the sacramental ingestion of the cactus button medicine from Prohibition-era laws regulating medicinal substances (Stewart 1987). They did so not as starry-eyed, newly made citizens of an American experiment in religious freedom but as actors wizened by a series of abrogations of treaties in the Southern Plains, seeking protection wherever they could find it within the American law. The strategy worked somewhat, in that practices associated with the incorporated Native American Church found legal protection in the courts, at least until the renewed drug wars of the late 1980s, when a newly established majority on the Supreme Court arguably went out of its way to review a case involving the ceremonial ingestion of peyote as a constitutionally privileged matter of religious exercise. As I will show, the seasoned contemporary Native activists discussed by Tracy Leavelle at the end of his chapter have had ample reason to be skeptical about the possibilities for the protection of Native traditions as religions.

That said, I emphatically do not offer this chapter as an analysis that, in turn, forecloses on future possibilities for fuller realization of equal protection of religious freedom under U.S. law. I will show how Native Americans have found success in statutory protections for the cultural resources and practices of tradition, whereas they have found little protection under constitutional provisions for the free exercise of religion per se. Because Native Americans made up less than 2 percent of the U.S. population in the 2000 Census, and are disproportionately poor at that, passage of such legislation could not rely on raw political muscle but, significantly, on arguments appealing to ideals of religious pluralism and human rights. To foreclose such possibilities in the context of the U.S. Constitution and U.S. law would be to construe the matter as a fait accompli rather than as a dynamic process shaped by political forces that may or may not change with understanding or shifting fortunes.

Especially since the resurgence of tradition in the 1970s, Native communities have been reasserting their identities and religious practices in highly visible ways. In nearly every corner of the country, Native communities have been emboldened to assert their claims in courts and legislatures to sacred lands, cultural property, and the free exercise of traditional practices. This chapter contends with an irony that also characterizes this moment. Put simply, Native American communities have found many (if not most) legal protections for their religious traditions by expressly not calling attention to their religiousness. I think this case is well worth contemplating in the larger discussion to which this book is dedicated. In part because the First Amendment has let them down; in part because their traditions have never been plainly, or solely, religious; in part because assertions of sovereignty, and the long history of federal Indian law that clarifies that sovereignty, matter, Native communities have sought and found further protection under federal Indian law, and under statutory regimes, especially historic preservation and environmental law, than they might have under the current state of First Amendment protection. This is not to speak of numerous sovereign assertions of self-determination, including tribe-specific traditions of law, and indigenous presence in venues of international law (Anaya 2004). To be sure, a fuller accounting of my subject would extend more deeply into these emerging strategies. Here I'll focus on aspects of U.S. law.

I begin with a truncated analysis of the limits of First Amendment protection, but I mean in this chapter to enrich that conversation by placing it in context with the other legal and political strategies that treat Native concerns not as those of religious individuals seeking individual rights of conscience, nor as those of a special interest group, but as sovereign communities with distinctive legal status. A teacher of mine has quipped that when Native claimants leave the more robust world of federal Indian law for the First Amendment, they are effectively likened to the "long haired guys with bongs and microbuses" that courts come to expect seeking costly accommodations under the free exercise clause of the First Amendment (Washburn 2007).

That clause is joined with the establishment clause to form the terse language of the First Amendment: "Congress shall make no law respecting an establishment of religion, or prohibiting the free exercise thereof." If it is unconscionable that the religions of First Americans find so little protection under the Constitution, it is unsurprising in light of a long and consistent history of U.S. Indian policies that, at best, actively discouraged Native religions and, more egregiously, overtly criminalized them. Although Congress uniformly extended citizenship to American Indians in 1924, and formal assimilation policies were reversed in 1934, Native people and their traditional practices have experienced more than the usual share of government regulation, as well as recognition of distinctive political status, and in this they are different from other minority religions (Deloria and Lytle 1983).

But there are also definitional issues involving Native traditions and the concept of religion. I can identify at least six facets of Native traditions that present difficulties for those defining religion in conventional ways: Native religions are many, not one. Native traditions often involve widely divergent beliefs even in one community. They are decidedly oral traditions, and consequently they have few clear lines of orthodoxy or institutional structures that might clarify right belief or practice. They are integrated with other, less visibly religious aspects of lifeways where the sacred is not so clearly set apart from profane matters of economic livelihood or political decision making. They are oriented toward sacred lands in ways that elude most Jewish or Christian analogies. They are often the province of communities rather than clear matters of individual conscience. They have often been interrupted traditions whose resurgence has called into question, at least among opposing interests, Native claims to authentic tradition. And these features have posed a difficult fit to the interpretive schemes for the First Amendment that courts have developed under other circumstances.

NATIVE RELIGIOUS FREEDOM IN THE COURTS

Indeed, it is worth underscoring that the major decisions by which the Rehnquist Court withdrew the scope of free exercise jurisprudence for religious minorities generally were cases involving Native religions, most notably *Lyng v. Northwest Cemetery Protective Association* (1988) and *Employment Division v. Smith* (1990). These cases, in turn, fell on the heels of a series of precedents in which appellate courts ruled fairly consistently against Native free exercise claims concerning sacred sites (*Badoni v. Higginson* [1980]; *Sequoyah v. T.V.A.* [1980]; *Wilson v. Block* [1983]).

If it has proved a steep hill to climb for Native communities to win meaningful protection for the legal category of religion, it is hardly a foregone conclusion that the First Amendment cannot protect them. And thus, my chapter decidedly will not proclaim a postmortem on the possibilities for constitutional and statutory protections of Native traditions qua religion. Indeed, after a century of activism seeking to protect sacred places, practices, and remains, Native people had reason to celebrate Congress's passage in 1978 of the American Indian Religious Freedom Act (AIRFA). This legislation clarified for government agencies, and presumably the courts, that Native traditions, their distinctiveness notwithstanding, count as religion worthy of constitutional safeguards: "It shall be the policy of the U.S. to protect and preserve for American Indians their inherent right of freedom to believe, express, and exercise the traditional religions of the American Indian, Eskimo, Aleut, and Native Hawaiians, including but not limited to access to sites, use and possession of sacred objects, and the freedom to worship through ceremonials and traditional rites" (42 U.S.C. 1996).

LYNG V. NORTHWEST CEMETERY PROTECTIVE ASSOCIATION (1988)

If it sounded clear as day, and if the courts had discretion to interpret the statute more broadly, AIRFA was found to lack teeth that might be enforceable in the courts. After AIRFA arguments failed to persuade courts in several other cases, the Supreme Court ruled ten years later in *Lyng v. Northwest Cemetery Protective Association* (1988) that AIRFA offered no basis for protection of California sites sacred to the Yurok, Karok, and Tolowa from a planned logging road, and ever since, AIRFA has been interpreted as conferring no "special religious rights on Indians," a resolution that continues to inform federal agency policies but contains no legal teeth by way of a formally recognized "cause of action" (*Lyng*, 485 U.S. at 455).

But the *Lyng* decision went further than to restrict the possible reach of AIRFA. It ostensibly did not dispute that the Indians' "beliefs are sincere and that the Government's proposed actions will have severe adverse effects on the practice of their religion" (*Lyng*, 485 U.S. at 447). Still, by means of applying and reasoning from the precedent in *Bowen v. Roy* (1986), a decision in which the Supreme Court did not recognize an unconstitutional burden claimed by a Native man whose private belief was that his daughter's spirit would be harmed by being given a Social Security number, the *Lyng* majority concluded that the logging road would not burden the religion of three entire Native tribes whose well-documented traditions of the Chimney Rocks High Country involved beliefs that its sanctity was needed for the renewal of the universe.

Part of the gap between the majority opinion in *Lyng*, authored by Justice O'Connor, and the spirited dissent, authored by Justice Brennan, stems from their disagreement about the applicability of *Bowen v. Roy*. The *Bowen* Court did not overtly question the sincerity of Roy's belief that his daughter's soul would be damaged by the assigning of a Social Security number, but it concluded that "the Free Exercise Clause simply cannot be understood to require the Government to conduct its own internal affairs in ways that comport with the religious beliefs of particular citizens," and this logic was applied to the facts in *Lyng*. What Justice O'Connor's opinion does not make explicit in *Lyng* is an unstated assumption that the cases are closely related because Roy was a Native American professing Native American religious beliefs. No ethnohistorians or anthropologists were needed to determine the depth or breadth of the belief in that case; it could read to the justices like any other free exercise claim by an upstart new religious movement or a maverick, if fervent, believer in the "church of me." But here is the point: The Court's logic is that *Roy* involves an odd belief by an individual that makes excessive demands on the state's ability to conduct its internal affairs. By the logic that both *Roy* and *Lyng* are "Native American" cases, the analogy is extended to the facts in *Lyng*: "However much we might wish that it were otherwise," O'Connor's decision goes, "government simply could not operate if it were required to satisfy every citizen's religious needs and desires." "The crucial word in the constitutional text is 'prohibit,'" O'Connor writes, "for the Free Exercise Clause is written in terms of what the government cannot do to the individual, not in terms of what the individual can exact from the government" (*Lyng*, 485 U.S. at 439). Because the Native communities were not "coerced" into violating their beliefs by the government actions, the majority in the *Lyng* Court held, the adverse effects were not constitutionally burdensome (*Lyng*, 485 U.S. at 476–477).

Justice Brennan's dissent took issue, at least partly, with the controlling analogy of *Bowen v. Roy*:

> Today the Court professes an inability to differentiate *Roy* from the present case. . . . In *Roy*, we repeatedly stressed the "internal" nature of the Government practice at issue. . . . We likened the use of such record-keeping numbers to decisions concerning the purchase of office equipment. Federal land use decisions, by contrast are likely to have substantial external effects that government decisions concerning office furniture and information storage obviously will not. (*Lyng*, 485 U.S. at 472)

And thus Brennan stopped short of differentiating *Roy* in the starker terms, even though his dissent drew extensively on the ethnographic report describing the urgency of the Native practices in the sacred precincts of the High Country. The controlling analogy that these are both Native American cases trumps what common sense would find patently obvious: that the claim by one Native American man that a Social Security number will rob his daughter of her spirit—and apparently the only Native person to have come forward with this concern—carries the same weight as the claims of three entire Native communities that a "marginally useful" road would destroy a sacred precinct where the cosmos is ritually renewed, where visions are sought, and where medicines are gathered. Applying the precedent of *Roy* to *Lyng* leads to what Brennan called the "cruelly surreal result" that "governmental action that will virtually destroy a religion is nevertheless deemed not to 'burden' that religion" (*Lyng*, 485 U.S. at 472).

In a scathing dissent, Justice Brennan argued that the majority had fundamentally misunderstood the claims of Native religions. Discussing the land-specific nature of Native religions and the inapplicability of creeds or other authoritative statements of what is central or orthodox belief, and drawing on a consultant's report about the specific religious significance of the High Country in question for the Karok, Yurok, and Tolowa, Brennan found the majority's reading of the free exercise clause "wholly untenable" (*Lyng*, 485 U.S. at 476–477).

EMPLOYMENT DIVISION V. SMITH (1990)

What the *Lyng* decision began with respect to sacred lands was finished off with respect to restricting free exercise more broadly in *Employment Division v.*

Smith (1990). Despite nearly a century of specific protections of the Peyote Way, the Court found against the claims to unemployment compensation by two Oregon substance abuse counselors who had been fired because they had ritually ingested peyote at Native American Church ceremonies as part of their own wellness and religious discipline (Long 2001). The Court found that Oregon's right to enforce its drug laws outweighed the free exercise rights of the Peyotists but actively went beyond applying a long-established balancing test, the so-called *Sherbert* test, to arrive at its result. Writing for the majority, Justice Scalia held as constitutional "valid and neutral laws of general applicability" that do not expressly deny free exercise rights even if they have the effect of the same (*Smith*, 494 U.S. at 872).

As critics from across the religious spectrum have made clear, the *Smith* Court effectively gutted the free exercise clause as it pertains to adherents of minority religions for whom often no clear line exists between inviolate beliefs and the practices that do more than merely express them. It also significantly devalued the religion clauses as distinctive terrain within the First Amendment, giving them credence only when conjoined in bundles of hybrid rights with the freedom of speech. Scalia wrote that any society would be "courting anarchy" were it to privilege claims such as those of the Peyotists. "We cannot afford the luxury," he writes, "of deeming presumptively invalid, as applied to the religious objector, every regulation of conduct that does not protect an interest of the highest order" (*Smith*, 494 U.S. at 888).

Plenty of critics, including Justice Blackmun in his strong dissent, call into question the slippery slope concern, noting that peyote exemptions in particular have seldom generated challenges to the government enforcement of drug laws (*Smith*, 494 U.S. at 917). Here, my interest is in identifying why a case involving American Indian practices should trigger Scalia's doomsday scenario of "courting anarchy." A generous argument could be made that Scalia's decision was even-handed in its explicit reluctance to involve the courts deeper and deeper in the business of evaluating the centrality of various religious beliefs and practices to ascertain their relative weight in balancing tests such as the *Sherbert* test. Scalia writes,

> It is no more appropriate for judges to determine the "centrality" of religious beliefs before applying a "compelling interest" test in the free exercise field, than it would be for them to determine the "importance" of ideas before applying the "compelling interest" test in the free speech field. What principle of law or logic can be brought to bear to contradict a believer's assertion that a particular act is "central" to his personal faith? Judging the centrality of different religious practices is akin to the unacceptable "business of evaluating the relative merits of differing religious claims." (*Smith*, 494 U.S. at 886–887)

But as with the *Lyng* case, the result that follows from this logic is "cruelly surreal": Substance abuse counselors are denied free exercise protections even though they are involved with a religious tradition known to promote sobriety and vetted under so much historic scrutiny as to be specifically exempted in federal controlled substance laws and those of many other states. Here the burden of proof, it seems, is on the outlier State of Oregon.

I am convinced that deep-seated myths about the vanishing Indian remain controlling, if implicit, frames of understanding of Native American claims in courts. I think Scalia's "courting anarchy" concern, as well as O'Connor's hasty application of the *Bowen v. Roy* analogy to the facts of *Lyng*, are shaped by this myth as well. The logic goes something like this: "Real Indians" vanished long ago, and contemporary Native religious practitioners have been degraded by a tragic history of dispossession. At best these claimants are "inventing" traditions and at worst making novel and thin claims to sacred places, or to beliefs such as Roy's about the spiritual threat of a Social Security number. Against this backdrop, Native peoples claiming First Amendment protections seem emblematic of the far-fetched demands that many wizened judges come to associate with religious mavericks. An argument can be made that the designation of religion as such is not the source of the problems addressed in this chapter so much as how much particular courts concerned with the larger issues have been willing to accept a broad semantic range of the term. If so, then the courts and society are educable, and a pluralist model for the recognition of religious diversity is not without continued merit.

For all intents and purposes, though, the lesson of *Smith*, and even of *Lyng*, is that when Native American communities have sought protections for their religious and cultural traditions under the First Amendment, they wind up being conflated with those "long-haired guys with bongs and microbuses." That the *Lyng* and *Smith* decisions explicitly do not take issue with the sincerity of the Native American beliefs at hand is belied by the extent of their miscalculation of how centrally their decisions obstruct Native free exercise.

If *Lyng* and *Smith* are among the principal cases by which the emerging majority on the Rehnquist Court withdrew the reach of free exercise clause generally, and thus represent a kind of opportunism by critics of an earlier jurisprudence that extended the free exercise protections up through *Wisconsin v. Yoder* (1972), it is also true that appeals to First Amendment protections of Native American religions came up short even in the heyday of the expansive free exercise protections.

Native American communities faced especially insurmountable difficulties persuading courts to uphold free exercise protections for sacred lands. In *Sequoyah v. Tennessee Valley Authority* (1980), the Sixth Circuit Court of Appeals remained unconvinced by claims that a proposed dam's flooding of nonreservation sites, graves, and medicines along the Little Tennessee that were sacred to the Cherokee violate the free exercise clause. The *Sequoyah* court found that the violated beliefs and practices failed to meet a standard of "centrality" to Cherokee religion, instead viewing the claims by members of Oklahoma-based Cherokee communities who had been forcibly removed from the Tennessee Valley in the early nineteenth century to be "essentially cultural" in nature.

That same year, in *Badoni v. Higginson* (1980), the Tenth Circuit ruled against Navajo claims about unconstitutional federal management of water levels at a dam desecrating Rainbow Arch in Utah by enabling tourist boats to interfere with sanctity and flooding other sites believed to be in themselves divine, "drowning gods," in effect. The appellate court overruled the lower court's position that the Navajo lacked standing because they demonstrated no "property interest" in the affected sites, and thus addressed the two distinct First Amendment arguments. With regard to the issue of lake levels drowning gods and prohibiting access to submerged prayer spots, the court held that the federal government demonstrated a "compelling government interest" that outweighed the free exercise prohibition in the *Sherbert* balancing test. With regard to the issue of the desecrating tourist traffic, the Tenth Circuit found that Navajo free exercise had not been burdened. "The First Amendment protects one against action by the government, though even then, not in all circumstances; but it gives no one the right to insist that in the pursuit of their own interests others must conform their conduct to his own religious necessities. . . . We must accommodate our idiosyncrasies, religious as well as secular, to the compromises necessary in communal life" (*Badoni*, 638 F.2d at 172).

Three years later, in *Fools Crow v. Gullet* (1983), the Eighth Circuit affirmed a district court's decision that found unconvincing Native claims that their religious free exercise was constitutionally burdened at Bear Butte, a major sacred precinct and vision quest site where construction and regulation requiring permits and rules for prayer on the South Dakota state park atop the site infringed on Cheyenne and Lakota practices. Such rulings have all but foreclosed further First Amendment constitutional challenges, but not surprisingly these places remain contested sites, with Bear Butte in particular a place of seemingly perennial gatherings of Native religious activists concerned with subsequent development schemes, such as a proposed gun range and expansive campground, music stage, and biker bar at the base of the butte, catering to the annual motorcycle rally in nearby Sturgis. If such desecrations—and it is uncanny how often the challenged developments are so crassly opposed to Native religious interests—have burdened Native religious exercise, they have also had the effect of rekindling spirited resistance. Indeed, according to Suzan Harjo, a Cheyenne–Muscogee journalist and advocate important to the passage of AIRFA and subsequent related legislation, the strategic efforts of Native communities to assert their religious freedom claims began with spiritual gatherings at Bear Butte in the 1970s (personal communication, 2009).

ESTABLISHMENT CLAUSE CHALLENGES

An additional difficulty facing government accommodation of Native traditions as religions has been the triggering of numerous legal challenges under the establishment clause. High-profile challenges have been brought in the courts against management plans of the Park Service and Forest Service that even modestly accommodated Native American concerns for proper ceremonial access to sacred sites on federal lands. In no small part, these agency accommodations followed AIRFA, or President Clinton's 1993 executive order "to accommodate access to and ceremonial use of Indian sacred sites by Indian religious practitioners and avoid adversely affecting the physical integrity of such sacred sites" (Executive Order 13007). In one major case, a coalition of tourism and property interests fought a plan at Devil's Tower National Monument that placed a voluntary ban on climbing during the month of June to accommodate the Lakota and others who consider Mato Tipila, Bear Lodge, to be sacred and who at the very least requested quiet for this month of intensive ceremonial activity (*Bear Lodge Multiple Use Association et al. v. Babbitt* [1990]).

In 1995, after consultations with the tribes, the Park Service enacted a policy banning licenses for June climbing under the auspices of commercial outfitters. Several outfitters filed suit in federal court challenging the policy as a government establishment of Native religion on public lands, and a judge's preliminary injunction in 1996 led officials to reduce the climbing ban to a voluntary one in which permit seekers merely were required to listen to a scripted sentence about the Native American concerns and a request that they refrain from climbing in June. Even this measure was challenged as a violation of the establishment clause, with the backing of the Mountain States Legal Foundation, an organization funded heavily by mining and timbering interests with a stake in public land management.

In 1998, a district court judge affirmed the constitutionality of the voluntary ban, and this was reaffirmed on appeal. Still, this was only a modest victory because even government managers willing to negotiate accommodations with tribes must keep a vigilant eye on these potential claims; others may avoid the hassle altogether.

Several years later, a private timber company challenged a Forest Service amended management plan prohibiting timbering and road construction within a certain radius of the medicine wheel atop a peak in Wyoming's Bighorn Mountains, a site sacred to the Arapaho, Shoshone, Cheyenne, and Crow. The comment period for an environmental impact study process produced significant criticism of the impacts on Native American cultural resources for a Forest Service plan for timber harvest in the area, criticism that led to changes in the government management plan. The company challenged the government's amended plan, arguing in part that the Forest Service had in effect established Native American religions in their weighing of multiple uses of public lands. In *Wyoming Sawmills, Inc. v. U.S. Forest Service* (2004), the Tenth Circuit affirmed a 2001 district court decision that held against the corporation on a number of accounts. As regarded the First Amendment claims, the district judge found that Wyoming Sawmills, Inc., lacked standing as to the First Amendment claims because the court could not remedy the constitutional wrongs the company had alleged, which amounted to financial hardship. The Tenth Circuit Court of Appeals agreed, finding the purely economic injury sustained by the corporation as an "artificial person" to be insufficiently analogous to other cases in which courts recognized standing to bring an establishment claim against the government (*Wyoming Sawmills*, 383 F.3d at 1247).

As with *Bear Lodge*, the *Wyoming Sawmills* case gave accommodations to Native religious free exercise some breathing room from claims of violations of the establishment clause. But it was refuted on grounds that did not lay a firm and broad foundation for future accommodations of Native American claims to religious free exercise in public land management decision making.

EAGLE FEATHERS AND THE UNIVERSALITY OF RELIGION

Still another problem has accompanied legal protections of Native American traditions as religions. Local religious traditions of indigenous peoples are ill suited for the universalism expected of religions, and in U.S. law that becomes clear as courts are asked whether protections of Native traditions as religions extend to non-Indian practitioners or practitioners who are racially Native but not members of federally recognized Indian tribes. This happened in a cluster of cases involving the possession of eagle feathers, which are exempted from criminal penalties under endangered species and eagle protection statutes through a permitting process available to "card carrying" members of federally recognized Indian tribes.

In *United States v. Hardman* (2002), the Tenth Circuit incorporated three cases challenging, on religious freedom grounds, a permitting process that excluded any practitioner of a Native religion who was not a member of a recognized tribe.[1] The court found that the religion of one of the three had been burdened, as he was a lineal descendant of an unrecognized Apache tribe, and that the burden could not be justified by the compelling state interest of a federal trust responsibility to "preserve Native American culture and religion." But a different circuit disagreed. One year later, in a similar challenge by a Canadian member of the Salish Nation, the Ninth Circuit held that limiting permits to members of federally recognized tribes was a lawful way to accomplish the government's trust responsibility (*United States v. Antoine* [2003]).[2]

THE DISTINCTIVE LEGAL STATUS OF NATIVE AMERICANS: NATIONS WITHIN A NATION

The federal trust responsibility, including a responsibility to "preserve Native American culture and religion," hinges not on the universality of religion or the racial makeup of Native Americans but on the distinctive political status of recognized tribes within U.S. law, and I turn now to consider the realm of Indian law as a legal regime by which many Native communities have found robust protections for religious traditions after the Rehnquist Court's stripping of the free exercise clause. Indian law is a vast and intricate field; here I wish only to introduce the cluster of group rights under the rubric of tribal sovereignty, rights enumerated in nearly 400 treaties, recognized over time by the courts, and implicating a special government-to-government relationship with recognized tribes.

SOVEREIGNTY

The sovereignty recognized by American courts has been a qualified one, rooted in foundational Supreme Court decisions under John Marshall that identify Indian tribes as "domestic, dependent nations" with confirmed rights of occupancy on their lands and extensive rights of self-determination that give treaties a robust legal status, but also with time delimiting those rights and ultimately assigning Congress "plenary power" over Indian affairs. If it seems oxymoronic to assert something like "quasi-sovereignty," it surely is; indeed, it is rooted in the contradictions of the "Doctrine of Discovery" formally incorporated into U.S. Indian law in *Johnson v. McIntosh* (1823). But even the subsequent qualifications on tribal sovereignty have triggered judicial review of federal actions for their accountability to a "trust responsibility" that has many implications for the protection of Native American interests that are arguably if not plainly religious.

First I would like to frame the matter of tribal sovereignty by focusing on a series of cases involving salmon fishing rights that link treaty rights, sovereignty, and the religious and cultural dimensions of activities that are also economic in nature. In 1905, the Supreme Court confirmed the treaty rights of Native people in Washington State to access what a series of treaties had designated their "usual and accustomed places" in order to take salmon, even on ceded reservation lands that fell into private hands. In *United States v. Winans* (1905), the Supreme Court defined "reservations" not merely as enclosures of lands not ceded but as clusters of enduring reserved rights, and the Court clarified a judicial interpretation of treaties that continues to challenge much conventional wisdom: "The treaty was not a grant of rights to the Indians, but a grant of rights from them—a reservation of those not granted" (*Winans*, 198 U.S. at 371).

In the 1970s, this logic was extended in another generative off-reservation salmon fishing case involving treaty rights, *United States v. Washington* (1974). This decision, often referred to as the Boldt decision for the district judge who rendered the opinion, held that Native tribes who were signatories to a series of treaties in the 1850s were entitled to one half the harvest of salmon on rivers that were their "usual and accustomed grounds and stations," quite apart from the presumptions of the State of Washington to assert its authority to regulate the fish harvest.

This decision carried tremendous consequences for the economic livelihood of the salmon fishing tribes and cleared ground for an expansive judicial protection of treaty-specified off-reservation hunting and fishing rights elsewhere. Although the decision hardly rested on the ceremonial nature of the salmon fishing practice, Boldt's decision made explicit reference to traditional religious and cultural practices in order to help establish the depth and reach of the Native peoples' concerns beyond those of subsistence in the making of the treaty language:

> The first-salmon ceremony, which with local differences in detail was general through most of the area, was essentially a religious rite to ensure the continued return of salmon. The symbolic acts, attitudes of respect and reverence, and concern for the salmon reflected a ritualistic conception of the interdependence and relatedness of all living things which was a dominant feature of native Indian world view. Religious attitudes and rites insured that salmon were never wantonly wasted and that water pollution was not permitted during the salmon season. (*Washington*, 384 F. Supp. 352)

After Boldt, the courts more formally came to recognize three "canons of construction" guiding the proper interpretation of Indian treaties. First, "ambiguous expressions must be resolved in favor of the Indian parties concerned." Second, "Indian treaties must be interpreted as the Indians themselves would have understood them"; finally, Indian treaties ought to be "liberally construed" in favor of the Indians.

In 1934, Congress passed the Indian Reorganization Act (IRA), which rejected the assimilation policy's allotment of communal land, dissolution of tribal governments, and criminalization of Indian languages and ceremonies. The IRA established a process by which Indian communities could incorporate as federally recognized Indian tribes, creating the legal framework for contemporary tribal governments in which the legal corpus of sovereignty is recognized. Many of these tribes have rewritten their constitutions in closer keeping with traditional forms of governance, and indeed such matters of self-governance and political self-determination can even carry the force of the free exercise of traditional practices.[3]

But the courts also placed limits on tribal sovereignty, recognizing in *Lone Wolf v. Hitchcock* (1903) that Congress holds the primary authority over Indian affairs and in some cases can abrogate treaties unilaterally. Thus equipped with what the Supreme Court called plenary power, Congress could conceivably do away with sovereignty "in one grumpy afternoon," to use Sam Deloria's expression (Washburn 2007). This principle of congressional plenary power was invoked in a number of twentieth-century cases, including one that bears, if indirectly, on First Amendment concerns addressed in other venues. In *United States v. Dion* (1986), the Supreme Court reversed a circuit court's decision that the express treaty rights of a Yankton Sioux man hunting eagles on reservation land trumped the extent of Congress's power to enforce a variety of eagle protection acts. Although a First Amendment claim had been denied Dwight Dion in the lower courts and did not reemerge on appeal, the Supreme Court affirmed that the doctrine of plenary power could extend to "quiet abrogations" of treaty provisions without Congress doing so expressly.

If twentieth-century courts have stepped up to acknowledge tribal sovereignty in a number of important respects, the language of plenary power continues to reach into Native American communities and lives. For example, it was congressional action, in 1924, that applied citizenship to Indians. It is congressional authority, and that delegated to the executive branch, that can offer (and, in many cases, withhold) the federal recognition of Native communities as tribes, so crucial to enjoyment of the recognized political status that triggers matters of sovereignty and of the trust responsibility. And it was congressional action in 1968 that extended the protections of the Bill of Rights to Native Americans on reservations vis-à-vis tribal governments.[4]

TRUST DOCTRINE AS SOURCE OF BOTH TRIBAL RIGHTS AND FEDERAL CONTROL

The courts have come to regard the federal government as a trustee of Indian interests. Rooted in the ward–guardian language of *Cherokee Nation v. Georgia* (1831), the trustee relationship surely suggests a deep paternalism, and trust law typically extends to the management of real property.[5] Yet the law makes trustees legally accountable for their conduct in ways that have been useful to tribes seeking to advance religious and cultural interests in the domains of law and policy.

In the 1970s, for example, a Nevada tribe won an important case that asserted that the United States had violated its trust responsibility in a dam management plan that failed to allocate enough water to replenish Pyramid Lake, both the major source of economic livelihood to the tribe and a sacred body of water intricately related to tribal identity. In *Pyramid Lake Paiute v. Morton* (1972), a district court judge found the United States had failed to live up to "the most exacting fiduciary standards" as trustee and, in effect, set a precedent that means the executive branch, in making any domestic policy, can never take off its hat as trustee of American Indian interests.

The courts have extended trust accountability to congressional actions as well. In *United States v. Sioux Nation* (1980), a case involving Lakota claims to the Black Hills, or *Paha Sapa*, "the heart of everything that is," the Supreme Court found that government actions to right the wrongs through monetary compensation for unlawful abrogations of the Fort Laramie Treaty (1868), in which Lakota signatories expressly had secured the Black Hills from American encroachment, had failed the trust responsibility. Lowering the standard from "exacting fiduciary standards" merely to a standard of "good faith," the Court nonetheless sided with the Lakota in their major claim that the government had not acted in good faith as a trustee when it converted land into money payments. Ironically, in keeping with the practices of the statute authorizing the Indian Claims Commission, the Court awarded hundreds of millions of dollars to the Lakota, but the Lakota nations party to the suit have refused payment, and to this day the money sits in escrow, despite the raging poverty on South Dakota reservations. Shannon County, for example, in which Pine Ridge is situated, consistently ranks as among the poorest counties in the United States.

FEDERAL INDIAN LAW AND CIVIL RIGHTS

If the trust responsibility and tribal sovereignty have given some shelter to Native religious claims where the First Amendment has failed them, the foundation of Indian law is also to be contrasted with the Fourteenth Amendment civil rights regime of equality under the law, which Winnifred Fallers Sullivan (2005), among others, has identified as a promising basis for religious freedom generally in the future.[6]

As Charles Wilkinson (1991:378) puts it, "Indian issues veer away from other questions of race. The most cherished civil rights of Indian people are not based on equality of treatment under the Constitution and the general civil rights laws." American Indian survival as peoples relies on treaties, statutes, and executive orders recognizing a range of special prerogatives. Wilkinson shows the symmetry between the field of Indian law and indigenous claims that religion and peoplehood are seamlessly woven together in ways of life:

> The same essential questions and their answers apply not only to walleyes and muskellunge in Wisconsin, but also to . . . salmon and steelhead in Washington and Oregon; eagles in Wyoming and Idaho, water in California and Nevada; tax collection in Minnesota and Nebraska; peyote in Utah and New Mexico; custody of young Indian children in Montana and Illinois; land title in Maine and New York; economic development in Florida and Oklahoma; tribal taxation and court jurisdiction over non-Indians in Arizona and the Dakotas; Native sovereignty in Alaska and Hawaii. (Wilkinson 1991:378)

HISTORIC PRESERVATION: TRADITIONAL CULTURAL PROPERTIES

In concert with the legal strategies invoking the distinctive legal status of federally recognized Indian tribes, the two statutory frameworks of historic preservation and environmental law have also offered Native communities considerable protections of traditions, places, and practices outside the discourse of religious freedom. Under the National Historic Preservation Act (NHPA, 1966), sites that are sacred to Native people count because they are considered cultural resources of value to Americans generally, but amendments to the regulations have transformed what had long extended only to archaeological sites to a network of protections for cultural resources of concern to living communities.

NHPA, originally passed in 1966 to protect historic buildings from urban renewal, emerged through a series of amendments and procedures as a productive framework for properties of interest to architectural historians and archaeologists. The mechanism for protection is procedural: required processes of review assessing potential adverse affects to properties deemed eligible for the National Register of Historic Places, consultation with interested parties and the public, and possible mitigation or at least memoranda of agreement.

Reforming the process in 1990, the National Park Service clarified what is eligible for the National Register of Historic Places to include what it designated a Traditional Cultural Property (TCP): "One that is eligible for inclusion in the National Register because of its association with cultural practices or beliefs of a living community that (a) are rooted in that community's history, and (b) are important in maintaining the continuing cultural identity of the community" (Parker and King 1990:38).

Two years later, Congress amended the act to further instruct government agencies that properties of religious and cultural importance to Indian tribes and Native Hawaiian organizations were eligible for the register and that tribes were to be consulted under the NHPA's mandatory consultation procedure. Although no specific mention is made of Native Americans, a majority of designated TCPs are Native sites. And important for our purposes, there is a studious avoidance of the term *sacred* in the regulations. Thomas King (2003:7), one of the authors of the regulations designating TCPs, reflected, "Even where places are ascribed . . . spiritual qualities, are sanctified by practice or belief, I've become wary of calling them "sacred." The term carries a great deal of semantic freight in Western culture that may be counterproductive to load on a place, even one to which supernatural power is ascribed."

For King, this is in part because *sacred* is too wooden a term to signify the variety of ways in which indigenous people can regard significant landscapes: Some places are so sacrosanct that people just do not go there, others are sacred but also open to other uses, such as for economic livelihood, and still others are sacred in terms of certain times of year. But avoiding reference to "the sacred" in the TCP regulations also has to do with King's (2003:9) concern that the fashionable movement to protect significant places as "sacred sites" insists on "standards of inviolate protection which, in the realities of a secular and pluralist democracy, will result in fewer such places receiving protection in the first place."

Perhaps it is because of these pragmatic insights that the TCP designation has proved so useful to Native communities seeking to protect places they consider sacred or significant, for through the consultation and negotiated agreements that can ensue, Native religious interests can be accommodated without the headlines, scrutiny, and probable losses of a First Amendment claim.

ENVIRONMENTAL LAW

Like the consultations with tribes mandated under NHPA, the environmental impact review process under the National Environmental Protection Act (NEPA, 1969), as well as an executive order on environmental justice directing government agencies to evaluate environmental ills disproportionately borne by low-income and minority populations (Executive Order 12898), has offered footing for Native efforts to assert some control over sites of significance to their traditions, and not only where environmental damage is concerned. NEPA review procedures involve consideration of the "human environment," which expressly includes impacts on cultural as well as natural resources. But environmental laws can do more to protect Native religious interests than merely establish procedures of consultation, as shown in a case involving the Pueblo of Isleta, whose traditional lands straddle the Rio Grande just miles downstream from Albuquerque (*City of Albuquerque v. Browner* [1996]). Authorized by a 1987 amendment to the Clean Water Act that recognized Indian tribes as states for the purposes of setting clean water standards that apply to upstream governments, Isleta Pueblo leaders went ahead and set stringent standards for Rio Grande water that were challenged by Albuquerque, which faced a $250 million improvement in treatment technology to comply.

Among the "designated uses" requiring the higher cleanliness standard, the Pueblo cited "Primary Contact Ceremonial Use." In keeping with its traditions of the secrecy of sacred knowledge, the Pueblo offered no details of the ceremonial usage, only that it is for "religious or traditional purposes by members of the Pueblo of Isleta" and that it could involve "immersion and intentional or incidental ingestion of water" (*City of Albuquerque*, 97 F.3d at 428). They didn't need to disclose the details; this wasn't a First Amendment claim. Calling Isleta's justification too "vague" and even "irrational," Albuquerque challenged Environmental Protection Agency (EPA) approval of the standards with a cocktail of claims that are typical of those countering assertions of tribal rights: violations of administrative procedure, an unconstitutional establishment of Pueblo religion, and a claim that if Isleta were not disingenuous about its ceremonial usage, it would have sought an even higher standard of "safe for drinking."

The district court made quick work of rejecting Albuquerque's claims, and the Tenth Circuit made equally quick work in affirming. The establishment clause was not violated because ceremonial usage was but one among a range of uses, most of them secular in intent, requiring stringent clean water standards. The courts also found that EPA approval advanced the Clean Water Act, not Isleta Pueblo religion, adding that "if anything, the agency's approval furthers the free exercise of religion" as clarified by AIRFA, and that the EPA was not becoming excessively entangled with Pueblo religion when it issued future permits in keeping with the Isleta standards.

Finally, the courts dismissed the claim that sincere claims to ceremonial use would set a drinkable standard, noting that Isleta was not designating raw Rio Grande water as its drinking water supply, only trying to ensure that ceremonial uses and "incidental" ingestion were protected to a "fishable/swimmable" standard. And the strong result has persuaded other tribes to pursue this strategy, including Pacific Northwest tribes challenging the impacts of dams on migrations of salmon that are at once matters of economic, religious, and cultural significance.

Beyond environmental statutes, environmental arguments have enabled public servants to manage public lands in ways that effectively accommodate Native religious claims without overtly doing so and thus triggering the challenges on establishment grounds. For example, at Cave Rock on Lake Tahoe, regarded by the Washoe as their spiritual birthplace, officials expressly avoided reference to free exercise in a management plan banning popular practices of public climbing and picnicking on the site.

CONSULTATION, NOT RIGHTS

It should be made clear here that the bulk of the protections under environmental law and historic preservation law amount to consultative procedures, ones that incorporate tribal governments in decision making and foster conditions for negotiated settlements. That they *should* mandate consultation and that they *can* foster such negotiated agreement does not mean that they invariably *do* bear such fruit. Because the review processes relating to these protections have become very technical, even Byzantine; because their legal teeth take shape only through the difficult-to-establish claims of administrative discretion under the Administrative Procedure Act; and especially because the consultants who collect and analyze data work under agencies that are proponents of the projects under review, it takes resources, expertise, and vigilance to ensure that the procedures are followed in a way that appropriately consults with tribes and effectively takes their concerns into account. Tribes have won from the courts some modest judicial review of lapses of administrative discipline in cultural resource processes, as in a Tenth Circuit decision finding that the U.S. Forest Service had not adequately consulted tribes merely by sending a notification letter requesting detailed markings of maps of sacred sites for a proposed recreation and road expansion in a canyon of deep significance to members of Sandia Pueblo

(*Pueblo of Sandia v. United States* [1995]; *Pit River Tribe et al. v. U.S. Forest Service* [2006]). The importance of consultation with federally recognized tribal governments has also been clarified as a general matter by executive order (Executive Order 13175).

But the consultation promoted by NHPA and NEPA at its best relies on responsible government, and it is disciplined to work as it ought in terms of tribal interests by little case law, and case law that turns on the language of the statutes and their accompanying regulations, not on recognized fundamental religious freedom rights Native people might enjoy under more robust free exercise protection.

BEFORE "AFTER PLURALISM"

Before we begin a postmortem on the legal protection of Native American traditions as religions, we should reckon with recent legal gains that the freedom of Native traditions qua religions have made under statutory protections. The Native American Graves Protection and Repatriation Act (NAGPRA, 1990), for example, marks a formidable piece of human rights legislation that regards the remains of Native Americans as human remains and not "archaeological resources" and that mandates the repatriation from museums of funerary objects, items of cultural patrimony, and culturally identifiable sacred objects that have not only righted numerous past wrongs but occasioned the healing of social ills and revival of Native religions. NAGPRA is formidable in my view because in the face of powerful contestation from the archaeological, scientific, and museum sectors, Native advocates persuaded Congress, in part through specific tribal narratives of historical injustice but also in part through narratives of universal human rights to religious freedom and the integrity of the dead (Johnson 2007). What is more, NAGPRA creates space for weighing indigenous ways of knowing in making determinations of cultural affiliation, including consideration of oral historical traditions as well as scientific data, in its regulations. The full reach of such tribal claims to cultural affiliation has been contained by an appellate court in *Bonnichsen v. United States* (2004), the case involving the disposition of the remains of so-called Kennewick Man, or Ancient One, as Native claimants regard him, and surely NAGPRA processes have produced some difficult claims and counterclaims of cultural affiliation by multiple Native communities. But as Gregory Johnson (2007) and others have ably shown, NAGPRA has profoundly reshaped the terrain on which Native claims to the dead and to the sacred are negotiated with other interests (see also

Fine-Dare 2002; Ridington and Hastings 1997). I could and should extend this analysis, along with that of other legislative interventions by Congress, such as the return of Blue Lake to Taos Pueblo, a decision that was informed by the trust responsibility but also by the persuasiveness of religious pluralism and its language of the sacred.

More particularly, congressional attempts to restore an approach to the free exercise clause before the Rehnquist Court's narrowing jurisprudence of *Lyng* and *Smith* may promise to serve Native claims in prisons and sacred lands better than they do for other religious minorities. A broad coalition of religious freedom groups left and right persuaded Congress to pass the Religious Freedom Restoration Act (RFRA) in 1993, reapplying the three-pronged *Sherbert* test to cases in order to reverse jurisprudence in the wake of *Smith*. Although the Supreme Court ruled in *City of Boerne v. Flores* (1997) that the statute exceeded Congress's constitutional authority as it applied to states and localities, most Native claims reliably pertain to federal agencies and statutes, and many states reacted by passing their own RFRA-like legislation. In 2006, the newly configured Roberts Court affirmed the constitutionality of RFRA as applied to federal law in a case whose factual record resembled closely that of the *Smith* peyote case (RFRA 1993).

An amendment to RFRA went even further to make room for free exercise protection for Native Americans. In 2000, with the Religious Land Use and Institutionalized Persons Act (RLUIPA), Congress responded to *Boerne* by narrowing the reach of RFRA to land use decisions and prison administration, the latter easing the exceptionally difficult path Native inmates have faced in securing accommodations for their free exercise rights behind bars. But RLUIPA also extended (indeed amended) RFRA's definition of the "exercise of religion" to include "any exercise whether or not compelled by, or central to, a system of religious belief" (RLUIPA § 2000bb 2 (4)). For favorable courts, anyway, this semantic move helps Native claimants address the nearly insurmountable precedents set in the 1980s sacred land cases discussed earlier (*Badoni* [1980]; *Sequoyah* [1980]). And where the *Lyng* Court drastically narrowed the scope of the meaning of *prohibit* in the free exercise clause, statutory protections under RLUIPA and RFRA as amended set the discussion atop a standard of "substantial burden."

The possibilities and limits of the U.S. courts' capacity to protect Native religious freedom since RLUIPA and RFRA are perhaps best seen in the shifting fortunes of *Navajo Nation et al. v. U.S. Forest Service* (2006). The case involved the claims against federal land use decisions believed to desecrate Arizona's San Francisco Peaks by the Navajo, Hopi, Havasupai, White Mountain Apache, and Hualapai nations, who are among thirteen tribes who consider the massif to be a sacred mountain. At issue was Forest Service approval of a plan to pump up to

100 million gallons of Flagstaff's sewage effluent to make artificial snow, in order to ensure more predictable and profitable skiing on the peaks, where drought conditions in the winter of 2001–2002 had allowed only four skiable days. Although there were some challenges to the propriety of the NEPA and NHPA review procedures in rendering the go-ahead, at the appellate level the case turned on the question of whether the snowmaking scheme violated RFRA. In 2006, an Arizona federal district court ruled in favor of the Forest Service and its permitting of the snowmaking scheme, citing the precedents of *Lyng* and making ample note of an appellate court ruling in *Wilson v. Block* (1983) against a free exercise of religion challenge to development of the ski area on the peaks in the first place (apparently it mattered little that these precedents were matters of First Amendment interpretation, not the RFRA statute).

In March 2007, a three-judge panel of the Ninth Circuit Court of Appeals unanimously and vociferously reversed in favor of the tribes, illuminating and emboldening this section of my argument at the time I first drafted it, but the Ninth Circuit, having chosen to rehear the case en banc, issued a decision in August 2008 superseding its three-judge panel on precisely the RFRA matters in question, finding that Native religion was not "substantially burdened" by the spraying of sewage effluent on a sacred mountain, and Judge Fletcher's three-judge panel opinion remains as a dissent. Because other circuit courts had differed with the Ninth Circuit on the precise meaning of RFRA's "substantial burden" language, the Supreme Court agreed to receive certiorari petitions to consider hearing the case on appeal, but in June 2009, the High Court denied the petitions, so the Ninth Circuit en banc opinion stands.

The en banc majority reasoned that Congress intended, through its appeal in RFRA to language of "substantial burden," to tie that statute to the courts' particular understanding of substantial burden in its First Amendment decisions, including especially *Lyng* and others cited earlier. Judge Fletcher's sixty-one-page dissent, a revision of the 2007 three-judge panel ruling, documents in detail the specific nature of the sacredness of the San Francisco Peaks for the affected tribes, in terms of how the physical and spiritual contamination would substantially burden particular ceremonial practices but also more broadly in terms of how contamination would "lead to the inability to maintain daily and annual religious practices comprising an entire way of life, because the practices require belief in the mountain's purity or a spiritual connection." The three-judge panel opinion had laid claim to the definitional expansions of RFRA and RLUIPA and signaled in dicta that *Lyng* need no longer control future cases concerning sacred sites.

> The Court in *Lyng* denied the Free Exercise claim in part because it could not see a stopping place. We uphold the RFRA claim in this case in part because otherwise we

> cannot see a starting place. If Appellants do not have a valid RFRA claim in this case, we are unable to see how any Native American plaintiff can ever have a successful RFRA claim based on beliefs and practices tied to land that they hold sacred. (*Navajo Nation v. U.S. Forest Service* 06-15371 [March 2007] at 10106)

The August 2008 en banc ruling held otherwise and advanced a strikingly narrow view of RFRA's definition of religious exercise and untenable burdens:

> The sole effect of the artificial snow is on the Plaintiff's subjective spiritual experience. That is, the presence of the artificial snow on the Peaks is offensive to the Plaintiff's feelings about their religion and will decrease the spiritual fulfillment Plaintiffs get from practicing their religion on the mountain. Nevertheless, a government action that decreases the spirituality, the fervor, or the satisfaction with which a believer practices his religion is not what Congress has labeled a "substantial burden"—a term of art chosen by Congress to be defined by reference to Supreme Court precedent—on the free exercise of religion. Where, as here, there is no showing the government has coerced the Plaintiffs to act contrary to their religious beliefs under the threat of sanctions, or conditioned a governmental benefit upon conduct that would violate the Plaintiffs' religious beliefs there is no "substantial burden" on the exercise of their religion." (*Navajo Nation*, 535 F. 3d at 1063)

The en banc ruling went on to paraphrase the slippery slope concern that Justice Scalia sounded in *Smith*. Were there to be a showing of substantial burden, the Ninth Circuit found, "any action the federal government were to take, including action on its own land, would be subject to the personalized oversight of millions of citizens," each holding "an individual veto to prohibit the government action solely because it offends his religious beliefs, sensibilities, or tastes, or fails to satisfy his religious desire" (*Navajo Nation*, 1535 3d. at 1063).

Judge Fletcher's spirited dissent argues instead that a plain reading of Congress's intent in passing RFRA in the first place was anything but a ringing endorsement of the courts' previous interpretation of "substantial burden," and given some variance in the appellate courts' interpretations of the RFRA statute on this threshold question, I think the issue will reemerge. If the language of the en banc ruling in the San Francisco Peaks case suggests the ultimate weakness of the pluralism model of protected religious exercise as matters of "subjective experience," "feeling," and "spiritual fulfillment," before we move to what should come after pluralism, I want to take stock of the statutory gains that Native peoples have secured on these matters, gains that must rely less on their electoral presence than on their ability (by means of pluralist discourse) to lay claim to the religiousness, the sacredness of their interests. Put simply, if religion has not served Native people well as an effective category of constitutional protection, it has been important as a means of persuasion in their efforts to garner the political and moral support to protect certain high-profile sacred sites as matters at the heart, not the fringe, of this American experiment in religious freedom.

If, as in AIRFA, the end result of that rhetorical advantage in the political and legislative process has not amounted to much when squared off against powerful economic interests of tourism and extractive industries in the case of sacred lands, or when confronted by powerful myths that real Indians and real Indian religions vanished in a tragic past, there are some possibilities here that at least some Native people do not want to forgo. If I conclude on a note of equivocation, I suspect I am not alone in a discussion contemplating a world that is at once "after" and "before" pluralism.

NOTES

The author would like to thank the editors, other participants in this forum, and Kevin Washburn for helpful suggestions. I would like to add that it is outrageous that Native people receive so little relief under the First Amendment, and nothing in this chapter should be regarded as undermining Native First Amendment claims to religious freedom.

1. Joselius Sainz was a lineal descendant of the Chiracahua Apache, a federally unrecognized tribe whose eagle feathers were confiscated and not returned in the absence of a permit. The other two claimants were non-Native: Samuel Ray Wilgus and Raymond Hardman. Hardman lived on a Utah reservation, and his children and former wife were members of a federally recognized tribe, but he was convicted of possessing eagle feathers connected with a funeral for his children's godfather when his ex-wife tipped off authorities.

2. Leonard Antoine served a two-year prison sentence for having brought eagle feathers without a permit into the United States for a potlatch ceremony. A member of the Cowichan Band of Salish in Canada, Antoine was ineligible for a permit because he was not a member of a federally recognized Indian tribe. The Ninth Circuit Court did not believe that applying the Religious Freedom Restoration Act (RFRA) to the permit process should result in nonrecognized Native Americans being included in the process. The *Antoine* court stuck by a decision it had made in 1997 upholding the requirement that Native members of federally recognized tribes go through the permitting process even if it presented possible delays. It refused to follow Antoine's argument that his situation presented different difficulties altogether: "We do not believe RFRA requires the government to make the showing the Tenth Circuit demands of it. Although the record contains no data on the number of nonmembers who would seek permits if eligible, the consequences of extending

eligibility are predictable from the nature of the repository program" (*Antoine*, 318 F.3d at 922, note 5).

3. In some cases, even where individual civil rights actions against the tribes have emerged, the federal courts have supported the sovereignty of those recognized tribal governments. See *Santa Clara Pueblo v. Martinez*, 436 U.S. 49, 98 S. Ct. 1670, 56 L.Ed.2d 106 (1978); and *Lomyaktewa v. Hathaway*, 520 F.2d 1324 (9th Cir. 1975), *cert. denied* 425 U.S. 903 (1976). I should add that sovereignty thus recognized in U.S. courts comes under significant challenge by Native people claiming forms of inherent sovereignty other than that developed in U.S. law.

4. On the latter point, the Indian Civil Rights Act legislatively addressed the Supreme Court's holding in *Talton v. Mays* (1896), in which the Court understood tribal sovereignty as meaning that the U.S. Constitution's Bill of Rights did not apply to the tribes. As concerns religious free exercise, the act included a version of the free exercise clause of the First Amendment, with a habeas corpus provision for a remedy in federal court, but notably excluded establishment language: "No Indian tribe in exercising powers of self-government shall—1) make or enforce any law prohibiting the free exercise of religion, or abridging the freedom of speech, or of the press, or the right of the people peaceably to assemble and to petition for a redress of grievances" (*Talton*, 25 U.S.C. § 1302, as amended).

5. The legal framework of the trust doctrine was based on *Cherokee v. Georgia* (1831). It was significantly elaborated in a 1942 case in which a contemporary tribal council sued the U.S. government for failing to hold a nineteenth-century tribal council to account for corruption in the administration of treaty payments. In *Seminole Nation v. United States* 316 U.S. 286 (1942), the U.S. government was apprised that the courts would hold it accountable to rigorous fiduciary standards as a trustee, arguing that there is a "distinctive obligation of trust incumbent upon the government in its dealings with these dependent and sometimes exploited people. Under a humane and self-imposed policy which has found expression in many acts of Congress and numerous decisions of this Court, it has charged itself with moral obligations of the highest responsibility and trust" (*Seminole Nation*, 316 U.S. at 296).

In *United States v. Mitchell*, 463 U.S. 206 (1983), the Court extended the trust responsibility and heightened federal accountability for its actions, to be in force wherever the government exercised "elaborate control or supervision."

6. This special legal status has on several occasions trumped the civil rights legal regime of the Fourteenth Amendment. In *Morton v. Mancari* (1974), a decision with numerous implications for subsequent Indian law cases, the Supreme Court upheld an Indian hiring preference policy of the Bureau of Indian Affairs and distinguished the legal basis for much of Indian law and policy as one not applying to a special racial group or interest group:

> The preference, as applied, is granted to Indians not as a discrete racial group, but, rather, as members of quasi-sovereign tribal entities whose lives and activities are governed by the BIA in a unique fashion. On numerous occasions this Court specifically has upheld legislation that singles out Indians for particular and special

treatment. As long as the special treatment can be tied rationally to the fulfillment of Congress' obligation toward the Indians, such legislative judgments will not be disturbed. Here, where the preference is reasonable and rationally designed to further Indian self government, we cannot say that Congress's classification violates due process. (*Morton*, 417 U.S. at 535)

WORKS CITED

American Indian Religious Freedom Act. 1978. 42 U.S.C. (1996).

Anaya, S. James. 2004. *Indigenous Peoples in International Law*. 2nd ed. New York: Oxford University Press.

Badoni v. Higginson, 638 F.2d 172 (10th Cir. 1980).

Bear Lodge Multiple Use Association et al. v. Babbitt, 2 F. Supp. 2d 1448 (D. Wyo. 1998), *affirmed*, 175 F.3d 814 (10th Cir. 1999), *cert. denied* 529 U.S. 1037 (2000).

Bonnichsen v. United States, 217 F. Supp. 2d 1116, 1125–1126 (D. Or. 2002), 367 F.3d 864 (9th Cir. 2004).

Cherokee Nation v. Georgia, 30 U.S. 1 (1831).

City of Albuquerque v. Browner, 97 F.3d 415 (10th Cir. 1996), *cert. denied* 522 U.S. 965 (1997).

City of Boerne v. Flores, 521 U.S. 507 (1997).

Deloria, Vine, Jr., and Clifford Lytle. 1983. *American Indians, American Justice*. Austin: University of Texas Press.

Employment Division, Department of Human Services State of Oregon v. Smith, 494 U.S. 872 (1990).

Fine-Dare, Kathleen. 2002. *Grave Injustice: The American Indian Repatriation Movement and* NAGPRA. Lincoln: University of Nebraska Press.

Fools Crow v. Gullet, 706 F.2d 856 (8th Cir. 1983), *cert. denied* 464 U.S. 977 (1983).

Johnson, Gregory. 2007. *Sacred Claims*. Charlottesville: University of Virginia Press.

Johnson v. McIntosh, 21 U.S. 8 Wheat. 543 543 (1823).

King, Thomas. 2003. *Places That Count: Traditional Cultural Properties in Cultural Resource Management*. Walnut Creek, Calif.: Alta Mira Press.

Lone Wolf v. Hitchcock, 187 U.S. 553, 23 S. Ct. 216, 47 L.Ed. 299 (1903).

Long, Carolyn. 2001. *Religious Freedom and Indian Rights: The Case of* Oregon v. Smith. Lawrence: University Press of Kansas.

Lyng v. Northwest Cemetery Protective Association, 485 U.S. 439 (1988).

Morton v. Mancari, 417 U.S. 535, 94 S. Ct. 2474, 41 L.Ed.2d 290 (1974).

Native American Graves Protection and Repatriation Act. 1990. 25 U.S.C. 3001 et seq. Relevant Regulations: 43 CFR 10.

National Environmental Protection Act. 1969. 42 U.S.C. 4321. Relevant Regulations: 40 CFR 1500–1508.

National Historic Preservation Act. 1966. 16 U.S.C. 470. Relevant Regulations: 36 C.F.R. 800.

Navajo Nation et al. v. U.S. Forest Service, 408 F. Supp. 2d 866 (D. Ariz. 2006) [Unrecorded 3 Judge Panel Decision of Ninth Circuit 06-15371 (March 2007)], 535 F.3d 1058 (9th Cir. en banc 2008), *cert. denied.*

Parker, Patricia, and Thomas King. 1990. Guidelines for Evaluating and Documenting Traditional Cultural Properties. *National Register Bulletin* 38.

Pit River Tribe et al. v. U.S. Forest Service et al., 469 F.3d 768 (9th Cir. 2006).

Pueblo of Sandia v. United States, 50 F.3d 856 (10th Cir. 1995).

Pyramid Lake Paiute v. Morton, 354 F. Supp. 252 (U.S. Dist. Court, D.C. 1972).

Religious Freedom Restoration Act. 1993. 42 U.S.C. §. 2000bb.

Religious Land Use and Institutionalized Persons Act. 2000. 42 U.S.C. § 2000cc.

Ridington, Robin, and Dennis Hastings (In'aska). 1997. *Blessing for a Long Time: The Sacred Pole of the Omaha Tribe*. Lincoln: University of Nebraska Press.

Sequoyah v. Tennessee Valley Authority, 620 F.2d 1159 (6th Cir. 1980).

Stewart, Omer. 1987. *Peyote Religion: A History*. Norman: University of Oklahoma Press.

Sullivan, Winnifred Fallers. 2005. *The Impossibility of Religious Freedom*. Princeton, N.J.: Princeton University Press.

United States v. Antoine, 318 F.3d 919 (9th Cir. 2003), *cert. denied* 124 S. Ct. 1505 (2004).

United States v. Dion, 476 U.S. 734 (1986).

United States v. Hardman, 297 F.3d 1116 (10th Cir. 2002).

United States v. Sioux Nation of Indians, 448 U.S. 371 (1980).

United States v. Washington, 384 F. Supp. 312 (W. Dist. Washington 1974), *affirmed* 520 F.2d 676 (9th Cir. 1975), *cert. denied* 423 U.S. 1086, 96 S. Ct. 877, 47 L.Ed.2d 97 (1976).

United States v. Winans, 198 U.S. 371 (1905).

Washburn, Kevin. 2007. Federal Indian Law [class lecture]. University of Minnesota School of Law, Minneapolis.

Wenger, Tisa. 2009. *We Have a Religion*. Chapel Hill: University of North Carolina Press.

Wilkinson, Charles. 1991. To Feel the Summer in the Spring: The Treaty Fishing Rights of the Wisconsin Chippewa. *Wisconsin Law Review* 1991:375.

Wilson v. Block, 708 F.2d 735 (D.C. Cir.), *cert. denied* 464 U.S. 956 (1983).

Wisconsin v. Yoder, 406 U.S. 205 (1972).

Wyoming Sawmills, Inc. v. U.S. Forest Service et al., 383 F.3d 1241 (10th Cir. 2004), *cert. denied*, 546 U.S. (2005).

10. SAVING DARFUR

Enacting Pluralism in Terms of Gender, Genocide, and Militarized Human Rights

ROSEMARY R. HICKS

On a December evening in 2006, shrieking rape whistles pierced the air outside the Sudanese embassy in Washington, D.C. Mobilized by the Save Darfur Coalition (SDC) and its partners, the whistle blowers and other activists demanded intervention to halt certain incidents of sexual violence that followed rebel insurgencies and a government counterinsurgency in western Sudan. Appealing to international treaties created after the Holocaust and atrocities of the 1990s, and contesting the 2005 UN Security Council conclusion that the conflict did not constitute genocide, the SDC argued that "rape and sexual violence [are] used as a tool of genocide" in Darfur. It therefore required UN military intervention. Beginning in 2006, the additional emphasis on rape helped expand support for intervention despite contestations over the racial and religious categories used to define the conflict, various refutations of its scale, and debates over the effectiveness of military responses.

Ultimately, in 2009, the International Criminal Court (ICC) rejected accusations of genocide. Until then, the SDC pursued a two-pronged strategy involving private Washington lobbyists and advertising firms, and more popular-level attempts to forge alliances between Jewish Americans and evangelicals. The latter included African Americans in the Sudan Campaign Coalition, which had lobbied for the 1998 International Religious Freedom Act and persuaded Congress to label the Darfur conflict genocide in 2004

(Eichler-Levine and Hicks 2007; Gustafson 2009; Mamdani 2009b; McAlister 2008). As we shall see, SDC narratives of rape by "Arab" government militias rather than "African" refugees and rebels (or, worse, UN peacekeepers) were constructed out of continually changing complex situations and read through ideas about authentic religion and liberal global governance. While their strategies mobilized legislative bodies and broadened alliances, they also narrowed the span of American pluralist inclusion. Furthermore, they reinforced long-standing trends of making both Islamic law and gendered bodies grounds for international intervention in sovereign states.

In designating the Sudanese crisis a genocide, the SDC and its funded organizations had to delineate both victims and victimizers. These dichotomizing labels ignored the colonial history and continuing messiness of ethnic and tribal identities in Sudan and obscured the ever-expanding environmental, economic, and political complexities of the situation. Between 2004 and 2007, religious groups, academics, policy experts in the region, and legislative bodies contested SDC analyses on both factual and policy grounds (Aidi 2005; Ban 2007; Faris 2007; Flint 2007; Flint and de Waal 2005; Mamdani 2007a, 2007b; Sachs 2005), and a *New York Times* article praised the SDC for raising awareness but criticized it for having "hampered aid-delivery groups, discredited American policy makers and diplomats and harmed efforts to respond to future humanitarian crises" (Dealy 2007:WK 10). Significantly, just as some SDC officials began to recognize the complexities in Sudan and seek to change tactics, the organization engaged larger international structures with the powerful and simplified charge of genocidal rape.[1] In 2006, the SDC heightened its claims of genocide by framing rape through inaccurate binaries detailing innocence (Darfuri rebels) and guilt (Sudanese government), victim (African) and victimizer (Arab), and justice (international law) and injustice (Islamic law). As both ardent SDC supporters and detractors ultimately recognized (Kristof 2009; Mamdani 2009b), this effectively hid the violent atrocities committed by multiple parties to the conflict.[2] Furthermore, SDC distinctions between proper and improper Islam continued to structure national and racial identities and understandings of gender, despite the fact that the organization had ceased citing Islam as motivating the violence (a narrative borrowed from activists mobilizing American intervention in the Sudanese civil war) in 2006.

These multiple dynamics were evident in the SDC's "Faith Action Packets," Amnesty International's annual reports, and the 2007 Refugees International (RI) reports on sexual violence in Darfur. Amnesty International helped found the SDC and cosponsored the 2006 and later events around the world. RI, founded in 1979 as a "global voice for the world's dispossessed," accepted SDC funding to compose their reports and concluded their July 2007 work by petitioning the Sudanese government for permission to be the SDC representative there.[3] In SDC statements at rallies, action packets for religious practitioners, and partner reports, the Darfur redemption project was not always explicitly religious (saving non-Muslims from Muslims) or racial (saving Africans from Arabs). However, it remained both of those things when organizers framed intervention as saving tribal women from genocidal rape and the injustice of insufficient legal redress before Shari'a-based courts. As discussed in this chapter, these claims were shaped by developments in international law and previous American practices of building interreligious and pluralist coalitions. Bracketing American economic and strategic interests in Sudan (covered in Mamdani 2009b), examining the production and power of SDC narratives that framed American moral, religious, and political authority around intervention in genocidal sexual violence reveals both the possibilities and dangers of basing military intervention on ostensibly apolitical activism and the idioms of pluralism.

RACIAL CATEGORIES AND JUDEO-CHRISTIAN COALITIONS: A LONGER HISTORY

The SDC resulted from a meeting of the U.S. Holocaust Memorial Museum and American Jewish World Service on July 14, 2004. That year, museum director Elie Wiesel issued the organization's first "genocide alert" and labeled the fighting between rebel groups, militias, and government forces by that term. The thirteen original SDC Executive Committee members, described as representing all "major faiths and the Sudanese community," included Jewish and Christian associations, one Muslim society, and various human rights groups. By August, seventy organizations had signed the SDC "Unity Statement and Call to Action" to stop the conflict, in which more than 100,000 had died. The statement did not mention genocide. Nevertheless, this term flourished in SDC literature and other contexts (including congressional resolutions) just as the number of violent deaths dramatically declined (Flint and de Waal 2008). By 2006, more than 100 organizations belonged to the SDC (180 by 2007), which claimed to represent more than 100 million Americans. SDC interpretations of the crisis and thus solutions gained global attention through their media campaigns, political lobbying, and organizing among student and religious groups. These endeavors contributed to congressional passage of more than forty pieces of legislation between 2004 and 2008 (most of which labeled the situation genocide)[4] and were likewise instrumental in securing UN deployment of hybrid United Nations–African Union peacekeeping forces (Dealy 2007). The tremendous funding needed for these efforts was garnered through private (sometimes corporate) donations, SDC public rallies, and extensive e-mail appeals (de Waal 2009b; Mamdani 2009b). After the first rally in April 2006, however, some SDC signatories criticized the lack of Muslim representation among speakers and the simplified racial framing of the crisis. Thereafter, the SDC redoubled their emphasis on rescuing violated women.

In shifting the explicit grounds for American pluralist activism and military intervention from contested issues of race and religion to Shari'a-related sexual violence, the SDC and its partners reinvigorated diverse, longstanding narratives that establish American moral authority with military endeavors to save women from Islam. Before turning to these changes, we must first trace the longer history of building interreligious coalitions around military endeavors on behalf of victimized women. This history reaches back before the second Sudanese civil war and involves multiple racial and religious constructs (including Arab and black African identities). Elie Wiesel demonstrated this in using another history to mobilize action: distinctions between East and West, Arabs and Jews (Eichler-Levine and Hicks 2007).

The Protestant Reformation seems an unlikely period from which to draw insight into twenty-first-century debates; nevertheless, a brief review of intertwined racial, religious, and political categories is necessary here. Martin Luther and later Protestants perpetually grouped Jews, Muslims ("Turks" in earlier centuries, Arab Semites later), and Catholics together as overly dogmatic, ritualistic, and legalistic in their religious practices. These framings characterized debates about religious law and national inclusion in changing ways for centuries. During eighteenth- and nineteenth-century European colonial and domestic projects, philologists and political officials aggregated the category of Arab to, and then disaggregated it from, that of Semite. Meanwhile, India and Persia/Iran were incorporated into notions of Aryan, or Indo-European, identity (Anidjar 2003, 2008; Heschel 2008; Masuzawa 2005; Said 1978). This racial disaggregation enabled the post–Cold War "magical anti-Semitism" and "philo-Semitism" that Geneviève Zubrzycki discusses in her chapter on the significance of crosses in contests over Auschwitz–Birkenau and Polish identity (chap. 11, this volume). In the United States, the separation of the two was likewise solidified as particular kinds of Judaism were wedded to Protestant Americanness through inclusive, and limiting, notions of "Judeo-Christian" commonality. In the meantime, sub-Saharan Africa, the "dark continent" ostensibly devoid of civilization, was materially exploited and simultaneously excluded from histories of progress and cultural development (Mamdani 2004).

National and international politics figured centrally in transforming American Gilded Age Protestant cosmopolitanism into a tri-faith Protestant–Catholic–Jewish (or Judeo-Christian) model by the end of World War II (Kitagawa 1987; Schmidt 2006; Todd, chap. 8, this volume). Thereafter, the United States' emergence as a global power, participation in founding the United Nations, and tendencies to ally with Israel over other countries in the reconfigured "Middle East" (especially after the 1956 Suez crisis and 1967 war [McAlister 2005]) drew attention from various Cold War attempts to foster Jewish–Muslim–Christian conversations and highlight common "Abrahamic traditions" (Hicks 2010). Winnifred Fallers Sullivan and Terry Todd (chap. 3 and chap. 8, this volume) describe Islam as a recent factor in contemporary formations of American religion and law, both of which originated out of symbioses with particular kinds of Protestantism but evolved through negotiations with other traditions. Like Catholics, Jews, and members of other non-Protestant communities, they contend, Muslims have been interpolated into (or excluded from) "Americanness" and American social and legal structures in ways influenced by these origins. Late-twentieth-century combinations of "multiculturalism and globalization, theological and ecclesial changes within the Christian churches, international human rights movements, an expanded notion of what counts as religion in academic and political contexts, and larger social shifts toward egalitarian and horizontal relations" (Sullivan, chap. 3, this volume).

These American developments illuminate how SDC organizers (primarily Jewish and evangelical, in contrast to the mainline Protestants who guarded authentic religion and Americanness until the late twentieth century) were somewhat able to define American pluralism from positions of power instead of periphery (Eichler-Levine and Hicks 2007). Religious *practice* has historically been a sticking point for such pluralist inclusion, disrupting alliances based on supposedly shared understandings of "religion as conscience" (Sullivan, chap. 3, this volume) or religion as primarily ethical Judeo-Christian "faith" (Todd, chap. 8, this volume). SDC allowance for Muslim participation in the practice of pluralist activism recalled prior liberal Protestant invitations to Jews and African Americans. As discussed in the next two sections, these racial–political–religious histories bring SDC modes of including Muslims, which were influenced by portrayals of Muslim before, during, and after the Cold War and by subsequent changes in America's international standing (Marr 2006; McAlister 2005), into greater focus. Premised on the universal religiosity of particular human rights values and activist practice, the SDC's stated grounds for including Muslim pluralist partners hinged on racially marked understandings of Muslim attitudes toward gender and Shari'a, as well as Muslim willingness to submit faith and practice to international law.

LIBERALISM, INTERNATIONAL LAW, AND AMERICAN PLURALIST PRACTICE

The SDC's activism followed an era of cosmopolitan optimism (Calhoun 2003, 2007) wherein the United States emerged as the world's sole superpower and the international community turned its attention to crises in developing nations. Ethnic cleansing was a primary concern, but botched incursions into Somalia in 1993 contributed to UN and U.S. reticence to intervene in Rwanda in 1994 (Barnett 2003) or in Srebrenica in 1995, when Bosnian Serbs massacred Bosnian Muslims in the UN "safe area." In March 1999, the Clinton administration cited "indicators that genocide is unfolding in Kosovo" as justification for the NATO bombings (unsupported by the UN) that followed (Clines 1999). Following these developments, the ICC was created specifically to investigate and try war crimes and genocide. Older international institutions (World Bank, International Monetary Fund, UN, and NATO) expanded during this time, and new ones (World Trade Organization, ICC) developed with the power to arrange global governance around liberal (or American neoliberal) political and economic structures. The programs of these institutions sometimes sparked new conflicts with their attempts to shape subjects and nation-states into an "international community" whose mechanisms were not universally accepted (Barnett and Duvall 2005).

Pre–Cold War whispers of an international imperative to cross sovereign state boundaries so as to protect endangered citizens and internally displaced persons were reinvigorated by post–Cold War cosmopolitanism and became a stated international norm in 2001 (Barnett and Weiss 2008:27–28). The ICC was established in 2002 and (as longtime advocate Amnesty International argued) marked "the first time in history that serious crimes of violence against women . . . have been recognized as crimes against humanity and war crimes."[5] Though important in many respects, these new institutions of global governance also marginalized significant debates over international jurisdiction and the mechanisms by which only particular kinds of sexual violence merited redress (Halley 2008). SDC portrayals of the crisis were shaped in the wake of these political developments so as to effectively mobilize both average Americans and international legislative bodies. As the UN and World Health Organization maintained, Darfur was neither the most violent nor the least complicated crisis at the time. The majority of deaths resulted from starvation and disease in the wake of the thirty-year drought and famine (surely exacerbated by the conflict), and though still horrific, violent deaths after 2004 fell below emergency levels to between 100 and 300 per month (Flint 2007; Mamdani 2009b).

Nevertheless, the racial and religious identities narrated through SDC claims of genocide resonated strongly with Americans and others who pressured their legislatures, the UN, and the ICC to intervene in Sudan.

FORMULATING "FAITH-BASED" ACTION THROUGH AMERICAN PLURALIST POLITICS

In 2006, the SDC began furnishing religious leaders with resources via its Web site. These included "Christian Faith," "Jewish," "Interfaith," and "General Faith" action packets meant to educate American religious practitioners about the situation. No "Muslim" action packet was published, although an insert in the packets identified all the fatalities in Darfur as Muslims.[6] A "Muslim Faith Action Packet" was added between the April and September 2006 rallies, and references to "Arab" perpetrators were removed from all packets. Nevertheless, dichotomous narratives of "systematic *ethnic* cleansing of African Darfuris by the Sudanese Government and their proxy militia—the Janjaweed" remained, and the SDC redistributed these same materials for the 2007 Global Days for Darfur rallies and events.[7] Significantly, the packets addressed religious groups in terms of their moral authority and supposed relationships to genocide. For example, the Christian packet described its readers' divine "empowerment" to stop genocide and their burden to save others, whereas the Jewish packet emphasized Jews' special moral position as "quintessential victims" and responsibility to identify genocide wherever it occurs. Likewise, the differences between the revised packets and the new "Muslim" addition not only suggested the SDC Board of Directors' assumptions about the orientations various practitioners had toward the issue, they also complicate suppositions about the moral and political neutrality of American pluralist practice.

Following the April 2006 Washington, D.C., rally (criticized in the *Washington Post* and boycotted by the Council of American Islamic Relations for not including Muslims or Darfuris on the pre-released speakers list), the absence of Muslim representation among the SDC's directors[8] presented challenges for diversifying materials (Eichler-Levine and Hicks 2007). Imam Rashid Omar of Indiana had joined the April rally at the last minute and reiterated his 2004 message, titled "A Belated Muslim Response to the Humanitarian Crisis in Darfur."[9] Although Omar had described his response and that of the entire Muslim community as "belated," Egyptian imam Feisal Abdul Rauf of the American Society for Muslim Advancement (not present at the rally but, along with the Council on American–Islamic Relations and other Muslim groups, an original signatory to the 2004 "Unity Statement") contended that "we and other organizations horrified by the human rights violations have been urging specific actions since the crisis began."[10] Omar, an immigrant to the United States and a South African apartheid survivor, did not speak at later events. However, his three-year-old message was turned into a "Sample Sermon" for the Muslim packet and included with other materials that suggested a structural, but not substantive, similarity between Muslims and their Christian and Jewish collaborators.

Like the Jewish and Christian packets, the action packet for Muslims contained "Sample Prayers" and "Text Resources." Missing from the Muslim packet were specified Islamic prayers and the Jewish and Christian packet "Responsive Reading for the People of Darfur." This insert identified readers as "the faith community throughout America" empowered to stop "horrendous crimes, including gang rapes of women and girls, burning of homes and religious buildings, killing of babies and other atrocities . . . mass slaughter of human life, displacement, starvation, and rape as a means of ethnic cleansing in Armenia, the Holocaust, Cambodia, Bosnia, Rwanda [and n]ow in South Sudan and in Darfur" and united participants "in prayer, in action, in spirit, to let the Darfurian people know that they are not abandoned. Not on our watch will we stand idly by and have genocide occur. We pray that peace, protection, and mercy prevail in Sudan."

Additional differences were evident in the "Sample Prayers," which in the Christian packet emphasized confession and repentance and petitioned God to forgive Christians' failures to believe that "you have empowered *us* to protect our brothers and sisters." The lengthy supplemental prayer in the Jewish packet focused on identification with Darfuri victims, responsibility to stand in and speak for them, and commentary on the victimizers, which read in part:

Though we remember being slaves
We do not often think of the horrors of slavery
We pray because there are limits to what we can do

How can one look upon the faces of children and peaceful adults and respond with violence, death, and genocide?
How do we understand the hearts and minds of the oppressors?
Are they ignorant of their victims' humanity?
Do they not see themselves in their victim's eyes?

We pray that the people of Darfur regain their lives, their land, their hope.
We pray too, that the Sudanese military and the Janjaweed militia regain their humanity.
We pray that the World's leaders will not allow genocide to become an economic tool.
We must become tools of justice on behalf of these victims of genocide. . . .

> *We must raise our voices to speak out on behalf of the oppressed, for the victims who have no voice.*[11]

A Muslim "Du'a/Prayer for the People of Darfur, Sudan" included at the end of Omar's "Sample Jumu'ah Khutbah" (but not listed in the "Sample Prayers" section or table of contents) also pleaded for peace and an end to suffering but provided a different commentary on the Sudanese leadership:

> Lord of all Humankind, from what we have witnessed, grant us the grace to have a greater understanding and empathy for the suffering of innocent victims of the war in the Sudan, no matter their ethnicity, color or religion.
>
> All-wise and All-mighty God, Grant the leaders of the Sudan wisdom and guide them to use their power to serve the good of all and to fashion a more just and caring world. Amin.

In contrast to other prayers, Omar's prayer emphasized the Sudanese ability to likewise be instruments of justice. Furthermore, he did not use the term *genocide*.

The final difference between packets lay in their textual portions, wherein the various groups were exhorted to respond to oppression in different ways. The same passage from the book of Proverbs (3:27) topped all three "Text" and "Scripture" inserts, but there the agreement ended. Common scriptures with somewhat different translations marked the "Jewish Action Packet" and "Christian Action Packet." Among them were Isaiah 58:9–12, in which the chosen who respond to God's calling are guided, renewed, and restored as they end "oppression" (Christian) and "wickedness" (Jewish). In contrast to restorative themes, the texts in the Muslim packet focused on training Muslims to aid others, avoid *being* oppressive, and intervene when other Muslims oppress:

> And let there among you be a group of people who invite to all that is good, who enjoin what is right and forbid what is wrong.
>
> Surah 3:104

> The Prophet Muhammad (peace be upon him) said: "(God) has revealed to me that you should adopt humility so that no one oppresses another. (Riyadh-us-Salaheen)
>
> *Hadith* 1589 *(Riyadh-us-Salaheen)*

> The Prophet Muhammad (peace be upon him) said: "Help your brother, whether he is an oppressor or he is oppressed." People asked, "It is right to help him if he is oppressed, but how should we help him if he is an oppressor?" The Prophet said, "By preventing him from oppressing others."
>
> *Sahih Al-Bukhari*, 3:624

In these selections, SDC leaders' assumptions about the various member groups' attitudes toward violence became clear. Whereas texts in the Christian and Jewish action packets exhorted constructive activity (i.e., "restoring" and rescuing), texts in the Muslim packet focused primarily on restraining destructive activity (i.e., "prevention").

Distinctions between appropriate pluralist partners were not merely represented textually, as SDC members had forged their early alliances with African American Christians but not Muslims, thereby engaging debates over African American identity and Muslim American identity (Jackson 2003), as well as over Muslim inclusion in American pluralist projects. Eventually, the SDC ceased inaccurately describing the conflict as "Muslim" versus "Christian."[12] David Rubenstein (2007), then the SDC executive director, publicly asserted the impossibility of making simple distinctions between victim and victimizer. Nevertheless, the SDC's printed materials continued to distinguish true Islam from false and acceptable religion from irreligion by reproducing racial dichotomies (victimizing Arab Muslims and victimized African Muslims) and positioning Arab Muslims as particularly violent perpetrators who disregarded common human rights values. Thus, although SDC organizers attempted to include American Muslims in pluralist activism, the substance of their materials reflected continuing uneasiness about how to incorporate Muslims into "the faith community in America" and into liberal international structures of global governance. Furthermore, although SDC directors and rally speakers no longer identified the "Muslim government in the North" as responsible for the "ethnic-cleansing," this accusation remained salient in the work of SDC partners such as Refugees International, which presented genocidal rape as facilitated by Shari'a-based law under the Arab Sudanese leadership.[13]

VIOLATED WOMEN, MORAL AMERICANS, AND THE PROBLEM OF ISLAM

In 2006 and 2007, the SDC focused on particular violent acts as violations of womanhood, motherhood, and nationhood and thus framed them as both contrary to human rights and legal cause for military intervention. To be clear, narratives of sexual violence and aggrieved motherhood were prevalent before 2006 (Flint and de Waal 2005; Power 2004), and emphasis on racial dichotomies did not disappear between 2006 and 2009. Rather, during these years of declining death tolls and increasing contestation, racially coded Shari'a-facilitated rape became a more prominent argument for intervention and an ostensibly incontrovertible point around which to build pluralist activism. After an April 2007 performance of a Darfur-themed play at Manhattan's Public Theater, audience members (including one who insisted that Americans needed clear lines) asked David Rubenstein to define the sides in the conflict. Rubenstein argued that it was impossible to reduce the issue to simple binaries and that the only "good guys" were civilians in the refugee camps and those who intervened on their behalf. Josh Rubenstein of Amnesty International reinforced this distinction, noting that the danger to women lay *outside* the camps, where those ordered to find firewood became vulnerable to attack. Though horrific, rape as a weapon of war was not the only sexual violence that concerned local activists, Amnesty International, or Refugees International, however. Nor did the Darfur conflict approximate the scale of death and sexual violence happening in the Democratic Republic of the Congo, where 1,200 people died per day in 2006, some during and after vicious rape campaigns.[14] A look at the SDC's 2006 turn to sexual violence demonstrates the rhetorical power of connecting rape to Islam and will illuminate why Amnesty International and Refugees International (both grantees of the SDC) provided differing perspectives on the racial and religious aspects of the crisis.

During the September 2006 SDC–Amnesty International Global Days for Darfur rally, former secretary of state Madeline Albright highlighted the contestations preceding the SDC's shift in focus to sexual violence and in strategy to international law. Delivered on the grassy East Meadow of Central Park, Albright's address challenged those who argued against military intervention:

> The issue is not about trying to impose U.S. Western values on Sudan, for the protection of the innocent is a universal responsibility. Every major religion, culture, and legal tradition demands respect for people. This issue is *not* about trying to advance American interests in Darfur because our concerns have to be humanitarian, and this issue is not about trying to promote one religion or another because all the sides in Darfur are predominantly Muslims. In short, this is *not* about politics, this is about *people*.
>
> So this Coalition of all people meeting throughout countries in the world is a sign of international responsibility. Because we are not just Americans, but African and Arab and Asian and European and Latino, representing *everybody*. . . . [Therefore], President Bush at the United Nations General Assembly has to make *clear* that the United Nations has to go inside, into Sudan.

Albright's speech marked the turning of SDC and partner efforts from national to international intervention. Although she mentioned the importance of diplomacy, trade, and nongovernment humanitarian relief organizations, Albright emphasized the necessity of military solutions. She was not alone in asserting ostensibly apolitical humanitarian and religious mandates to act. Amnesty International USA executive director Larry Cox called for U.S. intervention, citing "the humanity of each and every one of us [that] is at stake." He then introduced special Amnesty International ambassador Mira Sorvino, whose speech on behalf of mothers and children indicated an important change in SDC and Amnesty International strategy. Sorvino recounted stories of rapes outside the camps and inserted an explicitly patriarchal metaphor into her plea for intervention:

> How could we let this occur? The lack of food, malnutrition, humanitarian access cut off. . . . Over two million victims of violence, and women continue to be raped as they forage for food. . . .
>
> Please think of these mothers and children. . . . Please forgive the analogy, but the government is like the head of a family, . . . the government in Khartoum like a sick, sociopathic parent. . . . It is time for us to stop treating the government as normal in its sovereignty . . . as if it's their people and their problem. . . . What do we have to be afraid of?
>
> We said "never again" to the Holocaust, . . . Rwanda. . . . Why is this any different? Why is the plight of these mothers and children any different?

The emphasis on sexual violence as grounds for intervention continued at later events, including the Amnesty International–sponsored rape whistle action outside the Sudanese embassy in December 2006 and "Weekend of Prayer for Darfur," a campaign coordinated with religious practitioners "to call for immediate protection of the Darfurian people.[15] Both initiatives stated that military intervention would protect Africans from community-destroying rape, and they presented intervention as the authentically religious and authentically American response to the situation. These descriptions and proposed solutions resonated with various religious Americans for multiple reasons, of course, but most significantly for this chapter in how they reproduced longstanding tropes wherein Americanness is demonstrated through military exercises against Muslims.

From the specter of bonded female captives under Barbary pirates that helped foster masculine Republican virtue, to the harem and polygamy so repudiated during the Victorian era, such images provided potent fuel for projecting American moral authority during troubled times (Marr 2006). As incursions into Afghanistan and Iraq demonstrated, the practice of building American national identity and economic and military power through endeavors to save women from Islam remained effective into the twenty-first century (Abu-Lughod 2002; Hirschkind and Mahmood 2002; Mamdani 2007b). Narratives presented at the rallies and in SDC publications intersected with these longer trajectories and involved contested claims to the moral authority and social capital of Americanness. Not only did organizers situate human rights as the substance of authentic faith and ostensibly apolitical activism as the center of pluralist practice, they defined the relationship of different religious Americans to each other under ideas about democratic pluralism and divine mandates. Over the course of 2006 and 2007, this included transforming pluralist America into a nation that did not simply witness genocide but actively intervened—in this case, to save Darfuri women from Arab Islam.

Notably, not all SDC partners cited the complicity of improper religion in the Darfur conflict. Islam was never mentioned in Amnesty International's annual reports on Darfur. Rather, the authors consistently presented the political and economic causes of the crisis (including continuing struggles over land, water, and oil wealth), avoided using the term *Arab*, and never used the word *genocide*.[16] Furthermore, the September 2007 Amnesty International report described the situation as complex and the violence as multifaceted. Although the organization did use the title *Janjawid*, they had ceased defining this as an Arab group in 2004 and maintained that "armed opposition [rebel] groups also carried out human rights abuses." However, the material on Amnesty International's SDC-funded Web site (http://eyesondarfur.com, launched in 2007) replicated the SDC's framing of Arabs versus Africans,[17] and in 2008 Amnesty International USA reorganized their primary Web site to highlight Darfur as a top priority, second only to stopping abuses carried out through the war on terrorism. In their 2008 report, Amnesty International noted that the conflict by that point involved more than thirty different armed factions. Although Amnesty International did describe some as "Arab" in 2008 (using the word for the first time since 2004), they immediately noted that "armed groups were *increasingly* divided along ethnic lines" (indicating that ethnicity was not inherent to the conflict but became salient through it). Meanwhile, Refugees International reiterated SDC framing in its *Laws Without Justice* report of June 2007 and intertwined assumptions about gender, race, and religion into accusations that the despotic Sudanese "regime" denied juridical justice to rape victims with a politicized derivation of Islam.[18]

The effect of such politicized discourses of rape allowed the persistence of genocide charges against Arabs, even though the SDC no longer used that racial designation. According to Refugees International, rape in Darfur's "traditional social structure" injures both a woman and her "entire tribe":

> Rape is an integral part of the pattern of violence that the government of Sudan is inflicting upon the targeted ethnic groups in Darfur. The raping of Darfuri women is not sporadic or random, but is inexorably linked to the systematic destruction of their communities. . . . These rapes are part of a calculated plan to humiliate women and their communities, including forced impregnation, the ultimate goal of which is to achieve ethnic cleansing in the region. (Fricke and Khair 2007:7)

Woman or mother was thereby presented as the symbol of the entire collectivity and violated womanhood the symbol of victimized group identity. Building this narrative, which was highlighted in the Refugees International reports featured in English-language media in the United States and Europe,[19] required neglecting multiple other incidents of sexual violence, including increased rapes occurring *inside* the refugee camps (within tribes and families) and rapes committed by UN soldiers. Refugees International tangentially acknowledged that rape had occurred within the camps but attributed it to the breakdown of "traditional" tribal society due to genocidal attacks. The dichotomous language of victim and victimizer allowed Refugees International and the SDC to maintain charges of genocide even while the death toll waned and greater attention to racial and religious complexities in the region made other binary distinctions untenable.

In concluding their report on the lack of juridical justice (simply defined as "justice") under Sudanese law, the Refugees International authors made explicit claims about the role of Islam in perpetuating gender-based "ethnic cleansing":

> It is vital to note that there is nothing inherently Islamic about the way Sudan's rape law is constructed. In fact, Pakistan, a country that imposes Islamic law, changed its rape law in 2006, allowing rape to be considered a crime distinct from *zina* [translated here as "adultery"]. Similarly, in 2006 the Republic of the Maldives took steps to reform its laws by commissioning a draft penal law and sentencing guidelines that, *though based on Islamic law*, still comply with international norms. The Government of Sudan must act immediately to prevent rape from occurring in Darfur, and, *like other Islamic countries seeking to improve justice for women* who have been raped, to revise the harmful laws that penalize both rape victims and those who support them. (Fricke and Khair 2007:13; italics added)

With this summation, the authors simultaneously denied the religious validity of Sudan's legal system and implied that injustice was part of even authentic interpretations of Shari'a. Thus, religiously authentic or not, Sudan must become "like other Islamic countries seeking to improve justice for women" by reforming their laws. As is evident here, even in well-intentioned attempts to stop violence, Refugees International (on behalf of the SDC) participated in defining Islam and adjudicating Sudanese authenticity against that ideal. They recommended international intervention partly on the grounds of lacking Sudanese compliance with "international best practices" (legal and medical) and partly on insufficient Sudanese compliance with reforms that fit their definition of authentic Islam. Although Refugees International worked with local Sudanese organizations, Refugees International also pointed to their inadequacies and the need to train locals in understanding the real impact of rape. According to the report, rape is an ethnically motivated violation that occurs primarily outside familiar settings and victimizes a woman's "entire tribe."

Refugees International's primary concern was that Sudanese women seeking "justice" (legal convictions) would be considered adulterers and face capital punishment if they failed to prove their cases. Their report repeatedly cited two unrelated death sentences for adultery, although it did not claim that those sentenced had made accusations of rape. The report's authors, by describing legal impediments to "justice" and legally facilitated rape (due to government employee immunity), implied that Sudanese judges had either no awareness of or no concern for the victims of mass atrocities. Judges in Sudanese courts, the report implied, were part of a genocidal regime based in Islamic law and culture. As such, they were incapable of assessing victims' innocence or of convicting "Arab" Janjawid of using rape as a weapon. Furthermore, the authors underplayed the internal dynamism of Shari'a (Ali 2006; Hallaq 2005; Tucker 2003) and as a consequence suggested that unreformed Islam and its law were human rights problems. SDC action packets and Refugees International reports determined that the solution was to reform American and Sudanese sensibilities and institutions and, when that failed, to mobilize military force.

Before involvement with the SDC and later in 2007, Refugees International issued reports urging the UN to persist in addressing the sexual violence committed by UN peacekeepers (including against children in southern Sudan) and African Union forces (accused in 2006 of sexual violence in Darfur). Refugees International's 2007 report, *Ending Sexual Violence in Darfur: An Advocacy Agenda*, continued to focus on rape outside the internally displaced persons settlements but also noted—after UN forces had been authorized—that rape inside them was an issue and that the identities of rebels were not clear. The report's author, Sarah Martin, contextualized wartime sexual violence as a perennial issue not unique to Sudan. Even as she laid out this larger frame, however, she connected violence in Sudan to an Islamic variety of misogyny that made such horrific crimes expected rather than exceptional: "The changing nature of the conflict and the face of gender-based violence in Darfur is also a result of the patriarchal culture in Sudan that treats women as lesser beings with few rights and as chattel to be taken during a conflict" (Martin 2007:1). Martin ignored or minimized Sudanese legal changes undertaken in response to the Darfur conflict, framed the sexual violence as genocide, and added, "As Darfur is a predominantly Muslim area, the stigma against rape, strong in any context, is particularly so there." Furthermore, despite noting that victims in the "less hostile" context of Chad reported rape less frequently than those in Sudan, Martin (2007:24) cited Shari'a and stoning as a primary reason some women sought economic redress over legal justice. In contrast, the Amnesty

International 2008 report specified that no executions for adultery had occurred in 2007 and that the unrelated death sentences highlighted in Refugees International reports were reportedly commuted.

SDC and Refugees International had partnered as early as 2005 in a letter Refugees International director Kenneth Bacon (the former Pentagon spokesman who defended the NATO bombings in 1999) sent to then–President Bush urging stronger action in Sudan. Like the SDC materials, the 2007 Refugees International reports were more nuanced than their previous advocacy papers. In their 2004 report, *Rape, Islam, and Darfur's Women Refugees and War-Displaced*, for example, the author asserted that "the fate of a raped woman in an Islamic fundamentalist society such as that in Sudan is already sealed" (Lumeye 2004:2). Their later change in tone reflected both organizations' continuing responses to criticism over anti-Muslim and anti-Arab bias, their recognition of the complexity of the crisis, and their subsequent attempts to broaden their coalitions. As with previous American coalitions, this pluralist expansion was simultaneously inclusive and regulatory. Although Refugees International correspondent Sarah Martin acknowledged at the end of 2007 that "the only solution to ending rape in Darfur is to find a political solution to end the conflict," Refugees International and the SDC continued to cite religious and racial motivations for the violence. Reform in keeping with international standards was still necessary, they argued, and so "it is critical to involve Muslim women activists from outside Sudan" in changing Sudanese laws (Martin 2007:ii). The next year, the SDC transitioned from supporting military intervention and social reform to more dramatic measures: arresting the acting Sudanese head of state.

PRACTICING AMERICAN PLURALISM, POLICING INTERNATIONAL LIBERALISM

This chapter has thus far drawn attention to how the SDC and Refugees International relied on multiple interwoven constructs of religion and race and a series of overlapping binaries that specified gendered norms of citizenship, simplified dynamics in Darfur into genocidal rape, and defined American pluralist practice in terms of human rights. Before concluding with the developments of 2009 and larger implications of these strategies, we turn to the international aspects important to these assertions of American identity, moral orientation, and political authority. Madeline Albright had posited American global leadership in 2006, and former SDC director David Rubenstein affirmed it in 2007, as both contended that international intervention was reliant on the American government. " The French ambassador to the UN doesn't care what we think," Albright had argued, and the Chinese ambassador doesn't care what you think, but they do care what the American government cares about. So it's our role to put that pressure on the American government, on our political leaders." This the SDC did by testifying before Senate subcommittees and UN Security Council and committee meetings and by making Darfur an active issue during the 2007–2008 presidential debates. In June 2007, senator and presidential candidate Barack Obama (also a speaker at the April 2006 SDC rally) underlined the "rightful" role of pluralist religious coalitions in America. Focusing on abortion, same-sex marriage, and school prayer was tantamount to "hijacking" the faith, he argued. In contrast, appropriate practices involved uniting Americans to address social problems such as poverty, AIDS, healthcare, and the "genocide" in Darfur (Goodstein 2007). One year later, the three top candidates signed a joint statement making the genocide a foreign policy priority for the next administration and elaborated their views in separate interviews for an SDC video.[20] Meanwhile, the UN approved deployment of UNAMID, a hybrid UN–African Union peacekeeping force, in Sudan on July 31, 2007.

At the 2007 UN General Assembly meeting, then-president George W. Bush extolled the Declaration of Human Rights and declared that the "United Nations must answer this challenge to conscience and live up to its promise to promptly deploy peace-keeping forces to Darfur."[21] He then connected such action to the moral mandate of American leadership in providing universal equality: "America will lead toward this vision where all are created equal, and free to pursue their dreams. This is the founding conviction of my country. It is the promise that established this body. And with our determination, it can be the future of our world. Thank you, and God bless."

The next day, the SDC sent a message to its 900,000 American e-mail subscribers affirming American authority in international affairs and urging activists to stay the course. "After years of frustrating delays," they argued, "we may finally be at a crucial turning point for the people of Darfur."[22] Indeed, the United States soon ceased to be alone in defining the crisis as genocide. Citing the pivotal ways civil society and nongovernment organizations had informed his analysis—and, for the first time, elaborating extensively on the use of rape as a government-sponsored strategy of targeted brutalization—ICC prosecutor Luis Moreno Ocampo (2008a, 2008b) detailed his plans to charge Sudanese officials with genocide.

In June and July 2008, the SDC pressed the case for genocidal rape in reports to UN Security Council officials (under U.S. presidency since June 1, 2008), in a statement to the U.S. Mission to the UN, and in their June 19, 2008, testimony before the Security Council Session on Women, Peace, and

Security. On July 14, 2008 (the fourth anniversary of the SDC), ICC prosecutor Moreno Ocampo described how rape was central to proving charges against Sudanese President Bashir for the same war crimes and crimes against humanity with which Sudanese and Congolese officials before him were charged. To these Moreno Ocampo also added genocide. Experts on the political situation in Darfur quickly decried Moreno Ocampo's comparison of Sudan to Nazi Germany, argued that the grossly overstated numbers buttressing baseless genocide charges would be seen as cover for regime change, and cautioned against actions that could further endanger civilians (de Waal 2008; Flint and de Waal 2009a, 2009b). ICC judges rejected the genocide accusation in 2009. Nevertheless, the Sudanese government responded to the remaining charges and arrest warrant as predicted. Citing complicity in intelligence gathering, President Bashir expelled international aid workers laboring to ameliorate the devastation of ecological crises and war, seized their assets, and shut down Sudanese human rights organizations.

While fostering a global network to call on the "American faith" and "international" communities, the SDC participated in defining authentic Americanness, authentic religion, and pluralist practice in terms of international human rights activism. In 2007, Jodi Eichler-Levine and I concluded that interreligious activism created grounds on which intertwined religious and national identities (all contingent on understandings of gender, ethnicity, and socioeconomic standing) are negotiated. Continually contested formations "converge dynamically in each interaction according to the various interpretations brought to and re-narrated *through* the event," we argued, with each interaction providing "fodder for the next round" of deliberating pluralism, religiosity, and Americanness (Eichler-Levine and Hicks 2007:731). As discussed here, arguments about genocidal sexual violence were central to the changing narratives through which the SDC formulated pluralist practice between 2006 and 2009, identified victims and victimizers, and assigned innocence and guilt. Once codified in congressional legislation, UN resolutions, and international legal documents, these formulations of racial, religious, and national identity lost a measure of fluidity and influenced international precedents for deploying military force and, for the first time ever, moving to arrest an acting head of state.

The UN had adopted the doctrine of "Responsibility to Protect," asserting the legality of crossing state boundaries to protect human lives and human rights, in 2005. Meanwhile, the SDC and its partners contributed to trends of defining pluralist projects in terms of human rights. (They were certainly not alone in this. In April 2006, for example, Pope Benedict XVI addressed the General Assembly and affirmed that the Responsibility to Protect and the

Universal Declaration of Human Rights were moral values authentic to all religious traditions.)[23] Nevertheless, in basing military action on the ostensibly genocidal motivations of Arab Muslims in Sudan, the SDC ratified diverse practitioners' anxieties about Arabs and Muslims more generally, some of which Elie Wiesel had articulated in his keynote speech at the April 2006 SDC rally. There, Wiesel had conflated al Qaida with Iranian Holocaust deniers, with the Sudanese government, and with threats to the Israeli state (Eichler-Levine and Hicks 2007). Furthermore, the SDC ignored repeated assertions that the conflict in Darfur was not simply racial, religious, or gender genocide, that it could be solved by political solutions rather than militarized intervention, and that tremendous violence (often categorized as "collateral damage" [Asad 2003]) and rape always coincide with peacekeeping efforts. Thus, SDC practices of pluralism, set within international structures of liberal global governance, regulated different identities in gendered and racially coded terms while positioning unreformed Arab Islam as morally lacking and problematic for human rights.

Pluralism is often articulated as an ethic essential to democratic practice and an appropriate framework for resolving national and international conflicts. Though a good in many respects, pluralism is a technique for making supposedly irreducible differences coexist, and therein lays its naturalizing power. In the case of the SDC, resonant appeals to static animosities elided the fluidity of religious and racial identities and the political circumstances under which differences become salient. Insistence on such static differences can then be used in the production of further violence, such as that categorized as "collateral damage" under military intervention, or as happened in Darfur with the adoption of ethnically coded narratives of violence late in the conflict. Finally, insisting that particular racial and religious differences cause horrific violence against women perpetuates the international practice of making gendered bodies the grounds of larger religious and national claims, military actions, and perhaps even regime change. In light of these concerns, it is worth considering whether American-led enforcement of liberal pluralism might be instrumental in producing just the opposite.

The Darfur crisis offers a cautionary tale. The lesson is not to ignore political conflicts, mass violence, or rape as a weapon of war. Rather, it is to consider how  efforts to enact American pluralist practice through liberal international structures may involve projecting various identities and interests rather than, or as much as, recognizing those unfolding in local contexts. Furthermore, one must consider how these modes may hide the power of liberal and neoliberal institutions of global governance to ignite, as well as ameliorate, conflicts and possibly perpetuate further crises by providing both figurative and dangerously literal "fodder for the next round."

NOTES

My thanks to Courtney Bender and Pamela Klassen, organizers of the conferences from which this chapter emerged and its careful editors; to Benjamin L. Berger and Jesse K. Rosenthal for many helpful comments; and to the organizers of and respondents at the 2007 American University in Cairo "Humanitarianisms" conference: Michael J. Barnett, Craig Calhoun, Janice Gross Stein, Raymond Duvall, and Pamela F. DeLargy.

1. In 2007, the SDC senior director of international policy and advocacy (among others) echoed Mamdani's concerns and sought Mamdani's advice on how better to address the situation. See "Mamdani Responds to His Critics II," http://blogs.ssrc.org/darfur/2009/05/12/mamdani-responds-to-his-critics-ii/.

2. Kristof excoriated Mamdani for arguing that the SDC linked humanitarianism more closely with the war on terrorism, and he prefers Flint and de Waal's analysis. Significantly, the latter also argue that the crisis does not constitute genocide and that the number of deaths was vastly overstated. Unlike Mamdani, I intend here to examine the turn toward sexual violence within American pluralist activism, not the war on terrorism or the history of the conflict in Sudan.

3. RI is "an independent, non-profit humanitarian advocacy organization based in Washington, D.C. [that does] not accept government or United Nations funding, relying instead on contributions from individuals, foundations and corporations." See "History" at http://www.refugeesinternational.org/section/aboutus/history (accessed July 17, 2007).

4. For a full list, see http://www.savedarfur.org/pages/passed_legislation/ (accessed June 26, 2009).

5. "About the International Criminal Court," http://www.amnestyusa.org/International_Criminal_Court/About_the_International_Criminal_Court/page.do?id=1021004&n1=3&n2=35&n3=1033 (accessed August 20, 2008).

6. "400,000 Muslims Have Been Killed in Darfur," http://millionvoicesfordarfur.com/pdf/Darfur%20Muslim%20Insert.pdf (accessed May 2, 2006). Although all inserts featured the same statistics, only this piece detailed the victims' religion. Originally accessed May 2, 2006, the action packets were subsequently removed or revised. Updated packets ("Christian Action Packet," "Jewish Action Packet," and "Muslim Action Packet") were available at http://www.savedarfur.org/pages/organize_your_congregation (first revisions accessed September 14, 2006; second revisions accessed April 3, 2007).

7. From the "Global Days for Darfur III: Background on the Global Days Concept" sections.

8. "Board of Directors," http://www.savedarfur.org/pages/board_of_directors (accessed September 17, 2007).

9. This 2004 message comprised the second "Sample Sermon, Homily, Dvar Torah, Jumu'ah Khutbah" component of the "Interfaith Action Packet."

10. Quoted in SDC Press Release, "Faith-Based Coalition to Hold 'Week of Prayer and Action for Darfur,'" March 21, 2006.

11. Authorship of the supplemental Christian prayer was anonymous. This Jewish prayer was credited to Morris Deutsch, Sherm Edwards, Barbara Luchs, Virginia Murphy, Fred Reiner, Melinda Salzman, Lynn Sweet, and Nelly Urbach.

12. Some evangelicals stressed this narrative throughout 2005 and 2006, but others disputed it. As late as April 2006, the coalition provided press statements evoking this distinction (specifically, that of World Evangelical Alliance International director Geoff Turncliffe, included in the SDC "Press Packet").

13. Quoted in Richard Cizik (National Association of Evangelicals vice president of governmental affairs) and Rabbi David Saperstein (SDC Executive Committee member), "Human Rights Opportunity for Bush" [op-ed], *Washington Times*, November 14, 2005.

14. See Amnesty International annual reports on the situation at http://www.amnesty-usa.org/By_Country/Congo_Dem_Rep_of/page.do?id=1011136&n1=3&n2=30&n3=886 (accessed August 15, 2008) and the 2006 UNICEF report (quoted in Mamdani 2009b:20).

15. SDC Press Release, "Advocates Rally in the Nations Capital Against Rape and Sexual Violence in Darfur," December 10, 2006, http://www.savedarfur.org/newsroom/releases/advocates_rally_in_the_nations_capital_against_rape_and_sexual_violence_in/ (accessed June 12, 2007).

16. Amnesty International used the word *Arab* once in its 2004 report and noted in 2005 that the Arab League had sent a fact-finding mission drawing attention to the issue. Amnesty International Annual Reports (titled "Sudan") available at http://www.amnestyusa.org/annualreport.php?id=ar&yr=2005&c=SDN (2005, covering 2004), http://www.amnestyusa.org/annualreport.php?id=ar&yr=2006&c=SDN (2006), http://www.amnestyusa.org/annualreport.php?id=ar&yr=2007&c=SDN (2007), and http://www.amnestyusa.org/annualreport.php?id=ar&yr=2008&c=SDN (2008). See also "Darfur: 'When Will They Protect Us?' Civilians Trapped by Violence in Sudan," September 2007, AI Index: AFR 54/043/2007, http://web.amnesty.org/library/index/engafr540432007 (accessed August 15, 2008).

17. See Amnesty International's interactive multimedia project "Eyes on Darfur" and its acknowledgment of SDC funding at http://www.eyesondarfur.org/about.html.

18. *Laws Without Justice* uses the term *regime* interchangeably with *Government of Sudan* and almost exclusively in sections 5, "Immunity for Government Affiliated Perpetrators and Other Deficiencies in the Legal Regime," and 7, "Harassment of NGOs Working on Issues of Sexual Violence" (Fricke and Khair 2007:11, 15, 16, 17). This perhaps reflects the influence of former SDC executive director David Rubenstein (2007), who purposefully substituted the word *regime* for the more neutral term *government*.

19. *Laws Without Justice* was covered in the *New York Times* (Nicholas D. Kristof, "Spineless on Sudan," July 9, 2007) and on the BBC News International Web site ("Sudan Rape Laws 'Need Overhaul,'" June 29, 2007, http://news.bbc.co.uk/go/em/fr/-/2/hi/africa/6252620.stm [accessed August 20, 2008]).

20. SDC Press Release, "Clinton, McCain, Obama Joint Statement 'We Stand United on Sudan,'" May 25, 2008, http://www.savedarfur.org/newsroom/releases/

clinton_mccain_obama_joint_statement_we_stand_united_on_sudan/ (accessed August 18, 2008).

21. "President Bush Addresses the United Nations General Assembly," http://www.whitehouse.gov/news/releases/2007/09/20070925-4.html (accessed September 26, 2007).

22. Colleen Connors, SDC, "First Words, Now Action" (September 26, 2007, electronic communication).

23. Catholic News Service provides the full text of the speech at http://cnsblog.wordpress.com/2008/04/18/text-of-pope-to-un-general-assembly/ (accessed August 18, 2008).

WORKS CITED

Abu-Lughod, Lila. 2002. Do Muslim Women Really Need Saving? Anthropological Reflections on Cultural Relativism and Its Others. *American Anthropologist* 104:783–790.

Aidi, Hishaam. 2005. Slavery, Genocide and the Politics of Outrage: Understanding the New "Racial Olympics." *Middle East Report* 234. http://www.merip.org/mer/mer234/aidi.html (accessed February 24, 2010).

Ali, Kecia. 2006. *Sexual Ethics and Islam: Feminist Reflections on Qur'an, Hadith, and Jurisprudence*. New York: Oneworld.

Anidjar, Gil. 2003. *The Jew, the Arab: A History of the Enemy*. Stanford, Calif.: Stanford University Press.

Anidjar, Gil. 2008. *Semites: Race, Religion, Literature*. Stanford, Calif.: Stanford University Press.

Asad, Talal. 2003. *Formations of the Secular: Christianity, Islam, Modernity*. Stanford, Calif.: Stanford University Press.

Ban, Ki-moon. 2007. A Climate Culprit in Darfur. *Washington Post*, June 16, p. A15.

Barnett, Michael. 2003. *Eyewitness to a Genocide: The United Nations and Rwanda*. Ithaca, N.Y.: Cornell University Press.

Barnett, Michael, and Raymond Duvall. 2005. Power in Global Governance. In *Power in Global Governance*, ed. Michael Barnett and Raymond Duvall, 1–33. New York: Cambridge University Press.

Barnett, Michael, and Thomas G. Weiss. 2008. Humanitarianism: A Brief History of the Present. In *Humanitarianism in Question: Politics, Power, Ethics*, ed. Michael Barnett and Thomas G. Weiss, 1–48. Ithaca, N.Y.: Cornell University Press.

Calhoun, Craig J. 2003. "Belonging" in the Cosmopolitan Imaginary. *Ethnicities* 3, no. 4:531–553.

Calhoun, Craig J. 2007. *Nations Matter: Culture, History, and the Cosmopolitan Dream*. New York: Routledge.

Clines, Frances X. 1999. Crisis in the Balkans: The Overview; NATO Hunting for Serb Forces; U.S. Reports Signs of 'Genocide. *New York Times*, March 30, p. 114.

de Waal, Alex. 2006. I Will Not Sign. *London Review of Books*, November 30, pp. 17–20.

de Waal, Alex. 2008. Moreno Ocampo's Coup de Theatre. SSRC Making Sense of Darfur blog. http://blogs.ssrc.org/darfur/2008/07/29/moreno-ocampos-coup-de-theatre/ (accessed August 20, 2009).

de Waal, Alex. 2009a. Data for Deaths in Darfur. SSRC Making Sense of Darfur blog. http://blogs.ssrc.org/darfur/2009/02/26/data-for-deaths-in-darfur/ (accessed August 20, 2009).

de Waal, Alex. 2009b. Does "Save Darfur" Feed Darfur? SSRC Making Sense of Darfur blog. http://blogs.ssrc.org/darfur/2009/06/29/does-save-darfur-feed-darfur/ (accessed August 20, 2009).

Dealy, Sam. 2007. An Atrocity That Needs No Exaggeration. *New York Times*, August 12, p. WK 10.

Eichler-Levine, Jodi, and Rosemary R. Hicks. 2007. As "Americans Against Genocide": The Crisis in Darfur and Interreligious Political Activism. *American Quarterly* 59, no. 3:711–735.

Faris, Stephan. 2007. The Real Roots of Darfur. *Atlantic Monthly*, April, pp. 67–69.

Flint, Julie. 2007. In Sudan, Help Comes from Above. *New York Times*, July 6, p. A15.

Flint, Julie, and Alex de Waal. 2005. *Darfur: A Short History of a Long War*. New York: Zed and International African Institute.

Flint, Julie, and Alex de Waal. 2008. *A New History of a Long War*. New York: Zed.

Flint, Julie, and Alex de Waal. 2009a. Case Closed: A Prosecutor Without Borders. *World Affairs* 171, no. 4:23–38.

Flint, Julie, and Alex de Waal. 2009b. To Put Justice Before Peace Spells Disaster for Sudan. *Guardian*, March 6, p. 32.

Fricke, Adrienne L., and Amira Khair. 2007. *Laws Without Justice: An Assessment of Sudanese Laws Affecting Survivors of Rape*. Washington, D.C.: Refugees International.

Goodstein, Laurie. 2007. Faith Has Role in Politics, Obama Tells Church. *New York Times*, June 24, p. A22.

Gustafson, Marc. 2009. Calling Darfur as They See It. *Oxonian Review* 9, no. 3. http://www.oxonianreview.org/wp/calling-darfur-as-they-see-it/.

Hallaq, Wael. 2005. *The Origins and Evolution of Islamic Law*. Cambridge: Cambridge University Press.

Halley, Janet. 2008. Rape in Berlin: Reconsidering the Criminalization of Rape in the International Law of Armed Conflict. *Melbourne Journal of International Law* 78, no. 9:78–124.

Heschel, Susannah. 2008. *The Aryan Jesus: Christian Theologians and the Bible in Nazi Germany*. Princeton, N.J.: Princeton University Press.

Hicks, Rosemary R. 2010. Creating an "Abrahamic America" and Moderating Islam: Cold War Political Economy and Cosmopolitan Sufi Muslims in New York City After 2001. Ph.D. diss., Columbia University.

Hirschkind, Charles, and Saba Mahmood. 2002. Feminism, the Taliban and the Politics of Counter-Insurgency. *Anthropological Quarterly* 2:339–354.

Jackson, Sherman. 2003. Black Orientalism: Its Genesis, Aims, and Significance for American Islam. In *Muslims in the United States*, ed. Philippa Strum and Danielle Tarantolo, 21–38. Washington, D.C.: Woodrow Wilson International Center for Scholars.

Kitagawa, Joseph. 1987. The 1893 World's Parliament of Religions and Its Legacy. In *The History of Religions: Understanding Human Experience*, ed. J. Kitagawa, 352–368. Atlanta, Ga.: Scholars Press.

Kristof, Nicholas D. 2009. What to Do About Darfur. *New York Review of Books*, July 2. http://www.nybooks.com/articles/22771 (accessed June 24, 2009).

Lumeye, Fidele. 2004. *Rape, Islam, and Darfur's Women Refugees and War-Displaced*. Washington, D.C.: Refugees International.

Mamdani, Mahmood. 2004. *Good Muslim, Bad Muslim: America, the Cold War, and the Roots of Terror*. New York: Pantheon.

Mamdani, Mahmood. 2007a. Blue-Hatting Darfur. *London Review of Books*, September 6, pp. 18–20.

Mamdani, Mahmood. 2007b. The Politics of Naming: Genocide, Civil War, Insurgency. *London Review of Books*, March 8, pp. 5–8.

Mamdani, Mahmood. 2009a. Mamdani Responds to His Critics II. SSRC Making Sense of Darfur blog. http://blogs.ssrc.org/darfur/2009/05/12/mamdani-responds-to-his-critics-ii/ (accessed June 20, 2009).

Mamdani, Mahmood. 2009b. *Survivors and Saviors: Darfur, Politics, and the War on Terror*. New York: Pantheon.

Marr, Timothy. 2006. *The Cultural Roots of American Islamicism*. New York: Cambridge University Press.

Martin, Sarah. 2007. *Ending Sexual Violence in Darfur: An Advocacy Agenda*. Washington, D.C.: Refugees International.

Masuzawa, Tomoko. 2005. *The Invention of World Religions: Or, How European Universalism Was Preserved in the Language of Pluralism*. Chicago: University of Chicago Press.

McAlister, Melani. 2005. *Epic Encounters: Culture, Media, and U.S. Interests in the Middle East Since 1945*. Berkeley: University of California Press.

McAlister, Melani. 2008. The Politics of Persecution. *Middle East Report* 249. http://www.merip.org/mer/mer249/mcalister.html (accessed June 26, 2009).

Moreno Ocampo, Louis. 2008a. Seventh Report of the Prosecutor of the International Criminal Court to the UN Security Council Pursuant to UNSCR 1593 (2005). The Hague: International Criminal Court.

Moreno Ocampo, Louis. 2008b. Statement by Mr. Louis Moreno Ocampo, Prosecutor of the International Criminal Court. Statement to the United Nations Security Council Pursuant to UNSCR 1593 (2005)—5 June 2008. The Hague: International Criminal Court.

Power, Samantha. 2004. Dying in Darfur. *New Yorker*, August 30, p. 58.

Rubenstein, Josh. 2007. A Conversation with David Rubenstein, the Save Darfur Coalition, Moderated by Josh Rubenstein, Amnesty International, April 21, 2007.

http://www.publictheater.org/static/CODdavidrubenstein.pdf (accessed July 16, 2007).

Sachs, Jeffrey. 2005. *The End of Poverty*. London: Penguin.

Said, Edward. 1978. *Orientalism*. New York: Vintage.

Save Darfur Coalition. 2006a. Christian Faith Action Packet. http://millionvoicesfordarfur.com/pdf/Darfur%20Christian%20Faith%20Action%20Packet%202006.doc (accessed May 2, 2006, but since removed).

Save Darfur Coalition. 2006b. General Faith Action Packet. http://millionvoicesfordarfur.com/pdf/Darfur%20General%20Faith%20Action%20Packet%202006.doc.

Save Darfur Coalition. 2006c. Interfaith Action Packet. http://millionvoicesfordarfur.com/pdf/Darfur%20Interfaith%20Faith%20Action%20Packet%202006.doc.

Save Darfur Coalition. 2006d. Jewish Faith Action Packet. http://millionvoicesfordarfur.com/pdf/Darfur%20Jewish%20Faith%20Action%20Packet%202006.doc.

Schmidt, Leigh Eric. 2006. Cosmopolitan Piety: Sympathy, Comparative Religions, and Nineteenth-Century Liberalism. In *Practicing Protestants: Histories of Christian Life in America, 1630–1965*, ed. Laurie F. Maffly-Kipp, Leigh E. Schmidt, and Mark Valeri, 199–221. Baltimore: Johns Hopkins University Press.

Tucker, Judith E. 2003. *In the House of the Law: Gender and Islamic Law in Ottoman Syria and Palestine*. Berkeley: University of California Press.

11. WHAT IS RELIGIOUS PLURALISM IN A "MONOCULTURAL" SOCIETY?

Considerations from Postcommunist Poland

GENEVIÈVE ZUBRZYCKI

What does pluralism mean in a society whose citizens are 96 percent ethnically Polish and 95 percent Catholic?[1] And what is religious pluralism in a society where 96 percent of citizens declare that they believe in God and 75 percent participate in religious services at least once a month?[2] If one were to look only at these statistics, Poland would appear to be a monocultural society where the issue of religious pluralism simply does not exist. But as expected with many descriptive statistics, as soon as we scratch beneath the surface of the numbers, we find a very different picture, in this case one shaded not only by varying degrees of commitment to the faith and its creeds but also by different types of Catholicisms adopted by individuals and divergent orientations coexisting within the Polish Catholic Church itself (Zubrzycki 2004, 2005).

I suggest that we need to dig even deeper to unearth the challenges of pluralism in a place like Poland. As a point of departure, to understand the cultural and social dynamics around the issue of pluralism and its political implications, we must take into account the processes through which that nation's current demographic makeup was achieved and naturalized. Indeed, for most of its history, Poland was actually quite diverse in the most straightforward sense, populated by people belonging to different ethnic, linguistic, and religious communities. With the arrival of World War II this was dramatically changed: Jews, who in 1931 constituted approximately 10 percent of the population, were exterminated during the Holocaust or emigrated after the war, as many survivors became targets of pogroms (Gross 2006) or of state-sponsored anti-Semitic campaigns (Stola 2000). The Polish state's borders also shifted west after World War II; Ukrainian, Belarusian, and Lithuanian minorities were incorporated into the Soviet Union, and German populations in the West were expelled. As a result, ethnic Poles, who in 1931 constituted approximately 65 percent of the Second Republic's population, by 1946 accounted for about 95 percent of the People's Republic. The population's religious makeup was also dramatically changed by World War II and its aftermath: In 1931 Catholics composed 65 percent of Poland's population, but by 1946 the proportion of Catholics had increased to 96 percent of the population within the new borders (Michowicz 1988; Tomaszewski 1993).

Poland's current ethnic and religious "homogeneity" is therefore the byproduct of recent historical events and political processes. But this radically new reality was successfully naturalized and normalized in the postwar period. Indeed, the communist party-state, in search of legitimacy, prided itself on the formation of an ethnic Poland and effectively erased even the memory of diversity by repressing that past. Meanwhile, the Catholic Church could justifiably claim to represent civil society and portrayed itself as the authentic "nation's keeper," in opposition to a state imposed from outside and from above. Combined, these processes further tightened an ideological link between Polishness and Catholicism.

World War II and its aftermath therefore mark the dividing line between a diverse "before" and a homogeneous "after," demographically speaking. However, this "after" is far from being what the title of this volume refers to. "After pluralism," as defined by Pamela Klassen and Courtney Bender in the introduction to this volume, refers to an ideological and normative space; not a sociological one. It refers to a moment when pluralism, as a value, has been internalized to such an extent that one can interrogate what is to follow. In this sense, then, Poland's "after" is actually an ideological space and a historical moment *before* pluralism because there is no widespread commitment to pluralism and its virtue. In fact, I will show that there is significant resistance and opposition to the idea of pluralism, and the idea of pluralism has been a contested issue in various public debates that have punctuated the postcommunist period.

One of these key debates concerned the nature of the newly independent and democratic state. In the contest to define the core values on which the state was to be built, the postcommunist period has been shaped by a society-wide debate in which the Catholic right and the official hierarchy of the Catholic Church emphasized the "objective" homogeneity of Poland's population, whereas intellectuals and politicians on the left, the center, and liberal Catholics stressed the nation's ideological heterogeneity.[3] While the former pointed to a concrete set of values associated with the nation's Christian heritage, which they argued would be best protected in a "confessional state," the latter argued that in a plural society religion is one among many value systems. They therefore demanded the confessional neutrality of the state in order to protect the rights of minorities, atheists, or nonpracticing Catholics, and ensure citizens' equality de jure and de facto. That position, in turn, was qualified by at least one prominent archbishop as "democratic totalitarianism," because a minority of nonbelievers would determine the constitutional path followed by the overwhelming majority of Poles (Archbishop Michalik in *Nasza Polska*, February 19, 1997 [quoted in Zubrzycki 2001]).

These debates occurred in the context of, and as a consequence of, the radical opening of the institutional settings of public discourse since the fall of communism. This had substantial repercussions for the Church, whose authority in the public sphere has declined significantly with the liberalization of society and with the introduction of a plurality of institutions in civil society. At the same time, however, religious discourses and symbols have become familiar weapons in the hands of ethno-Catholic nationalists—often supported by the conservative and fundamentalist wings of the Catholic Church—in their attempt to re-create the "us versus them"[4] master frame that successfully mobilized masses under communism but that now impedes constructive, consensual institution building.

In contemporary Poland, therefore, the very idea of pluralism is contested, as the conservatives and the far right refuse to think of Poland in those terms, insisting that the country is monolithically defined from a core set of values, a single root system from which the nation grows. Many wield Poland's demographic statistics ("95 percent Catholic") to bolster claims of monolithic unity and legally enforce a very narrow vision of Poland. In the most notorious set of events, such statistics were used to support and justify the inclusion of an *invocatio Dei* in the 1997 Constitution (Zubrzycki 2001) and were often invoked to defend the state's aggressive policing of social movements deviating from an imagined national norm. It is with the help of statistics, for example, that gay pride parades were banned in Warsaw and that strict legislation on abortion is maintained. Because Catholicism, for historical reasons, has traditionally played an important role in defining the symbolic boundaries of the Polish nation, the question of who truly belongs, according to conservative Catholics, depends to a great extent on religious affiliation and commitment. Thus religious discourse in present-day Poland generally is not being used to advocate the building of an open society, as it had under communism, but rather to exclude those considered unworthy of full membership. "Jews" occupy a privileged place in that debate, as they serve as a foil for debates on Polish national identity.[5]

In this chapter, I address the ways in which various Polish groups articulate, in their discourses and through their practical uses of religious symbols, the relationship between Polishness and Catholicism. I do so by examining a controversial event, when self-defined "Poles–Catholics" erected hundreds of crosses just outside the walls of the Auschwitz–Birkenau Museum in Oświęcim.[6] I first describe the so-called War of the Crosses and discuss its significance; I then show how some social actors used religious symbols to emphasize, maintain, and strengthen the link between Polishness and Catholicism and to exclude those who advocate pluralism in Poland, and analyze the various and shifting significations of the cross in the postcommunist period. Finally, I consider the challenges Poland's apparent homogeneity and Catholicism's traditional role in defining and bounding that homogeneity pose to the creation of an open, plural society.[7]

THE WAR OF THE CROSSES: DEFINING THE EVENT AND ITS SIGNIFICANCE

Before I describe the War of the Crosses and what motivated it, a few words must be said about why Poles would care about Auschwitz at all; after all, Auschwitz is a key site of the Shoah and a universal symbol of evil (Alexander 2002). Poles actually have a close relationship to the former camp, as it was initially created for Polish political prisoners. Not until the Final Solution was implemented in 1942 was the camp given the additional and henceforth main function of death camp for the European Jewry, through the creation of Auschwitz II–Birkenau two miles away. Although the camps in Treblinka, Bełżec, Chełmno, and Sobibór became synonymous with the extermination of Jews in Polish consciousness (because this is primarily where Polish Jews from the liquidated ghettos of Warsaw, Cracow, Łódź, and Lublin were killed), "Oświęcim" became and remained the symbol of Poles' martyrdom during World War II, representing the attempt by Nazis to physically and culturally annihilate the Polish nation. After the war, the communist state built onto this already common understanding of the camp by creating the State Museum Oświęcim–Brzezinka in 1947 on the basis of a law "on the remembrance of the martyrdom of the Polish Nation and other Nations." As the name of that law suggests, Poles, although not the camp's only victims, were its main martyrs. The museum was indeed squarely Polish from its inception, but the national narrative was told in the socialist mode and according to socialist parameters. In it, "Victims of Fascism" from Poland and twenty-seven other states were exploited and exterminated at the camp, later liberated by the victorious and just Soviet army. In this narrative, the extermination of Jews was forced into the background, and the extent of Polish suffering was brought closer to the fore. Polish Jews were counted as Polish victims. Conflating Polish Jews and gentile Poles into the category "Polish citizens," or sometimes simply "Poles," implied that Poland had the largest death toll. The museum has revised its narrative since the fall of communism and the opening of Soviet archives. It has dropped most of the socialist rhetoric, and, most importantly, it now stresses that Jews constituted 90 percent of the camp's victims. However, for Poles, who for three generations were socialized to the notion that they had constituted the majority of prisoners and victims of the camp, this revision of history is not easily or unquestioningly accepted.[8]

It is in the context of Auschwitz's narrative revision and, more broadly, of the reexamination of Polish national identity's relationship to Catholicism, after the fall of communism, that in the summer of 1998 self-defined "Poles–Catholics" erected hundreds of crosses just outside Auschwitz, in the backyard of what was, from 1984 to 1993, an infamous Carmelite convent.[9] The War of the Crosses was spurred by rumors, a few months earlier, to the effect that a large cross, commonly called the papal cross, would be removed from the grounds of the former convent, at the request of Jewish organizations.[10] A series of commentaries by political figures immediately followed and were thrust into the public arena. A well-known right-wing political figure qualified the intended removal as "religious profanation and national humiliation." One hundred thirty deputies and a group of senators from right-wing parties signed a petition to the government advocating the continued presence of the cross at the gravel pit, and Lech Wałęsa spoke out against the removal of the cross in a letter to Bishop Tadeusz Rakoczy, under whose jurisdiction the town of Oświęcim falls. By mid-March, popular mobilization was under way: Some parishes celebrated special Masses for "the respect and protection of the papal cross," alongside vigils for the defense of crosses in Poland. At the annual Jewish-sponsored "March of the Living" in April that year, banners and posters with slogans such as "Defend the Cross" and "Keep Jesus at Auschwitz" (in English) were displayed on the gravel pit fence.[11] By the spring, the issue had become an affair involving, at the domestic level, government officials, the opposition, the Catholic Church, and various civic organizations.

In June, Kazimierz Świtoń, ex-Solidarity activist and former deputy of the right-wing Confederation of Independent Poland, initiated a hunger strike at the gravel pit that lasted forty-two days, demanding from the Catholic Church a firm commitment that the cross would remain.[12] After failing to secure such a commitment, Świtoń appealed to his fellow Poles to plant 152 crosses on the grounds of the gravel pit, both to commemorate the (documented) deaths of 152 ethnic Poles executed at that specific site by Nazis in 1941 and to "protect and defend the papal cross."[13] This appeal proved successful: In the summer and fall of 1998, the gravel pit in Oświęcim was transformed into the epicenter of the War of the Crosses, as individuals, civic organizations, and religious groups from every corner of Poland (and from as far away as Canada, the United States, and Australia) answered Świtoń's call to create a "valley of crosses," encouraged by the popular and controversial radio station Radio Maryja. By the time the Polish army finally removed them in May 1999, 322 crosses stood at the gravel pit.

During that summer, the site became the stage for prayer vigils, Masses, demonstrations, and general nationalist agitation. It was the destination of choice for pilgrims, journalists, and tourists in search of a sacred cause, a good story, or a free show, respectively. Religious images of the national Madonna (Our Lady of Częstochowa) and secular symbols such as red-and-white Polish flags and national coats of arms commonly adorned the crosses and added to their symbolic weight and complexity. The papal cross itself was transformed into an improvised altar, with flowers, candles, and small flags spread at its foot. The fence surrounding the area, where crowds of the curious gathered to observe the spectacle, was similarly covered with political banners and flowers.

At the national level, the fourteen-month "war" was marked by a series of debates and legal battles, numerous declarations from public officials, and accusations and counteraccusations that embroiled the government in conflict with the opposition, Polish public intellectuals, Polish Jewish activists, groups from the far-right, the Catholic Church, and a schismatic brotherhood claiming to represent "true Catholicism in defense of the Nation." At first, the government stood on the sidelines, invoking the principle of separation of church and state as defined in the Concordat of 1997 in arguing that the papal cross was the property of the Catholic Church, which was responsible for the use of its religious symbols. The Church countered that the crosses stood on government property and that the Catholic Church had no monopoly over the symbol of the cross, which belonged to the entire Christian community of believers. Over time, however, as a growing number of crosses appeared at the gravel pit, the crisis became more acute for both the government and the Church. For the Church, it was rendered more acute by the disobedience of Catholics to the Episcopate's request, in late August, to stop planting crosses, and by the persistent involvement of the Society of St. Pius X, a schismatic group.[14] For the government, the situation was exacerbated by demands from Israel and pressure from representatives of the U.S. Congress to remove all crosses from the proximity of Auschwitz at precisely the time when Poland was negotiating the terms of its NATO membership.

In the end, the Polish government and the Catholic Church made concerted attempts to find a solution and regain control of the gravel pit. After many legal battles and the passage of a law regarding "the protection of the grounds of former Nazi camps" on May 7, 1999, a 330-foot zone was established around Auschwitz, giving the government the legal means to evict Kazimierz

Świtoń from the gravel pit, where he had been encamped in a trailer for nearly a year, while the Church arranged for the crosses to be relocated to a nearby sanctuary. However, the papal cross remained. There was thus no resolution of the initial conflict concerning the presence of that specific cross. For this reason, the social action of cross planting could therefore be qualified as "successful" and is regarded as such by Świtoń himself. By escalating the conflict and radicalizing the demands—from the retention of one cross to the retention of hundreds—the Defenders of the Cross successfully changed the terms for what a compromise would entail. In fact, by the end of the affair, removal of the papal cross was not even considered an option and was not open to negotiations; the removal of Świtoń and the 300-odd crosses was the principal objective of most of those involved. If at the outset the papal cross's presence at the gravel pit was not inevitable and different authorities considered the possibility of its removal and relocation, by the drama's conclusion its presence at that site had been naturalized and been made a permanent monument in the landscape of Auschwitz's perimeter.

The War of the Crosses was fought on several fronts but structured along two main axes. The first one, the most apparent, was played out between Poles and Jews concerning the contested meaning of "Oświęcim/Auschwitz" and the problematic presence of a Christian symbol at that site of the Holocaust. The second axis concerned the contested meaning of the cross and, more broadly, of the nation in postcommunist Poland and involved a serious debate among Poles. Although the War of the Crosses was without a doubt an interreligious and interethnic (or international) conflict, the controversy was also an intranational and even intra-religious crisis: It highlighted and sharpened conflicts between ethno-religious and civic–secular nationalists, between members of the Church hierarchy and clergy who supported the action and those who did not, and between the institutional Church, self-defined Poles–Catholics planting crosses, and a schismatic group celebrating religious services at the site. In fact, the War of the Crosses became *the* occasion for Poles to debate the place of religion and religious symbols in an open society and the relationship between Polish national identity and Catholicism more broadly.[15] Even though it was initiated by marginal characters, the event did mobilize support, and the issues it raised were not marginal but rather became a lightning rod for mainstream commentary and discussion of Polishness, its traditional association with Catholicism, anti-Semitism, and the state of Catholicism in postcommunist Poland. It brought to light with unusual clarity the challenges of building a plural society in a postcommunist society as it revealed the insidiousness of narratives propagated by the communist regime and the pervasiveness of ethno-Catholic myths of the nation. It also highlighted the extent to which Manichean views of the world and rhetorical styles still shape public debates about the nation, religion, and the state.

POLONIZING AUSCHWITZ AND CATHOLICIZING POLISHNESS

The men and women who brought crosses to the gravel pit chose to firmly anchor Auschwitz and its memory as specifically and indelibly Polish by marking it with a symbol that could not be shared with Jews. By choosing that symbol, they were commemorating the deaths of their co-religionists, but they were also attempting to ossify a vision of Polishness that has slowly been disintegrating since the fall of communism.

The great majority of the crosses erected at the gravel pit bore a small commemorating plaque indicating the name and prisoner number of the victim in whose memory the cross was erected, or a specific slogan, message, poem, biblical inscription, or testimony, such as "Defend the Cross," "For God and Fatherland," or "Only Poland." Most of them were signed by their sponsors, whether private individuals or organizations, but some preferred to remain anonymous. The most common theme expressed on the crosses' inscriptions was the martyrdom of Poles and the implicit claim to Poles' right to the site. By commemorating Polish victims, they contested the Jewishness of Auschwitz. A great many crosses emphasized the Polish identity of the victims and their suffering, in an attempt to counteract the recent revision of the camp's history. Recall that the cross-planting action was initiated by Świtoń, who invited Poles to commemorate the death of ethnic Poles executed at the gravel pit in July 1941, thereby sufficiently Polonizing the site such that the papal cross would remain. In this vein, one woman intended her cross as a testimony of the crimes against Poles; her cross's inscription read, "As an inhabitant of [nearby village], I was a witness of those brutal murders of Poles by Hitlerites in the camp and at the gravel pit. Let this birch cross attest that I remember you. Anna Chrapczyńsa."

Other crosses emphasized the Catholic identity of Poles by fusing, sometimes in creative ways, Catholicism and Polishness. In addition to a multitude of crosses bearing inscriptions such as "to the Poles–Catholics murdered at the gravel pit" and "Here died Polish patriots–Catholics," many were inspired by verses commonly attributed to Adam Mickiewicz, Poland's national bard:

Only under this cross
Only under this sign
Poland is Poland
and a Pole is a Pole.

One cross's author, in a significant inversion or Freudian slip, replaced the poem's last verse with the line "and a Catholic is a Pole," illustrating the complete conflation of national and religious categories.[16] Moreover, the cross is often described as Poland's protector and main attribute, its totem. Without it, Poland would no longer be Poland, as the short poem suggests, or no longer exist at all, as Świtoń argued: "This cross, it is for Poland to be or not to be" (quoted in *Rzeczpospolita*, July 20, 1998).

The aesthetics of the War of the Crosses—its symbols, rituals, and strategies of resistance—are strikingly reminiscent of those of the historic sit-in strike at the Gdańsk shipyard in 1980, which marked the birth of Solidarity and the beginning of the end of communism in Poland and Eastern Europe. The Defenders of the Cross created an event that borrowed from a repertoire of actions and symbols that could easily be recognized by participants and observers alike. Hunger strikes, political speeches, prayer vigils and Masses, flags, pictures of the Lady of Częstochowa and of the pope, flowers and candles, posters, banners, and leaflets distributed at the gate repeated a well-known script in an effort (conscious or not) to re-create—or at least give the impression of re-creating—the power of August 1980, a rare moment of collective effervescence and unprecedented social solidarity (itself replicating a Romantic script developed during the nineteenth-century insurrectionary period). By borrowing well-established aesthetics, the Defenders of the Cross placed themselves in a long lineage of "Poles–patriots" that include Adam Mickiewicz, the pope, and Solidarity's heroes, thereby attempting to generate a strategic narrative link with other significant historical events such as national insurrections, the pope's first visit to Poland, and the "Polish August."

Through the manipulation of key symbols and through ritual performances, Świtoń and the Defenders of the Cross generated emotional responses that mobilized a certain group of Poles to social action. In their discourse, the Defenders of the Cross attempted to re-create the "us versus them" master frame that had proved mobilizing under communism and transfer it to a new conflict. However, that new frame was used not only to differentiate "us, Poles" from "them, Jews" but also to distinguish "we, the Catholic nation, real Poles" from "them, atheist communists, fake Poles" and even "us, true Catholics" from "them, washed-out Catholics or crypto-Jews," as I analyze in the next section. Posters on the gravel pit's fence offered promises to the pope to defend the cross from the "hierarchists," insinuated to be communists. A list of high-ranked Polish officials from the left *and* the right was boldly stretched on a banner, with the warning to them that "He who fights the cross dies under the cross." This marginal and extreme group attempted to hijack the meaning of Polishness by portraying itself as "the nation": "*We* are the nation," the Defenders of the Cross proclaimed at the gravel pit, attempting to create the illusion of unity against external Others (American and Israeli Jews) and internal Others (communists, atheists, masons, and "Jews"), at a moment of intense social, economic, and political divisions in the country.

Although they were successful in their immediate goal—to ensure that the papal cross would remain at the gravel pit—Świtoń and the Defenders of the Cross failed at the their second objective, namely to revitalize and ossify a vision of Polishness that is slowly eroding. In fact, their strategy further contributed to the erosion it sought to stop. Although Poles remain overwhelmingly religious, the cross they now bear is no longer the symbol of their historical Passion, nor that of the union of their faith with national identity, but rather—and quite counterintuitively—a contested symbol expressing deep social tensions regarding Polish Catholicism.

DEBATING POLAND BY DEBATING THE CROSS

The practice of erecting crosses to sacralize a site and protect oneself from a potential repression from the state was not new, nor was the use of religious symbols to affirm Polish national identity. But the meaning of those practices and their moral valuation have certainly changed with the fall of communism and the construction of a sovereign state.

Under communism, the presence of the cross in the public sphere was seen as something desirable by many Poles opposed to the communist regime, including atheists and Jews. This was especially true in the 1980s, when the secular left took pride in the Polish pope and his human rights message, supported workers demonstrating with religious symbols in Gdańsk, and more generally embraced the Church after the declaration of martial law in 1981. In 1983, for example, during the fortieth anniversary of the Warsaw Ghetto Uprising, Marek Edelman, the uprising's last living leader, decided that Solidarity's independent commemoration of the event should be marked by the laying of a cross with flowers at the Ghettos' Heroes monument. In that gesture, the cross was used not as a Christian symbol but as a national one. It meant to demarcate Solidarity's commemoration of the event from the official, state commemoration and to underline the "genuine" Polishness of the trade union, as opposed to the state's "foreignness."

Moreover, the cross was widely understood as a sign of diversity against an imposed monolithic worldview, and its physical presence served as a reminder of the regime's fragility. Catholicism and its primary symbol, the cross, were regarded by a great number of Polish citizens as good because they marked the line dividing atheist colonizers from "authentic Poles" and marked an area of relative freedom from the state. Engaging in religious practices and articulating religious discourse in the public sphere were activities that, de facto, created a "plural" society in place of the totalizing society the communist party-state endeavored to construct and impose.

In the post-1989 context, that signification is no longer persuasive. The cross in the public sphere now signifies for liberal intellectuals from the left (and for some liberal Catholic circles) the imposition of a set of values and intolerance toward Others. It stands as the rejection of the principles of the *Rechtsstaat*, where particular allegiances are relegated to the private sphere—an opinion that was similarly expressed in debates about the Constitution's preamble (Zubrzycki 2001). For them, the symbol of the cross at Auschwitz in particular stands for an ethno-Catholic vision of Poland that not only excludes Jews from its present and past but also excludes all those who do not think of themselves or of Poland in those terms. For liberal Catholics associated with the Catholic publications *Tygodnik Powszechny*, *Znak*, and *Więź*, such as Stefan Wilkanowicz, the large papal cross is a political instrument, a provocation contrary to the Christian meaning of the symbol (*Gazeta Wyborcza*, August 7, 1998), and for others it is the shameful expression of Polish nationalism.

For editors of far-left, anticlerical publications such as the satirical weekly *Nie*, the cross stands for fundamentalist tendencies in Poland since the fall of communism and represents the "narrow-minded clericalism and bigotry" of the so-called Catho-right. In the words of Jerzy Urban (1998:35), *Nie*'s owner and editor-in-chief, the "crossomania" is a comedy in which the crusaders, like madmen escaped from mental institutions, play "Cathonationalist gardeners . . . planting crosses on gravel, like dogs and cats feeling the need to mark their territory."

In the discourse of conservative Catholic groups, however, attempts to remove the cross are still associated, at least rhetorically, with the communist past of forced atheization and religious repression. The presence of the cross in the public sphere here still signified, in an interesting twist, religious freedom and religious *pluralism* associated with Western culture and values, as expressed in this Catholic organization's declaration against the removal of the papal cross from the gravel pit:

> Signs and symbols are the testimony of [the living's] faith and national identity, their dignity and freedom, their endurance and hope. For Christians, for the majority of Poles, the cross is such a sign. In our forefathers' history, the partitioning powers or the occupants more than once have fought against the presence of the sign of the holy cross on Polish land. Today, in a free and independent European country, in a state based on the rule of law and democracy, the battle with the symbols of religious faith is contrary to the spirit of Europe and the expression of lack of respect for people

of other faith or nationality. (Civitas Christiana, in *Katolicka agencja informacyjna*, no 12 [1998])

A few things in this statement are noteworthy: the identification of the cross as a religious and *national* symbol, the emphasis on demographic "facts" to make the argument for the presence of the cross at Auschwitz (the majority of Poles are Christian), the historical analogy drawn between current (Jewish) attempts to remove the cross and religious repression by several occupiers, and the claim that fighting the presence of the cross is antithetical to democracy. If that last point made sense under communism, it is clearly anachronistic in post-communist Poland. Nevertheless, the message found a ready audience.

CONCLUSION: SYMBOLIC EXCLUSION IN A "MONOCULTURAL" SOCIETY

Although many used descriptive statistics to justify the presence of the cross in Polish public space or to fight for the institutionalization of Catholic doctrine in the 1997 Constitution (Zubrzycki 2001), the War of the Crosses shattered the myth of Polish society's homogeneity: Poland's population may be 96 percent ethnically Polish and 95 percent Catholic, but what Polishness and Catholic identity are is polysemous and contested. Contrary to the myth of Poland's intrinsic Catholicism and of the Church's monolithic authority in that country, tension, fissures, and lines of division run deep within Polish society and within the Church itself.[17] The Pole–Catholic association of identifications is reproduced only by determined cultural work on specific symbols, events, and their meanings. Moreover, this cultural work is carried out by specific social groups and performed on their media staging grounds to create "communities of discourse" (Wuthnow 1989), the formulations of which are disseminated—yet not necessarily assimilated—more or less successfully throughout the population at large.

Debates about the cross within Poland concerned not only whether religious symbols should be present at Auschwitz or its immediate proximity—which is at the core of theological arguments between Christians and Jews—but what the cross in Poland means. In other words, for Poles the debates about the crosses at Auschwitz were debates about the association of the national and religious dimensions and its appropriateness and legitimacy in the postcommunist context. The discussion rarely directly involved Poles and Jews in dialogue, although Jews remained the implicit (and often explicit) external and internal Other in exchanges between Poles. Jews and Jewishness served as a foil for the discussion of Polishness and of the role of Catholicism in defining and shaping the latter.

As my analysis of the War of the Crosses demonstrates, Catholicism and its symbols in postcommunist Poland are no longer used to unite and include with the objective of building an open society against a totalitarian state but rather are used by ultranationalist Catholics to exclude those who are not considered worthy of full membership. In addition to Jews, Poland's traditional internal Other, "bad Catholics," "cosmopolitan secularists," and Freemasons have also become categories of symbolic exclusion to the nation, with the last two categories used as code words for Jews. Religion therefore is used by these groups to define the symbolic boundaries of the "Polish nation": Who truly belongs depends to a great extent on one's commitment to a very specific, narrow vision of Polishness, that of the Polak–katolik.

In this context, Jewishness itself becomes a symbol, standing for a civic–secular Poland. Through a complex chain of associations, a "Jew" is anyone who does not adhere to a strictly exclusive ethno-Catholic vision of Poland. Even certain bishops are accused of being "crypto-Jews." In these circles, the European Union is similarly identified by the right as a machination by Jews to institutionally, structurally annihilate nation-states. From this perspective, Poland is ruled by "Jews"—by symbolic Jews. Those opposed to the ethno-Catholic vision of the nation and those proponents of a plural, civic–secular Poland are accused of being "Jews" through a series of associations and double-entendres. Ideological difference is thereby ethnicized. Adam Michnik (1999:73) calls this peculiar phenomenon magical anti-Semitism: "The logic of normal, correct and healthy anti-Semitism is the following: Adam Michnik is a Jew, therefore he is a hooligan, a thief, a traitor, a bandit etc. . . . Magical anti-Semitism however works this way: Adam Michnik is a thief, therefore he is most probably a Jew." Jewishness serves as an ethno-religious category opposed to the Polak–katolik that is used to exclude unwanted ideological elements.

This points to an interesting paradox. The category of Polishness is generally understood in ethnic terms, following the German, romantic model of nationhood but also in ideological–political terms.[18] Certain Poles, because of their political allegiances and ideological positions (mostly with the liberal left), are deemed un-Polish or anti-Polish or qualified as "fake Poles" or "Jews" by the conservative far-right. Whereas this type of symbolic exclusion is typical of places where the nation is understood in civic terms and where, therefore, one's national identity—at least ideally—is determined by his or her adhesion to the principles of the social contract,[19] it seems unlikely and ill befitting a place where the nation is understood primarily in ethnic terms, where national identity is thought to be primordial, transmitted by birth and flowing through one's veins. Following that conception, national identity can be neither chosen nor escaped; it is constitutive of the self. How is it possible, given this understanding of national identity, to have ideological forms of exclusion from the ethnic nation? How is the tension reconciled between these two modes of exclusion, one based on blood and culture, the other based on ideological orientations and political bonds?

In the Polish case, ideological difference is ethnicized: An "un-Polish" or "Polish-speaking" (i.e., "non-Polish") liberal intellectual advocating a civic–secular Poland becomes a "Jew." "Magical anti-Semitism" is activated against a specific set of values: capitalism and communism, both perceived as threats to a traditional, conservative way of life and religious values, both associated with cosmopolitanism, and both associated with Jewishness. Thus we witness the strange phenomenon of anti-Semitism in a country virtually without Jews, but also philo-Semitism, its mirror image.[20]

The emergence of Jewish festivals, the opening of Jewish restaurants, and the popularization of Klezmer music reveal not merely the folklorization of Jews and things Jewish in Poland but also the attempt to reclaim a past that has been ideologically erased and suppressed by the socialist state in its effort to legitimize and naturalize the new borders and new demographic makeup of the postwar nation-state. That past is continually negated by the right in current-day Poland. The plural mosaic of the First and Second Republics represents for that ideological formation an anomaly that needed correction and must be prevented at all costs from returning. If for the right "Jews" are the figures of nightmares, auguring a pernicious civic vision of the nation, for the left "Jews" are the symbol of an emancipating civic vision. Although the diversity that characterized Poland for most of its history is unlikely to return, the recognition of that history and its legacy is seen as highly desirable for civic nationalists. It is a means of signaling pluralism (with all the international cachet that term carries) in the present through the contemporary return of a repressed past of diversity. Yet that civic vision also gestures toward the hope for some of a future postethnic horizon.

NOTES

This chapter adapts selected materials from my book *The Crosses of Auschwitz: Nationalism and Religion in Post-Communist Poland* (Chicago: University of Chicago Press, 2006).

1. According to the 2002 census data. It goes without saying that ethnic, national, and religious identities are constructed and that such bounded categories are no more real or objective than others that are deemed subjective. It should therefore be clear that I do not take demographic homogeneity as a fact but as a social construction sometimes invoked for ideological and political purposes.

2. The numbers on religiosity (belief and practice) were obtained from Centrum Badania Opinii Społecznej (2006). In addition to the statistics cited here, 77 percent of Poles over the age of fifteen consider religion an integral part of their everyday life. Conversely, only 12 percent of them consider religion to have little meaning in their life.

3. Poland is even "overpluralist" according to Danuta Waniek (1991:14), who used the term to refer to the proliferation of political parties and ideological positions represented in the public sphere in the early phase of the postcommunist transition. Giovanni Sartori's concept of "polarized pluralism" has also been used in the Polish context. See Seleny (1999) and Jasiewicz (2000).

4. "Us" was the nation, united behind Solidarity and the Catholic Church, and "them" the elite in power, perceived as serving the interests of the Soviet Union rather than that of Poland.

5. The quotation marks indicate the symbolic and discursive nature of the category. It is the *image* of Jews and *representations* of Jewishness that are used to define Polishness, not real, existing Jews—even when actual Jewish people are referred to or even verbally and symbolically abused. I discuss this issue in the last section of the chapter.

6. Pronounced "Osh-VYEN-chim." Oświęcim is a small town (pop. 50,000), fifty miles from Krakow. It was part of the Incorporated Territories during World War II and is better known in the world by its German designation, Auschwitz, where the Nazis built an elaborate network of concentration and mass extermination camps.

7. The evidence for this chapter was collected via archival research, fieldwork interviews, and participant observation. I reviewed and analyzed editorials and letters to the editor in Polish newspapers (dailies, weeklies, and monthlies) from diverse political and ideological orientations, covering a wide spectrum from left to right. Other primary documents include official Church publications, pastoral letters, sermons, homilies, and texts of "spontaneous" public prayers; political speeches and pamphlets; inscriptions left on the crosses and placards brought to the site of the War of the Crosses; and other, nontextual artifacts such as posters, postcards, icons, and altars. For a discussion of the data and methods used for this study, see Zubrzycki (2006:30–32).

8. For an analysis of the various layers of meaning Oświęcim has for Poles and for a discussion of recent trends at the museum, see Zubrzycki (2006:chap. 3). On the respective meanings of Auschwitz and Oświęcim, see also Goban-Klas (1995), Huener (2003), Kucia (2001), Novick (2000), Sułek (1998), Tanay (1991), Webber (1992), and Young (1993).

9. For a summary of the Carmelite convent dispute, see Zubrzycki (2006:2–7). For detailed accounts, see Bartoszewski (1991), Głownia and Wilkanowicz (1998), and Rittner and Roth (1991). For a conservative pro-Polish view, see Raina (1991).

10. The "papal cross" was originally erected in the yard of the convent—the so-called gravel pit—to protest the planned relocation of the Carmelite nuns. It was brought there by a local priest and a group of former (Polish Catholic) Auschwitz prisoners. The cross had been part of an altar on the grounds of Birkenau, Auschwitz's sister camp two miles away, where John Paul II celebrated Mass in 1979 during his first,

historic visit to Poland as pontiff, hence the cross's popular name (papal cross). The cross had been dismantled and stored in a local church's basement during the decade between the pope's Mass at Birkenau and the night it appeared in the convent's yard. It was erected at that site without witnesses and without any public or known ritual and ceremony. Although we cannot say with certainty that social actors did not act out of religious motivations, we can say that the practice was also, if not primarily, politically motivated. Indeed, the planting of crosses to sacralize a site, to give it sacred immunity, had been a common practice under communism. Most often, this tactic was used to defend church property, but the symbol was also used as a "protective weapon" against the communist state during protests and rallies. In this case, the erection of the papal cross in the yard of the Carmelite convent was clearly a tactic and form of protest against the planned relocation of the Carmelite nuns.

11. The gravel pit is the fenced area just outside the walls of Auschwitz where the papal cross is and where the hundreds of other crosses were erected in 1998–1999. The area takes its name from its function during World War II. It is also the former Carmelite convent's backyard.

12. Kazimierz Świtoń (b. 1931) organized in 1978 the first Committee of Free Professional Unions in People's Republic of Poland (Komitet Wolnych Związków Zawodowych); he was a member of Solidarity from 1980 to 1989 and a deputy in the Sejm from 1991 to 1993. He participated in several hunger strikes in the late 1970s and throughout the 1980s. His hunger strike in the defense of the papal cross should thus be understood as the continuation of a popular strategy of resistance to the authorities under communism.

13. Approximately 100,000 ethnic Poles were prisoners at Auschwitz, of whom 70,000 were killed. About 1.1 million people died at Auschwitz–Birkenau, 90 percent of whom were Jewish (Piper 1992).

14. The Society of St. Pius X was founded in 1970 by Archbishop Marcel Lefebvre, who refused to submit to the teachings of Vatican II and was excommunicated by John Paul II in 1988 for schism. Its members are commonly referred to, in Polish, as Lefevrists.

15. My focus here is exclusively on the lines of conflict between Poles. For an analysis of the Polish/Christian–Jewish axis of the controversy, see Zubrzycki (2006:chaps. 3 and 5).

16. I was unable to find the origins of these verses, but it is certain that they are part of a well-known hymn that was frequently sung in the 1980s not only in pilgrimages and Masses for the homeland but also during vigils, demonstrations, and strikes (Rogozińska 2002:28).

17. On the divisions within the Polish Catholic Church that were exacerbated by the War of the Crosses, see Zubrzycki (2006:183–199).

18. Of course, even though its ideologues insist on its primordial character, the ethnic nation is nonetheless, like any other form of nation, a social construction. Whereas the civic nation is conceived as a construct, the ethnic nation is conceived of as a given. However, this is not what I am underlining here. Rather, I am pointing out the ideological criteria used by the right in determining one's Polishness and the ten-

sion such criteria entail for the (ideally) ethnically defined nation. For a discussion of ethnic and civic nationalism, see Brubaker (1992), Nielsen (1999), Schnapper (1994), Yack (1996), and Zubrzycki (2001).

19. The American case is the paradigm of ideologically defined national identity, where "being American" means supporting a specific set of values and practices, and therefore where it is possible to be "un-American," say, for supporting communism during McCarthyism or, more recently, for criticizing the Bush administration in the post–September 11 United States. For an analysis of this mechanism, see Lipset (1990).

20. It is very difficult to establish the exact number of Jews in Poland, and estimates vary greatly from one source to another, ranging from 1,055 (2002 Polish Census) to 40,000 (*American Jewish Year Book*). The wide variation in these data depends on how Jewishness is determined: self-declaration in the Census, formal membership in Jewish organizations, or ancestry. The numbers have also steadily grown in the last decade, as better sources became available and as the Jewish community has witnessed a cultural, religious, and institutional renaissance. In 1989 and 1990, the *American Jewish Year Book* estimated the total Jewish population of Poland to be 5,000, of which nearly 2,000 people were registered with Jewish communities. That figure was widely cited in Polish publications throughout the 1990s. During that decade, the total number of Jews in Poland was re-estimated to be closer to 10,000 (*American Jewish Year Book* 1992, 1995). By the beginning of the new millennium, the number of Polish Jews registered with the community, belonging to Jewish organizations, or receiving aid from the American Jewish Joint Distribution Committee had nearly quadrupled, to between 7,000 and 8,000. Between 10,000 and 15,000 people showed interest in rediscovering their Jewish ancestry, and as many as 40,000 Polish citizens are now thought to have some Jewish ancestry (*American Jewish Year Book* 2002, 2003). The numbers cited by Piotr Kadlčik, president of the Jewish community in Warsaw and president of the Union of Jewish communities in Poland, are slightly more conservative. According to him, there are now 4,000 to 6,000 "registered Jews" (people with formal ties to one or more organizations of the Jewish community) and approximately 20,000 to 25,000 Polish citizens of Jewish descent who do not maintain a formal connection to these institutions. For Polish census data, consult http://www.mswia.gov.pl/mn_narod_zydzi.html; for other Polish estimates, see Łodziński (2003:30).

WORKS CITED

Alexander, Jeffrey C. 2002. On the Social Construction of Moral Universals: The "Holocaust" from War Crime to Trauma Drama. *European Journal of Social Theory* 5, no. 1:5–86.

Bartoszewski, Władysław T. 1991. *The Convent at Auschwitz*. New York: Braziller.

Brubaker, Rogers. 1992. *Citizenship and Nationhood in France and Germany*. Cambridge, Mass.: Harvard University Press.

Centrum Badania Opinii Społecznej. 2006. *The Meaning of Religion in the Life of Poles*. Warsaw: CBOS.

Głownia, Marek, and Stefan Wilkanowicz, eds. 1998. *Auschwitz: Konflikty i dialog*. Kraków: Wydawnictwo Św. Stanisława.

Goban-Klas, Tomasz. 1995. Pamięć podzielona, pamięć urażona: Oświęcim i Auschwitz w polskiej i żydowskiej pamięci zbiorowej. In *Europa po Auschwitz*, ed. Zdzisław Mach, 71–91. Kraków: Universitas.

Gross, Jan T. 2006. *Fear: Anti-Semitism in Poland After the Holocaust*. New York: Random House.

Huener, Jonathan. 2003. *Auschwitz, Poland, and the Politics of Commemoration, 1945–1979*. Athens: Ohio University Press.

Jasiewicz, Krzysztof. 2000. Dead Ends and New Beginnings: The Quest for a Procedural Republic in Poland. *Communist and Post-Communist Studies* 33:101–122.

Kucia, Marek. 2001. KL Auschwitz in the Social Consciousness of Poles, A.D. 2000. In *Remembering for the Future: The Holocaust in an Age of Genocide*, ed. John K. Roth and Elisabeth Maxwell, 632–651. New York: Palgrave.

Lipset, Seymour Martin. 1990. *Continental Divide: The Values and Institutions of the United States and Canada*. Washington, D.C.: Canadian-American Committee.

Łodziński, Sławomir. 2003. Dyskryminacja czy nierówność: Problemy dyskryminacji osób należących do mniejszości narodowych i etnicznych w Polsce po 1989 roku. In *Integracja czy dyskryminacja? Polskie wyzwania i dylematy u progu wielokulturowości*, ed. Krystyna Iglicka. Warsaw: Instytut Spraw Publicznych.

Michnik, Adam. 1999. Wystąpienie. In *Kościół polski wobec antysemityzmu, 1989–1999: Rachunek sumienia*, ed. Bohdan Oppenheim, 69–76. Kraków: WAM.

Michowicz, Waldemar. 1988. Problemy mniejszości narodowych. In *Polska Odrodzona, 1918–1939*, ed. Jan Tomicki, 285–321. Warsaw: Wiedza Powszechna.

Nielsen, Kai. 1999. Cultural Nationalism, Neither Ethnic nor Civic. *Philosophical Forum: A Quarterly* 28, no. 1–2:42–52.

Novick, Peter. 2000. *The Holocaust in American Life*. New York: Mariner.

Piper, Franciszek. 1992. *Ilu ludzi zginęło w KL Auschwitz: Liczba ofiar w świetle źródeł i badań, 1945–1990*. Oświęcim: Wydawnictwo Państwowego Muzeum w Oświęcimiu.

Raina, Peter. 1991. *Spór o klasztor sióstr karmelitanek bosych w Oświęcimiu*. Olsztyn: Warmińskie Wydawnictwo Diecezjalne.

Rittner, Carol, and John K. Roth, eds. 1991. *Memory Offended: The Auschwitz Convent Controversy*. New York: Praeger.

Rogozińska, Renata. 2002. *W stronę Golgoty: Inspiracje pasyjne w sztuce polskiej w latach, 1970–1999*. Poznań: Księgarnia Św. Wojciecha.

Schnapper, Dominique. 1994. *La Communauté des citoyens: Sur l'idée moderne de la nation*. Paris: Gallimard.

Seleny, Anna. 1999. Old Political Rationalities and New Democracies: Compromise and Confrontation in Hungary and Poland. *World Politics* 51:484–519.

Stola, Dariusz. 2000. *Kampania antysyjonistyczna w Polsce, 1967–1968*. Warsaw: Instytut Studiów Politycznych Polskiej Akademii Nauk.

Sułek, Antoni. 1998. Wokół Oświęcimia: Spór o krzyże na tle wyobrażeń Polaków o sobie i Żydach. *Więź* (November):61–70.

Tanay, Emanuel. 1991. Auschwitz and Oświęcim: One Location, Two Symbols. In *Memory Offended: The Auschwitz Convent Controversy*, ed. Carol Rittner and John K. Roth, 99–112. New York: Praeger.

Tomaszewski, Jerzy. 1993. The National Question in Poland in the Twentieth Century. In *The National Question in Europe in Historical Context*, ed. Mikulas Teich and Roy Porter, 293–316. Cambridge: Cambridge University Press.

Urban, Jerzy. 1998. *Nie* 35.

Waniek, Danuta, ed. 1991. *Problemy socjologii konstytucji*. Warsaw: Instytut Studiów Politycznych Polskiej Akademii Nauk.

Webber, Jonathan. 1992. *The Future of Auschwitz: Some Personal Reflections*. [First] Frank Green Lecture. Yarnton: Oxford Centre for Postgraduate Hebrew Studies.

Wuthnow, Robert. 1989. *Communities of Discourse: Ideology and Social Structure in the Reformation, the Enlightenment, and European Socialism*. Cambridge, Mass.: Harvard University Press.

Yack, Bernard. 1996. The Myth of the Civic Nation. *Critical Review* 10, no. 2:193–211.

Young, James E. 1993. *The Texture of Memory: Holocaust Memorials and Meaning*. New Haven, Conn.: Yale University Press.

Zubrzycki, Geneviève. 2001. "We, the Polish Nation": Ethnic and Civic Visions of Nationhood in Post-Communist Constitutional Debates. *Theory and Society* 30, no. 5:629–669.

Zubrzycki, Geneviève. 2004. The Broken Monolith: The Catholic Church and the "War of the Crosses at Auschwitz" (1998–99). In *Religion und Nation: Beiträge zu einer unbewältigten Geschichte/Nation and Religion: An Unfinished History*, ed. Michael Geyer and Hartmut Lehmann, 176–204. Göttingen: Wallstein-Verlag.

Zubrzycki, Geneviève. 2005. "Poles–Catholics" and "Symbolic Jews": Jewishness as Social Closure in Poland. In *Studies in Contemporary Jewry*. Vol. 21, *Jews, Catholics, and the Burden of History*, ed. Eli Lederhendler, 65–87. New York: Oxford University Press.

Zubrzycki, Geneviève. 2006. *The Crosses of Auschwitz: Nationalism and Religion in Post-Communist Poland*. Chicago: University of Chicago Press.

12. THE CURIOUS ATTRACTION OF RELIGION IN EAST GERMAN PRISONS

IRENE BECCI

At the margins of a small town in Brandenburg, the region surrounding Berlin, there is a prison with a bloody past.[1] It is a recent building, constructed in the early days of the Nazi regime as one of the most modern prisons in Europe, meant to hold about 1,800 inmates. During the war, it was occupied by about three times as many people. They were mostly exploited to build weapons. Thousands of inmates were executed in this prison during the war, and hundreds died of diseases (Wachsmann 2004). The German Democratic Republic (GDR) uncannily continued to use the building as a prison. In the early 1950s, about 3,000 people were imprisoned here, in many cases for political reasons. Just before entering the building, one still passes by two landmarks of the Socialist era: a "house of culture,"[2] named after a socialist hero who was executed there in 1944, and a Soviet tank serving as a reminder of the Red Army troops who fought against Nazism in the area.

In the immediate aftermath of the fall of the Berlin Wall, the inmates of this prison moved from a meeting in the chaplaincy to occupy the roofs, eventually striking for general amnesty.[3] Still in operation today, the prison keeps about 850 inmates in various sections (e.g., high security, pretrial detention, open detention). When I first visited the prison in 2003 I was impressed by the grayness of the building and its visible security system. I had long conversations with the Catholic chaplain,[4] who had been providing spiritual care in the prison since the 1980s and who had played a major role in mediating the strikes. Once, when asking him about his impression of the role of spirituality in prison, I wondered whether inmates were more religious than the people outside. I knew that the Brandenburg population kept its distance from religious involvement. The loud public resistance to the introduction of Christian teaching as a compulsory school subject after unification was only one example illustrating the secular and areligious mood among the population.[5]

The chaplain's answer to my question was straightforward: "Yes, one can say that. . . . I would say," he went on, "that here the religious question is much clearer. Outside, it is put aside by the load of work or by TV or by drinking beer; here it manifests itself. Well, I would say the religious question can here be seen very well and some experience it extremely intensively."[6]

To underpin his impression, he added that in this huge prison, where he had regular contact with hundreds of inmates, he knew "at least five or six inmates who read the Bible three to four hours every day. I know two inmates" he continued, "who are strongly involved in religion, one in the Orthodox religion, the other reads a lot of literature from the Pentecostal movement. He wants to become a preacher in a Pentecostal church one day."

It may seem strange to many readers that the existence of a few religiously active inmates out of several hundreds can be interpreted as a sign of religious vitality. And yet, in the particular context of eastern Germany,[7] such a claim makes perfect sense. In order to see how, let us take a few steps back in time.

RELIGION AND THE SOCIALIST HERITAGE IN EASTERN GERMANY

The religious history of the area that is today eastern Germany is long and rich. Some diversity existed within Christianity since its instantiation as the main religious denomination of the population and without it, notably through the early presence of Jewish communities. The Reformation (Martin Luther lived in this very area) lessened the pervasiveness of the ecclesiastical hold on people[8] and allowed the emergence of a large number of Protestant denominations. Religious conflicts and even wars between denominations—basically between Lutherans, Calvinists, and Catholics—have since then contributed to define German history. In 1555 religion was territorialized following the principle of *cujus regio ejus religio*, which organized religious diversity on a civil level by linking political and religious authorities. The different Protestant denominations, such as Pietism and Janseism, deeply shaped German modernity by promulgating and practicing such values as education and philanthropy. The Weimar Republic then introduced religious freedom for all citizens and abolished any state church. Despite the regular violent attacks and persecutions against Jews since the Middle Ages, Jewish culture continued to live and intermingled deeply into German modernity, especially in its cosmopolitanism, until Nazism. As in many European countries before and after World War II, local political and ecclesiastical authorities were strongly linked, making the Christian orientation of state institutions thereby "natural," in the sense theorized in Winnifred Fallers Sullivan (chap. 3, this volume).[9] As Geneviève Zubrzycki argues for the case of Poland (chap. 11, this volume), postsocialist countries illustrate clearly the artificiality of this process of naturalization.

At the end of World War II, the occupation of eastern Germany by Soviet troops and the western part by the Allied forces split the country also at a religious level. In the West, the majority of the population was Catholic, and its economy favored immigration from Turkey on a large scale. In the East, most remaining Germans had a Protestant affiliation, except those living in the Catholic enclaves in Saxony and Thuringia. For more than forty years, a socialist–atheistically oriented government marginalized religion and to some extent repressed religious activities. Socialist ideology had to reunite all people, whatever their cultural and religious background. The ideology had to supplant any other transcendental worldview and cultural practice. Socialism has changed the religious landscape of eastern Germany in a spectacular way. Church membership rates in the region steadily and drastically declined, as table 12.1 shows. After unification, religious participation rates did not rise, nor did they remain the same, as happened in post-Soviet Poland. Likewise, according to regular surveys, nontraditional religiosity, such as New Age practices, has not taken hold among East Germans.

TABLE 12.1 Religious Affiliations

	GDR[a]		Eastern Germany	
	1949	1989	1997[b]	2004[c]
Protestant	80.5%	25%	21.5%	20%
Roman Catholic	11%	4–5%	4.9%	4.8%
Other religious affiliation	<1%	<1%[d]	Ca. 2.5%	Ca. 2%
No religious affiliation	7.6%	70%	Ca. 67%	Ca. 70%

[a]Pollack (1994:373–424).
[b]Knippenberg (2005:67).
[c]Landesbetriebe für Datenverarbeitung und Statistik Land Brandenburg (2005:582–583).
[d]Ramet (1998:56).

The religious plurality brought into western Germany by immigrants has no correlate in eastern Germany. The socialist government controlled immigration tightly. Most of the immigrants were actually invited to perform specific technical tasks within the broader picture of collaboration between socialist countries, and they could not settle in the GDR because their families were left behind and their length of stay was limited. The greatest challenge the socialist regime had to face came from the large number of East Germans who wanted to leave the Republic. To do so without permission was considered a crime. When the wall fell, the exit wave continued, with the exceptions of some cities and towns such as Berlin and Dresden. At the end of 2007, about 2.4 percent of the people in eastern Germany were "non-Germans."[10] Unlike the rest of the population, most of these "non-Germans" are affiliated with one religion, most often with the Orthodox Church, Buddhism, or an Islamic community. The total percentage of "other" religions remains very low, however; only in larger towns, particularly in Saxony and in Berlin, are there a few mosques or pagodas. Unlike in western Germany, where more than 70 percent of the population is affiliated with Christian churches, in the East the religious norm is "non-belonging."[11] Although there was no change at this level, religion underwent a radical transformation at two other levels after 1989: an institutional level and a social and political one.

First, although state–church relations were very tense since the beginning of the socialist era and even more so after a strict separation between church and state was instituted in 1968, with unification the separation was transformed into a "limping" one (Mangoldt 1997:83), as it is in western Germany. Pressure on the churches was removed, and collaboration with the state encouraged the accomplishment of common tasks. Several Christian holy days were restored as state holidays, and church-related organizations received a privileged status to shape and implement welfare and social service programs (Becci 2008). With regional variations, today "the different Protestant land churches, plus some Orthodox ones, and the Roman Catholic Church, are bodies defined by the public law" (Aires 2004:109). This legal recognition had an indisputable impact on the churches' public role and their social perception. A large number of East Germans could no longer see in the church a potential ally against the injustices coming from state actors. Rather, they started to associate the church with the capitalist Western world. However, some East German religious actors tried to reaffirm their own understanding of the churches' social role, and where possible they rejected many privileges in order to show their distance from the state: For instance, prison chaplains in eastern Germany stand under the authority of the church, although they are paid by the state ministry, whereas in western Germany they are often state employees in all regards.

The motivations behind this attitude become clear if one considers the changes that occurred at the level of the churches' political role in society. During the GDR and especially during its breakdown, religion had a crucial political importance for civil activists (Neubert 2000). Although the Socialist Unity Party closely controlled high-ranking church authorities, the local parishes hosted social movements. This church-based, often urban opposition occupied a large number of political fields, such as international politics (peace, NATO, civil service), ecological concerns (pollution, nuclear energy), gender issues (abortion, homosexuality), and human rights (political prisoners, freedom of speech and of movement). Christian Joppke (1995:83) argues that opposition "was tolerated as long as it remained within the church, but it faced stiff persecution as soon as it stepped outside the church." However, the repression often continued within church groups as well: Infiltrations, bureaucratic harassment, and manipulations were common, as was discrimination against Christians in education and work. Still, the churches were the only places where some free cultural activity was allowed, and church groups increasingly became very active in mobilizing around the issue of political prisoners. When the wall was opened, however, numerous members of peace and environmental groups, who used the church for their meetings and political mobilization, abandoned any religious involvement.

All these developments have led to a unique situation. In terms of religious practice and affiliation, today East German society is among the most secularized and areligious ones in Europe. Today, most East Germans have not belonged to any religious community for generations. Yet at the level of state institutions, the established churches have a privileged status. What impact does this have on the prison institution and its relation to religion?

RELIGIOUS PLURALITY IN EAST GERMAN PRISONS

In my numerous and repeated visits to different prisons in eastern Germany, I observed that inside, unlike the outside society, religion holds an important place. For example, when accompanied by a chaplain or by volunteers working with the chaplaincy, I was controlled much less than when I was a regular visitor. It was not rare to see Catholic nuns enter or leave the building. The rooms of the chaplaincy were well marked and usually spacious and nicely decorated. Often I saw tattoos of crosses on many prisoners' arms and legs, which according to them symbolized death. The prison libraries held a large range of religious and esoteric books. I also visited some cells, where inmates had Buddha statues, rugs for their prayers to Allah, Orthodox icons, or posters quoting biblical verses on the walls. Religious services were attended by a large number of inmates, although many of them showed interest in conversation with their fellow inmates. All these observations stand in sharp contrast to the outside world, where churches, the only visible religious signs in the landscape, are usually empty and poorly equipped; most of the time, they are used for concerts and arts exhibitions.

Some of the interviewed inmates who were regularly involved in religious activity—more than half of all those I interviewed—clearly stated that their level of religious practice had increased in prison compared to the outside, where they "didn't go to church as often."[12] Others had never had any religious practice at all before being imprisoned. Religious categories were used in hybrid ways to label others and oneself; for example, one inmate considered himself Jewish–Christian.

For chaplains, the greater interest in religion that inmates manifest is strongly connected to the specific context of the institution. A prison chaplain in Saxony[13] told me that he actually perceived the change not so much in terms of increased religiosity; rather, he said that inmates are "more direct, more accessible and in some way also self-conscious." As an example he told about some inmates' reaction to his sermons. They challenged him with sentences such as "That's not true what you're saying about the good Jesus. I don't buy that." He went on to say that no member of his parish outside would ever question so directly what he says.

Inmates indicated a wide range of reasons why their religiosity had increased after they entered prison. Some of the narratives tell of a profound conversion, others stress the fact that religious practice in prison is one of the few possible ways to spend time in a fruitful way. They would then explain their recourse to religion by pointing to the lack of alternative activities offered to help with rehabilitation. There were also inmates who affirmed that they went to see the chaplain only to receive tobacco or a slice of cake. In any case, it seemed that the distance from religion that most East Germans had learned during their socialization was suspended in prison. Their relationship to religion in prison appeared easier and more intense than that outside.

This finding raises the question of how such a relationship is embedded in the very specific context of East German prisons. This question is particularly salient because in eastern Germany today, there is a numerical overrepresentation of "non-Germans" in prison.[14] In the prisons of Brandenburg, the percentage of inmates having nationalities other than German stood at around 17 percent in 2005, which is about ten times higher than their proportion of the wider society. According to estimates made by chaplains, the majority of the non-German inmate population is Polish, Algerian, Russian, Romanian, or

Vietnamese.[15] As a consequence, religious affiliations are more numerous and more diverse in prison than outside.[16]

In what follows, I shall document how the relationship to religion in prison can be framed by using Erving Goffman's concept of total institution in a critically revised form. These two steps shall lead to some theoretical elaborations based on Michel Foucault's idea of pastoral power. Interestingly, in "secular" prisons, East German states are confronted by religion in a more intense and diverse way than in any other institution, or even simply in society. How, I therefore ask, is chaplaincy and spiritual care more generally organized currently in East German prisons? And to what extent does its organization take this religious plurality and intensity into consideration?

PRISON CHAPLAINCY: RELIGION IN A TOTAL INSTITUTION

As a consequence of the general reestablishment of the churches, today chaplaincy has a central and affirmed role to play in East German prisons. During socialism the presence of chaplains in prison was informal, minimal, or very dubious.[17] Officially religious freedom was guaranteed to prisoners, but in practice very few party-loyal chaplains were allowed periodically to celebrate—under strict surveillance—religious services in prison. Today, they are recognized as fully integrated into prison life. As a matter of fact, in every East German prison the presence of at least one Protestant and one Catholic chaplain, as well as one church or chapel, is legally guaranteed. Christian chaplains are the only permanent employees as far as religious matters are concerned. They have their own office in the prison building, can move freely, and are protected by the right to keep their conversation with inmates confidential. The state directly or indirectly contributes to their salary, but, as indicated earlier, they are under the authority of the church. Chaplains have to be treated as colleagues by staff members (Eick-Wildgans 1993:182), and they are responsible for the spiritual life of the whole institution, that is, for inmates and staff. They are the only religious actors participating in the committee that makes decisions about the treatment of individual prisoners.

Prison authorities consider inmates' participation in the activities organized by chaplains to promote rehabilitation. However, this is not necessarily the case for those who exercise their right to religious freedom independently from chaplaincy. According to the new German prison law, no matter which religion they belong to, inmates have today the right to spiritual care, to participate at religious services, and to possess religious writings and objects.[18] The right to follow religious dietary rules is granted, but the prison establishment has no obligation to cook particular meals if there is another way (a self-organized cooking area in a prison unit, for instance) for the inmates to obtain them. Legally, all recognized religious communities are allowed to provide spiritual assistance in prison, and since 1990, smaller religious groups, such as Adventists, Baptists, and Buddhists, have been recognized as public corporations. According to the law, a recognized religious community should communicate the names of its representatives to prison administrators, who then contact them and give them access to the prison if inmates request spiritual assistance. In practice, such requests entail bureaucratic procedures that have a dissuasive effect on religious communities and inmates. As a consequence, inmates who are religiously active either use the chaplaincy or organize autonomously.

How does this new setting influence the relationship to religion, or do inmates and staff use the new privileges linked to religion for other purposes? What effect do these privileges have on the power configurations in prison? In order to problematize these questions and to further my analysis of particular cases, I adapt Erving Goffman's theory of total institutions to come up with a revised set of characteristics of total institutions. This shall allow me to make clear what is specific about religion in prison compared with the outside. After this description, I propose a critical reevaluation of the relationship to prison chaplains on the basis of Michel Foucault's idea of pastoral power.

In *Asylums*, Erving Goffman (1991) counts prisons as total institutions. His definition is quite inclusive, referring in particular to the fact that in such organizations, all "aspects of life are conducted in the same place and under the same single authority"; each "phase of the member's daily activity is carried on in the immediate company of a large batch of others, all of whom are treated alike and required to do the same thing together"; and all activities make sense within the proclaimed aim of the institution (Goffman 1991:17). This definition points to space ("in the same place") and time ("phase of . . . daily activity"). Moreover, Goffman (1991:104) argues that total institutions encourage "the assumption that staff and inmate are of profoundly different human types."

Scholars inspired by Goffman have identified additional characteristics in their study of prisons in terms of total institutions (McEwen 1980). For my purposes, the most important of these is that high barriers to social intercourse with the outside are erected. As Goffman writes, total institutions can be distinguished according to the aim they proclaim and according to which they are organized. Prisons are places of coercion, punishment, rehabilitation, and control.

To sum up, we shall keep in mind the specificity of prisons in terms of space and time, the strict distinction within prisons between staff and inmates, their contact with the outside, and their aim. A consideration of how chaplaincy is situated in prison with regard to these aspects in eastern Germany shall allow us to locate, more generally, the role of religion for both inmates and the prison administration.

SPACE

The space in prison is scrupulously subdivided so as to allow the most efficient accomplishment of specific activities, such as cells to sleep, courtyards to walk, corridors to link units, shower areas, library, and chaplaincy. Inmates depend on the staff for all their movements; they do not possess any keys, and all doors and gates are locked. Each time I visited a prison I had to enter at least ten thick doors and gates to get to the room where I was heading, and each door had to be opened and closed again by a guardian accompanying me. The physical restriction on movement entails also a psychological dependency. Inmates learn that they have to wait and obey and that they receive what they need only bit by bit. These experiences of prison space forge what Alison Liebling and Helen Arnold (2004:165) call "symbolic and significant constructions of the state's relationship with the individual." According to the interviewed inmates, in prison they learn blind obedience instead of autonomy, responsibility, and critical judgment.

Chaplains and their chaplaincies disrupt the scrupulous spatial organization of prisons. Whereas all other rooms look the same, those for the chaplaincy often appear as an oasis; they are carefully decorated (with flowers, plants, colorful pictures, and candles) and transmit a feeling of welcome (the smell of coffee and cookies) and harmony (smiling people). Unlike most prison officers, who have a limited number of keys, chaplains have keys for most of the doors and gates in prison and in many cases also the doors of inmates' individual cells. This permits them to follow inmates in every kind of situation (high-security cells for example) and to meet them in private (by meeting them in their cells or taking them individually to their office). Inmates see the chaplain as not having any spatial obstacle in prison, which makes him very attractive to them. An inmate expressed this idea in a nutshell by saying that the chaplain, contrary to others, "takes us out of the cell from time to time" (*holt uns mal aus der Zelle raus* [my translation]). Under these circumstances chaplaincy offers the possibility to escape from daily routine, from the regulations, and from isolation.

Chaplains also open up space insofar as they help inmates obtain prison leaves, giving them the possibility, on special occasions, to get out of the prison for one day (e.g., when a relative dies). This capacity to reach out of the institution has a huge importance for inmates, who often ask chaplains to help them in working out their relationships to family and friends living in the outer society.

The chaplaincy also appears as a place where spatial restrictions can be broken in terms of sociability within the prison. For example, often it is possible through the chaplaincy to meet other inmates whom one is not allowed to meet according to the rules of the institution. The inmates know that the chaplain will not ask about exactly what happens during such a meeting. There is an implicit agreement not to ask as long as everything is kept quiet and order is maintained. To summarize, by smoothly disrupting the organization of space in prison, chaplains stand out as distinctive figures. A short look at the cadence of prison time leads to a similar conclusion, as I shall demonstrate.

TIME

For Pierre Bourdieu (2000:206–245), mastering the time of others is a sign of power. Absolute power is in the hands of those whose actions are in no way predictable by others and who own their, and others', time. Waiting for someone else's permission to use one's own time means being subordinated. In prison, time is totally mastered by the administration.[19] The authorities decide how the days and the hours are structured. Moreover, in many cases, the actual length of the sentence can be changed without plausible reasons. Therefore inmates develop a great sense of dependency in regard to time while also profoundly experiencing its arbitrariness. Time in prison also means repetition, routine, and monotony. Visitors bring relief, but they are very rare. One further particularity of prisons is that the unemployment rate is extremely high. Working is compulsory in German prisons, but on average only about 20 percent of the detained population works.[20] Nonworking inmates have almost unlimited spare time.

It seems misleading to argue—as many do—that inmates start practicing religion in prison just because they have time to do so. On the contrary, in order to understand properly the recourse to religion, I suggest linking the question of time in prison to that of identity. Religion has its own rhythm during a day (prayers), a week (religious services), or a year (religious holidays); thus it connects the inmate to an imagined community that exists outside prison and that lives according to a different time than that of the prison. The religious rhythm interrupts the bureaucratic routine of prison, it particularizes inmates out of an undifferentiated human mass and links them to another world.

In prison the presence of chaplains is regular, their help is immediate, and the relationship to them can be long term. Chaplains have no serious temporal obstacles; they are almost always there to help. Some chaplains follow the inmates they care for to the various institutions in which they are incarcerated. This way, they create strong and long-lasting personal ties with the inmates. Most convicts have experienced relational interruptions their whole life, because of their various incarcerations or because of forced or chosen clandestineness, as is the case in particular for illegal immigrants. Under such conditions a long-term perspective gains particular importance. The chaplains' intervention appears as lasting also because their action is not seen as that of a single person but rather of an institution. Inmates realize that the offer coming from the chaplaincy is supported by the church, which stands as a backbone for the chaplains' action. This allows chaplains to offer support to inmates even after they are released. The chaplain thus appears as a person one can count on. This reliability distinguishes the chaplaincy from other services offered in prison. It is a definite advantage and creates the conditions for chaplains to have a more intimate dialogue with inmates.

Chaplains also organize special initiatives for Christian holidays, such as Easter and Christmas. They usually offer a parcel to all inmates on these occasions.[21] Catholic chaplains also celebrate minor dates on the ecclesiastical calendar, such as prayers for Mary. Observing these rituals at the same time as the whole Catholic community fosters a synchronic link between inmates and the Church community and alludes to the belonging of the prisoners to a larger community, here that of the Catholic Church. The creation of links between otherwise separated units has a strong symbolic value that can also be observed in the established distinctions between staff and inmates.

THE DISTINCTION BETWEEN STAFF AND INMATES

According to Goffman, the smooth functioning of a total institution is based on the most fundamental and strict distinction between staff and inmates. What Goffman did not consider, however, were intermediate figures, such as chaplains. As I alluded to earlier, in East German prisons, chaplains can be clearly distinguished from the staff and inmates. Chaplains' margins of liberty stand in strong contrast to those of other staff members. Unlike staff, the chaplains do not give orders, nor do they oblige anybody. They give hints and suggestions, offer space for emotions, and seek consensus. Chaplains not only are different from staff; they also bridge the cleavages between staff and inmates. As mentioned, according to new regulations, not only is the chaplain responsible for the spiritual well-being of all inmates, but he (or she)[22] is also supposed to support staff members spiritually. As a matter of fact, the term prison chaplaincy clearly refers to the institution as a whole and not to the inmates. To see how this bridging works, consider the case of prison bureaucracy. Commonly, if a prisoner makes a request—such as seeking a visit from a minister of his faith or asking for a prayer rug—he has to do it in writing and follow a strict and lengthy procedure. An answer usually takes at least a week, and further authorizations are required. During this time, the inmate may have contact only with the guards, who channel the requests and the answers. Chaplains are able to reduce such bureaucratic obstacles; for instance, they invite representatives of other religions to meetings of the chaplaincy or provide rugs for pious Muslim inmates without going through all the bureaucratic steps. By doing so, they often prevent potential conflicts between staff and inmates. One reason why it is easier for some chaplains to break bureaucratic barriers is because their relationship to the administration is based on reciprocal recognition and respect. For instance, attendance at the Sunday service (which is higher than outside the prison) does not require any complicated written request. The services are in some cases (mostly in smaller prisons) also free of direct supervision by officers and offer the possibility for chaplains to reach a wide range of people.

Chaplaincy also appears as a protected place, a place of trust, and probably the only place in prison to offer inmates authentic relationships. As inmates recount, when they meet the chaplain, they feel free to talk about whatever they want and do not need to struggle to be taken seriously. Inmates related that in their experience of being accused, tried, and imprisoned, they went through many situations in which they were not believed. Their word had to be proved systematically. Therefore, for them to be simply believed by the chaplain has a huge symbolic and emotional importance. One element that puts chaplains in a position of trust, according to inmates, is precisely that they are perceived as being detached from the prison staff, as standing outside or beyond the prison system. The chaplains themselves greatly contribute to creating an understanding of themselves as exterior to the power relation between inmates and the prison institution, as providers of universal care. In eastern Germany, where religious affiliation, participation, and knowledge have been very low for generations, the confessional character of chaplaincy has become quite irrelevant for chaplains. What is at stake for chaplains is almost never a confessional issue; rather, the question of trust as a universal human need plays a crucial role.

CONTACT WITH THE OUTSIDE

Although prison is a closed institution, there are many ways to create contact with the outside world. One way is through the people who enter prison on a daily basis. However, prison staff are clearly in a power relation (be it control or diagnosis) with inmates. Outside any power relation there are family members, friends, and volunteers—often invited by the chaplains—who come to visit inmates or sing at religious services. For inmates, the closer the place of incarceration is to one's home, the more visits are likely. Obviously, recently immigrated inmates receive fewer visits and therefore are more isolated. Moreover, when inmates are moved frequently from one prison to another (this is used as a strategy to break existing inmate networks), keeping regular contact with the outside is almost impossible. Less personal windows to the outside world are mass media, which reflect and reinforce prejudices (including religious prejudices). In general, inmates are overexposed (compared with people on the outside) to television and radio. Almost every cell has a television or radio, and in most cases it is switched on all day. The role of mass media, particularly television, in prison is amplified by the totality of the institution: Inmates are not able to confront the impressions gained through television with other media sources or with people who have other sources of information. Newspapers are also a source of information about the outside. Some inmates can subscribe to a newspaper, but this is rarely the case with non–German-speaking inmates, for whom foreign newspapers are a luxury. Chaplains are often the main source of foreign newspapers.

Chaplains are allowed to bring some material into the prison. They provide inmates with all sorts of objects and services they need but cannot otherwise get in prison because they don't have the money or the authorization: tobacco, coffee, books, socks, underwear, trousers, stamps, or the ability to make a telephone call, send a fax, or repair clothes. Some goods and services are available only through the chaplains.

Most chaplains are very active politically outside prison on issues of incarceration. They present papers at conferences,[23] relate their experiences, and publish articles in ecclesiastical newspapers and political publications.

From its intermediate position, and thanks to its many advantages, chaplaincy has come to symbolize a space of freedom for inmates in a wide range of aspects. Engaging with the chaplaincy allows inmates to reach out of prison discursively, materially, spatially, temporally, and relationally.

REHABILITATION AND CONTROL

As we have seen, the relationship to the chaplain is primarily a relationship of trust. Not only do inmates trust the chaplains, but chaplains are also on good terms with the prison administration. The peculiar character of this relationship can be theorized, by using a Foucaultian framework, as a pastoral relationship in which pastoral power is at work.

It is very important to be aware of the question of power because the Goffmanian approach actually referred to an ideal type of total institution. When it comes to the study of a concrete prison setting, one should be careful not to assume that prisons function perfectly according to their formal organization. Rather, the opposite is often the case, as Donald Clemmer demonstrated in his study *The Prison Community* (1940). As the title of his book indicates, he observed a community in prison. According to him, the imprisoned create their own cultural life; it is not completely determined by the disciplinary setting of the institution. Some resist the all-encompassing power of the prison by using their social and cultural capital, to use Bourdieu's (1979) vocabulary, whereas others organize themselves along class distinctions, prison experience, type of crime, and other distinctions. The total control at which the administration aims is rarely possible; incidents are not isolated or rare events but a commonplace. Moreover, because modern prisons discursively aim at rehabilitating, that is, at reconciling criminals with society, it is necessary for them to influence not only the body but also the mind of the detained. When it comes to the mind, religion certainly plays a crucial role, and so do the religious actors who mediate religious care. For Foucault, care is always connected to power, and this is why pastoral care and pastoral power are the two sides of the same coin.

Michel Foucault (2007:123) argued that the pastorate developed first in the East, "in a pre-Christian East . . . Mediterranean East." There, pastors used to guide a "flock," to watch over it "and avoid the misfortune that may threaten the least of its members" (Foucault 2007:127). They used to protect and feed the whole community and were ready to even sacrifice themselves in order to ensure individual salvation.[24] They would favor harmony among the members on the way and gain their allegiance not by threatening, scaring, terrorizing, or forcing them but by dedicating care and attention to every single one (Foucault 2000:303). They would therefore know all members intimately and personally by "exploring their souls" (Foucault 1983:214). According to Foucault (2007:128), this form of power is individualizing, unlike massifying forms of power—which were typical in ancient Greece—because the pastor convinces every member of the flock individually, with personalized arguments. He follows every single individual throughout life. The relationship the pastor constructs with the single individual is therefore moral and complex, because it aims at persuading him, and hence at finding a consensus (Foucault 2007:128). For the pastor, within the flock harmony must prevail over antagonism or competition. Foucault writes that this form of power "was introduced into the Western world by way of the Christian Church" (Foucault 2007:129). For centuries it was confined to the ecclesiastical organization, but with the emergence of "the state in the modern sense of the word" (Foucault 2000:313), this form of power was extended to various nonreligious institutions. With the rise of the welfare system, it smoothly became a common practice in state structures, such as prisons. His role of mediator, his constant presence and discretion put the chaplain in a clear position of pastoral power.

In prisons, rehabilitation stands in for salvation; however, because the coercive power of the state is so obvious, pastoral power cannot be exercised by a state actor but only by chaplains. More than any other staff member, chaplains have a certain power over inmates' minds, and this power is identified and cherished by the staff. The pastoral power of chaplains is particularly attractive to those who seek to control inmates, where, as Clemmer wrote, total control is very difficult. In a certain way, prison administration seems to depend on the action of chaplains to harmonize prison life. For instance, chaplains are often called to intervene in the most painful moments, such as after a fight or an attempted suicide. The chaplains' influence on inmates is certainly pivotal in terms of preventing destructive situations, whoever the victim is. According to some convicts' narratives, in the chaplaincy they learned to focus on ideas that are nonviolent, or do not lead to illegality, and to master self-control. A perhaps unintended consequence of this action is that chaplaincy finally contributes to "stabilizing the total institution" (Günther 2005:322).

My impression is that chaplains are absolutely aware of this risk, and in response they attempt in many different situations to push the limits set by the institution further and further. For its part, the administration keeps constant pressure on chaplains to gain their collaboration and appropriate their knowledge. The administration appears to be trying out all sorts of possibilities to reach the particular knowledge that the chaplain has accumulated through his experience and proximity with inmates, as it actually used to be with pastors more generally during the GDR. This could be part of the reason why being in prison was "the continuation of the GDR on a smaller scale" (*die Fortsetzung der DDR auf engerem Raum* [my translation]), as one inmate stated during a group meeting in the chaplaincy, provoking a round of laughter from the other detainees.

On one hand, chaplains rely heavily on the institutional position they have thanks to the establishment of their church; on the other, they act as people who can face inmates independently from the administration and who are able to use their personal space to resist the submission of their position to the disciplining power of the prison administration. For representatives of other religions, entering prison only sporadically for their visits, it is impossible to fulfill such a function.

In sum, chaplaincy strengthens inmates' capacity to get through the prison experience without seriously criticizing why such an experience is so devastating at a structural level. Rather, it encourages inmates to face their crimes individually and take responsibility. For the prison administration, chaplaincy is a good way to shape inmates in accordance with prison requirements. This does not mean that the commitment of chaplains and inmates is not authentic or that the figure of the chaplain is not appreciated. On the contrary, because self-control, human relations, contact with the outside, and trust are crucial for prisoners' rehabilitation, chaplaincy becomes a felt source of support, whatever one's religious affiliation is.

Interestingly, some religious pluralism is experienced and develops in a lively way despite institutional attempts to control and contain religion in prison. As mentioned earlier, prisons seem to produce religious changes. In some cases the change can cause a real, profound, and lasting conversion. Inmates whose religiousness has not been touched by the experience of detention are in the minority among those I met. In prison, they show a greater openness toward religion, a certain curiosity. Religion is a common topic of discussion among inmates, and comradeship develops, often across confessional and religious boundaries. Apparently religion, in its institutionalized form, attracts the curiosity of the generally nonreligious East Germans once they are imprisoned.

CONCLUSION

The question of religious pluralism in eastern Germany is particularly interesting because its society has reached a unique level of secularization. The recent change in religion that occurred with the political turn of 1989 is a good opportunity to follow closely the introduction of prescriptive discourses on religion. Since then, despite the high level of secularization among the population, state-run institutions have been reconstructed on the basis of the anthropological assumption that religious needs are universal and that they can best be cared for by the established religions. In prison, this means that Christian chaplaincy receives important privileges in terms of freedom of action and intervention, but chaplaincy also remains in the hands of the established religions. The official chaplaincy dominated by Protestant and Catholic chaplains appears as very inclusive and it is actually supposed to take care of inmates of all religions. Through institutional arrangements, chaplaincy now has a confirmed structural position that opens up a large freedom for chaplains but also puts them in a relation of pastoral power that attracts the administration. During socialism and its breakdown, East German chaplains experienced religion as a source for resistance against the state but also as a realm in which the state could infringe on people's personal lives. Although the prison institution attempts to control the religious lives of inmates, it reaches its limits when meeting the hybrid and plural forms of religious engagement that actually take place in prison. Despite this control, religion seems to open up a space in prison where control is difficult, where a certain vitality can develop, and where inmates partly experience what rehabilitation could mean.

NOTES

1. In 2003 I carried out part of my fieldwork in different prisons in Brandenburg, Berlin, and Saxony as a doctoral student of the European University Institute. In 2006–2007 I came back to East Berlin and Saxony-Anhalt with a project on former inmates as a postdoctoral fellow of the Max-Planck Institute of Social Anthropology. In 2003–2004 I participated in group meetings of the prison chaplaincy and interviewed sixteen inmates, thirteen chaplains, and two prison wardens. Two chaplains were women, and all other interviewees were men. All interviews were transcribed verbatim and coded partly on the basis of the questionnaire, partly in vivo, following the ideas of the grounded theory paradigm. More details about the results and analyses can be found in my dissertation (Becci 2006).

2. These cultural centers were managed by state authority and existed in all urban areas and major settlements in the GDR and in all socialist countries.

3. The occupation of the prison roofs as a tactic to force prison authorities to listen to prisoners' demands was adopted in different East German prisons around 1990. See Arnold (1995).

4. Three chaplains work in this prison, two Protestants and one Catholic.

5. The compromise was to create an inclusive subject called "life-conduct, ethics, religion." Only pupils certifying their participation in a parochial teaching can opt out of this compulsory course. For a discussion of this case in light of the reorganization of the church–state relations in eastern Germany, see Becci and Willems (2009).

6. This and the following quotes taken from my interviews are my translation.

7. Since German unification in 1990, social scientists have not yet come to a clear consensus on how to best designate the regions that once formed the GDR and their inhabitants. Some use the expression "new German states" (Neue Bundesländer), thereby actually meaning the regions having from the point of view of East Germans their former names again: Thuringia, Saxony, Saxony-Anhalt, Brandenburg, Mecklenburg, eastern Pomerania, and to some extent Berlin. It is clear that many East Germans find this expression alien, although it makes sense for Westerners. Some sociologists, such as Detlef Pollack and Wolfgang Engler, writing on their own society, do not hesitate to use the expression *East Germans*. As Wolfgang Engler (2002:22) points out, the citizens of the GDR did not call themselves "East Germans." They started to do so only years after the fall of communism. They have created this new

identification by using an existing collective way of thinking and behaving in society. For this reason, today it seems to be one of the most plausible terms used. It has not a nostalgic but a descriptive character. Being East German means having a certain perspective on the world, a perspective enriched by the experience of political and social change.

8. One often-mentioned example is the Protestant reduction of the number of sacraments from seven to two: communion and baptism. See Zylstra (1992).

9. Before Sullivan, Mary Douglas (1986:90) wrote that institutions can "naturalise" what is actually socially constructed, such as "prevailing political values."

10. The expression "non-Germans" is used in official statistics to refer to people registered in Germany but with no German nationality. Most of these people are of Turkish, Italian, or Polish nationality. They were born in Germany and did not apply for German nationality or were born abroad and are living in Germany on a long-term or temporary basis. This percentage is much lower than the average of non-Germans in the whole of Germany, where it stood at about 8.8 percent. Being both eastern and western, Berlin is a unique case, with 14 percent "non-Germans." See http://www.destatis.de/jetspeed/portal/cms/Sites/destatis/Internet/EN/Navigation/Statistics/Bevoelkerung/Bevoelkerungsstand/Bevoelkerungsstand.psml.

11. More on the normality of nonbelonging is in Wohlrab-Sahr and Schmidt (2003).

12. This quote is taken from an interview with an East German inmate, about forty years old, who attended not only the weekly services but also other activities organized by the chaplain.

13. The Saxon prison where he worked was initially built for 200 people at the beginning of the nineteenth century as a house of correction, and it expanded quickly to include a female population. In the nineteenth century about 500 people, criminals as well as simply poor or disabled people, were kept there. At the end of the century, it became a military prison, and during World War II it was the scene of horrible executions. During the GDR, the place was the destination for political prisoners, who were also tortured. In some cases prisoners were killed and buried in mass graves. At the places that were later identified as former mass graves, there is today a memorial. In the last two decades of the GDR, some buildings of this prison were used as a house of work for youth, the so-called Jugendwerkhof. Today it is located in the suburbs of a small town, and it houses about 500 prisoners. It has also a high-security section. The two chaplains working there, one Catholic and one Protestant, have a common room, with a kitchen and a prayer and meeting room. It is located close to the prison library.

14. The national average rate of non-German inmates stands at about 25 percent. Unlike in the wider society, these are more likely to be second-generation residents and illegal immigrants (Federal Criminal Police Office 2003). See also Wacquant (1999).

15. Obviously, there is a significant difference between rural and urban areas. In the largest prison of the country, Tegel in Berlin, about 32 percent of inmates were foreign-born at the end 2006. See http://www.berlin.de/jva-tegel/02_UeberUns/03_Statistische_Angaben/index.html. According to estimates by a member of Entegra, a Berlin association supporting Muslim inmates, in 2000 at least one third of the prisoners in town were Muslims. See http://www.entegra-ev.de.

16. The emergence of religious diversity in prison has drawn the attention of social scientists to spiritual care. For England, Wales, France, and Norway, see Beckford and Gilliat (1998), Beckford et al. (2005), and Furseth (2001).

17. One important and officially appointed chaplain during the GDR is suspected of having collaborated with the state security at the expense of prisoners (Beckmann and Kusch 1994). More than one interviewed inmate shared this suspicion.

18. Inmates have the right to possess objects having a particular moral or affective value for them, as long as they are not of high commercial value. These kinds of limitations, which in themselves sound neutral, can be discriminatory, as one can imagine in the case of persons belonging to the Sikh faith.

19. For a longer analysis of the relationship to time in prison, see Wahidin (2006).

20. See German Prison Act, §§ 41 and 37. The job should correspond to the inmate's skills and be profitable. However, the wage is less than 1 euro per hour. A third of it is put aside and given to the inmate on release. Whenever the possibility to work existed in prison, the work paid much less than the lowest wages outside (usually only 20 percent of it). The law states that if the institution cannot provide enough work for the inmates, they can occupy themselves otherwise. No further specifications are given.

21. This is actually specially legislated by the federal administrative provisions concerning the German Prison Act, § 33.

22. About 17 percent of the Protestant chaplains are women. See http://www.gefaengnisseelsorge.de/personensuche.html. In the case of Catholics, according to the Bundeskonferenz der Katholischen Seelsorgerinnen und Seelsorger im Justizvollzug, the proportion is a little smaller. Female chaplains care for male prisoners, who make up 95 percent of the total inmate population, as well as for female prisoners. The question of religion is different when it comes to female prisoners in regard to both their religious affiliation and the type of religious care they receive (Lösch 1994).

23. For instance, see Friedrich Ebert Stiftung (2002).

24. *Salvation* stands here for the French word *salut*, which conveys both safety and religious salvation.

WORKS CITED

Aires, Wolf. 2004. Germany's Islamic Minority: Some Remarks on Historical and Legal Developments. In *Regulating Religion: Case Studies from Around the Globe*, ed. James Richardson, 103–112. Amsterdam: Kluwer Academic/Plenum.

Arnold, Jörg. 1995. Corrections in the German Democratic Republic: A Field for Research. *British Journal of Criminology* 35, no. 1:81–94.

Becci, Irene. 2006. *Religion and Prison in Modernity: Tensions Between Religious Establishment and Religious Diversity: Italy and Germany*. Florence: European University Institute.

Becci, Irene. 2008. *Collapse and Creation: The Rise and Fall of Religion in East German Offender Rehabilitation Programmes*. Halle Saale: Max Planck Institute for Social Anthropology.

Becci, Irene, and Joachim Willems. 2009. Gefängnisseelsorge in Ostdeutschland im gesellschaftlichen Wandel. *International Journal of Practical Theology* 13:90–120.

Beckford, James. A., and Sophie Gilliat. 1998. *Religion in Prison: Equal Rites in a Multi-Faith Society*. Cambridge: Cambridge University Press.

Beckford, James A., Danièle Joly, and Farhad Khosrokhavar. 2005. *Muslims in Prison: Challenge and Change in Britain and France*. New York: Palgrave Macmillan.

Beckmann, Andreas, and Regina Kusch. 1994. *Gott in Bautzen: Gefangenenseelsorge in der DDR*. Berlin: Links.

Bourdieu, Pierre. 1979. *La Distinction: Critique sociale du jugement*. Paris: Minuit.

Bourdieu, Pierre. 2000. *Pascalian Meditations*. Trans. Richard Nice. Cambridge: Polity.

Clemmer, Donald. 1940. *The Prison Community*. Boston: Christopher.

Douglas, Mary. 1986. *How Institutions Think*. Syracuse, N.Y.: Syracuse University Press.

Eick-Wildgans, Susanne. 1993. *Anstaltseelsorge: Möglichkeiten und Grenzen des Zusammenwirkens von Staat und Kirche im Strafvollzug*. Berlin: Druncker & Humblot.

Engler, Wolfgang. 2002. *Die Ostdeutschen als Avantgarde*. Berlin: Aufbau Verlag.

Federal Criminal Police Office. 2003. *Police Crime Statistics 2003 of the Federal Republic of Germany*. Wiesbaden: Federal Criminal Police Office.

Foucault, Michel. 1983. The Subject and Power. In *Michel Foucault: Beyond Structuralism and Hermeneutics*, ed. Hubert L. Dreyfus and Paul Rabinow, 208–228. Chicago: University of Chicago Press.

Foucault, Michel. 2000. "Omnes et singulatim": Towards a Critique of Political Reason. In *Power*, ed. James D. Faubion, 298–325. Vol. 3 of *Essential Works of Foucault, 1954–1984*. New York: New Press.

Foucault, Michel. 2007. *Security, Territory, Population: Lectures at the Collèges de France, 1977–1978*. Ed. Michel Senellart. Basingstoke: Palgrave Macmillan.

Friedrich Ebert Stiftung. 2002. Forum Berlin, *Gemeinnützige Arbeit statt Knast*.

Furseth, Inger. 2001. *Muslims in Norwegian Prisons and the Defence*. Trondheim: Tapir Akademisk Forlag.

Goffman, Erving. 1991. *Asylums: Essays on the Social Situation of Mental Patients and Other Inmates*. New York: Penguin.

Günther, Ralf. 2005. *Seelsorge auf der Schwelle: Eine linguistische Analyse von Seelsorgegesprächen im Gefängnis*. Göttingen: Vandenhoeck & Ruprecht.

Joppke, Christian. 1995. *East German Dissidents and the Revolution of 1989: Social Movement in a Leninist Regime*. New York: Macmillan.

Knippenberg, Hans, ed. 2005. *The Changing Religious Landscape of Europe*. Amsterdam: Het Spinhuis.

Landesbetrieb für Datenverarbeitung und Statistik Land Brandenburg. 2005. *Statistisches Jahrbuch 2005*. Potsdam: Landesbetrieb für Datenverarbeitung und Statistik.

Liebling, Alison, and Helen Arnold. 2004. *Prisons and Their Moral Performance: A Study of Values, Quality, and Prison Life*. Oxford: Oxford University Press.

Lösch, Manfred, ed. 1994. *Als Mann und Frau, Seelsorgerin und Seelsorger im Gefängnis*. Vol. 3 of *Reader Gefängnis-Seelsorge*. Hannover: Evangelischen Konferenz für Gefängnisseelsorge in Deutschland.

Mangoldt, Hans von. 1997. *Die Verfassungen der neuen Bundesländer: Einführung und synoptische Darstellung; Sachsen, Brandenburg, Sachsen-Anhalt, Mecklenburg-Vorpommern, Thüringen*. Berlin: Duncker & Humblot.

McEwen, C. A. 1980. Continuities in the Study of Total and Nontotal Institutions. *Annual Review of Sociology* 6:85–143.

Neubert, Ehrhart. 2000. *Geschichte der Opposition in der DDR: 1949–1989*. Bonn: Bundeszentrale für Politische Bildung.

Pollack, Detlef. 1994. *Kirche in der Organisationsgesellschaft: Zum Wandel der gesellschaftlichen Lage der evangelischen Kirchen in der DDR*. Stuttgart: Kohlhammer.

Ramet, Sabina P. 1998. *Nihil obstat: Religion, Politics, and Social Change in East-Central Europe and Russia*. Durham, N.C.: Duke University Press.

Wachsmann, Nikolaus. 2004. *Hitler's Prisons: Legal Terror in Nazi Germany*. New Haven, Conn.: Yale University Press.

Wacquant, Loic. 1999. "Suitable Enemies": Foreigners and Immigrants in the Prisons of Europe. *Punishment and Society* 1, no. 2:215–222.

Wahidin, Azrini. 2006. Time and the Prison Experience. *Sociological Research Online* 11, no. 1. http://www.socresonline.org.uk/11/1/wahidin.html.

Wohlrab-Sahr, Monika, and T. Schmidt. 2003. Still the Most Areligious Part of the World: Developments in the Religious Field in Eastern Germany Since 1990. *International Journal of Practical Theology* 7:86–100.

Zylstra, Sape A. 1992. Protestantism: Theology and Politics. In *Protestantism and Politics in Eastern Europe and Russia: The Communist and Postcommunist Eras*, ed. Sabrina Petra Ramet, 11–39. Durham, N.C.: Duke University Press.

SELECTED BIBLIOGRAPHY

Abbott, Andrew. 1995. Things of Boundaries. *Social Research* 62:857–882.

Abu-Lughod, Lila. 2002. Do Muslim Women Really Need Saving? Anthropological Reflections on Cultural Relativism and Its Others. *American Anthropologist* 104:783–790.

Aires, Wolf. 2004. Germany's Islamic Minority: Some Remarks on Historical and Legal Developments." In *Regulating Religion: Case Studies from Around the Globe*, ed. James Richardson, 103–112. New York: Kluwer Academic/Plenum.

Alexander, Jeffrey C. 2002. On the Social Construction of Moral Universals: The "Holocaust" from War Crime to Trauma Drama. *European Journal of Social Theory* 5:5–86.

Ammerman, Nancy. 2005. *Pillars of Faith: American Congregations and Their Partners*. Berkeley: University of California Press.

Asad, Talal. 1993. *Genealogies of Religion: Discipline and Reasons of Power in Christianity and Islam*. Baltimore: Johns Hopkins University Press.

Asad, Talal. 2003a. *Formations of the Secular: Christianity, Islam, Modernity*. Stanford, Calif.: Stanford University Press.

Asad, Talal. 2003b. What Might an Anthropology of Secularism Look Like? In *Formations of the Secular: Christianity, Islam, Modernity*, 21–66. Stanford, Calif.: Stanford University Press.

Ayoub, Mahmoud M. 1990. The Islamic Context of Muslim–Christian Relations. In *Conversion and Continuity: Indigenous Christian Communities in Islamic Lands*,

Eight to Eighteenth Centuries, ed. Michael Gervers and Ramzi Jibran Bikhazi, 461–477. Toronto: Pontifical Institute of Mediaeval Studies.

Baird, Robert J. 2000. Late Secularism. *Social Text* 18:123–136.

Banchoff, Thomas, ed. 2007. *Democracy and the New Religious Pluralism*. New York: Oxford University Press.

Baumann, Martin, and Samuel M. Behloul, eds. 2005. *Religiöser Pluralismus: Empirische Studien und analytische Perspektiven*. Bielefeld: Transcript.

Becci, Irene. 2006. *Religion and Prison in Modernity: Tensions Between Religious Establishment and Religious Diversity: Italy and Germany*. Florence: European University Institute.

Beckford, James A., and Sophie Gilliat. 1998. *Religion in Prison: Equal Rites in a Multi-Faith Society*. Cambridge: Cambridge University Press.

Bender, Courtney. 2010. *The New Metaphysicals: Spirituality and the American Religious Imagination*. Chicago: University of Chicago Press.

Berger, Benjamin L. 2008. The Cultural Limits of Legal Tolerance. *Canadian Journal of Law and Jurisprudence* 21:245–277.

Berger, Peter, Grace Davie, and Effie Fokas. 2008. *Religious America, Secular Europe? A Theme and Variations*. Aldershot: Ashgate.

Bhabha, Homi. 2004. *The Location of Culture*. Routledge Classics Edition. London: Routledge.

Bhargava, Rajeev, ed. 1998. *Secularism and Its Critics*. Delhi: Oxford University Press.

Bial, Henry. 2005. *Acting Jewish: Negotiating Ethnicity on the American Stage and Screen*. Ann Arbor: University of Michigan Press.

Bilgrami, Akeel. 1994. Two Concepts of Secularism. *Yale Journal of Criticism* 7, no. 1:211–227.

Borrows, John. 2008. Living Law on a Living Earth: Aboriginal Religion, Law, and the Constitution. In *Law and Religious Pluralism in Canada*, ed. R. Moon, 161–216. Vancouver: UBC Press.

Bourdieu, Pierre. 1984. *Distinction: A Social Critique of the Judgement of Taste*. Cambridge, Mass.: Harvard University Press.

Bowden, Henry Warner. 1981. *American Indians and Christian Missions*. Chicago: University of Chicago Press.

Bramen, Carrie. 2001. *The Uses of Variety: Modern Americanism and the Quest for National Distinctiveness*. Cambridge, Mass.: Harvard University Press.

Brooks, Vincent. 2006. *You Should See Yourself: Jewish Identity in Post-Modern American Culture*. New Brunswick, N.J.: Rutgers University Press.

Brown, Wendy. 2006. *Regulating Aversion: Tolerance in the Age of Identity and Empire*. Princeton, N.J.: Princeton University Press.

Cadge, Wendy, and Elaine Howard Ecklund. 2007. Immigration and Religion. *Annual Review of Sociology* 33:359–379.

Calhoun, Craig J. 2003. "Belonging" in the Cosmopolitan Imaginary. *Ethnicities* 3, no. 4:531–553.

Calhoun, Craig J. 2007. *Nations Matter: Culture, History, and the Cosmopolitan Dream*. New York: Routledge.

Campbell, David, and Morton Schoolman, eds. 2008. *The New Pluralism: William Connolly and the Contemporary Global Condition*. Durham, N.C.: Duke University Press.

Casanova, José. 1994. *Public Religions in the Modern World*. Chicago: University of Chicago Press.

Chambers, Simone. 2007. How Religion Speaks to the Agnostic: Habermas on the Persistent Value of Religion. *Constellations* 14:210–223.

Connolly, William E. 2005. *Pluralism*. Durham, N.C.: Duke University Press.

Dallmayr, Fred. 1996. *Beyond Orientalism: Essays on Cross-Cultural Encounter*. Albany: State University of New York Press.

Davie, Grace. 2002. *Europe: The Exceptional Case: Parameters of Faith in the Modern World*. London: Darton, Longman, and Todd.

Deloria, Vine, Jr. 1999. *For This Land: Writings on Religion in America*. Ed. James Treat. New York: Routledge.

Eck, Diana. 2002. *A New Religious America: How a "Christian Country" Has Become the World's Most Religiously Diverse Nation*. San Francisco: HarperSanFrancisco.

Eck, Diana. 2007. Prospects for Pluralism: Voice and Vision in the Study of Religion. *Journal of the American Academy of Religion* 75:743–776.

Ecklund, Elaine, and Wendy Cadge. 2007. Immigration and Religion. *Annual Review of Sociology* 33:359–379.

Edgell, Penny, Joseph Gerteis, and Douglas Hartmann. 2006. Atheists as "Other": Moral Boundaries and Cultural Membership in American Society. *American Sociological Review* 71:211–234.

Eichler-Levine, Jodi, and Rosemary R. Hicks. 2007. As "Americans Against Genocide": The Crisis in Darfur and Interreligious Political Activism. *American Quarterly* 59:711–735.

Eisenberg, Avigail. 2005. Identity and Liberal Politics: The Problem of Minorities Within Minorities. In *Minorities Within Minorities: Equality, Rights, and Diversity*, ed. Avigail I. Eisenberg and Jeff Spinner-Halev, 249–270. Cambridge: Cambridge University Press.

Emon, Anver M. 2006. Conceiving Islamic Law in a Pluralist Society: History, Politics and Multicultural Jurisprudence. *Singapore Journal of Legal Studies* 136:331–355.

Fessenden, Tracy. 2007. *Culture and Redemption: Religion, the Secular, and American Literature*. Princeton, N.J.: Princeton University Press.

Fish, Stanley. 2007. Liberalism and Secularism: One and the Same. *New York Times*, September 2. http://fish.blogs.nytimes.com/2007/09/02/liberalism-and-secularism-one-and-the-same.

Forst, Rainer. 2004. The Limits of Toleration. *Constellations* 11:312–325.

Gilsenan, Michael. 2000. Signs of Truth: Enchantment, Modernity, and the Dreams of Peasant Women. *Journal of the Royal Anthropological Society* 6, no. 4:597–615.

Golebiowska, Ewa A. 2004. Religious Tolerance in Poland. *International Journal of Public Opinion Research* 16:391–416.

Habermas, Jürgen. 2006. Religion in the Public Sphere. *European Journal of Philosophy* 14:1–25.

Halberstam, Joshua. 1982–1983. The Paradox of Tolerance. *Philosophical Forum* 14:190–207.

Hamburger, Philip. 2004. *Separation of Church and State*. Cambridge, Mass.: Harvard University Press.

Herberg, Will. 1955/1983. *Protestant–Catholic–Jew: An Essay in American Religious Sociology*. Chicago: University of Chicago Press.

Hollinger, David. 2001. Not Universalists, Not Pluralists: The New Cosmopolitans Find Their Own Way. *Constellations* 8:237–248.

Howe, Mark deWolfe. 1965. *The Garden and the Wilderness: Religion and Government in American Constitutional History*. Chicago: University of Chicago Press.

Hurd, Elizabeth Shakman. 2007. *The Politics of Secularism in International Relations*. Princeton, N.J.: Princeton University Press.

Hutchison, William. 2003. *Religious Pluralism in America: The Contentious History of a Founding Ideal*. New Haven, Conn.: Yale University Press.

Huxley, Andrew, ed. 2002. *Religion, Law and Tradition: Comparative Studies in Religious Law*. London: RoutledgeCurzon.

Iyigun, Murat. 2006. *Ottoman Conquests and European Ecclesiastical Pluralism*. Discussion Paper no. 1973. Bonn: Forschungsinstitut zur Zukunft der Arbeit/Institute for the Study of Labor.

Jakobsen, Janet R., and Ann Pellegrini, eds. 2008. *Secularisms*. Durham, N.C.: Duke University Press.

James, William. 1909. *A Pluralistic Universe*. London: Longmans, Green.

Jung, Courtney. 2001. The Burden of Culture and the Limits of Liberal Responsibility. *Constellations* 8:219–235.

Kaplan, Benjamin. 2007. *Divided by Faith: Religious Conflict and the Practice of Toleration in Early Modern Europe*. Cambridge, Mass.: Harvard University Press.

Klassen, Pamela E. 2011. *Pathologies of Modernity: Medicine, Healing, and the Spirits of Protestantism*. Berkeley: University of California Press.

Knippenberg, Hans, ed. 2005. *The Changing Religious Landscape of Europe*. Amsterdam: Het Spinhuis.

Kniss, Fred, and Paul Numrich. 2007. *Sacred Assemblies and Civic Engagement: How Religion Matters for America's Newest Immigrants*. New Brunswick, N.J.: Rutgers University Press.

Kraut, Bennie. 1989. A Wary Collaboration: Jews, Catholics, and the Protestant Goodwill Movement. In *Between the Times: The Travail of the Protestant Establishment*, ed. W. R. Hutchison, 193–230. New York: Cambridge University Press.

Kühle, Lena. 2003. Religious Pluralism in Multireligiosity. In *Theology and the Religions: A Dialogue*, ed. Viggo Mortensen, 419–429. Grand Rapids, Mich.: Eerdmans.

Kurien, Prema. 2007. *A Place at the Multicultural Table: The Development of an American Hinduism*. New Brunswick, N.J.: Rutgers University Press.

Kymlicka, Will. 1995. *Multicultural Citizenship: A Liberal Theory of Minority Rights*. Oxford: Clarendon Press.

Kymlicka, Will. 2001. *Politics in the Vernacular: Nationalism, Multiculturalism, and Citizenship*. Oxford: Oxford University Press.

Kymlicka, Will. 2003. Canadian Multiculturalism in Historical and Comparative Perspective: Is Canada Unique? *Constitutional Forum* 13, no. 1:1–8.

Leavelle, Tracy. 2007. "Bad Things" and "Good Hearts": Mediation, Meaning, and the Language of Illinois Christianity. *Church History* 76:363–394.

Levitt, Laura. 2007. Impossible Assimilations, American Liberalism, and Jewish Difference: Revisiting Jewish Secularism. *American Quarterly* 59:807–832.

Levitt, Peggy, 2007. *God Needs No Passport*. New York: New Press.

Lippy, Charles. 2000. *Pluralism Comes of Age*. Armonk, N.Y.: Sharpe.

Long, Carolyn. 2001. *Religious Freedom and Indian Rights: The Case of* Oregon v. Smith. Lawrence: University Press of Kansas.

Mahmood, Saba. 2006. Secularism, Hermeneutics, and Empire. *Public Culture* 18, no. 2:323–347.

Mamdani, Mahmood. 2004. *Good Muslim, Bad Muslim: America, The Cold War, and the Roots of Terror*. New York: Pantheon.

Martin, David. 1969. *The Religious and the Secular: Studies in Secularization*. New York: Schocken.

Marty, Martin. 2007. Pluralisms. *Annals of the American Academy of Political and Social Science* 612:13–25.

Masuzawa, Tomoko. 2005. *The Invention of World Religions: Or, How European Universalism Was Preserved in the Language of Pluralism*. Chicago: University of Chicago Press.

McAlister, Melani. 2005. *Epic Encounters: Culture, Media, and U.S. Interests in the Middle East Since 1945*. Berkeley: University of California Press.

McAuliffe, Jane Dammen. 1990. Fakhr al-Din al-Razi on Ayat al-Jizya and Ayat al-Sayf. In *Conversion and Continuity: Indigenous Christian Communities in Islamic Lands, Eight to Eighteenth Centuries*, ed. Michael Gervers and Ramzi Jibran Bikhazi, 103–119. Toronto: Pontifical Institute of Mediaeval Studies.

McCarthy, Kate. 2007. *Interfaith Encounters in America*. New Brunswick, N.J.: Rutgers University Press.

Meyer, Birgit, and Annelies Moors, eds. 2006. *Religion, Media, and the Public Sphere*. Bloomington: Indiana University Press.

Mitchell, Timothy, ed. 2000. *Questions of Modernity*. Minneapolis: University of Minnesota Press.

Mittermaier, Amira. 2011. *Dreams That Matter: Egyptian Landscapes of the Imagination*. Berkeley: University of California Press.

Modood, Tariq. 2007. *Multiculturalism: A Civic Idea*. Cambridge: Polity.

Modood, Tariq, and Geoffrey Levey, eds. 2008. *Secularism, Religion, and Multicultural Citizenship*. Cambridge: Cambridge University Press.

Most, Andrea. 2004. *Making Americans: Jews and the Broadway Musical*. Cambridge, Mass.: Harvard University Press.

Needham, Anuradha Dingwaney, and Rajeswari Sunder Rajan, eds. 2007. *The Crisis of Secularism in India*. Durham, N.C.: Duke University Press.

Okin, Susan Moller, ed. 1999. *Is Multiculturalism Bad for Women?* Princeton, N.J.: Princeton University Press.

Ong, Aihwa. 2006. *Neoliberalism as Exception: Mutations in Citizenship and Sovereignty*. Durham, N.C.: Duke University Press.

Pandolfo, Stefania. 2000. The Thin Line of Modernity: Some Moroccan Debates on Subjectivity. In *Questions of Modernity*, ed. Timothy Mitchell, 115–147. Minneapolis: University of Minnesota Press.

Pecora, Vincent. 2006. *Secularization and Cultural Criticism: Religion, Nation and Modernity*. Chicago: University of Chicago Press.

Peters, John Durham. 1999. *Speaking into the Air: A History of the Idea of Communication*. Chicago: University of Chicago Press.

Philpott, Daniel. 2002. The Challenge of September 11 to Secularism in International Relations. *World Politics* 55:66–95.

Porterfield, Amanda. 2008. Religious Pluralism, the Study of Religion, and "Postsecular" Culture. In *The American University in a Postsecular Age*, ed. Douglas Jacobsen and Rhonda Jacobsen, 187–202. New York: Oxford University Press.

Réaume, Denise G. 2001. Legal Multiculturalism from the Bottom Up. In *Canadian Political Philosophy: Contemporary Reflections*, ed. Ronald Beiner and Wayne Norman, 194–206. Oxford: Oxford University Press.

Sarna, Jonathan D., ed. 1998. *Minority Faiths and the American Protestant Mainstream*. Urbana: University of Illinois Press.

Sassen, Saskia. 2006. *Cities in a World Economy*. Thousand Oaks, Calif.: Pine Forge Press.

Schmidt, Leigh Eric. 2003. The Making of Modern Mysticism. *Journal of the American Academy of Religion* 71:273–302.

Schmidt, Leigh Eric. 2006. Cosmopolitan Piety: Sympathy, Comparative Religions, and Nineteenth-Century Liberalism. In *Practicing Protestants: Histories of Christian Life in America, 1630–1965*, ed. Laurie F. Maffly-Kipp, Leigh E. Schmidt, and Mark Valeri, 199–221. Baltimore: Johns Hopkins University Press.

Scott, Joan Wallach. 2007. *The Politics of the Veil*. Princeton, N.J.: Princeton University Press.

Seljak, David, and Paul Bramadat. 2005. *Religion and Ethnicity in Canada*. Toronto: Pearson Longman.

Shachar, Ayelet. 2001. *Multicultural Jurisdictions: Cultural Differences and Women's Rights*. Cambridge: Cambridge University Press.

Sheppard, Colleen. 2006. Constitutional Recognition of Diversity in Canada. *Vermont Law Review* 30:463–487.

Stewart, Charles, and Rosalind Shaw, eds. 1994. *Syncretism/Antisyncretism: The Politics of Religious Synthesis*. New York: Routledge.

Stout, Jeffrey. 2004. *Democracy and Tradition*. Princeton, N.J.: Princeton University Press.

Sullivan, Winnifred Fallers. 2005. *The Impossibility of Religious Freedom*. Princeton, N.J.: Princeton University Press.

Sullivan, Winnifred Fallers. 2009. *Prison Religion: Faith-Based Reform and the Constitution*. Princeton, N.J.: Princeton University Press.

Taylor, Charles. 2007. *A Secular Age*. Cambridge, Mass.: Harvard University Press.

Tinker, George E. 2004. *Spirit and Resistance: Political Theology and American Indian Liberation*. Minneapolis, Minn.: Fortress Press.

Tully, James. 1995. *Strange Multiplicity: Constitutionalism in an Age of Diversity*. Cambridge: Cambridge University Press.

Viswanathan, Gauri. 2008. Secularism in the Framework of Heterodoxy. *PMLA* 123:466–476.

Williams, Bernard. 1999. Tolerating the Intolerable. In *The Politics of Toleration in Modern Life*, ed. Susan Mendes, 65–76. Durham, N.C.: Duke University Press.

Wuthnow, Robert. 2005. *America and the Challenges of Religious Diversity*. Princeton, N.J.: Princeton University Press.

Zubrzycki, Geneviève. 2006. *The Crosses of Auschwitz: Nationalism and Religion in Post-Communist Poland*. Chicago: University of Chicago Press.

CONTRIBUTORS

IRENE BECCI studied social sciences at the universities of Lausanne and Rome. She defended her doctoral dissertation on religious practices in German and Italian prisons in 2006 at the European University Institute in Florence. Between 2006 and 2009, she was a postdoctoral fellow at the Max Planck Institute for Social Anthropology in Halle, Germany, conducting research on morality and religion in eastern German offender rehabilitation programs. She currently leads a research team on religious pluralism in Switzerland's prisons, sponsored by the Swiss National Science Foundation.

COURTNEY BENDER's research focuses on the social and cultural processes that shape religious practice, experience, and interaction in contemporary American life. She is the author of *Heaven's Kitchen: Living Religion at God's Love We Deliver* (University of Chicago Press, 2003) and *The New Metaphysicals: Spirituality and the American Religious Imagination* (University of Chicago Press, 2010). She recently (2009–2010) served as the co-chair of the Social Science Research Council's initiative on Spirituality, Political Engagement and Public Life, funded by the Ford Foundation.

BENJAMIN L. BERGER is an associate professor of law at the University of Victoria, Canada. He received his J.S.D. from Yale University and has written extensively in his principal areas of research: constitutional and criminal law and theory, law and religion, and the law of evidence. A member of the editorial board of the *Canadian Journal of Law and Society*, he is co-editor of *The Grand Experiment: Law and Legal Culture in British Settler Societies* (UBC Press, 2008), and his recent publications include articles in the *Supreme Court Law Review*, *Journal of Comparative Law*, and *Law, Culture and the Humanities*.

ANVER M. EMON is an assistant professor in the Faculty of Law, University of Toronto. His research focus is on premodern and modern Islamic law and legal theory, premodern modes of governance and adjudication, and the role of Shari'a both inside and outside the Muslim world. He is the author of *Islamic Natural Law Theories* (Oxford University Press, 2010) and the founding editor of *Middle East Law and Governance: An Interdisciplinary Journal*.

ROSEMARY R. HICKS is currently a Mellon Postdoctoral Fellow at the Center for the Humanities, Tufts University. She received her Ph.D. in 2010 from the Department of Religion at Columbia University, where her dissertation focused on Islam in the United States and genealogies of moderation. Her research focuses on how Americans respond to increased religious and ethnic diversity and disagreements over secularism, multiculturalism, and issues of gender and sexuality. She was a 2007–2008 American Fellow with the American Association of University Women and a 2007–2009 Mellon Fellow with the Institute for Social and Economic Research and Policy at Columbia. She has published in *American Quarterly* (2007), *Comparative Islamic Studies* (2007), and the *Journal of Feminist Studies in Religion* (2004).

JANET R. JAKOBSEN is director of the Center for Research on Women and teaches women's studies at Barnard College, Columbia University. Beginning in 2009, she is serving as dean for faculty diversity and development. She is the author of *Working Alliances and the Politics of Difference: Diversity and Feminist Ethics* (Indiana University Press, 1998) and editor (with Elizabeth Castelli) of *Interventions: Activists and Academics Respond to Violence* (Palgrave Macmillan, 2004). With Ann Pellegrini, she is author of *Love the Sin: Sexual Regulation and the Limits of Religious Tolerance* (New York University Press, 2003) and editor of *Secularisms* (Duke University Press, 2008). She has been a fellow at the Udall Center for Public Policy at the University of Arizona, the Center for the Humanities at Wesleyan University, and the Center for the Study of Values in Public Life at Harvard Divinity School. Before entering the academy, she was a policy analyst, lobbyist, and organizer in Washington, D.C.

PAMELA E. KLASSEN is an associate professor in the Department for the Study of Religion and director of the Religion in the Public Sphere Initiative at the University of Toronto. Her books include *Blessed Events: Religion and Home Birth in America* (Princeton University Press, 2001) and *Pathologies of Modernity: Medicine, Healing, and the Spirits of Protestantism* (University of California Press, 2011). In 2008–2009, she was a Jackman Humanities Institute Fellow at the University of Toronto, where she began work on a new project titled "Protestant Experiments with Truth: Testimonies of the Spirit in a Scientific Age."

TRACY NEAL LEAVELLE is an associate professor of history and co-director of the American Studies Program at Creighton University in Omaha, Nebraska. He has published essays in *Church History, American Quarterly,* the *Journal of Religion & Society, American Indian Quarterly,* and other venues. He is working on two book manuscripts. The first, "Colonial Conversions: Religious Encounters and Cultural Translation in French and Indian North America," examines ambiguous religious encounters and the fluidity of cultural boundaries in a colonial environment of shifting power relations. The second is a brief history of Native American religions for Wiley-Blackwell. He is also collaborating with astronomer Salman Hameed (Hampshire College) on a study of conflicts between Native Hawaiians and scientists over the disposition of Mauna Kea, a sacred peak and world-class center for observational astronomy.

MICHAEL D. MCNALLY is an associate professor of religion and chair of the Religion Department at Carleton College. He is author of *Honoring Elders: Aging, Authority, and Ojibwe Religion* (Columbia University Press, 2009), *Ojibwe Singers: Hymns, Grief, and a Native Culture in Motion* (Oxford University Press, 2000; Minnesota Historical Society Press, 2009), and a number of articles, and the editor of *Art of Tradition: Sacred Music, Dance, and Myth of Michigan's Anishinaabe, 1946–1955* (Michigan State University Press, 2009).

AMIRA MITTERMAIER is an assistant professor in the Department for the Study of Religion and the Department of Near and Middle Eastern Civilizations at the University of Toronto. She completed her undergraduate studies in Islamic studies at the Eberhard-Karls-Universität, Tübingen, Germany, and her M.A. and Ph.D. in sociocultural anthropology at Columbia University. Before joining the University of Toronto, she held a Mellon Fellowship in the Society of Fellows in the Humanities at Columbia University. Her interests include modern Islam, Sufism, modernity and postcolonialism, the anthropology of religion, and anthropologies of the imagination. Her book *Dreams That Matter: Egyptian*

Landscapes of the Imagination is being published by the University of California Press (2011).

ANDREA MOST is an associate professor of American literature and Jewish studies in the Department of English at the University of Toronto. Her first book, *Making Americans: Jews and the Broadway Musical* (Harvard University Press, 2004), received the 2005 Kurt Weill Prize for distinguished scholarship on musical theater. She is currently at work on "Theatrical Liberalism," a book-length study of the relationship between Jews and popular entertainment in twentieth-century America.

WINNIFRED FALLERS SULLIVAN is an associate professor of law and director of the Law and Religion Program at the University at Buffalo Law School, the State University of New York. She received her J.D. and Ph.D. from the University of Chicago. She studies the intersection of religion and law in the modern period, particularly the phenomenology of modern religion as it is shaped in its encounter with law. She is the author of *Paying the Words Extra: Religious Discourse in the Supreme Court of the United States* (Harvard University Center for the Study of World Religions, 1994), *The Impossibility of Religious Freedom* (Princeton University Press, 2005), and *Prison Religion: Faith-Based Reform and the Constitution* (Princeton University Press, 2009).

J. TERRY TODD is an associate professor of American religious studies at Drew University, where he also directs the Center on Religion, Culture & Conflict. He has written many articles on religion and American lives, and his research and teaching focus on the history of American forms of Christian faith and practice, particularly as they developed in twentieth-century urban contexts. He is especially interested in the influence of religious ideas on U.S. nationalism and representations of Jesus produced by American media.

GENEVIÈVE ZUBRZYCKI is an associate professor of sociology at the University of Michigan. Her research focuses on the role of symbols in national mythology and the linkages between national identity and religion at moments of significant political transformation. Through an investigation of memory wars between Poles and Jews at Auschwitz, her book *The Crosses of Auschwitz: Nationalism and Religion in Post-Communist Poland* (University of Chicago Press, 2006) examines the historical constitution of the relationship between Polish national identity and Catholicism and its reconfiguration after the fall of communism. It received the American Sociological Association's Distinguished Book Award from the Sociology of Religion section, the American Association for the Advancement of Slavic Studies' Orbis Best Book Prize, and the Polish

Studies Association's Best Book Award. Zubrzycki's next project is a historical ethnography of the triadic relationship among religion, nationalism, and state (re)formation in Poland and Quebec, through the examination of the "careers" of religious symbols and their ritual use in religious processions, popular parades, and political protests.

INDEX

Abbott, Andrew, 14
Abella, Rosalie, 119–121
abortion, 51n.10, 268, 279, 300
Abu-Lughod, Lila, 189, 196n.10, 263
accommodation, of religion: in Canada, 4, 105; and law, 83, 84, 98–101, 113, 117–119; and Native Americans, 174, 227, 234, 235, 245; as resistance, 16
acculturation, 129, 134
Afghani, Jamal al-Din al-, 179, 181, 195n.1
Ahmad, Al-Hagg, 178–183, 185, 193
Aidi, Hishaam, 253
Aires, Wolf, 299
Albright, Madeline, 262, 267, 268
Alexander, Jeffrey C., 280
Ali, Kecia, 266
Allouez, Claude, 161
American Indian Religious Freedom Act (AIRFA, 1978), 170–173, 228–234, 243, 248
American Indians. *See* Native Americans
Americanism, Americanness, 211–212, 269; exclusion from, 256
American values, 45; and immigration, 46; and Muslim women, 263–264; and Sudan, 262
Ammerman, Nancy, 24n.10, 38
Anaya, S. James, 227
Anidjar, Gil, 255
Annie Get Your Gun (play), 147–148
anti-Catholicism, 84, 92, 93
anti-Muslim, 253, 254, 267
Antin, Mary, 150n.15
anti-Semitism, 208, 213, 283, 290; and antitheatricality, 137
antitheatricality, 136, 137, 140
Armstrong, Margaret, 212
Arnold, Helen, 304
Asad, Talal, 3, 17, 50nn.7,8, 111, 131, 180, 182, 270
assimilation: and Islam, 75; and Judaism, 129; and Native Americans, 102,

assimilation (*continued*) 103, 108, 164, 165, 167, 168, 227, 238; resistance to, 166
Auschwitz, 280–284, 287, 288, 291nn.6,8,10, 292n.11
Austin, E. L., 204
authority, ontological, 65
autonomy, 42; and community, 42, 43; and normativity, 43
Axtell, James, 164
Ayer, William, W., 214

Badoni v. Higginson (1980), 233, 245
Baer, Marc David, 7
Baird, Robert J., 131, 132
Bakhtin, M. M., 186, 187, 197n.19
Banchoff, Thomas, 9
Banerjee, Neela, 95
Ban Ki-moon, 253
Barak, Aharon, 105
Barish, Jonas, 136–137
Barnett, Michael, 257
Barroso, José Manuel, 11
barzakh, 194
Baumann, Martin, 6, 11
Bayor, Ronald H., 201, 208
Bear Lodge Multiple Use Association et al. v. Babbitt (1990), 234, 235
Beatty, David M., 105
Belasco, David, 142, 143, 151n.23
Bentham, Jeremy, 7, 8, 14, 23
Berger, Peter, 6
Bergreen, Laurence, 127
Berkhofer, Robert F., Jr., 159
Berlant, Lauren, 38
Berlin, Irving, 127, 147, 148, 149
Bhabha, Homi, 15
Bible, 35, 87, 162, 173, 204, 216–217, 297; King James Version of, 40
Bickel, Alexander M., 112
Bilgrami, Akeel, 53n.29
biopower, 39, 40
Board of Education of Kiryas Joel Village School District v. Grumet (1994), 89
Bonnichsen v. United States (2004), 244
Bouchard, Gérard, 4
Bourdieu, Pierre, 149n.6, 305, 309
Bowden, Henry Warner, 164
Bowen v. Roy (1986), 229, 230, 232
Brady, Mary Pat, 52n.23
Bramadat, Paul, 10
Bramen, Carrie, 18
Broder, John M., 51n.16
Brown, Wendy, 24n.9, 60, 100, 111, 182
Brunini, John, 208, 210, 211, 216, 217
B.(R.) v. Children's Aid Society of Metropolitan Toronto (1995), 109–110
Buhle, Paul, 149n.3
Bush, George W., 35, 47, 84, 262, 267, 268
Bush, Laura, 47, 53n.26
Butler, Judith, 52n.24
Byrd, Robert, 40

Calhoun, Craig J., 257
Calloway, Colin, 168
Campbell, David, 3
Cantor, Eddie, 213–214
Carr, Steven Alan, 150n.11
Catholics, 95, 136, 144, 149n.5; exclusion of, from "Americanness," 256; and fall of communism, 279; in Germany 297, 298–301, 304; identity of, 284, 289; and immigrants, 45; and Jews, 201–220; as overly dogmatic, 255; in Poland, 277–290; and Polishness, 278, 285–286; and prison, 296, 302, 306, 311; and Protestants, 7, 11, 50n.9, 51n.10, 91, 151n.26, 201–220; and theater, 136
Certeau, Michel de, 189
Chambers, Simone, 4
Cherokee Nation v. Georgia (1831), 239, 249n.5
Chidester, David, 169–170
Christianity, 11, 35, 85, 163; conservative, 84; denominational differences in, 110; in Germany, 298, 299, 300; and Native Americans, 157, 173 (*see also* assimilation: and Native Americans; colonial-

ism: and Native Americans; religious freedom: and Native Americans); Puritan, 162–163; and sexuality, 37
Church of England, 6, 7
City of Albuquerque v. Browner (1996), 242
City of Boerne v. Flores (1997), 245
Clemmer, Donald, 309, 310
Clines, Frances X., 257
colonialism, 53n.25; and Bentham, 7, 23; as conquest, 102; and evangelization, 162; history of, 15, 253; and Native Americans, 156, 168–173 (*see also* Deloria, Vine, Jr.; Native Americans)
colonization: continuing, 171; and pluralism, 175
Connolly, William, 9–10, 12, 18, 54n.30, 117, 182, 196n.9
conquest, 102, 103
conversion, 213; and cross-cultural encounter, 102, 103, 104, 106–108, 121n.4; and Islam, 75; and law, 112, 116, 120; in prison, 301, 311; to the stage, 135, 140
Corliss, Richard, 127
Coso Hot Springs (Calif.), 168–170
Cover, Robert M., 116
Crapanzano, Vincent, 194

Dallmayr, Fred, 102–104, 108, 112, 116, 117
Dalrymple, William, 53n.28
Davie, Grace, 91
Dealy, Sam, 253, 255
Deliette, Pierre, 158–162
Deloria, Vine, Jr., 172–174
democracy, 208–209, 218, 241; and Anglo-Protestant culture, 44–45; and law, 119, 287–288; and pluralism, 32, 33, 181, 203; and tolerance, 105, 202
de Waal, Alex, 253, 254, 255, 261, 269, 271n.2
Dewey, John, 145
DiCenso, James, 194
Dinshaw, Carolyn, 54n.30
Dirks, Nicholas, 3
diversity, 18, 23, 214, 220, 290; in Canada, 10, 105, 119; and Catholicism, 278, 287; cultural, 103, 104, 105, 113, 116, 120, 160, 181; and Islam, 181–182; and law, 98–100, 104, 105–108, 118; and Native Americans, 232; religious, 1–5, 11–14, 17, 20, 32–33, 108, 297; in U.S., 9, 16, 31, 170, 204–205, 211, 213
Dolan, Jay, 201
Dolan, Mary Jean, 86
dreams: interpretation of, on television, 186–189; and Muslim identity, 178; and unconscious, 189–192. *See also* Freud, Sigmund
Duggan, Lisa, 38
Duranti, Marco, 203

eagle feathers, 235–236, 238
Eastman, Charles, 167, 168, 172
Eck, Diana, 9, 12, 170, 219
Edgell, Penny, 85
Eichler-Levine, Jodi, 253, 255, 256, 258, 269, 270
Eick-Wildgans, Susanne, 302
Eisenberg, Avigail, 6
Ellenberger, Henri, 197n.22
Employment Division v. Smith (1990), 230, 232, 245, 247
encounter: and law, 99–104, 110, 114–116, 119–121; as metaphor, 16; and tolerance, 106–108
Engler, Wolfgang, 312n.7
Environmental Protection Agency (EPA), 242–243
equality: in Canada, 99, 107, 109, 115, 118; and Civil Rights Movement, 211; gender, 5, 75; and governance, 14, 44–47, 114; and law, 240; in U.S., 32, 45, 95, 268. *See also* multiculturalism
ethnography, 12, 21, 22, 179, 181, 183, 193, 194, 230
European Union, and marginalized religions, 11

faith, 42, 60, 85, 90, 95, 117; and acting, 147; and dress, 108; and health, 87–88; and Judaism, 132–133; and Protestantism, 131; and White House, 84, 92
family, 42, 141, 308; and gender, 36; and law, 11; "traditional," 42
Faris, Stephan, 253
Feiner, Shmuel, 138
Ferber, Edna, 127, 140
Ferguson, Roderick, 39, 52n.17
Fessenden, Tracy, 5, 18, 24n.10, 50n.9, 157
Fine-Dare, Kathleen, 244–245
First Amendment, 83, 90, 93–95, 170, 225–228, 231–246
Fitchett, George, 90, 94, 95
Flast v. Cohen (1968), 92–94
Flint, Julie, 253, 254, 257, 261, 269, 271n.2
Foner, Eric, 46
Fools Crow v. Gullet (1983), 233
Ford, Richard T., 116
Forst, Rainer, 106
Fort Laramie Treaty (1868), 239
Foucault, Michel, 38, 39–41, 51n.16, 52n.18, 184, 302, 303, 309, 310
Fowler, James W., 88
Freedland, Michael, 127
Freedom from Religion Foundation (FRFF), 89, 91, 92, 95
Freedom from Religion Foundation v. Nicholson (2007), 86–92, 94
freedom of religion, 252, 287; in Canada, 4, 98, 104, 105, 106–109; in Europe, 11; and Judaism, 128, 131, 133–134, 140, 145; and law, 98, 104, 105, 106–109; and Native Americans, 171, 225, 228 (*see also* American Indian Religious Freedom Act); in U.S., 10, 45, 144
Freud, Sigmund, 178, 179, 184–186, 189–190, 192, 194, 197nn.22,24
Fricke, Adrienne L., 264, 265
Friedlaender, Israel, 131
Frothingham v. Mellon (1923), 92–93
Furia, Philip, 127
gender, 37, 38, 39, 41, 46; equality, 5, 75; and religious communities, 48; and religious discourse, 48, 261–267; and pluralist discourse, 12, 21, 37–40
genocide, 170, 252, 253, 254, 257–260, 264–269
Gerteis, Joseph, 85
Gilman, Charlotte Perkins, 42
Gilmore, Michael T., 137
"God Bless America" (Berlin), 127–128, 147
Goffman, Erving, 302–309
good, 65, 66, 72
Goodstein, Laurie, 268
Gordon, Judah Leib, 139
Graf, Friedreich Wilhelm, 16
Grant, George, 104
Great Depression, 203
Gross, Jan T., 278
Gulliford, Andrew, 171, 173
Günther, Ralf, 310
Gustafson, Marc, 253

Habermas, Jürgen, 4, 34, 182
Hakim (Egyptian psychoanalyst), 186–190, 192
Halberstam, Joshua, 106
Hall, David D., 163–164
Hallaq, Wael, 266
Halley, Janet, 257
Halperin, David, 43
Hamburger, Philip, 50n.9, 84
Hammerstein, Oscar, 139, 140, 146
Haquem, Amber, 179
Harjo, Joy, 157, 158, 166, 170, 175
Harnick, Sheldon, 145
Hartmann, Douglas, 85
Hastings, Dennis, 245
Hauser, O., 204
Hein v. Freedom from Religion Foundation (2007), 91–94
Hennessy, James, 208
Herberg, Will, 202
Heschel, Abraham Joshua, 142, 143, 144, 145, 146

Heschel, Susannah, 255
heteronormativity, 38, 39, 44
Hicks, Rosemary R., 253, 255, 258, 259, 270
Hirschkind, Charles, 263
Hitchens, Christopher, 5
Hollinger, David, 6, 16
homonormativity, 38
Horace, Lillian B., 212
human rights, 261, 264, 266–270, 286; and law, 119; and Muslims, 259, 261; and Native American burial grounds, 244; and religious freedom, 82, 105, 181, 226, 300
Hunter, Stanley A., 217
Huntington, Samuel, 31, 32, 34, 45–46
Hurd, Elizabeth Shakman, 17
Hutchison, William, 6
Huxley, Andrew, 82
hybridity, 85, 121

immigrants, 129; Eastern European, 132; as equal to native-born, 45; and Islamic law, 76; Jewish, 132, 145; and religious practices, 85; in western Germany, 299
immigration, 3, 11, 45–47, 299; of Latinos, 45; and reform, 31
Indian Religious Crimes Code, 166
Indian Reorganization Act (IRA, 1934), 238
International Criminal Court, 252, 257, 258, 268, 269
interreligious or interfaith dialogue, 3, 5, 16, 21, 43–44, 202, 208–210, 214–216, 258
Irwin, Lee, 166, 167
Islam: accommodation of minorities by, 75; and *fiqh*, 61; and identity, 60; and *jizya*, 74, 75, 78nn.15,17; and legal analysis, 61, 71, 74–76; and misogyny, 266; as morally problematic, 270; and *niqab*, 75; as overly dogmatic, 255; "proper" and "improper," 253; and scientific thought, 179–180, 185; as sealed tradition, 179; and U.S., 34, 37, 253, 256
Iyigun, Murat, 7

Jackson, Sherman, 261
Jacobson, Matthew Frye, 150n.10
Jaenen, Cornelius, 161
Jain, Kajri, 4
Jakobsen, Janet R., 17, 20, 34, 35, 50nn.9–10, 131
James, William, 7–8
Jazz Singer, The (film), 135, 141
Jehovah's Witnesses, 109–111
Jesuits, 160, 161, 163
Jews: acting Jewish, 142–145; and Catholics, 201–220; in Hollywood, 129, 133, 140, 150n.20; Jewishness, 132, 284, 289–290, 291n.5, 293n.20; and Protestants, 133, 201–220, 255; Russian, 139; Spanish, 138. *See also* Judaism
Johnson, Gregory, 244
Johnson v. McIntosh (1823), 50n.9, 236
Joppke, Christian, 300
Judaism: and culture creation, 128, 129; in Europe, 11; instruction in, 143; as overly dogmatic, 255; and Protestant model, 131–132; "secular," 129, 130; secularization of, 132–133; and sex, 143; and theater, 134, 138; in U.S., 132–149, 210–212, 215; *values of, 128, 141
Judeo-Christian, construction of category of, 21, 52n.19, 201–220, 256
Jung, Courtney, 5, 15
jurisprudence, 82, 228, 232, 245; American, 83, 84, 90, 93; Canadian, 104–105, 108, 115; Islamic, 61, 62, 64, 71, 72, 75, 77n.2

Kahn, Paul W., 113, 118
Kaplan, Benjamin, 7
Kaplan, Mordecai, 132
Kazan, Elia, 218
Kelley, Robin D. G., 46

Khair, Amira, 264, 265
Kidwell, Clara Sue, 174
King, Thomas, 241
kirpan, 108–109
Kitagawa, Joseph, 256
Knippenberg, Hans, 299
Kraut, Benny, 202, 207
Kristof, Nicholas D., 253, 271n.2
Kühle, Lena, 6, 8
Kupperman, Karen Ordahl, 162, 163, 164
Kurien, Prema, 15
Kymlicka, Will, 6, 10, 114–116

Lacan, Jacques, 186, 190, 194, 197n.22
Lafitau, Joseph François, 160, 161
La Guardia, Fiorello, 206, 208, 209, 213
Lambek, Michael, 195n.6
law: authority of, 117–118; and culture, 100; as culture, 99, 120; and dominance, 113; environmental, 242–243; and Native American religion, 157; and norms, 109; religious, 255; and religious studies, 82; as shaper of meaning, 112; and Sudan, 252–270; and U.S. religious practice, 84; and values, 108. *See also* accommodation: and law; conversion: and law; democracy: and law; diversity: and law; equality; family: and law; human rights; multiculturalism: and law; natural law; religion: and law; Shari'a
Leavelle, Tracy, 159, 203, 226
Le Boullenger, Jean, 161
Lepore, Jill, 164
Levey, Geoffrey, 4
Lévi-Strauss, Claude, 189
Levitt, Laura, 52n.21, 132–133
Levitt, Peggy, 4
Lippy, Charles, 6, 16
liberal: governance, 60; norms, 48; rule of law, 59; values and power, 47
liberalism, 47, 103; and Judaism, 133; Protestant American, 130; and tolerance, 114
liberation theology, of Native Americans, 156, 175
Liebling, Alison, 304
Linenthal, Edward T., 169, 170
Locke, John, 144, 182
Lone Wolf v. Hitchcock (1903), 238
Long, Carolyn, 231
Lösch, Manfred, 314n.22
Luhrmann, Tanya, 185
Lumeye, Fidele, 267
Lutherans, 212–213
Lyng v. Northwest Cemetery Protective Association (1988), 171–172, 228–230, 232, 235, 245–246

Mahmood, Saba, 17, 263
Mamdani, Mahmood, 17, 18, 253, 254, 255, 257, 263
Mangoldt, Hans von, 299
Mann, Thomas, 182
Marr, Timothy, 256, 263
marriage: as constructed by politicians, 40; as norm, 39
Martin, Joel W., 167, 171
Martin, Sarah, 266, 267
Marty, Martin, 9, 16
Masuzawa, Tomoko, 3, 131, 255
Mayhew, Thomas, Jr., 163–164
McAlister, Melani, 253, 256
McCarthy, Kate, 15
McDermott, W. F., 205
McEwen, C. A., 303
McKean, Erin, 130
media, 36, 86, 179, 185, 197n.17, 254, 265; in prisons, 308
Medved, Michael, 37, 51n.13
Meier, Walter A., 213
Mendelssohn, Moses, 144
Messick, Brinkley, 198n.26
Meyer, Birgit, 4
Michnik, Adam, 289
Michowicz, Waldemar, 278
military intervention, 254, 263
minority cultures, 114

missionaries, 159, 160, 164
Mitchell, Timothy, 3
Mittermaier, Amira, 194
Modood, Tariq, 3, 115
Monaghan, Frank, 203
Moore, Deborah Dash, 202
Moors, Annelies, 4
Moreno Ocampo, Louis, 268, 269
Mormons, and Hollywood, 37
Morrison, Kenneth M., 159
Morsy, Soheir, 179
Morton v. Mancari (1983), 249n.6
Muhammad, Prophet, 260; and dreams, 179, 184, 191, 197n.25
Multani v. Commission Scolaire Marguerite-Bourgeoys (2006), 108–109
multiculturalism, 101–102; and anthropologists, 182; in Canada, 105–106; and law, 98–100, 112, 116–120, 181; social costs of, 116; theories of, 113, 114; and women, 115
Muslims: arguments of, for natural law, 61; and dreams, 178–195; in Europe, 11; exclusion of, from pluralism, 258; and Hollywood, 37; jurists, 60, 61, 62, 76; post–September 11, 34; and race, 261; as religious marker, 11; voluntarist jurists, 68, 69, 70; and Western knowledge systems, 193

Nabil, Shaykh, 189–193
Nandy, Ashis, 184
National Conference of Christians and Jews, 202, 206, 217
National Environmental Protection Act (NEPA, 1969), 242, 244, 246
National Historical Preservation Act (NHPA, 1966), 240–242, 244, 246
Native American Church, 167, 225, 226, 231
Native American Graves Protection and Repatriation Act (NAGPRA, 1990), 244
Native Americans: bias against, in the courts, 232; healers among, 163; and interreligious dialogue, 174; and Jesus, 161; and liberation theology, 156, 175; oral tradition of, 163; and Protestants, 157, 164; sacred land of, 169, 172, 173, 227 (*see also* Traditional Cultural Property); and salmon, 237, 240, 243; and sovereignty, 3, 5, 156, 168, 175, 226, 236–238, 240, 249nn.3–4,6; as superstitious, 158–160, 163, 164, 165. *See also* assimilation: and Native Americans; colonialism: and Native Americans; religious practice: of Native Americans
natural law, 67, 72, 76; hard naturalism, 62, 68, 69, 70; and jurisprudence, 64; and reasoning, 68; soft naturalism, 70
Navajo Nation et al. v. U.S. Forest Service (2006), 245, 247
Neubert, Ehrhart, 300
Newcomb, Steven T., 50n.9
New York World's Fair (1939–1940), 127, 201, 203, 217, 218
Nietzsche, Friedrich, 137, 178, 179, 193
North Atlantic Treaty Organization (NATO), 257, 267, 282, 300

Obama, Barack, 31, 33, 84, 195n.7, 268, 272n.20
Ong, Aihwa, 54n.30
Ortiz, Simon J., 168, 169
Osborn, William Church, 205, 206, 208
Other, 76, 181

Pagden, Anthony, 161
Page, Jack, 171
Pandolfo, Stefania, 180, 194
Parker, Patricia, 241
Parrish, Michael, 207
pastoral power, 309–311
Patel, Geeta, 35, 53n.27
Peace of Westphalia (1648), 17
Pecora, Vincent, 18
Pellegrini, Anne, 17, 34–35, 131
Pennington, W., 7
Peters, John Durham, 23

peyote, 167, 225, 226, 231, 240, 245
Philpott, Daniel, 17
Pit River Tribe et al. v. U.S. Forest Service (2006), 244
pluralism, 1, 2, 6, 59, 256; "after," 2, 32, 77, 248, 278; alternatives to, 36; and anthropologists, 8; in Canada, 10; as colonialism, 156; and colonization, 175; vs. diversity, 10; ecclesiastical, 6; exclusion of Muslims from, 258; inadequate, 33; mapping of, 9; as normative goal, 9; and norms, 42; "official," 7; and political theorists, 3, 8; post-pluralism, 31, 94, 95; practical, 16; practices and norms of, 22; prescriptive, 12; problematic, 107, 182; and religion, 5; in U.S., 6, 18, 31, 83, 202, 257–270; values of, 44; and Western values, 287
Pocahontas, 16
Pollack, Detlef, 299, 312n.7
Porterfield, Amanda, 9
power: and norms, 39, 44; and tolerance, 203. *See also* jurisprudence; law; pluralism; religion; secularism
Power, Samantha, 261
prisoners: Muslim, 5; and space, 304–305; and staff, 306–307; and time, 305–306
prisons: chaplains in, 299–311, 312n.1, 313n.13, 314n.22; spirituality in, 297, 300–301, 311
Protestant Reformation, 34
Protestants, 82, 131, 164; and Catholics, 7, 11, 50n.9, 51n.10, 91, 151n.26, 201–220; culture of, 145; denominations of, 297–298; and ecumenism, 204; identity of, 31; and Jews, 133, 201–220, 255; liberal, 130; and moral values, 35, 205; and Native Americans, 164, 172; and normativity, 90
Prucha, Francis Paul, 166, 171
psychoanalysis, 184–185, 189, 196n.13
Puar, Jasbir, 38, 39, 52n.17
Pueblo of Sandia v. United States (1995), 243–244
Puritanism, 162–163; and theater, 136–137
Pyramid Lake Paiute v. Morton (1972), 239

Québec, 4, 6, 10
queer theory, 36, 38–44, 46–49; and norms, 49
Qur'an, 61, 68, 74, 75, 180, 184, 189, 190, 191, 195n.2; and Freud, 179

Rajan, Rajeswari Sunder, 51n.12
Ramet, Sabina P., 299
rape. *See* sexual violence
Raphaelson, Samson, 135
Raustiala, Kai, 116
Réaume, Denise G., 113
Refugees International, 253, 261, 262, 264–267
religion: and authenticity, 14, 21, 42, 52n.21, 165, 173, 228, 253, 256, 263–265, 269, 270; categories of, 15; as form of resistance, 157; framework for understanding of, 60, 66; and hybridity, 14; and identity, 85; and law, 100; as natural, 3, 84, 94, 160, 164; as performance, 142–143; as policed, 95; and political identity, 5; and public discussions, 4; and race, 253–254, 256, 258, 260, 261, 264–265, 267; relegation of, to the past, 173; as subject of inquiry, 1; universalism of, 235; and U.S. government, 84; "wars of," 1
religiosity, 35, 40, 269, 291n.2, 298, 301; of African Americans, 212; universal, 256
religious community, 41
religious difference, 1, 5, 47, 98; and immigrants, 45; vs. openness, 46; and public sphere, 33; and race, 252–255; and tolerance, 107; "units" of, 32, 41
religious diversity, 4, 99; studies of, 16
religious ethics, and gender and sexuality, 47

religious freedom, 82, 287; and American Jews, 133; in Canada, 99, 104–107, 109, 110; and First Amendment, 83, 225, 235; in France, 75; and Native Americans, 170, 172, 174, 240, 244, 245 (*see also* American Indian Religious Freedom Act); in prisons, 302–303; in U.S., 91, 201, 203, 215; in Weimar Republic, 298. *See also* human rights
Religious Freedom Restoration Act (RFRA, 1993), 245–247
Religious Land Use and Institutionalized Persons Act (RLUIPA, 2000), 245–246
religious liberties, 109–111
religious practice, 109, 256; of Muslims, 256; of Native Americans, 157, 159, 163, 165, 225–248
religious symbols, 83, 167, 211, 213, 279, 280, 282, 283, 285–289
Richter, Daniel, 164
Ridington, Robin, 245
Riesebrodt, Martin, 51n.14
Rockefeller, John D., Jr., 208–209, 214, 216
Rodinson, Maxime, 191
Rubenstein, David, 261, 262, 267, 272n.18
Rubenstein, Josh, 262
Rubin, Gayle, 43

Sachs, Jeffrey, 253
Said, Edward, 3, 255
Salisbury, Neal, 162, 163
Sandrow, Nahma, 138
Sassen, Saskia, 3
Save Darfur Coalition (SDC), 252–270
Schenkel, Albert, 209
Schmidt, Leigh Eric, 8, 256
Scholem, Gershom, 138
Schoolman, Morton, 3
Scott, Joan Wallach, 18
Seager, Richard H., 204
secularism, 130; Christian, 35; as framework for interaction, 34; Hindu, 35; Jewish, 129, 130, 132–133; liberal, 76; norms of, 47; "open," 4; vs. pluralism, 17; and sexuality, 47; in U.S. and Europe, 17
Seidman, Naomi, 132–133
Seljak, David, 10
Seminole Nation v. United States (1942), 249n.5
September 11, 2001, 34, 52n.17, 127, 219, 293n.19
Sequoyah v. T.V.A. (1980), 228, 232, 233, 245
sexuality: and ethics, 38; and secularism, 47
sexual regulation, 35, 37, 40, 41
sexual violence, 252–255, 261–267
Shachar, Ayelet, 115–116
Shari'a: in Canada, 36; and reasoning, 61–62, 67, 70, 71, 73–77; in Sudan, 254–256, 261, 265–266
Shaw, Rosalind, 15
Sheen, Fulton J., 212
Sheppard, Colleen, 121n.4
Show Boat (play), 139–141, 146
Silk, Mark, 202
Silverman, David J., 164
socialism, 133, 280, 281, 290, 296–311, 312n.2
Sohrab, Mirza Ahmad, 215, 216, 220
Spencer, Robert, 220
spiritual healing, 88
Spivak, Gayatri Chakravorty, 49n.4
Stewart, Charles, 15
Stewart, Omer, 226
Stola, Dariusz, 278
Stout, Jeffrey, 23
Subramaniam, Banu, 35, 53n.27
Sudan, 252–270, 272nn.16,18–19; arguments against military intervention in, 262; civil war in, 255; rape law in, 264–265. *See also* Shari'a: in Sudan
Supreme Court of Canada, 105, 119
Susman, Warren, 139, 150n.17
Świtoń, Kazimierz, 281–282, 283, 284, 285, 286, 292n.12

Talmud, 143
Talton v. Mays (1896), 249n.4
Taylor, Charles, 4, 73, 78n.14, 95
Temple of Religion, 201–219; architects of, 209–210; exclusion of Buddhists and Baha'is from, 203, 214, 216, 217; Twilight Hour in, 210
Ten Commandments, 144
terrorists: bombing in London by, 34; Christian and Muslim, 5
text: interpretation of, 73; of Save Darfur Campaign resources, 259–261
theater: and faith, 147; and Jewish law, 138; and morality, 140; as sacred space, 134, 141; as sinful, 137
Tinker, George E., 156, 157, 170, 175
tolerance, 98, 106, 107, 109–120, 181; and conversion, 112; and liberalism, 114; limits of, 111, 112, 182; and power, 203
Tomaszewski, Jerzy, 278
Tomkins, Calvin, 205
Traditional Cultural Property (TCP), 241
Tucker, Judith E., 266
Tully, James, 14, 24n.10, 108, 118, 119, 120

United Nations, 252–253, 255, 257, 258, 265, 266, 268, 269, 272n.14
United States: government of, 83–85, 226, 267–268; and international affairs, 268, 270; and Islam, 34, 37, 253, 256; and Judaism, 132–149, 210–212, 215; and military intervention, 47, 253, 254, 255; as model of diversity, 16, 201–208; and Native Americans, 157–175, 225–248; not "after" pluralism, 31; popular culture of, 127–149; as superpower, 257; and values, 45–46, 50n.9, 210–213, 217, 255, 262, 264, 269. *See also* diversity: in U.S.; freedom of religion: in U.S.; pluralism: in U.S.; religious freedom: in U.S.; United States Supreme Court
United States Supreme Court, 50nn.9–10, 52n.19, 83, 89, 90–95, 151n.27, 171, 226, 229, 236–239, 245–247, 249n.4. *See also individual cases*
United States v. Antoine (2003), 236, 248n.2
United States v. Dion (1986), 238
United States v. Hardman (2002), 235
United States v. Mitchell (1983), 249n.5
United States v. Sioux Nation (1980), 239
United States v. Washington (1974), 237
United States v. Winans (1905), 237
Urban, Jerzy, 287

veterans, and spiritual care, 86–91
Veterans Administration, 86–90
Villarejo, Amy, 39, 52n.17
Viswanathan, Gauri, 18
Vizenor, Gerald, 168

Wachsmann, Nikolaus, 296
Wall, Wendy, 202, 219
Waniek, Danuta, 291n.3
Warner, Michael, 38, 41
War of the Crosses (Poland), 280–289
Warrior, Robert, 168
Washburn, Kevin, 227, 238, 248
Watt, W. Montgomery, 191
Weaver, Jace, 168
Weber, Donald, 149n.3
Weber, Max, 148
Wenger, Tisa, 225
White, Richard, 161
Wiesel, Elie, 254, 255, 270
Wilkanowicz, Stefan, 287
Wilkinson, Charles, 172, 240
Williams, Bernard, 106, 110
Williams, Lacey Kirk, 212
Williams, Michael, 205–206, 212
Williams, Raymond, 193, 198n.27
Williams, Roger, 162–163
Wilson, Waziyatawin Angela, 156, 174
Wilson v. Block (1983), 246
Wisconsin v. Yoder (1972), 232
World Parliament of Religions, 204, 215

World War II, 86, 169, 202, 217, 256, 277, 278, 280, 291n.6, 292n.11, 298, 313n.13
Wuthnow, Robert, 9, 288
Wyoming Sawmills, Inc. v. U.S. Forest Service (2004), 235

Yellowbird, Michael, 156, 174
Yiddish, 138
Young, Iris Marion, 49n.4

Zernike, Kate, 51n.15
Ziarek, Ewa, 41
Zinberg, Israel, 150n.16
Zitkala-Ša, 167–168, 172
Ziwer, Mustafa, 184, 186, 189, 190